D0961857

Mexico

The publisher gratefully acknowledges the generous contribution to this book provided by the Literature in Translation Endowment Fund of the University of California Press Foundation, which is supported by a major gift from Joan Palevsky.

Mexico

A Brief History

Alicia Hernández Chávez

Translated by Andy Klatt

UNIVERSITY OF CALIFORNIA PRESS

Berkeley / Los Angeles / London

University of California Press, one of the most distinguished university presses in the United States, enriches lives around the world by advancing scholarship in the humanities, social sciences, and natural sciences. Its activities are supported by the UC Press Foundation and by philanthropic contributions from individuals and institutions. For more information, visit www.ucpress.edu.

University of California Press
Berkeley and Los Angeles, California

University of California Press, Ltd.
London, England

Originally published in Spanish as *México: Breve Historia Contemporánea* by Fondo de Cultura Económica, copyright © 2000.

Library of Congress Cataloging-in-Publication Data
Hernández Chávez, Alicia.
    [México. English]
    Mexico : a brief history / Alicia Hernández Chávez ; translated by Andy Klatt.
        p.   cm.
    Includes bibliographical references and index.
    ISBN 0-520-23321-2 (cloth : alk. paper).—ISBN 0-520-24491-5 (pbk. : alk. paper)
    1. Mexico—History.   I. Title.
F1226.H4613   2006
972—dc22   2004062002

Manufactured in the United States of America
15   14   13   12   11   10   09   08   07   06
10   9   8   7   6   5   4   3   2   1

To my granddaughters,
PAOLA, SOFÍA, *and* ALICIA

Contents

Maps

Figures

Tables

Preface

One of the great aspirations of historians, especially those who research and teach, is to communicate their own vision of history. One way to communicate this vision of the past is through a general but relatively brief history, one that incorporates information about the different historical periods without engaging in the kind of oversimplification that insults the intelligence of the reader. With this in mind, I have tried to set forth the principal events of Mexico's history and offer my interpretation of both their meanings at the time they occurred and the meanings they have acquired since that time.

Great historical transformations are usually followed by new general histories that reflect on and revise our view of the past from a vantage point that includes new horizons. There is also much to be learned from the histories penned by past generations of writers. They, too, compiled past events and projected them into the historian's present in order to illuminate the circumstances they found themselves in and the historical conjunctures they faced.

My generation lived through the initial breakdown of a political system born out of the reputedly popular revolution of 1910–1920. In 1959 and 1968, popular protest was repressed and intellectuals or political opponents were imprisoned. We were thus positioned to contrast the official history we were taught with the everyday life we experienced: extreme poverty in the face of extravagant wealth, honest and hardworking families in contrast to overnight millionaires, and arbitrariness in defiance of the rule of law.

The end of the Cold War and the new era of globalization have accentuated the breakdown of traditional party systems, political representation, the role of the State, and the role of governments, bringing about a new international instability. Important advances in Mexico's democratic life occurred in the 1980s, and Mexico's entrance into the global market has imposed a different historical tempo. In the first years of the twenty-first century, a new generation of Mexicans is learning to live in a rapidly changing world of relative uncertainty and insecurity. This phenomenon is affecting people all around the globe. Mexico is probably experiencing the end of a cycle that began in the nineteenth century and produced one of the greatest transformations in history, leading to a secular society where individual actors act jointly in the pursuit of social interests in a market economy.

As a historian, I have felt compelled to reflect and write in order to understand Mexico's past and present, and thereby to visualize contemporary Mexico moving in a global world. To conceptualize and produce a general history of a single country, one must take into account the wide range of historical works that have already been produced, including one's own. One must also incorporate the perspectives of anthropologists, political scientists, economists, sociologists, and psychologists, for the historian should produce an account of the past that includes the perspectives of all the social sciences. Only thus does a national history become a part of the history of mankind.

Several works have in the past taken on this challenge. Octavio Paz produced the two greatest syntheses of Mexican history in *The Labyrinth of Solitude* and *Posdata* (also known as *The Other Mexico: Critique of the Pyramid*), which I have read and reread and from which I learned that our Mexicanness is the outgrowth of a wider, universal history as well as our own national experience.

I did not have the privilege of working directly with Paz, but from his writings I learned to examine the critical or determinative elements of the past, which do not necessarily correlate with the temporal divisions of conventional history. I also learned to prefer a recounting of history on the basis of certain elements—continuity, innovation, and transformative moments—which means history with a minimum of names and dates. Thus, in order to present the most illuminating elements of Mexico's history, I have studied the record of past events and selected the most significant moments, eschewing political or ideological motivations. In this way, I hope to have restored to historiography some of its civilizing function.

Much of the thinking that has guided this brief history has matured through the course of my life. I grew up playing on explosive terrain. As a child, I lived in Dinamita, Durango, a volatile nitroglycerine factory town in the crevasses of the Sierra Madre. During my youth and adulthood, Mexico and the world experienced convulsive change. At the same time, the fields of economics, anthropology, political science, sociology, and psychology were becoming ineluctable elements in the writing of history. The historical narrative was transformed from a list of dates, names, and events into a description of the tensions experienced by human societies and the human response to those pressures. This synthesis is an individual work in which I hope to reflect the progress made toward that goal by the collective efforts of Mexican and Mexicanist scholars. More than anything else, I hope that this book reflects the opening of historiography to the contributions of other social sciences. My intention is to present the evolution and the most important transformations in the lives of the Mexican people through that methodological lens.

I have had the good fortune to benefit from the wisdom of those who have gone before me and to learn from my maestros; in addition, I have profited tremendously from the help of my friends and colleagues. Under no other circumstances could I have dared to relate the events of six centuries, an account whose goal is to understand my country's present on the basis of its historical past in order to illustrate the nature of Mexico's full transition to contemporaneity. I have tried to avoid a moralistic or judgmental tone toward the actions of any historical actor, or the passing of judgment on any social actor or actors in the course of recounting their specific actions. Classifying social actors as good or bad contributes little to an understanding of the historical junctures or challenges they faced, or to knowing how they met those challenges or appreciating the ongoing effects of the choices that they made. By setting moral judgment aside, in fact, it becomes that much easier to get close to the actual historical experiences, from those of the conquest to those that have concerned Mexico in recent years—the recurrent crises that often seem to threaten all that her people have built with no small effort.

As I have said, this general history provides only the most basic information. The reader will not find interminable lists of dates, generals, and rulers. It is intended as a short presentation of the attitudes and behaviors adopted by the Mexicans, both those who occupied positions of political, economic, or cultural authority and those who worked, studied, and made Mexican history without attracting any extraordinary attention to themselves. In short, I offer the reader a history of the Mexican people. Nevertheless, this work is limited in scope; it is a historical summary and thus emphasizes what I consider to be the relevant aspects of Mexico's history. The writing of a complete general history of Mexico would require the participation of a large group of historians and social scientists. Thus my goal is limited: to offer a text that can be appreciated by the largest possible number of readers while providing up-to-date, clearly organized, and well-presented information on Mexico's political, social, and economic history, together with an interpretation of the historical processes in play. It should be easy for the reader to take in the information presented and form his or her own judgments upon it.

The history of a country is like the biography of an individual: it can be understood by distinguishing its significant stages. I hope that the reader will find the chapter structure of this book helpful in this regard. For instance, in the chapter centered on the independence period, the reader will also find a description of significant factors leading to the events of 1800–1824 and their origins in the colonial order described in the previous chapter. Thus there is a focus on both continuity and rupture. The chapter then presents a framework for understanding the development of mid-nineteenth-century Mexico as described in the following chapter. The division of history into periods reflects my understanding and personal interpretation of historical processes.

Studying a set of events on a timeline divided into historical periods helps us to better understand the unfolding of history at each stage of its development. However, I have also made a special effort to link historical situations and events to the defining element of each period, be it the conquest, colonial society, independence, the revolution, nationalism, statism, neoliberalism, or globalization. I have tried to avoid one of the common weaknesses of brief histories by organizing events within a specific historical process that logically incorporates political, social, and economic factors. The logic of this narrative structure should illuminate the characteristics and organizing principles of each period in question. A narrative history organized around the continuity of processes has two advantages: events are organized logically, and the reader is provided with space in which to formulate his or her own conclusions, which he or she is then free to measure against the conclusions proposed by the author throughout the work.

A brief selected bibliography is provided at the end of the work. I hope it will pique the reader's interest in examining and learning more about the history of Mexico. While the bibliography does not include all the important works published on the topic, I believe that it is a good foundation for further study.

I particularly want to recognize the invaluable criticisms and suggestions of Marcello Carmagnani and John Womack Jr. We have had numerous memorable conversations around the subject matter of this book and other topics, and I owe them an endless intellectual debt. In different ways, Manuel Miño Grijalva and Jaime Rodriguez have played significant roles in the making of this book, and I thank them. Of course, none of my colleagues is in the least responsible for any error on my part. I had the good fortune to work on this edition with Andy Klatt, a very knowledgeable and skilled translator. I also thank Laura Harger and the staff of the University of California for their careful work on the presentation of this book.

My parents, Óscar and Alicia Hernández Chávez, and my sons, Ricardo and Adolfo Orive Hernández, have given me continual and unconditional support amid the ceaseless changes that we have all endured. They have all made life ever more exciting.

CHAPTER I

The Indigenous World

When the Spanish stepped onto the American mainland, they encountered a complex cultural tapestry. Some indigenous cultures were thriv-
ing, some retained vigorous traditions, and others were in decline, but
each had its own rich and unique features. Some twenty million people
inhabited the Mesoamerican area, concentrated in large interdependent
urban centers with outlying clusters of agricultural settlements.

The cities had differentiated themselves from the countryside in the
Classic period, between 200 and 900 A.D. Although the numerous agricultural settlements were small, people tended to group themselves into
villages with strong internal social distinctions. The rural areas were dependent and subordinate to the city-states, which were inhabited by elite
social strata. Political, administrative, religious, and artisanal activities
were concentrated in the cities, and services could be obtained there. The
urban elites had developed the capacity to organize and direct complex
labor relations.

The growing population and the sophisticated social organization
stimulated the development of new technologies, such as improved seed
stock and agricultural irrigation in the countryside. The evolution of
urban planning led to new construction technologies and the building of
plumbing infrastructure in the cities. Stone conduits carried water to
both the cities and the fields. In the Mayan area, canals were fed from
cenotes, naturally occurring spring-fed limestone sinkholes. On the large
lakes of the Valley of Mexico, fresh water was fed to *chinampas,* artificial
earthen islands like those still seen in Xochimilco, to the south of Mexico

I

City, that were anchored by live *huejote* trees and fertilized with lichen, aquatic vegetation, and mud from the lake bed. Elsewhere, water was supplied to terraced fields carved into mountainsides. Water reserves, intended to produce high agricultural yields, were stored in enormous earthenware vessels, in small dammed ponds, and in *cenotes*. A system of internal roads provided transportation within large urban areas. These are still observable in pre-Hispanic archeological sites. Another road system linked together the far-flung urban centers. These innovations and natural resources served the daily needs of villages and of the cities that began to expand around 200 A.D., a development that stimulated productivity through the employment of more intensive and extensive sowing and harvesting methods, and satisfied both cultural and religious needs through the widespread exchange of goods.

The use of animal power and of the wheel were unknown to indigenous society when the Spanish arrived. In their place was a complex organization of labor that spread throughout the villages and cities and produced marked social differentiation. Political organization also became more complex as nobles came to govern large areas and developed the means to dominate rural society. Soon they were able to establish kinship relations and form alliances with the nobles of different ethnicities in distant regions.

Wars between nobles' domains, minor kingdoms, and ruling dynasties were constant, but complex military institutions did not develop because the politico-religious aspects of conflict predominated over the strictly military. Shifting alliances and matrimonial pacts, rather than warfare itself, were instrumental in the rise and fall of ruling families and capital cities.

Long-distance trade relations were another fundamental characteristic of pre-Hispanic society. Complex religious, political, and family networks were organized in order to develop and maintain these relations, facilitating a certain degree of population mobility.

The Ancestors

Archeological evidence tells us that there were human settlements twenty thousand years ago in present-day Mexico and part of Central America. In this sense, the history of Mexico began several millennia ago, if by *history* we mean the story that began the moment humans were first able to transform their physical environment to sustain and reproduce families, engage in art and religion, and develop social relations among family lines.

The first population groups spent most of their time and energy gathering wild fruits and vegetables and hunting for meat. They organized themselves into bands of twenty to thirty families under the authority of a chief, to whom they attributed superior, and perhaps religious, qualities. These bands moved within wide areas, since a family of five required nearly four-tenths of a square mile in order to maintain and reproduce itself. The bands' mobility can also be explained by the need to defend themselves against other humans who entered their territory. These hunter-gatherers also spent time in the manufacture of wooden domestic utensils and weapons such as bows, arrows, and blowpipes. Group activities were accompanied by religious rites and ceremonial meals.

Archeological finds indicate that human settlements were dynamic and multiplied over time, presumably due to population growth and the increasing size of the bands. It was probably at this "macroband" stage that the social and political authority of the chief began to be differentiated from the politico-religious function of magical healers who were responsible for the well-being of the group.

About seven thousand years ago, during the fifth millennium B.C., the Indians of Mexico began to cultivate the plants that they had up until then gathered in the wild. These plants formed the basis of the Mesoamerican diet. Most of them, like corn, beans, onions, squash, chilies, avocados, and tomatillos, would by colonial times enrich the human diet worldwide, along with the Andean potato.

Like the conversion to the socially more complex macrobands, the switch from hunting and gathering to agriculture was gradual. It was not a simple transmission of knowledge from one generation to the next. It was the outcome of complex processes involving the selection of plant species, their genetic mutation, and the ability to remember and predict weather patterns and their implications for the availability of plant and animal food.

The transition from nomadic to seminomadic life took several millennia, from 5000 to 2500 B.C. During this time, members of macrobands developed the agricultural skills necessary for intermittent farming and, subsequently, the additional sophisticated skills that could support permanent cultivation and settlement. Hunters still ventured from these settlements seasonally in order to bring back meat and products obtained in trade with other bands. The macrobands diversified their activities and eventually became tribes with elaborate social hierarchies, living in villages and building wattle-and-daub structures.

The development of agriculture stimulated important inventions, such as farming tools and other objects carved from stone, and earthenware containers for the storage and preservation of seeds and produce. It has been said that the Indigenous women of Mexico invented fired clay and transformed wild corn into domestic varieties. The illustrious botanist George Wells Beadle indicated that in breeding corn from a native species of grass called *teosintle,* the Indigenous people of the region produced the greatest morphological change in any cultivated plant and extended its range over a wider area than any other staple crop.[1] Another significant contribution of the Mesoamerican Indians was the domestication of cotton and the production of textiles from its spun fiber, replacing the use of maguey. By 1300 A.D., Mesoamericans were cultivating a variety of crops sufficient to provide a balanced diet of vegetable proteins and fatty oils: corn, beans, squash, and avocados.

Over time, the population became primarily sedentary and a common Mesoamerican religion spread, characterized by ceremonial burials and abundant figurines—lucid expressions of the Mesoamerican imagination and the construction of a symbolic world.

The Birth of Mesoamerica

Almost five thousand years ago, between 3000 and 2500 B.C., the cultures living on the stretch of land between Guatemala and the American Southwest began to divide into two cultural areas. Sedentary agriculture became well established in the Mesoamerican cultures from southern Guatemala to northern San Luis Potosí, while hunting and gathering persisted in what we call the Arid American cultures, which were located from Tamaulipas, Mexico, above the twenty-first parallel north to the Californias, Utah, Colorado, and Texas.

The cultural differences among the peoples of these large areas did not create conflict among them. On the contrary, goods, knowledge, and cultural practices flowed across their extensive and permeable frontiers, as they do across the political boundaries today. Ethnic and cultural recom-

---

1. George Wells Beadle, *The Language of Life* (Chicago: University of Chicago Press, 1967).

bination produced new multiethnic and multicultural communities. This permeability of the cultural boundary was due in part to the fact that it was never fixed but rather fluctuated in accordance with climatic cycles. In dry times, the people of the border region took up nomadism, while in temperate and humid times, they settled down and practiced agriculture.

Arid America was an ecological mosaic. Deserts alternated with fertile plains in areas contiguous to Mesoamerica. Its people traveled long distances. For example, hunters of the North American plains and fishermen of the Pacific Northwest moved throughout the Californias.

Map 1.1 suggests the possibilities for economic and cultural exchange between Mesoamerica and Arid America, a characteristic shared by the U.S.–Mexican border today. Responding to the demographic pressure produced by their own expansion, about 2000 B.C. sedentary agriculturalists began to extend the leading edge of Mesoamerican culture to the northern states of Mexico and the U.S. states of Arizona, New Mexico, and California. At this time, new settlements sprang up, and pockets of oasis agriculture prospered along the rivers in valleys and on plains in the southwestern United States and northwestern Mexico.[2]

In the twenty-seven centuries between 2500 B.C. and 200 A.D., Mesoamerican villages evolved into complex organizations. Agricultural villages began the period as settlements of twenty or so huts, living from agriculture based on seasonal rains and the silt deposited by rivers. They engaged in trade with other villages, but trading was still precarious at this stage. The existence of a symbolic world was underscored by protective deities. Agricultural and hydroengineering techniques for the construction of terraces, dams, and canals spread in the eight hundred years between 1200 and 400 B.C., what we call the Middle Preclassic period, making truly permanent and socially differentiated settlements possible. Agricultural cycles were regularized and additional plants were domesticated. The combined effect of new domestic plant species, regular harvests, and greater productivity stimulated both local and long-distance trade, and the acquisition of prestige goods became possible. Economic specialization and social differentiation appeared, along with political and religious hierarchies that organized and channeled the population's activities and energies. A partial writing system and the initial calendar registers were invented, and the first great ceremonial centers were built. To-

2. Further explanation is found in Alfredo López Austin and Leonardo López Luján, *Mexico's Indigenous Past* (Norman: University of Oklahoma Press, 2001), pp. 15–21.

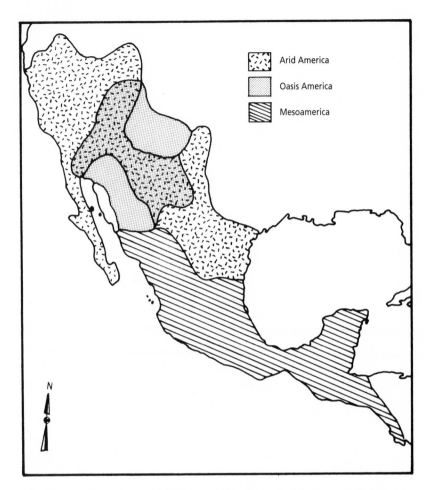

MAP 1.1. Ancient Mexico and its three cultural superareas. (Source: Alfredo López Austin and Leonardo López Luján, *El Pasado Indígena* [Mexico City: Fideicomiso Historia de las Américas—El Colegio de México—Fondo de Cultura Económica, 1996], p. 16.)

gether these developments produced the first pan-Mesoamerican culture, the Olmec.

Map 1.2 illustrates the original areas of Olmec culture in the region around Veracruz and Tabasco on the Gulf Coast. Olmec influence soon crossed the Valley of Mexico, Oaxaca, and Chiapas to reach the Pacific, ranging as far north as the border of Jalisco and as far south as Costa Rica. It was spread by long-distance trade in obsidian, jade, the basalt used for

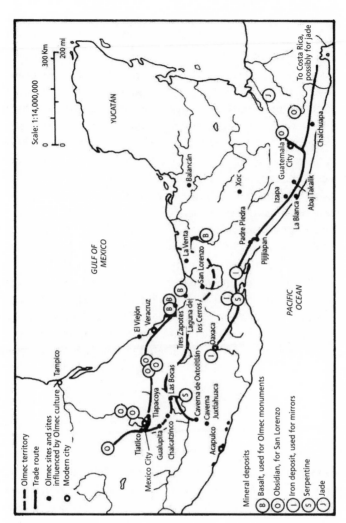

MAP 1.2. Olmec settlements and cultural influence. (Source: Michael Coe, Dean Snow, and Elizabeth Benson, *Atlas of Ancient America* [New York: Facts on File, 1986], p. 133.)

monuments, and the iron used for mirrors—all of them new, highly valued, and prestigious materials for many peoples.

Olmec art reflects a culture dominated by its religion and its powerful nobility, most famously through a large number of colossal stone heads. Recent finds indicate the existence of a great many divinities with similar attributes. In Las Limas, Veracruz, for example, a figure that dates from 800 to 400 B.C. portrays the accession to the throne of a young man represented as a jaguar in the arms of a noble, indicating his royal status. Four totemic divinities representing God the Creator are sculpted on the back and the knees of the jaguar-boy. The direct descendants of the royal line were obliged to perpetuate the memory of this God the Creator and to fulfill his commitments to the people. This kind of sculpture is a key to understanding Olmec iconography.

Olmec beliefs permeated other cultures. Its concept of a hierarchical society and government dominated by an elite group dedicated to a cult of gods and ancestors spread to various Mesoamerican regions, first by conquest and trade, and later through missionary zeal. The hierarchical conception of political life took particularly strong root in the Zapotec and Mayan civilizations. Without a doubt, the Olmec culture stimulated significant cultural changes, beginning around 1200 B.C., producing the relative cultural homogeneity in Mesoamerica that astonished the first Spanish invaders.

The Classic Period in Mesoamerica

Between 200 B.C. and 900 A.D., various aspects of Mesoamerican civilization matured. The population grew as production and regional trade increased. Outlying villages were integrated into the hierarchical systems of large urban centers. This process reached its apogee in the first few centuries A.D., most notably in the organization of territories surrounding architecturally monumental cities such as Teotihuacán, Monte Albán, and the Mayan cities of Uxmal, Copán, and Palenque.

Many reasons have been offered for the flowering of these great Mesoamerican cultures—most prominently, that there was an expansion of production sufficient to sustain larger numbers of people within the polity. We know of no new technologies that were comparable in impact to those of the Preclassic; however, during this period, trade, conquest, and cultural mimesis spread variations of existing technologies over the entire Mesoamerican region.

Recent studies of Mayan culture have suggested that the great ceremonial cities did not have continuous control over their surrounding areas. It seems that outlying areas would affiliate with whichever city offered them the greatest advantages at a given time. Thus urban elites had to constantly maintain positive relations with secondary settlements, lest village-level nobles incite rebellion against the authority of the capital.

The power of the calendar was crucial to political, governmental, cultural, and religious domination in every Mesoamerican culture. An understanding of meteorology, and of time and its calendrical expression, along with theocratic control of this knowledge comprised a major technocultural achievement of the extended historical period. Religion and calendrical calculation were combined in divinatory practices that drove fundamental changes in social and political organization. They gave rise to complex and hierarchical societies based on lineage and territorial rights. Kings were surrounded by nobles, priests, and sorcerers. The nobles, or *pipiltin*, were hereditary leaders who ruled over separate communities of *macehualtin*, or commoners. Both cosmic and worldly qualities were attributed to those who governed. Priests interpreted the religious calendar, the oracles, and divination cycles, while kings and nobles explained the significance of the agricultural calendar, supervised the functioning of the community, and administered its territory. Soldiers and merchants, in addition to their primary activities, performed diplomatic duties in the areas where they traveled. The strategy of sending members of the royal family to live permanently in other kingdoms may have begun at this time as a way to guarantee alliances. It was also an adaptation of the rule that royals could marry only other royals.

There were also local particularities during the thousand years of Classical Mesoamerican culture. In terms of the calendar, there were two major systems, that of Teotihuacán and that of the Maya. Teotihuacán maintained a relatively simple system that combined a 365-day religious-agricultural cycle with a 260-day sacred almanac, a divinatory calendar. The Maya, however, calculated the sequences and correspondences of their own two calendars much more precisely and elaborately. The two traditions were also distinguished by what Alfredo López Austin and Leonardo López Luján call "the symbolization of mental representations" in the case of Teotihuacán, and "the symbolization of verbal expressions" in the case of the Maya.[3] Put another way, Teotihuacán

3. López Austin and López Luján, *Mexico's Indigenous Past;* for the Mayan calendar, see pp. 150–53; for central Mexico, pp. 240–41.

ideograms, or figurative symbols, were used to represent ideas, while Mayan logograms represented words, which in turn represented ideas. The Classic was undoubtedly a period of fundamental and qualitative change. The impact of its religion and its social, cultural, and political organization lasted until the conquest. Map 1.3 illustrates the diffusion of Classic cultures in the center of Mexico. Teotihuacán culture was the most dynamic and was best situated for geographic diffusion, while the Monte Albán and Gulf Coast cultures were more geographically isolated.

Teotihuacán, in the Valley of Mexico, was a large metropolis of 170,000 to 200,000 people living in an area of less than eight square miles. It was the largest city in the Americas, powerful by virtue of its control over deposits of obsidian, an enormously valuable commercial commodity, as well as its ceramic and obsidian manufactures and long-distance trade. The population was fed through high-yield agriculture carried out on *chinampas,* artificial islands constructed in swampy areas.

Unlike the Mayan cities, Teotihuacán was multiethnic, divided into ethnically based residential neighborhoods that preserved individual languages and cultural practices. The presence of multiple ethnicities may explain the city's ability to spread its influence throughout the territories seen in map 1.3. A series of transportation corridors led to Jalisco, the Gulf and Pacific coastal regions, and southeast to Oaxaca and Chiapas. We do not know if one ethnic group governed the others or if noble succession was along family lines. We know only that there was a governing elite.

The city of Monte Albán, in the Oaxaca cultural area, had a longer life and greater continuity than Teotihuacán. It began to develop in 400 B.C. and reached its highest cultural development in 600 A.D. It had an intricate and complex culture, with a calendar similar to that of Teotihuacán and a rich and elaborate religious symbolism. The capital city dominated the entire Valley of Oaxaca through a well-structured political system, also exercising indirect control over Mixtec kingdoms in the nearby mountains. Monte Albán was divided into fifteen large districts based on lineages and occupational groups. Each district organized its own economic activities. The writing system was linear, pointing to the importance of syntax in the language. Stone inscriptions chronicle the exploits and conquests of Monte Albán's nobles and their alliances with other noble families.

Let us consider the features that fostered the movement and expansion so characteristic of Mesoamerican cultures. Map 1.4 illustrates the prominence of the Mayan city-states, large urban centers that dominated their surrounding territories, and shows their layout in relation to one another and the local and regional roads that connected them. However, there

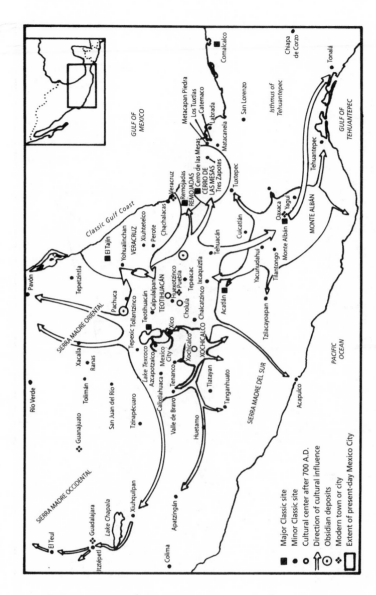

MAP 1.3. Mesoamerican cultures in the Classic period. (Source: Michael Coe, Dean Snow, and Elizabeth Benson, *Atlas of Ancient America*, op. cit., p. 105.)

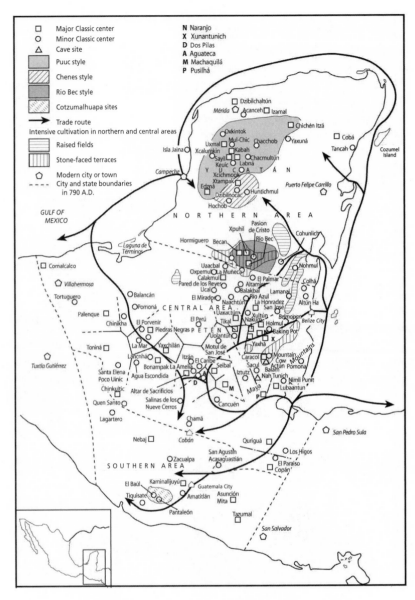

MAP 1.4. City-states of the Classic Mayan civilization. (Source: Michael Coe, Dean Snow, and Elizabeth Benson, *Atlas of Ancient America,* op. cit., p. 126.)

were also commercial routes by land and sea that linked the Mayan area with the center of Mexico. The fact that both of these large cultural areas developed quickly during this period strongly suggests that there was constant exchange between them.

Despite certain cultural commonalities with the rest of Mesoamerica, Classical Mayan civilization had its own particularities, developed over the five hundred years beginning about 400 A.D. Most city-states maintained links with each other through the intermarriage of royalty, with no one city dominating the others. Even Tikal, the major city of the Petén region, never imposed its will on the others. This explains how there came to be some twenty city-states, each with an urban center for its capital and each dominating its own territory, in the Mayan area around the first century A.D.

Like people in other indigenous cultural areas, by the first century A.D. the Maya had a high population growth rate. This spurred urban centers such as Tikal to develop new technologies and to transition from strictly seasonal to full-time, intensive, and diversified agriculture. Likewise, Mesoamericans in the Valley of Mexico began to terrace the land, reclaim marshland, and channel and store water for agricultural and urban consumption.

The political systems of Classic Mesoamerica grew ever more complex. Not only were royals distinguished from commoners, but there were hierarchical relations among different noble families operating according to strict rules of succession. Priests and warriors were also ranked. Lords were considered quasi-divine; the legitimacy of their power was totemic, deriving from the relationship between a divinity and a human group via the sacred link represented by the sovereign.

By the eighth century A.D., the Mayan territory contained a population of several million. Fifty thousand people lived in Tikal, an area of not much more than six square miles. The average noble family controlled an urban center of ten to fifteen thousand people. A king of kings, or *chulahuau,* presided over *ahauobo,* secondary kings of various ranks who governed in interdependent kingdoms of greater or lesser importance. Every smaller kingdom and lesser domain had a presence in the confederation, and its authority was represented in a major governing city. The lesser kings, established in a central city, delegated authority within their own jurisdiction to others of their lineage or to lesser nobles called *cahal,* but never to commoners. The unity and cohesion of the kingdoms, of which there must have been somewhere between twelve and sixty in the eighth century, were maintained by means of a complex web of noble families, all of them socially, economically, and culturally interrelated.

The main transportation route between the plateau and the Mayan lowlands was at first by river and along the coasts in wooden boats. Later, short- and long-distance trade roads were developed. Drought and floods were managed by means of complex reservoir and canal systems that ran under the cities, capturing rainwater and water from underground springs. The Maya also learned to utilize the huge limestone sinkholes called *cenotes* that collected underground spring water. Cultivated areas alongside rivers and marshes were elevated and heaped with rich swamp mud. The Maya grew lichen and raised fish in irrigation ditches running between the raised beds, using the lichen and fish excrement as fertilizers. The extensive organization of labor power implicit in these methods was rewarded with two or three harvests per year. These agricultural practices were so culturally salient that the kings adopted the water lily, typically found alongside the raised beds, as their symbol.

The jurisdictional boundaries between kingdoms were determined by wars fought exclusively in the dry season between January and May. At other times, people concentrated on agriculture, religious rituals, and other daily tasks. The Mayan calendar organized the cycle of life, which was said to last fifty-two years and was essential to the performance of rituals; the utilization of space; and strategies for trade, war, and marriage, as well as for the frequent conflicts of succession between ruling families. All things of importance were scheduled at auspicious times as determined by the stars and by omens. The Mesoamerican cultures had a cyclical and nonevolutionary rather than linear concept of time, reflecting their teleological worldview; that is, they believed that human events were divinely predetermined.

Deities were believed to sanctify the ritual spaces in cities and urban centers and to exalt them with their powers. At the conclusion of a cycle of life, intricate rituals were performed. Stelae were destroyed; houses and huts demolished; plates broken; and lilies, irises, and other flowers buried in natural caves. These rituals invoked the presence of the divinities and sanctified the sites where new cities would be built. They were intended to stimulate the emergence of a new ruling family, which would then be responsible for further renewal ceremonies and the planning of the future city. Similar ceremonies accompanied the spiritual burial of the deceased ruler. The earth's surface was perforated in order to renew human ties with the underworld. This was believed to enhance the grandeur of the new noble household. Likewise, ceremonies would be performed on elevated sites in order to facilitate the transmutation of the king and his shamanic passage across the three levels of the world.

The Decline of the Ancient World

Unlike previous periods, the Mesoamerican Postclassic, the period of the decline of the Indigenous cultures, produced an extensive written record. Thus we can date conquests and migrations, identify rulers by name, and even quantify tributes. The period is further distinguished by the introduction of metallurgy based on gold and copper, which seems to have arrived from South America about 800 A.D. This significant technological event led to the availability and use of new tools such as the ax, the chisel, the scalpel, the hoe, and the machetelike *coa*.

For reasons that are not yet clear, the great capital cities of central and southeastern Mexico fell or collapsed in the Postclassic period between 900 and 1500 A.D. The fate of two cities, one in the Mayan area and the other in the center, exemplify the events of the new period. The Toltec capital of Tula in central Mexico fell in 1150 to warriors from the north. In the southeast, the Mayan capital of Chichén Itzá fell to the Mexicas in 1250. The Mexicas and the warrior groups would dominate large areas of Mesoamerica until the arrival of the Spanish. This long period was characterized by increased social and geographic mobility, which explains the appearance of multiethnic power centers, and by political instability, intensified trade through expanded trading networks, and reconfigured interrelationships of religion, culture, and politics.

An appreciation of Postclassic society and its circumstances is essential to understanding the Indigenous reaction to the Spanish invasion. Cultural change intensified after 1000 A.D, when climatic changes drove seminomadic northern agriculturalists southward to central Mexico. Hunter-gatherers joined this migratory stream along the way. They belonged to many groups but were known collectively as *chichimecas,* or barbarians. As the migrants moved south in successive streams, they acquired much of the complex knowledge and adopted many of the technologies and practices that they encountered. They also stimulated increased militarism in the societies that they passed through or conquered.

The wave of northern peoples made a significant impact on political organization. They established new, highly organized power centers and focused more than ever on the political domination and subjugation of surrounding territories, accomplished by the establishment of subordinate kingdoms and the exaction of tribute. These new conditions explain the proliferation of conflict and rivalry leading to war in the Postclassic period. Subjugated peoples resisted domination by other ethnicities and the imposition of tributary relations. The Spanish would later be able to exploit these conflicts to their own advantage.

Militarism was widespread in the period. Warriors came from noble families, studied in special schools, and were organized by rank. They took on the attributes of fierce animals, becoming eagle-men, jaguar-men, or coyote-men, each pertaining to a corresponding religious cult. Warrior societies operated autonomously or at the service of power centers that called upon them to wage war. The result was continuous conflict, again a situation that the Spanish exploited in their military alliances with various ethnically based kingdoms or chieftainships.

The warrior societies participated in the cult of the god Plumed Serpent, who was the medium for the transmission of power to the new ruler-kings. Taking the name of this god, sovereigns in the center of Mexico now called themselves Quetzalcóatl, and in Yucatán, Kukulkán. Other myths served similar functions. The god Fifth Sun, for example, demanded that warriors capture prisoners for sacrifice. The art and architecture of the period were strongly influenced, and impoverished, by the dominant militarism.

Postclassic cultural forms were most forcefully expressed in central Mexico, where three waves of migration converged to transform the land and its political destiny. The Toltecs arrived in the tenth to twelfth centuries, the Chichimecas in the twelfth century, and the Mexicas in the fifteenth century. The Oaxaca culture was also modified by violent conflicts and by the shared occupation of its power centers by the agreement of various ethnic groups. In this period the Mixtecs infiltrated into Mitla and the fertile valleys of Oaxaca, and the Toltecs spread throughout Mesoamerica as far as Yucatán. The city of Chichén Itzá on the Yucatán peninsula shared many important characteristics with Tula, the Toltec capital in central Mexico.

There are two reasons for the inordinate attention paid to the Mexica people in any discussion of the Mesoamerican Postclassic. First of all, there is abundant archeological and documentary evidence to work with. Most importantly, they founded the empire that contested the Spanish invasion. However, their period of influence was brief. Between 1325 and 1430 the Mexicas, then subordinate to the Tepanecos, settled on some islands in Lake Texcoco. After defeating the kingdom of Atzcapotzalco in 1469, they constructed a confederation of kingdoms and expanded militarily until 1502. They would be overcome by the Spanish invasion less than two decades later.

Map 1.5 illustrates the formation and expansion of the Mexicas' Empire of the Triple Alliance. Its essential characteristics and its diffuse

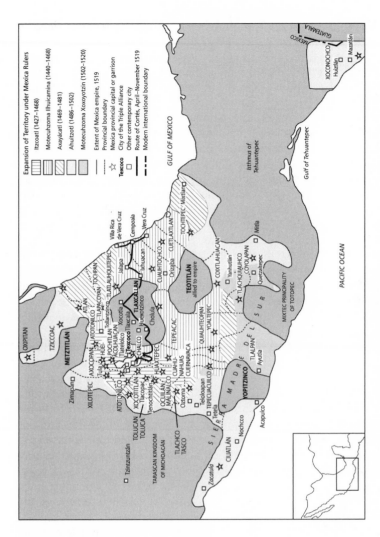

Expansion of Territory under Mexica Rulers

- Itzcoatl (1427–1468)
- Motecuhzoma Ilhuicamina (1440–1468)
- Axayácatl (1469–1481)
- Ahuitzotl (1486–1502)
- Motecuhzoma Xoxoyotzin (1502–1520)
- Extent of Mexica empire, 1519
- Provincial boundary
- Mexica provincial capital or garrison
- **Texcoco** City of the Triple Alliance
- Other contemporary city
- Route of Cortés, April–November 1519
- Modern international boundary

MAP 1.5. The empire of the Mexicas. (Source: Michael Coe, Dean Snow, and Elizabeth Benson, *Atlas of Ancient America*, op. cit., p. 146.)

territorial configuration of intermingling territories are best described by Pedro Carrasco:

After Tenochtitlan and Tetzcoco defeated the Tepanecs, their rulers Itzcoatl and Nezahualcoyotl decided to include Totoquihuatzin of Tlacopan as the third member of the alliance and thus established a new political order in the Basin. From the moment the Triple Alliance was founded, the decisions made by the victors illustrate the organizational features basic to the territorial structure of the new regime. Three of those features were aspects of the segmentary structure on which the Empire was based.

In each of the three capital cities the king would govern his own domain directly and without interference, continuing an already existing political and dynastic organization. Each of the three great kings kept under his rule a group of kingdoms, each with its own dynasty and ethnic tradition. The king of Tenochtitlan ruled the Colhua-Mexica kingdoms, the king of Tetzcoco the Acolhua-Chichimec kingdoms, and the king of Tlacopan the Tepanec kingdoms. In this way, each of the three parts of the alliance included a capital city with its great king and the lesser kingdoms with their dependent kings. A tripartite organization was thus established by the founding kings. The entire region that comprised the alliance was divided into three parts, each defined geographically as the domain of one of the three capitals.

Next this tripartite division was extended beyond the core area of the Basin. The three great kings decided that in all future conquests one of the three would be preeminent in one of the three sectors of the Empire. Beyond the Basin the area of each sector was adjacent to the domain of one of the ruling capital cities within the core area, with Tenochtitlan predominant in the south, Tetzcoco in the northeast, and Tlacopan in the northwest. Finally, in some of the areas first conquered by the Empire each capital took possession of separate towns, but as a rule the distant conquered regions paid tribute to the Empire as a unit, and their tribute was then shared by the three capitals. From the beginning there was, therefore, a series of distributions of conquered towns, of exchange of rights to the land, and of participation in tribute income that resulted in the scattering and consequently the intermingling of the territorial possessions of the three capitals, and of their rights to tribute, throughout the entire Empire. This intermingling constituted a third basic feature of the imperial structure. To a certain extent the three allied kingdoms were equivalent parts of the imperial structure, but a functional differentiation among them was established that gave predominance to the Tenochca king as director of the imperial armies. The proportion in which conquered lands and tribute were divided also favored Tenochtitlan, as did the practice of taking tribute from conquered areas to Tenochtitlan before distributing it among the three kingdoms.[4]

4. Pedro Carrasco, *The Tenochca Empire of Ancient Mexico: The Triple Alliance of Tenochtitlan, Tetzcoco, and Tlacopan* (Norman: University of Oklahoma Press, 1999), pp. 29–30.

Franciscan monk Fray Toribio Motolinía (?–1569) described the function of the large cities as seats of lineages in his *History of the Indians of New Spain:*

All the nobles who are subjects of the Mexican empire, who, as it is said, are thirty to one hundred thousand vassals and three thousand nobles of lands and many vassals were obliged to live in Mexico City a certain part of the year to be recognized at the court of Moteczumacin [Moctezuma]. And when they went to their lands and reigns, it was at the pleasure and will of the King. And they left a son or a brother for security and so that they would not rise up. For this reason all of them had houses in the city of Mexico-Tenuchtitlan [Tenochtitlan].[5]

The intermarried lineages linking each city with others meant that a given kingdom usually had additional seats of authority or possessions in other cities as well. This would have been a binding arrangement by which rights to land and tribute were interchanged, comparable to a diplomatic treaty between allied nobles. These common arrangements created labyrinthine relationships in the region. Several lords or confederated lordships would dominate territories within the boundaries of which there were also lands subject to other sovereignties. This checkerboard of sovereignties and ethnicities was sometimes the result of separate land distributions and migrations that took place over the course of time. But Carrasco defines the convoluted nature of land tenure as a conscious policy of the Triple Alliance to forge unity and establish overall clarity of control over its territory, a strategy he also attributes to previous polities, and which may have been general to Mesoamerica. This would explain the role of capital cities as centers of kingdoms having dependent kingdoms where either allied or subordinate nobles reigned, depending on the form of domination between the center and neighboring ethnic lordships and chieftainships.

Without a doubt, religion was an essential element of Mesoamerican societies. "The History of the Mexicans as Told by Their Paintings" is a Spanish translation of a pre-Columbian codex that juxtaposes numerous fragments of Indigenous art that illustrate a teleological view of when and by whom the world was created:

The four brethren gods, sons of Tonacateuhtli . . . all committed to Quetzalcóatl and Huitzilopochtli the performance of this task, in compliance with which they

5. Toribio Motolinía, *History of the Indians of New Spain* (Washington, D.C.: Academy of American Franciscan History, 1951), p. 83.

created, under the orders and judgment of the others, fire. This being done they made the half-sun. . . .

Presently they created a man and a woman; the man they called Uxumuxo, and the woman, Cipactonal. And they commanded them to till the ground, and they commanded her to spin and weave. . . . And that the *macehualtin* [commoners] should be born of them and that these should be not idle, that they be ever toiling.[6]

The idea of the divine origin of their society was not unique to the Mexicas. Indeed, it was common to many Mesoamerican cultures. The Mayan world had three levels: heaven, earth, and the underworld, all closely interrelated and sharing a common divine origin. The plane of human existence was sacred. It was defined by four cardinal points relative to a fundamental center. A tree, with its concentric rings, represented the four points. Its trunk stood on the earth. Its roots penetrated the underworld, and its branches extended laterally to touch the lowest reaches of the heavens. Human communities existed in the earthly dimension, which encompassed plains, mountains, lakes, and the subterranean *cenotes*, as well as the cities, palaces, and temples that humans themselves constructed. The sacredness of this human space was underscored by the existence of caves and mountains, centers of power complementing and materializing the concentricity of divine creation and its four cardinal points. We can describe the fundamental Mesoamerican conception of the world as divided along a horizontal cross section, with everything above belonging to heaven and everything below being terrestrial. Humankind, inhabiting a narrow strip between these realms, was created by the conjunction of all things, fathered by the sky that is, and conceived by the earth. The procreative process could be analyzed into four steps: the semen's descent from heaven, the conception of mother earth, childbirth, and the horizontal dispersal of the offspring to form the many peoples and fulfill God's plan.

How was the teleological principle expressed in Mesoamerican society? According to López Austin, God the Creator of all humankind, known as Quetzalcóatl in the Nahuatl-speaking world and by a different vernacular name in each community, assumed the role of God the Protector in the act of spilling his blood.[7] The function of God the Protec-

6. "Historia de los Mexicanos por Sus Pinturas," in Angel María Garibay, *Teogonia e Historia de los Mexicanos* (Mexico City: Porrúa, 1965), p. 25.

7. Alfredo López Austin, *Hombre-Dios: Religión y Política en el Mundo Náhuatl* (Mexico City: UNAM, 1989), p. 53.

tor was to lead the human community to the chosen land; by this means he became the Heart of the People.

López Austin does not tell us that God's status as protector was inherited by his direct descendents, the kings or supreme lords known as *tlatoani*, but Linda Schele and David Freidel report that the Maya believed this to be the case.[8] Nevertheless, all agree that men related by blood along patrilineal and endogamous kinship lines formed a community, and these communities were then hierarchically organized as kings or principal lords, priests, military chieftains, censors, and teachers. The community was not necessarily isolated. In fact it could be integrated with other human groups, such as *calpulli* in the Mexica area, or clan lineages among the Maya, to enjoy greater social benefits or establish a workable balance of population, agricultural resources, and trade.[9] The organization of Mesoamerican cities indicates a clear separation between ceremonial centers and agricultural (i.e., peasant) settlements. Within the cities, neighborhoods were organized on the basis of ethnicity or occupation, whether artisanal or commercial.

The Mesoamerican social fabric was sustained by reciprocity within the extended family and by a hierarchical organization based on the divine origin of the community. This enabled the nobility, called *pipiltin* in the Mexica area and *cahualob* among the Maya, to live off tributes assessed on the basis of agricultural surpluses and the availability of prestige goods. The existence of the nobility also had a basis in teleology, since "The god who is guardian and provider of water to the farmer is also he who sets the responsibilities of specialists and delivers them their instruments."[10] Each trade or craft had its own particular protector, its *nahual*.

The four cardinal points provided the conceptual parameters of a quadrilateral and concentric universe within which all social and territorial spaces were arranged and all social activities were framed. The overall space was both general and particular, each space within it a part of the whole. There was no abstract idea of a unitary space, only of different spaces with specific properties. We can say the same of time. There was

8. Linda Schele and David Freidel, *A Forest of Kings: The Untold Story of the Ancient Maya* (New York: William Morrow, 1990), pp. 64–95.

9. The word *calpulli* is usually interpreted in one of two ways: as a kinship organization with residential or territorial implications, or as an administrative division of cities intended to organize labor resources and the collection of tributes. See López Austin and López Luján, *Mexico's Indigenous Past*.

10. Jacques Soustelle, *La Pensée Cosmologique des Anciens Mexicains* (Paris: Hermann, 1979), p. 137.

no abstract idea of time, since each physical space was associated with a particular time. "Thus the Mexicas knew of space and time not as abstractions, but as places and events. The properties of each space were those of the time to which it was related, and vice versa." The temporal quadrants presented in the Mayan calendar "directly reflect the direction and color of their spatial organization."[11]

The two Mesoamerican calendars, as instruments for orientation in time and space, were indispensable to the regulation of human activity. The 260-day calendar, called *tonalpohualli* by the Mexicas and *tzolkin* by the Maya, was used to keep track of daily influences. The second calendar, of two 365-day years, was called *xiuhpohualli* by the Mexicas and was a guide to the future, and consequently was used in scheduling public events. The calendars served two purposes: "on the one hand, to regulate the ritual behavior that maintained the position of human beings in their space; on the other, to defend them from bad times and to instruct them in how to benefit from good ones."[12]

The nature of the concept of space and time in Mesoamerican societies helps us to understand their political and territorial organization. Among the Mexicas we see numerous towns and cities, or *altepetl,* comprising ceremonial centers with temples and palaces of the governing elite, along with rural settlements of peasants and tributaries. Sometimes the *altepetl* were grouped into larger political-territorial entities that exercised control over individual city governments and were ruled from a dominant city.[13] All of the cities that formed the Triple Alliance—Tenochtitlan of the Mexica people, Tetzcoco of the Acolhua-Chichimeca, and Tlacopan of the Tepaneca—were themselves the end result of the domination of many smaller political entities.

Territoriality was historically dynamic, but territories expanded and contracted without affecting the social groups that comprised them. This territorial dynamism allowed for the coexistence of various subethnicities within an overall ethnic unit and for the coexistence of multiple *calpulli,* which provided "a demarcation that permitted the conservation of their territorial rights and the autonomy of their inhabitants."[14]

Under the concept of territoriality, sons inherited their fathers' trade, craft, or office. Among the village-dwelling *macehualtin,* or commoners,

11. Schele and Freidel, *A Forest of Kings,* p. 78.
12. López Austin, *Hombre-Dios,* p. 79.
13. For a discussion of the *altepetl,* see Carrasco, *The Tenochca Empire of Ancient Mexico.*
14. Carrasco, *The Tenochca Empire of Ancient Mexico,* pp. 386–87.

the great majority tilled the land, labored in fields cultivated for the benefit of the State, and toiled on public works projects. People whose work was specialized, such as artisans or merchants, owed the State a portion of the goods they produced or traded but were exempt from labor on public works projects. The *pipiltin,* the managerial or noble strata, performed State functions and lived off the tribute of the village-dwelling *macehualtin.*

The privileged position and authority of the *pipiltin* were legitimated by the belief in their direct descent from original migrant founders, who were often believed to have come from a mythical site. They were said to be the favorites of a divine patron. Thanks to their privileged position, they followed special family dispensations, were entitled to use prestige goods, and occupied distinguished homes appropriate to their leading role. The *macehualtin* attended schools called *telpochcalli* to prepare for war and public labor, but the *pipiltin* attended their own schools, the *calmecac,* where they were prepared for government positions, the judiciary, leadership in war, and important religious posts.

The division between the *pipiltin* and the *macehualtin* did not prevent the latter from aspiring to positions of privilege. Members of the *pochtecah,* the merchants' *calpulli,* enjoyed rights otherwise reserved for *pipiltin,* because the *tlatoani,* or chief rulers, valued their knowledge and advice. The importance of the *pochtecah* was due to their strategic function in the organization of long-distance trade and the espionage that they performed in distant territories. Distinguished artisans and warriors could ascend to higher status rankings on the basis of outstanding merit. At the time of the Spanish invasion, 7 percent of all family heads in the region of Tlaxcala were *pipiltin,* a proportion similar to that of the nobility in other ancient societies.

The nature of the social classes and their organizational logic were related to the religious-territorial and political aspects of the social order. A *tlatoani,* invested with divine power, governed each *altepetl,* the urban space to which a surrounding territory was subject. He selected his own first deputy, the *cihuacóatl,* who was also a representative of divinity. The *cihuacóatl* carried out financial, judicial and cultural responsibilities. The *pipiltin* nobles served both principal rulers as senior counselors, those closest to the *tlatoani* being rewarded with conquered lands. These lands were not the private property of the *pipiltin,* however. They were worked by landless sharecroppers known as *mayeques.* The *mayeques* were exempt from tribute payments to the *tlatoani* and from labor duties on public works. They were not chattel of the *pipiltin,* and the latter did not have personal control over them. The *mayeques* could transfer to another *pi-*

piltin or to a *pochtecah* the rights that they obtained from the *tlatoani.* The lowest-status *mayeques* were known as *tlatlacotin,* whom the Spanish mistakenly took to be slaves. In fact, they were indentured servants who were bound, either with or without their families, to an individual until they could make good on their outstanding debts, perhaps incurred by gambling or as a fine for drunkenness or some other crime.

The mechanisms that wove together the societies of Mesoamerica brought an essential religious element into territorial and political matters. This explains the hierarchical organizing principle that spread in the Postclassic period, from the tenth to the sixteenth centuries. Reciprocity among the members of *calpulli* was still important, but by the time of the Spanish invasion it lacked the cohesive influence that it had exercised in the Classic and Preclassic.

The spread of the hierarchical principle helps us to understand the Postclassic tendency to concentrate functions and official positions. The hegemony of Tenochtitlan in the Triple Alliance provides an example. When Texcoco lost its ability to dominate the northeast quadrant of central Mexico, Tenochtitlan was able to expand in all directions, although its authority had until then been limited to the southern quadrants. It is worthwhile to remember that when Tenochtitlan assumed its dominance in the first third of the fifteenth century, the three cities were governed by a *huey tlatoani,* an emperor or "great speaker" to whom all kings were subordinate.

The consolidation of the Triple Alliance reinforced the tendency to expansionism. At the end of the fifteenth century and beginning of the sixteenth century, the empire stretched from the Gulf of Mexico to the Pacific Ocean and from the border with Meztitlán and the Tarascan kingdom of Michoacán in the north to the Isthmus of Tehuantepec and the Soconusco, the Pacific coast of Chiapas, in the south. The expansiveness of the alliance's power discredits the hypothesis that the Tenochca empire suffered from lack of internal cohesion, political structure, and military organization. On the contrary, the empire was able to mobilize the *pipiltin* and the nonspecialized *macehualtin* both socially and militarily. Only the skilled artisans retained their autonomy. The growth of the empire benefited the *calpulli* who, like the founding migrants, took over new territories and colonized them. The *pipiltin* took up special functions in the new territories, in particular the remittance of tributes to the imperial center.

Clearly, the societies of the pre-Columbian world were continuously adapting to changing contexts. When Tenochtitlan assumed dominance of the empire, a variety of reforms followed. In religion, Huitzilopochtli gained prominence and eclipsed Quetzalcóatl; economic reforms affected the territorial rights of the *calpulli;* politically, power was concentrated in the hands of the *huey tlatoani* and the imperial family's council of four. "All these changes were to the advantage of the new leaders and the nobility. They concentrated wealth, social privilege, and political power in the hands of the governing *tlatoani,* his warriors, and the nobles. The religious reforms consolidated and legitimized these changes, providing an ideological context for the new institutions and the inspiration for a continued expansion of the State."[15]

The reforms affected the *calpulli,* especially at the beginning of the sixteenth century. They were organized into groups of one hundred, each one divided in turn into five groups of twenty. These were intended to strengthen the organization of the empire. Merchants and artisans were now compelled to render service to the palace. The abolition of debt slavery, beginning late in the fifteenth century, reinforced the power of the *tlatoani* over the peasantry.

All of these changes occurred during the last century of the Postclassic. They illustrate one of the principal Mesoamerican societies' capacity for renovation and accommodation to new circumstances. As the empire expanded beyond its original geographical limits, it became ever more centralized in the interest of preserving its hierarchical character. In the process, new tensions arose. There were rebellions in twenty provinces on some thirty occasions, frequently coinciding with dynastic succession.

Social contradictions and conflict arose as a result of the Tenochca empire's extremely hierarchical political-territorial structure, which entailed complex status-ranking with exclusive privileges assigned to the various levels. This was not class conflict, but conflict between territorially differentiated social units. Similar conflicts arose in the Andes with the expansion of the *yana* system and the existence of *mitimaes.* The *yanas* were individuals or families who were uprooted from their places of origin and put at the service of people who enjoyed the favor of the state. The *mitimaes* were fragments of ethnic groups, or even entire groups, that were relocated for political reasons. In both the Andes and the territory of the Triple Alliance, social control was consolidated not by plunder but by colonization and binding agreement. It was maintained by religiously inspired cohesion, the mechanisms of tribute and trade, and the trans-

---

15. Geoffrey W. Conrad and Arthur Demarest, *Religion and Empire: The Dynamics of Aztec and Inca Expansionism* (Cambridge: Cambridge University Press, 1984), p. 33.

portation infrastructure that made these feasible. It is not true that the Spanish found, in either of the empires, a "thirst for freedom" on the part of the Indians. More probably, Mesoamerican nobles and others in administrative roles thought that they could ally themselves on better terms with the Spaniards than with the empire. The Triple Alliance was the largest and strongest confederation in existence when the Spanish arrived, but the arrival of this new and powerful force ignited a smoldering internal conflict based on alliances of convenience and underlying rivalries.

CHAPTER 2

The New Kingdom

Conquest and Colonization

The fifteenth century A.D. brought many changes to Mesoamerica. These were the final years of the Postclassic era. Significant changes had taken place in Europe during the last decades of the fourteenth century, particularly on the Iberian Peninsula. The Mediterranean had become a trading nucleus as agriculture and settlement expanded on its islands. Coveted crops had been successfully adapted, and the islands became producers of sugarcane and sweet wine. Dyes for the textile industry were derived from seaweed and sunflowers. By the early fifteenth century, Genoese roundboats had replaced galleys and galleons, an innovation that made Atlantic travel technically and economically more feasible. Experienced merchants and statesmen, not only from the Mediterranean but also from Portugal, France, England, Holland, Scandinavia, and Germany, would soon be intensely engaged in the colonization of the Americas.

The Columbian enterprise of 1492 and the subsequent conquest thus came after several centuries of experience in settling new lands, adapting people and goods to new environments, and adjusting European law to the customs and conditions of new territories. The encounter between the European world and the world of the Americas was nonetheless traumatic for the Indigenous people of America, including the inhabitants of pre-Hispanic Mexico. The unraveling of their social, political, and economic order was accompanied by tremendous demographic and cultural destruction. Less than fifty years after the arrival of the Spanish, the population had been reduced by 90 percent.

How did the Indigenous populations survive and develop one of the most complex syncretic social phenomena of modern times? Despite the devastation and humiliation they suffered, the Mexicas, Mixtecs, Zapotecs, Maya, and almost every other Indigenous ethnicity managed to survive the physical and cultural onslaught. While the Indigenous political organization was dismembered, the family system, cultural beliefs, and elaborate territorial symbols were retained. The Mexican peoples rapidly appropriated the new labor-saving methods that the Spanish had introduced, including the use of horses, donkeys, and oxen, to save human energy and increase productive capacity. They reconstructed their cultures through a fusion with Spanish influences. Their symbols, their writing systems, and their political hierarchies survived and were renovated. They maintained the complexity of their societies and their remarkable capacity to confront challenges, even the new ones they were facing. In the end, the Indigenous Mexicans and the Spanish were somehow each subdued by the other, and the violent confrontation came to a standstill. Despite the clear hegemony of the Europeans, both groups moved toward a new form of livelihood.

The Internationalization of the Americas

We cannot understand the invasion, conquest, and settlement of Mexico by the Spanish without considering Indigenous history or without noting that the Spanish and Portuguese expeditions to America were part of a broader Iberian expansion westward into the Atlantic.

The four-hundred-year-long Reconquest of the Iberian Peninsula from Islam was completed in 1492 with the fall of the city of Granada in southern Spain. With this historic victory, the kingdoms of Castile and Portugal invested their accumulated experience and power in Atlantic expansion. In addition to the Portuguese inroads on the coasts of Africa, the two powers used their bases in the Canaries and the Azores to begin the navigational advances that would open sea lanes to the west from Seville, Cádiz, and Lisbon.

The Iberians used the body of navigational knowledge available to the peoples of the Mediterranean to take advantage of marine winds and currents and open up new sea lanes to connect the peninsula with America. The Spanish and Portuguese expeditions to America carried with them the historical Spanish, Portuguese, Catalan, and Genoese experience of Mediterranean and Atlantic navigation, conquest, colonization, and trade.

Crucially, they introduced sugar, an Asian crop transplanted in Cyprus. They imported the institution of slavery, which would expand well beyond its European variants and be decisive in colonial development in general and the cultivation of sugar in particular. Other than on São Tome, slave labor had not previously been organized systematically around every aspect of sugarcane cultivation and processing. In America it was.

The use of ships to cross the Atlantic required the importation of shipbuilding and sail-making technologies and the large guns used by merchant shipping to defend the ships from pirates. Spanish galleons brought skilled merchants, men knowledgeable in the organization of factories, others with the legal skills needed to adapt Iberian institutions to the new social environment, and men with technical skills developed in Spain's European wars. All of them dedicated themselves to the consolidation of Spanish imperial hegemony.

For more than a century, the Caribbean was akin to a Spanish Mediterranean. Exploiting the excellent winds and currents, Spanish ships traversed virtual transoceanic highways at almost twenty miles per hour. This facilitated travel from the Atlantic islands to the Caribbean and the American mainland and the construction of port cities that were interconnected more by sea than by land. Men, goods, and knowledge moved freely between Santo Domingo, Puerto Rico, Havana, San Juan de Ulúa, Portobelo, Cartagena de Indias, Maracaibo, Puerto Cabello, La Guaira, and Cumaná. The return voyage to Iberia was longer, however, because maritime winds and currents were less favorable and seasonal hurricanes battered the area. While the development of the Mediterranean had relied on the backup of a European hinterland, however, the Caribbean port cities were relatively isolated. This limited their possibilities for development.

As the seventeenth century began, the Caribbean was transformed from a Spanish to an international sea. Once the ships of other European powers began to ply its waters, they quickly consolidated their presence on the Antillean islands. The French established themselves in Martinique and Guadalupe, and the English did the same in Jamaica, the Bahamas, and along the coasts of the mainland. The resulting upsurge in contraband wrested what had been a commercial monopoly from the hands of the Spanish.

The Canaries and the Azores were points of westward departure for contraband goods, unauthorized people, and prohibited books. Informal but profitable trade among the European mercantile powers developed there and on Caribbean islands and American shores.

The Europeans reached America at a moment when their own societies were undergoing a great transformation—the unraveling of the medieval idea of empire and the departure from the notion of Christendom as a single political and religious entity to move into an era of competing nations. The first supposed division of the non-European world between Spain and Portugal, determined by Pope Alexander VI after Columbus's discovery of America, led to a conflict between the two powers over which specific meridian would divide their colonial areas. As it turned out, the division brought about more conflict than peace among the European powers throughout the sixteenth century, provoking conflicts involving theology, law, cartography, and history. The conflicts induced modifications in the administration of the metropolitan areas of Iberia, particularly Castile, and it opened the door to the occupation of North America, the West Indies, and even part of Brazil by non-Iberian powers.

New challenges to Spain's domination of its world territories led the Crown of Castile to create a "compound monarchy" encompassing the Old and New Worlds. The Castilian monarch ruled over a series of subsidiary kingdoms and other territories but recognized the authority of ethnic nobles, local rulers, and local practices of land tenure. Each territory maintained the right to establish its own laws, its own form of internal administration, its own language and social norms, but its officials were appointed by the Castilian sovereign. Together with his representatives, the sovereign guaranteed peace and good government to his subjects in all the kingdoms of the realm and was responsible for religious conversion, the spread of religion, and the judicial system. In recognition of the alliance between the sovereign and his kingdoms, he was entitled to demand the *quinto real,* a tribute paid through the administrative mechanisms of each kingdom in return for his support and services, including military services.

The Organization of the Compound Monarchy in America

The social, cultural, and political concepts behind the compound monarchy were European and Iberian. This system of government, similar to a commonwealth, was transplanted by the Castilians from the Iberian peninsula and its European dominions to the West Indies, and later to the American mainland, in a version informed by a four-century experience of reclaiming the Iberian peninsula from Muslim dominion.

This last point is significant because in both the Reconquest and the Mexican and other American conquests, the Castilians confronted people, whether in war or in peace, who were manifestly different from themselves and had cultures dramatically distinct from their own. In this way, the Iberians were culturally better prepared than the French or the English to confront and engage non-Europeans. France's sixteenth-century defeat in Brazil, for example, was due to the superior ability of the Portuguese to establish an alliance with the Tupi Indians.

Both the Reconquest of Islamic Iberia and the conquest of Indian America were privately financed and accomplished without the financial backing of the Crown. The private enterprises that carried out Castilian conquests in the Caribbean and on the American continent were granted royal concessions entailing opportunities for trade with the infidel Indians, the confiscation of foodstuffs, and the capture of slaves. In return, the conquistadors, known as *capitanes de conquista,* owed the throne one-fifth of all trade goods, property, and slaves so obtained. In this kind of royal charter, legally called a capitulation, the *capitán de conquista* made a commitment to enter, explore, and populate a particular region. In return, the king granted him a series of considerations. Sometimes the conquistador was given the right to found a city and name its authorities. No tax was due save the *quinto real,* the one-fifth part of all treasures "recovered" through trade, industry, or plunder. Raiding parties on horseback, known as *empresas de conquista,* were carried out on the islands and the mainland for barter and pillage and for the capture of Indian infidels as slaves.

The *capitán de conquista* could also be appointed governor of all the lands he discovered and populated. In that case, he was responsible for the religious conversion of the Indians under his tutelage, and his lieutenants would be named mayors, administrators, and judges. An *encomienda* was granted to the conquistador and his heirs, granting them the right to the tribute the native inhabitants owed to the king. While the intention had been for the conquistadors to establish hereditary local rule and live off of Indian tribute, the system barely lasted more than one generation due to the massive death rate of the native population.

Local governments known as *cabildos* were established to carry out executive and judicial functions. Being elective institutions, the *cabildos* represented all Spanish settlers and had the right to representation at the royal court. Both the viceroy and the governor, though, had the authority to appoint an officer known as *alcalde mayor* or *corregidor* to oversee the performance of elected officials. These principles of organization, born of the Reconquest, would take very strong root in the new hemisphere.

Years before the first expeditions of Hernán Cortés, the Caribbean islands began to be transformed from trading posts and bases for pillaging expeditions to permanent colonies, populated by settlers who had been granted the ownership of urban home sites known as *solares,* and land for crops and orchards, as well as the services of Indigenous inhabitants fulfilling their labor obligations. These settlers who had rights and duties within their communities were called *vecinos.*

The colonization in the West Indies proved disastrous, however, prompting the king's administrators to put controls on the excesses committed by Spaniards toward the Indians. Tributes owed the Crown by both Spaniards and Indians were regulated, and, for the first time, controls were imposed on trading practices between the Spanish Indies and Castile, Venice, Catalonia, Portugal, and their possessions by the newly established Casa de Contratación in Seville. The Casa de Contratación issued licenses for trade with Panama, Santo Domingo, Havana, and other ports, and asserted the authority of the king in his new territories by establishing a special court called the Audiencia, the supreme judicial and administrative tribunal presided over by the viceroy. The Consejo de Indias, or Council of the Indies—a council for matters related to governance in the "Indies" (that is, the Americas), based in Spain—was established in 1524. It was modeled on similar bodies that were part of the compound monarchy in Castile, Aragón, Italy, and Flanders. Its role was to inform and counsel the king concerning events in his New World realms in order to protect the Indians, eliminate abuses, defend the Catholic religion, and prevent the spread of Protestant heresies and the reversion of converted Indians to idolatry.

The Invasion of Mexico

Years before Hernán Cortés began his expedition, news had reached Cuba of a powerful kingdom on the American continent. Cortés and his soldiers were familiar with the experience in the West Indies and might have anticipated what awaited them on the continent. In his first letter from the expedition, though, Cortés wrote that the Mexican mainland was so different that his previous experiences were largely irrelevant. The capital city of Tenochtitlan, he said, was as large as Seville. Its ruling class, as fray Juan de Torquemada would write in the following century, lived in cities and towns with kings subject to an emperor, nobles subject to those kings, and vassals subject to those nobles. He reported that the kings had ruled for centuries. Like the European nobility and royalty, he said, they had ennobled their domains.

The arrival of Cortés in Veracruz marked the beginning of the initial conquest of Mexico, a process that lasted from 1519 to 1521. Faced with an unexpected and unpredictable situation, Cortés and his men feared defeat at the hands of the Triple Alliance. The Emperor Moctezuma sent gifts to Cortés in Veracruz and asked him to go back where he came from. The Spaniards had made a significant impression on the native population,

despite their few horses and their gunpowder that worked only inter-
mittently, frequently fizzling due to the humidity.

The Spanish were probably seen not as invaders but as potential allies
within a complex power network. In addition, Hernán Cortés was suffi-
ciently astute to familiarize himself with the constellation of kingdoms
and nobles, their relationships and their vulnerabilities, and to utilize that
information to further his cause. His first military victory was on the
Tabasco coast, where the defeated local noble then presented him with
gifts including jewels, food, blankets of finely woven cotton, and twenty
young women.

One of these young women was Malintzin, baptized doña Marina by
the Spanish and universally known today as la Malinche, who spoke
Nahuatl and Maya, and later learned Spanish. She and Gerónimo de
Aguilar, a Spaniard who had lived in Yucatán for some years, served as interpreters to Cortés, helping him to learn more about Mesoamerica and
its kingdoms. Cortés discovered that the Tenochca Aztec empire had pa-
pered over fierce rivalries among its peoples, and he exploited these, making alliances and pitting kingdoms and principalities against one another.
The cities of Tlaxcala and Cempoala, for example, allied themselves with
him against the Mexicas in order to liberate themselves from domination
and tributary obligations. The Chalca people recognized Cortés's authority, and he appointed their nobles to administrative positions and respected their capital cities. In this way the nobles of different Indigenous
groups were able to protect their own property and that of their communities. Some groups allied themselves with the Spanish as they extended their conquests, as we shall see later.

The defeat of the Acolhua kingdom and its capital, Texcoco, was accomplished by exploiting the rivalries among ruling families. Cacama,
Moctezuma's nephew and also lord of Texcoco, advised the emperor of
the Triple Alliance to seize the Spaniards as soon as they arrived and put
them back on their ships. Cuitlahuac, the ruler of Iztapalapa and ally of
the ruler of Coyoacán, disagreed, which allowed Cortés to divide brother
from brother and weaken the Acolhua ruling family to his own advantage. Moctezuma and Cacama were deposed, and Cuitlahuac ascended
the throne. Other Mesoamerican peoples, such as the Zapotecs of Oaxaca, the people of Tehuantepec, and those of Pánuco, Tuxtepec, and
Huatusco, all sent messengers to Cortés, expressing their friendship
and soliciting his support for their freedom from the Triple Alliance.

The rapid conquest of central Mexico, apparently accomplished by
1524, is understandable only in this light. But the fall of Tenochtitlan by
no means meant that all of Mexican territory would immediately fall

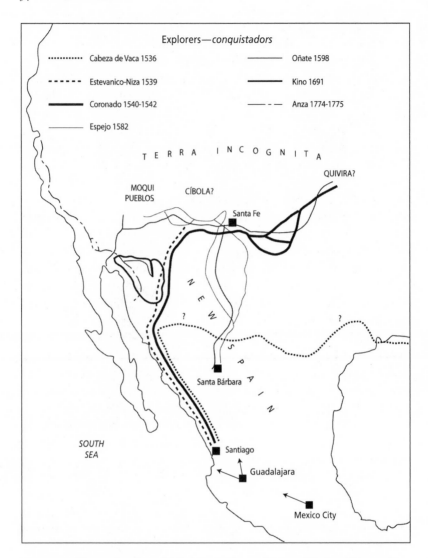

Explorers—*conquistadors*

·············· Cabeza de Vaca 1536	———— Oñate 1598
– – – – – Estevanico-Niza 1539	━━━━ Kino 1691
━━━━━ Coronado 1540-1542	—·—· Anza 1774-1775
——— Espejo 1582	

T E R R A   I N C O G N I T A

QUIVIRA?

MOQUI PUEBLOS   CÍBOLA?

Santa Fe

N E W

?   ?

S P A I N

Santa Bárbara

SOUTH SEA

Santiago

Guadalajara

Mexico City

MAP 2.1A. The exploration of Mexican territory. (Source: *National Geographic Magazine*, November 1982, p. 630.)

under Spanish control. The enterprise of conquest would last another century. Nevertheless, the decade of the 1520s saw the greatest expeditionary activity, as we shall see later.

With the fall of the imperial capital, the expeditionary forces left the central plateau and headed for the Pacific and Gulf coasts. (See maps 2.1a

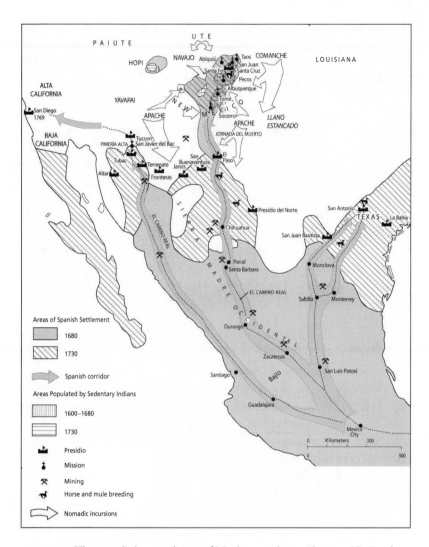

MAP 2.1B. The populations and uses of Mexican territory. (Source: *National Geographic Magazine,* November 1982, p. 630a.)

and 2.1b.) In the case of the Pacific, they were searching for a route to Asia. The conquest of the Gulf Coast extended to Texas and Florida. At this point, the conquistadors probably still believed the El Dorado myth of golden cities, but they soon stopped searching for them. From 1540 until the end of the century, they concentrated their efforts in the central plateau and the northern regions. In the former, they focused on Indigenous settlements and in the latter, on silver deposits. The discovery of these deposits would change the meaning of colonization, and would come to link New Spain to the world economy.

The Spanish advanced slowly, as they ran into stubborn resistance from nomadic Indians. The Indians established a front that ran along the twenty-first parallel north of Guadalajara and east toward San Luis Potosí. This line of resistance stretching between the Sierra Madre Occidental and the Sierra Madre Oriental remained stable until the Mixton War of 1540–1542, which was one of the first examples of an organized response by the Spanish government to Indian rebels regrouped in the north. The viceroy, don Antonio de Mendoza, amassed over thirty thousand men, including allied Indians and the conquistadors of eastern and central Mexico. This was also the first attempt by New Spain to expand northward into Chichimeca territory, and it was richly rewarded with the 1546 discovery of silver deposits in Zacatecas.

The Conquest of Mexico

Once the line of resistance was broken, various expeditions penetrated the north to conquer territory and search for new veins of silver. The roads, way stations, inns, and outposts they established led to the opening of agricultural lands in the Bajío, connected to the mining district of Zacatecas and to new veins of silver discovered to its north and east. Indian allies from central Mexico played a key role in the Spanish conquest and settlement of northern areas, which led to the founding of Nueva Galicia, Nueva Vizcaya, Nuevo León, and Nuevo México (New Mexico) between 1550 and 1590. A string of settlements linked Mexico City with new agricultural areas in the region known as the Bajío (in what is now the state of Guanajuato) and the mines of Zacatecas. The herding of domesticated and semidomesticated animals flourished, along with related activities such as shearing and tanning. The new towns themselves differed from those of central and southern New Spain. As direct vassals of the sovereign, their inhabitants enjoyed full *vecino* status. Thus they received generous land grants for themselves and their communities, which they exploited in connection with Spanish mining and commercial interests. Town hostels, or *mesones,* provided rest for weary travelers; beautiful colonial buildings were built for this purpose.

In the face of persistent Chichimeca threats and frequent belligerence, settlements further north necessarily differed from those in central and southern New Spain. Newly opened roads were provided with defensive outposts called *presidios,* and the towns built near the silver mines were fortified. Constant defensive measures were required in order to keep the roads open and maintain communication with the capital.

Any encounter between two civilizations inevitably entails the loss of life as well as economic and cultural losses. Every civilization, be it nomadic or sedentary, tribal or imperial, is constructed of a finely woven cultural fabric. In interaction with another civilization of a very different nature, this fabric stretches and ultimately either tears or unravels. In the process, both the aggressor civilization and that which it overruns are permanently changed.

We know that the conquerors were few in number, amounting to only about two thousand by 1530. Further migration from Spain was limited by a prohibition against the emigration of Castilian peasants. After the discovery of the mines their numbers increased, but not dramatically so. There were probably ten thousand Spaniards in New Spain by the middle of the sixteenth century, including both armed and religious conquistadors, clergy, administrators, and royal officials.

In order to prevail, this small number of men had to station themselves at geographically key points and had to seek the support of Indian allies. Between 1520 and 1539 they established their bases in Mexico City and on or near the coast at Veracruz, Pánuco, and Coatzacoalcos. In the 1540s they advanced again onto the plateau. The foundation of the town of Puebla de los Ángeles between Mexico City and Veracruz was part of their strategy to keep this route open in the event of Indigenous uprisings. The "spiritual conquest," or evangelization, of the Indigenous population, and the defense of the faith from attacks by Iberian Jews and foreign Protestants, was the great peaceful conquest carried out by Franciscans, Dominicans, and Augustinians of the regular clergy (those in the religious orders) and by the secular clergy (those outside the orders and therefore responsible directly to the bishop). The orders proliferated in every region. If we were to superimpose a map of monasteries over a map of Spanish cities, towns, and *presidios,* we would see that the monasteries were spread over all regions and that the *presidios* and towns were established at key points on the road system. By 1559, there were eighty Franciscan monasteries and houses, forty of Augustinians, and forty of Dominicans, housing a total of eight hundred ecclesiastics. To this number we must add the numerous Spanish and Indian secular brothers. There were about ten monasteries for every Spanish village.

Like the colonial towns, the monasteries were centers of spiritual teaching, evangelism, political ideas, and the distribution of goods. European animals, plants, and crops were raised there, and Indian products such as corn, chilies, and turkeys were also brought in for the Spaniards' use. The daily need for food was a powerful force that drew the two populations together.

Ecclesiastics taught the Indians that they had rights and that, as vassals, they enjoyed the protection and mercy of the king. Through a religious lens they created an image of the monarchy as more powerful than the conquistadors. Royal institutions in New Spain such as the Audiencia and the Juzgado de Indios, a special tribunal for matters relating to the Indians in the Americas, reinforced the authority of the Crown. From the mid-sixteenth to the late seventeenth century, the Juzgado de Indios rendered justice in response to lawsuits brought by Indigenous people against Spanish settlers.

The Birth of the New World

The conquest had unexpected and undesirable consequences for both the Indians and the Spaniards, in particular the spread of European diseases to which the Indians had no biological resistance. Beginning in the 1530s, population transfers, excessive work, and a wholly insufficient diet added to the effect of the epidemics. Compared with the estimated 20 million Indians living in Mesoamerica when Cortés arrived in 1519, there were 6.3 million in 1548 and barely one million at the turn of the century.

While the conquistadors and ecclesiastics had once dreamed of a New Spain ruled jointly by Spanish and Indian nobles, this idea was frustrated by the demographic catastrophe. The conquistadors' dream of a noble life supported by Indian tributes also turned to dust, and the ecclesiastics lost the hope, expressed by the first Franciscans, of creating a kingdom based on the dictates of the Gospels. The disaster also modified the Castilian monarchy's view of New Spain, the crown jewel of their empire. It demanded a reappraisal of strategies on the part of all parties: the Crown, the Church, the Spanish settlers, and the Indian rulers, in order to address the ongoing devastation.

The first challenge was the loss of the *encomiendas,* the rights to indigenous labor and tributes granted by the king to the *encomenderos*—the conquistadors and their descendants—in compensation for the costs of their expeditions of conquest, in return for which the *encomenderos* were expected to evangelize and protect the Indians. The king also responded to the abuses by some *encomenderos,* stripping them of their *encomienda* grants beginning in 1540. As a result, half of all Indian tributes, some 700,000 sixteenth-century pesos, were diverted from the coffers of *encomenderos* to the Royal Treasury. Within thirty years—by 1570—the majority of the Indians were direct vassals of the king. The demographic catastrophe had other, indirect effects on Indian society. Internal social order collapsed as Indigenous commoners, or *macehualtin,* ignored the rule of the nobles or fled their communities to seek relief in towns, cities, or mining centers, or better yet, entirely beyond the reach of Spanish authority.

The disintegration of the Indian hierarchy that had begun with the conquest of 1519–1540 obscured other dramatic changes that were under way, such as the transformation of Mexican agriculture. Cattle and sheep grazed where there had been a patchwork of corn, forests, and untamed grasslands, sometimes even preceding human settlement. Spaniards and Indians quickly realized the animals' increased value in the new environment and sought land grants for the purpose of building herds or renting to herders. Indians established a monopoly on cutting and selling local reeds for fodder. The new animal husbandry produced fresh meat for urban consumption, valuable hides, jerky, fat, tallow, and wool, all for a limited investment of both capital and labor. Indians raised sheep, goats, and pigs—smaller livestock whose meat was desirable to Spaniards and mestizos alike. Following the European tradition of seasonal grazing, herds were driven regularly from central Mexico to the northern territories and back, accompanied by men who thereby spread the influence of their innovative trades, customs, lifestyles, and beliefs.

The most important advantage provided by animal husbandry was the energy and transportation power that had previously been available only through the labor of Indians. In this sense, the presence of European animals compensated for the decline in the Indian population. With the use of animal power, ore was transformed into silver and goods were transported by wagon. Horses, in particular, facilitated communication. This form of animal power of European origin was really a technological revolution for both the Spanish and Indigenous populations. There would not be another innovation of equivalent importance until the railroad boom of the nineteenth century.

Animal power was responsible for the diversification of the different Mexican regions in the late sixteenth century. Vast *haciendas* were quickly consolidated in Nueva Galicia, Nueva Vizcaya, and Nuevo León to accommodate large herds of cattle and some sheep and goats. The enormity and wealth of the northern cattle country provided energy and food for the mining camps as well as power to pump water from mining shafts, timber to stabilize those shafts, and the firewood that powered the mining machines.

The great north, sparsely populated and home to hostile Indians, lacked many things, especially agricultural products other than wheat. It fell to the plateau around the viceregal capital and the mining and agricultural areas of the Bajío in the western lowlands to not only feed themselves but to produce a surplus to send north as well.

The economic geography of New Spain was strongly regional. In Puebla, for example, Indigenous and Spanish agriculture coexisted and complemented each other, while Spanish agriculture dominated the north. A special statute prohibiting land grants, or *mercedes,* to Spaniards was applied to Tlaxcala as a reward for its faithful alliance with Hernán Cortés. Thus a mixed Spanish and Indigenous agriculture of wheat and corn was able to prosper.

The Indian population did not collapse equally dramatically in all regions. The decline was more pronounced on the coasts and less so on the plateau, though it was still strongly evident in densely populated cities and in isolated sites where food was difficult to obtain. In Yucatán, the population had regained its preconquest level of some 200,000 inhabitants by the year 1600. Oaxaca's population was fairly stable, perhaps because its inhabitants benefited from the livestock economy, and women, children, and the elderly could find work in the silk and cochineal industries. (Cochineal is an insect native to Mexico that was used to produce a natural dye highly valued in New Spain and Europe.) Both of these, but particularly cochineal, required significant care and manual labor input. Communities in the colder regions of Oaxaca specialized in textiles for the regional market and for sale in central and northern New Spain. Cacao and some cochineal production prospered in Chiapas, where the demographic decline was also somewhat less dramatic.

The coexistence of Indigenous and European economies did not inevitably lead to domination by the European forms. Pedro Carrasco explains:

The markets, or *tianguis,* were maintained for Indigenous use and the same groups of pre-Hispanic merchants continued or even expanded their activities, adopting new means of transport and traveling to distant regions more easily and safely than in the old times. Cholula, for example, continued to be a large center for artisans and Indian merchants, with many busy *tianguis.* The markets pro-

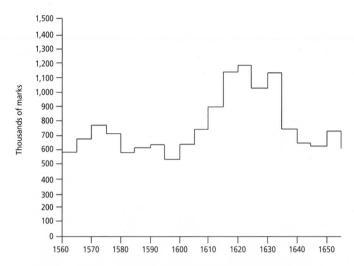

FIGURE 2.1. Silver production, 1560–1650. A silver mark (also known as the Castilian mark) weighed 230 grams. The information in this figure is based on the writings of Alexander von Humboldt (1769–1859), a German scientist and explorer who traveled in Mexico in the early 1800s. (Source: Peter John Bakewell, *Minería y Sociedad en el México Colonial: Zacatecas 1546–1700* [Mexico City: Fondo de Cultura Económica, 1976], p. 349.)

vided for the needs of the regional Indigenous population of the region and products imported from afar, like colorful *huipiles* from Campeche, the preferred clothing for most Indian women and girls in the city.[1]

While the local and domestic distribution of goods remained in Indigenous hands, wealthy Spanish merchants joined together at the end of the sixteenth century to form the trading guild or corporation known as the Tribunal del Consulado de la Ciudad de México. The tribunal took control of trade in silver and imported products such as mercury, iron, paper, textiles, and Mediterranean agricultural goods.

Mexico was the leading silver producer in the sixteenth century. Figure 2.1 tracks silver production in the principal silver-mining area of New Spain. As the figure indicates, production increased significantly in the sixteenth century, so much so that the value of coins printed by the mint in Mexico City went from a yearly average of 1.5 million pesos in the 1550s

1. Pedro Carrasco, "La Economía del México Prehispánico," in Pedro Carrasco and Johanna Brode, eds., *Economía Políticae e Ideología en el México Prehispánico* (Mexico City: Nueva Imagen, 1978), pp. 56–57.

to 3 million pesos by 1580 and 4.5 million at the beginning of the seventeenth century. Thanks to silver, Mexico was able to establish a role for itself in the Spanish imperial economy in Europe and beyond—in the Near East and particularly in India and China. Domestically, silver was the medium that tied regional economies together. They continued to be locally centered but traded among themselves.

Links between Societies

Once the initial shock of invasion and conquest had passed, Indian communities recovered their bearings and adopted various coping strategies. For example, they linked their communal corn and livestock economies to the tributary system, a Spanish holdover from the period of the Triple Alliance. While the Spanish levied tributes on individuals, it was the Indian elite who collected the necessary payments according to the number of inhabitants and retained their power over the general population. Indian leaders would deliver tributes to the *encomendero* first and then to the local Spanish authority, the chief magistrate. They would also collect the tribute due to *caciques* (traditional Indian leaders) and to *cabildo* officials, as well as contributions to a community fund. Thus the inhabitants of central Mexico preserved preconquest practices such as levying tributes according to the amount of property owned and the area of land under cultivation. When cooperating with the Spanish, Indian nobles could retain their titles, lands, and riches, and could maintain jurisdiction over towns and Indian populations.

Equally important was the fact that through the management of the Indian town council, Indigenous leaders were able to sustain and strengthen community bonds. They supported their own governing institution, paid for the town's religious services and festivals, and developed a fund to support Indian families at times of poor harvest or epidemic. Also very important was the fact that the so-called Indian republics established *cofradías*, or Catholic brotherhoods, dedicated to the village patron saint. In the treasuries of these *cofradías* revenue could be safeguarded from Spanish levies.

The Spanish administration was given the right to exact a levy on each head of family between the ages of fifteen and fifty, and Indian authorities were expected to collect and pay it. Indian authorities, on the other hand, tended to follow ancient custom by contributing to the pre-Columbian tributary register, the Matrícula de Tributos. Thus they preserved the practice of collective tribute based on overall community wealth and the amount of land under cultivation. It was the surplus generated from this collective tribute that provided for local government and services.

As an example, we can look at the 1549 expenditures of the Indigenous community of Otlazpan, subordinate to the village of Tepeji del Río in the state of Hidalgo. According to Pedro Carrasco, the *macehualtin* paid tribute in cash, cacao, firewood, and turkeys, all in proportion to the size of their plot of land. They also performed work in the communal *milpa,* or corn field. Women wove a given amount of cloth for *cabildo* and community officials. The governor, the four *regidores,* or local councilors, and the *mayordomo,* a local administrator, were paid in cash, but the *macehualtin* also provided them with firewood and agricultural labor. The scribe, cantors, and sacristans and a number of *tequitlatos* were also paid in cash. The *tequitlatos* were Indians who organized agricultural work in the fields of the *encomendero* and supplied his household. They also gathered the population for mass and catechism and made sure that children were baptized and that marriages were performed in church.

No matter how small a community was—and Otlazpan was small indeed—its existence was based on the principle that the authorities of each *pueblo,* or town, were responsible for tributary payments, and that community debts were the personal responsibility of the governor and members of the *cabildo.* If these authorities were unable to pay, their property was confiscated and they were imprisoned. The hierarchical pre-Hispanic social structure had survived. The *pipiltin* and the *macehualtin* continued to have distinct rights and obligations. Distinctions also survived within the Indigenous nobility, based on rank and tradition. One can understand why the Spanish approved Indian governors for lifelong terms; it allowed them to maintain ties with the Indigenous elite.

The autonomy of the Indian and Spanish republics was not a legal fiction. Each republic was independent and institutionally powerful, with authority residing in the *cabildo.* Both Spanish and Indian republics were endowed with land, water, and forest rights. The creation of two separate patterns of settlement with separate legislation, governing bodies, and jurisdictions was meant to preserve the integrity and autonomy of each ethnic group. Spaniards were banned from residing in the towns or villages of Indian republics. The *cabildo* was a Castilian institution, imported to the colony to give voice to the most prominent *vecinos,* whom the kingdom wanted to endow with the prestige and resources necessary to maintain their independence from otherwise powerful local authorities and institutions. To this end, they were given the authority to determine and manage the resources of their communities and regions.[2] The first *cabildo* in New Spain was established at Villa Rica de la Vera Cruz (now Veracruz) by conquistadors and other *vecinos*. From the very beginning it actively defended its interests before Hernán Cortés, the Audiencia, and the viceroys.

All Spanish *vecinos,* or male heads of families, were members of the *cabildo,* no matter what their status. The *cabildo* had jurisdiction over a district. A magistrate made legal rulings and administered the territory. Like their Indian equivalents, the *cabildos* were hierarchical institutions with particular social and political functions. At first, the *encomenderos* tried to dominate the *cabildos* in order to defend the privileges that the Crown was intent on denying them, and the struggle between *encomenderos* and other *vecinos* was ongoing. Still, they all agreed that the monarchy should not designate the members of the *cabildo,* that they should be elected annually as a counterbalance to the power of royal officials. In the Mexico City *cabildo,* founded in 1524, the *encomenderos* and other *vecinos* agreed that each group would name one *alcalde ordinario,* an administrative and judicial officer. The same compromise was reached in the provincial *cabildos* of Puebla, Oaxaca, and Mérida. The Spanish *cabildo* had jurisdiction at the district level and was presided over by the elected *alcalde ordinario,* but royal appointees such as *regidores* and *oidores* were a constant source of friction for the conquistadors and *vecinos,* who jealously defended their right to govern autonomously.

In the Indian republics, an Indigenous governor headed up the *cabildo* and was assisted by Indian *alcaldes, justicias, mayordomos,* and *regidores.* Principal elders, *caciques,* and former governors were called upon for their counsel when needed. Yet both the Spanish Recopilación de Leyes de Indias, a set of laws exclusive to the Americas, and customary Indian law bridged the passage between the two civilizations, Spanish and Indian.[3] The Indian *cabildo* also presented its interests to the king, who would attend to them and might satisfy their petitions if he could, fulfilling his role in the pact between sovereign and vassals.

The tension between the king's representatives and the *cabildo* of Mex-

---

2. A *vecino* was a male head of household who had a permanent residence and an established source of income in a town and thus had the rights and duties of a full citizen as well as the privileges of office, social, and cultural rank. A *vecino* could be either a Spaniard or an Indian.

3. The Recopilación de Leyes de Reinos de Indias, the Nueva Recopilación de las Leyes del Reino, and other sets of laws promulgated in 1567, 1640, and 1745 regulated the relations of the Spanish government with the Indian and non-Indian populations in the Americas.

ico City was so acute when Antonio de Mendoza served as viceroy in 1536 that either the governor or his lieutenant had to preside over the *cabildo* meetings. Later the *cabildo* opposed the dilution of its authority through the addition to its voting membership of a magistrate, or *oidor*, also appointed by the viceroy. The Spanish *cabildo* defended its autonomy, begging the king to order that such officers be denied the right to vote in *cabildo* meetings. In their petition, the members of the Mexico City *cabildo* argued that they had conquered and populated the land with their own economic resources, and that they best represented the interests of New Spain. This idea had such force that the *cabildo* of Mexico City was recognized as the leading legal body in New Spain, and its representatives to the Spanish court were authorized to defend the interests of all the *cabildos* in the viceroyalty.

According to historian José Miranda, official representatives of cities and towns in New Spain gathered on several occasions during the sixteenth century to consider matters of common interest and express their collective position to the king. These representative bodies, when acting jointly as Juntas de Procuradores, were notably similar to the Spanish Cortes, or parliament. There is little doubt that the *procuradores* conceived of themselves and their town councils as analogous to the Cortes. The first such representative council met in 1525 to discuss the unwanted participation of the governor's lieutenants on the *cabildos*. The councils also produced petitions to the royal Spanish court and designated representatives who would defend them there. Other recurring themes were the rights of the *cabildos,* the chartering of cities, and the call for the perpetuity of *encomiendas* granted to conquistadors and their descendants.

The participation and influence of the *cabildos* in the affairs of the viceroyalty were very great in the year of 1567. As a result, a new viceroy proposed that in return for a substantial contribution on their part, he would recommend to the king the establishment of a Court of New Spain. The proposal implicitly elevated New Spain to the status of a kingdom. Since the Middle Ages, every monarchy in Europe had had a parliament that advised the monarch and authorized and modified taxes and tributes. But it seems that the colonists declined to part with their considerable riches. After 1567, the united town councils known as Juntas de Procuradores lost political momentum.

The Spanish and Indian *cabildos* put institutional checks on the exercise of royal power in New Spain, as similar institutions did in other kingdoms of Spanish America and the Iberian Peninsula. They were the voice of the "kingdom," defending the interests of both *vecinos* and other residents of these political, social, and economic entities. The idea of New Spain as a kingdom referred not only to the territory but to all members of Spanish and Indian society. Again, the compound monarchy left the *cabildo,* the governing institution in the provinces of New Spain, in the hands of the *vecinos*—those men with full civil and political rights—and the *cabildo* had the right to representation at the royal court. The monarchy maintained royal institutions in New Spain like those that it would maintain in a commonwealth: the viceroyalty, the Audiencia, the Juzgado de Indios, and so on. As has also been explained, the royal court never successfully imposed absolutism in New Spain. Instead, it exercised a kind of indirect rule in which royal power was mediated by the representatives of the social estates of New Spain: the clergy, merchants, mine operators, those with aristocratic and honorary titles, *encomenderos,* and highly educated groups in the universities, the courts, and diplomacy. These groups governed themselves and defended their ranks, their privileges, and their social and economic positions in relation to the monarchy. An *encomendero* had more privileges, but also more obligations, than a merchant. The situation in Indian society was analogous. Important *pipiltin* and Indian officials had more privileges due to their status, but they also had more obligations than *macehualtin.* They had to put up their own property to guarantee the community payment of Indian tribute to the king or to an *encomendero.*

Colonial Institutions and Administration

Along with the other American regions, New Spain became a territory of the Spanish monarchy at a moment when the monarchy's power was becoming centralized and absolute. The transition from the limited and moderate parliamentary monarchy of the Late Middle Ages to the absolutist monarchy was slow, however, and its impact was never fully realized in the Americas. Even so, the king's expanding power gave him new prerogatives and responsibilities in New Spain. His representatives grew in number and took on new duties. Still, the Spanish State did not have an army or a navy in America, and the armed forces were not powerful institutions of colonial rule.

Hierarchy and authority were intrinsic to New Spain's status as a viceroyalty. Unlike a governor, magistrate, or mayor, the viceroy represented and embodied the "royal person" of the monarch. He was generally a royal protégé, a noble or related to one, a *hidalgo,* literally, the son of a renowned man. He ruled as a monarch over the political-administrative organization of the viceroyalty, and, like the king, he was obliged to protect the interests of all his subjects, to rule New Spain with justice and benevolence, and to defend the Indians, who were full vassals of the king but considered weak and lacking the capacity for reason.

The viceroy's responsibilities and power were limited and could be challenged by or before the Audiencia, which had judicial and administrative functions. The viceroy's budgetary authority, in particular, was subject to the approval of a council that included magistrates of the Audiencia and representatives of the Royal Treasury. At the end of his mandate, the viceroy's performance in office was subject to review by a representative of the king, a process that could also lead to legal proceedings against him. Beginning in 1519, the king's Council of the Indies was responsible for overseeing governance in the American territories and for the performance of all royal officials there.

The dominant colonial institutions were the royal Audiencias. The first Audiencia had been established in Santo Domingo. In New Spain there were two: the Mexico City Audiencia was founded in 1529, and that of Nueva Galicia in 1549. Chiapas fell under the jurisdiction of the Audiencia of Guatemala, founded in 1544. The Audiencias had judicial and administrative functions independent of the viceroy, and they could be petitioned to review his decisions. In effect, they supervised his administration. He was required to attend their general assemblies and receive their advice.

The distance from Spain and the difficulty of communication left the governing bodies of New Spain with significant practical autonomy, even with regard to decisions made at the royal court. That is not to say that the viceroy or the Audiencia disregarded the instructions of the Crown. On the contrary, they endeavored to minimize the objections to those instructions that might arise from the various social strata and groups in the kingdom. The Ordenanzas de Indias, a set of laws established in 1573, took account of this situation and explicitly allowed royal representatives in the colonies to act upon, moderate, or temporarily suspend their compliance with mandates from Madrid. This contradictory practice was described as "acceding but not complying": *Se acata mas no se cumple.*

Social and religious control was another challenge for the king's representatives. They acted with the full force of the law when it came to "the defense of the religion" among Spaniards and foreigners, all of whom were subject to the religious courts of the Inquisition. They were more tolerant of the Indigenous population's practice of their old religion, on the other hand, despite the fact that it was considered pagan and idolatrous. This tolerance doubtlessly contributed to the syncretism that left its mark on Indigenous and mestizo Catholicism. In this sense, two parallel religious systems developed in the sixteenth century: on the one hand, the traditional Catholic rite, on the other, Indian Catholicism, which accommodated itself to family and community life, with its celebrations of the life cycle and the agricultural cycle, hunting and healing rituals, and ceremonies marking changes of government. Both Indian officials and the leaders of *cofradías,* the religious brotherhoods so important in Latin American society, promoted the cults of numerous village and other saints. The leaders of the *cofradías* also assisted the ordained priests who conducted the orthodox masses of the official Church.

The tutorial policy of the Crown was decisive in relation to Spaniards, Indians, and work. Slavery was abolished in 1523, as was the personal servitude of Indians to their *encomenderos.* Added protection was afforded to Indians in 1542 with the introduction of what were called the New Laws. After a prolonged moral and theological dispute, Indians were finally held to possess souls and to be rational human beings. On the other hand, since they were viewed as lacking full reason, they merited royal mercy and were therefore not subject to slavery. Because they had recently become vassals of the king and were suffering under "wretched" conditions, they deserved royal protection, to be provided by the viceroy. When *encomiendas* were abolished, the conquistadors, their descendants, and all the *vecinos* vigorously opposed the imposition of these measures. They argued that their privileges were well deserved, the incorporation of New Spain into the empire having been entirely the fruit of their efforts.

Just as the king found it the better part of wisdom to be flexible when it came to Indian religious practices, so also his wish to abolish *encomiendas* foundered on the reality of colonial resistance. In the spirit of "acceding but not complying," the viceroy suspended the king's abolition of *encomienda* labor the same year that it was decreed. Then representatives of New Spain, of the Crown, and of *encomendero* interests opened negotiations. They reached a compromise, limiting the inheritance of *encomiendas* to one generation but at the same time reinforcing the ban on Indians providing labor to *encomenderos* in lieu of tribute. The terms of this compromise made it clear that Indian labor was not a monopoly of the *encomenderos;* it was available to whoever had the desire and the means to contract for it. This agreement went into effect in 1549, weakening the *encomenderos'* domination of the Indians. By the end of the century, a new labor system prevailed. Spanish officials and Indian authorities registered the available workforce and assigned day laborers to colonists who applied for their services. The authorities also took responsibility for collecting all wages from the employers and distributing them to the workers, thus insuring that they were paid.

At the time of the conquest and the foundation of New Spain, political attention was focused on the Indigenous population. Later, however, attention shifted to the defense of territories threatened by other European powers. New Spain, so very rich in silver, attracted the interest of foreign merchants and politicians. In addition to its wealth, it occupied a key position on the "Spanish lake" that linked Spain, its American colonies, and the Philippines. As a result, New Spain's Caribbean and Pacific coasts were subject to pirate attacks and incursions by corsairs, both supported by its colonial rivals.

Ports and ships needed to be protected from pirates and privateers, but that was not the crux of the problem. The privateers illegally imported European goods to sell in exchange for Mexican silver. It was not easy to stamp out this contraband activity, since it was a profitable way for merchants in New Spain to evade the heavy burden of the Crown's monopoly on trade, and the privateers offered goods at more favorable prices. But the monarchy badly needed silver to finance its European dominance and protect the powerful merchants in Seville. In order to protect the Sevillian trade monopoly and the remittances of silver, commercial shipping between Old Spain and New Spain was organized into convoys. Theoretically, convoys would arrive in Veracruz regularly, if acts of war did not delay them. They would provide New Spain with Spanish and European products and return bearing a corresponding amount of money and silver for the Crown.

For a central administration to control and govern such a vast and diverse territory as New Spain would have required the presence of civilian administrators in all its regions. In the absence of such an apparatus, Spanish and Indian *cabildos* tended to grow ever more autonomous. That is why provinces such as Nueva Galicia, Nueva Vizcaya, and Yucatán were administered by royally appointed governors. Even some smaller regions, like Veracruz and Tlaxcala, had their own governors. Each district—some one hundred of them by 1580—had an *alcalde mayor* or a *corregidor,* who replaced the *encomendero* in many regions. These men were responsible for, among other things, mediating between Spanish and Indian *cabildos* and representing their district's interests with higher authorities in Mexico City.

At first, the *alcaldes mayores* and *corregidores* were in every sense royal officers. They were named by the king and received regular salaries, while minor posts were handed out by the viceroy. They acted as judges in local disputes and maintained public order by summoning a militia from among the Spanish inhabitants. They were responsible for local administration and fiscal order. Soon, however, all this would change. The royal officers found it more lucrative to focus on commerce with Indian *pueblos* and communities, and the viceroys began to give the posts to relatives or use them as plum appointments in return for services rendered. Trade with the Indians was so profitable that these jobs continued to be desirable even after they became nonsalaried positions.

As was pointed out above, the transition in Europe toward a centralized monarchical State was never fulfilled in the Americas. The remoteness of the New World and the nature of its institutional structures impeded the development of anything like a civilian administration dependent on the king.

CHAPTER 3

The Colonial World

In the seventeenth century and the first years of the eighteenth century, Mexico underwent dramatic changes as a result of invasion and conquest. A new political, social, economic, and cultural order was established, one that would define the nature of the country for several centuries to follow.

During this period, a hierarchical order of ethnic and social categories brought into being by the conquest was spread throughout the regions. Catholicism was reinforced as a result of links between the royal authorities and the Church hierarchy.

The spread of the new order was made possible by the demographic recovery of the Indigenous population and the appearance of new sectors: the mulattos, the mestizos, and the *criollos* (the American-born descendants of Spaniards). The repopulation and Americanization of New Spain were possible due to both the expansion of mining and commercial agriculture and the inability of the monarchy to counter the autonomous growth of new local and regional forces. The *criollos* were the primary beneficiaries of the process, but the Indians also took advantage of the opportunity to complete their ethnic reconstitution, which had begun in the previous century.

The Shape of the Colonial World

The provincial capitals and the port cities were administered by viceregal officials. These were hubs on the network of roads and navigable rivers that connected mining districts and agricultural and cattle-raising areas to the harbors on the Gulf of Mexico and the Pacific coast. This transportation network delivered workers as well as material resources indispensable for the population's reproduction and survival, including salt, mercury, hides, food, and work animals.

Between these hubs, however, secondary areas were governed only indirectly by the viceroyalty. Elected Spanish and Indian *cabildos,* or town councils, governed independently in economic, social, and political matters. Spanish villages and towns alternated with mining centers and Indian *pueblos* in central New Spain, while the north-central region was more homogeneously Spanish colonial.

The number of towns represented on map 3.1 challenges the idea that New Spain was only thinly populated with Spaniards. While the Spanish population barely increased from ten thousand *vecinos* in 1570 to fourteen thousand in 1646, mostly in Mexico City, it rocketed to eighty thousand by 1774. Some say that Mexico City alone had fifty thousand *vecinos* by that time, although that figure is exaggerated. The word *vecino* specifically refers to the head of a family; we can presume that for every *vecino* there were three to four additional people.

By 1646, the Spaniards lived not only in the major cities and towns but also in smaller cities, towns, and villages strategically located throughout the colony in proximity to some fourteen hundred Indian communities, whose total population was greater. This pattern was probably strengthened with the policy of establishing Indian "congregations," groupings of people and towns with material resources sufficient for their own sustenance. This settlement policy was applied in 1550–1564 and again in 1593–1606. Terrible epidemics preceded those two periods, with the last large epidemic between 1578 and 1580. By that time the Indians had developed sufficient immunological defenses that the impact was less overwhelming. As a result, the second period of establishing Indian congregations had a longer-lasting effect than the first. With a population more resistant to disease, the matrix of colonial society was consolidated as a series of Spanish and Indian republics, each with its own legal code. Each Indian republic was organized around a principal town, the seat of the main town council or *cabildo;* secondary towns were known as *pueblos sujetos* (subject, or secondary, pueblos). The republics operated in the classical framework of direct self-government. Their self-sufficiency was ensured, as they were granted rights to natural resources such as farmland and water, and forest or pasture.

Although the Indian population was not growing at the turn of the

MAP 3.1. General map of New Spain in the seventeenth century. (Source: Jonathan I. Israel, *Race, Class, and Politics in Colonial Mexico, 1610–1670* [Oxford: Oxford University Press, 1975], p. 2.)

century, there is evidence of demographic recovery by 1630–1640. Population growth was undeniable by the end of the seventeenth century, with a total estimated increase of 28 percent between 1630 and 1700. This would suggest an Indian population of a million and a half by that time.

These figures do not reflect the social or economic changes or the dislocation brought about by the policy of Indian congregation. The movement of Indian populations into *pueblos* or places that offered better living conditions would indicate that their numbers grew a lot in some areas, while in others they stagnated, and in still others they dwindled. Some new *pueblos* were formed, some preexisting ones grew to be political centers, and others were reduced to dependency on larger towns. As a result of population growth, some brand-new Indian *cabildos* were formed, and some *pueblos sujetos* were separated from existing republics to form autonomous Indian republics.

The transition from population decline to population growth generated unanticipated social dynamics. Interaction among Indians, Spaniards, and mestizos increased. The population of mulattos and mestizos grew faster than any other sector, but these people were socially accepted only within a Spanish or Indian family network. If an Indian man married a mulatto or black woman, she was entitled to full *vecino* status within his village, whereas the reverse was not the case. Indian nobles were encouraged to marry into Spanish families. If a mixed-race individual built a fortune and contributed to the community, he could be granted *vecino* rights within the village. Yet non-*vecinos* lacking any permanent residence, whether Spanish, Indian, or mestizo, were considered a menace to the social order. If jobless, they were categorized as vagrants and were subject to captivity.

Social, political, and economic mobility in colonial society were expressed in many ways. Both Spanish towns and cities and Indian *pueblos* and *cabildos* acquired central roles as the administrative centers of areas under their jurisdiction and as units of social control.

The organization of Indigenous settlements reconstituted the familiar structures and spatial arrangements of urban *barrios,* or neighborhoods, secondary *pueblos,* and politically dominant *pueblos* in the different communities. The new social and spatial order was organized by officials appointed by the Crown called *comisarios* or *jueces de congregación,* who supervised Indian areas consisting of several *corregimientos.* After a visit of inspection, they would submit a development proposal for discussion to the local Spanish and Indian authorities and to the Spanish *vecinos* and *encomenderos.* After these consultations, the *comisario* or *juez de congregación* would formulate a modified plan for the congregation of towns, villages, and populations to be submitted to the viceregal authorities for their approval and for eventual implementation. Sometimes this process cost Indigenous authorities and nobles the respect of Indian commoners

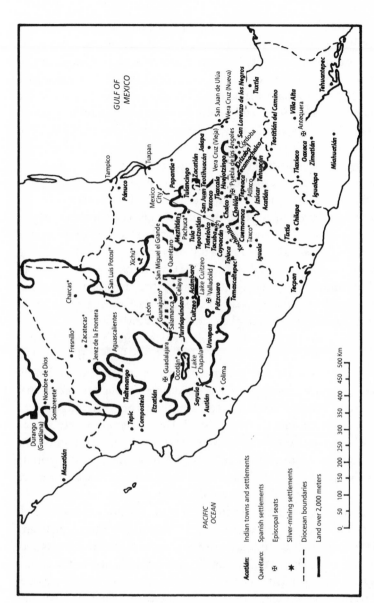

MAP 3.2. Central Mexico in the seventeenth century. (Source: Jonathan I. Israel, *Race, Class, and Politics in Colonial Mexico, 1610–1670*, op. cit., p. 34.)

because of their alleged collaboration with the *comisarios,* and in some cases, Indian commoners refused to make tribute payments.

We have a limited amount of information about the legal development of congregations in central Mexico. Bernardo García Martínez relates that it took five months to catalogue the Indigenous settlements in the mountains of Puebla State, and it took the two years of 1598 and 1599 to visit all of them.[1] The resulting document was passed to the Council of the Indies in 1600 for correction and approval. The next and final phase of the congregation process was not completed until 1608.

The length and complexity of the process were due to the need for consensus among the three parties: the Indians, the Spaniards, and the viceregal administration. It was imperative, though, to consolidate the core area of New Spain with the least amount of friction, and so the heart of the former Tenochca empire was colonized and a triple network established, consisting of Indians, Spanish, and royal officials. The Crown conceded broad autonomy to the Spanish and Indian sectors through their territorial administrations, the *cabildos.* On the regional level, though, the Crown governed indirectly and did not need to strengthen the administrative apparatus.

Nancy M. Farriss reports that in relatively marginal areas such as Yucatán, indirect government was established with little difficulty. The Crown prohibited the naming of magistrates, or *corregidores,* in that region to avoid conflict with the *encomenderos* and the religious orders that controlled the parishes. No intermediate positions between the governor and Indian communities were established. The *encomenderos* were remote figures who did not get very involved in the affairs of the community. The Indians did accord them respect, though, and rendered them tribute punctually. Chiapas and the Zapotec, Mixtec, and Mixe areas of Oaxaca also enjoyed independence from colonial magistrates.

The monarchy sought to depend on the "natural authorities" in each region of the Americas to resolve internal conflicts and to mediate any conflicts between royal officials and local or regional institutions. As a result, regional autonomy in New Spain was strengthened in the seventeenth and early eighteenth centuries, without, of course, weakening obedience to the king himself. Not even the sporadic Indigenous rebellions of the period challenged the fundamental loyalty to the king or to Catholicism. They simply opposed bad government and incompetent officials. When the king learned of these problems, he occasionally removed such officials from their positions.

---

1. Bernardo García Martínez, *Los Pueblos Indios y las Comunidades* (Mexico City: Centro de Estudios Históricos, El Colegio de México, 1991).

The New Geography of Indigenous Settlement

The Spanish State undertook a huge project in reorganizing the population along lines that were entirely new, conceived very specifically for New Spain and its other overseas possessions. The effects of this project were felt throughout the colony. The monarchy could control each segment of the population. The texture of material and cultural life was defined and enriched. Yet the innovative governmental and associational forms did not spring entirely from the new circumstances in New Spain. They corresponded to changes in the Spanish monarchy, which had entered into a decline during the reign of Felipe III, the son and heir of Felipe II. The first half of the seventeenth century was a time of powerful ministers who governed in the name of the king without convening the *consejos* of each realm. Between 1621 and 1643, King Felipe IV was represented by his most renowned minister, the Count Duke of Olivares. Olivares imposed an excessive tax burden and deprived the kingdoms of their accustomed liberties, which led to a crisis of the monarchy. Catalonia rebelled, Portugal opted for independence, and relations with the American provinces were strained. They lost their special charters, and obligations equal to those of the peninsular kingdoms were imposed upon them. The monarchy demanded greater contributions to strengthen its navy, and it wanted the American provinces to take responsibility for defending themselves against the constant military and commercial attacks by England, France, and the Netherlands. This attempted reorganization was a complete failure for the Crown, but as we will see, the power and autonomy of the recognized population sectors of New Spain, known as the estates, increased.

The Indians understood that they could exploit the political space opened up by the monarchy's declining power and economic weakness for their own ethnic reconstitution. Thus, decades after the early-seventeenth-century policy of Indigenous congregation, they reorganized their *pueblos* and affirmed the independence of their territories by paying large sums of money to the Crown in exchange for the *composition* of their land grants.[2] This speaks of a certain community wealth. In response to further demands for tribute, the Indians rebelled. The Indian rebellion in Oaxaca in 1660–1661 was an example of the Indigenous people's determination and capacity to oppose the attempts of *alcaldes*

---

2. *Composition* was a legal process for clarifying land titles in return for a fee paid to the king, in order to establish ownership and include certain lands that had been excluded from earlier grants of land-use rights.

mayores and *corregidores* to monopolize trade in regional products, particularly cochineal, the most lucrative among them.

The vigor of Indian communities was also manifested in their religious practices. There was a rebirth of what clerics called idolatry, which in fact was the nascent stage of religious syncretism, the cultural expression of a burgeoning ethnic reconstitution. At the same time, Indian religious and political practices began to merge through the spread of sainthood cults and their overlapping religious and civic expressions in the form of festivals jointly organized by the *cofradías,* or Catholic brotherhoods, and Indian governments.

The Indians' capacity to reorganize their communities gave them a real material and spiritual lift. They were better able to defend themselves from both Spaniards and mestizos, and they learned to benefit from the disputes between the clergy and the Crown over the latter's usurpation of Church prerogatives. Above all, the Indians appealed for the king's mercy in their "miserable" condition. Since all Indians were by definition considered minors, the king was empowered to protect their interests.[3] By various means, they also succeeded in concealing some of the community wealth of their *cabildos* and *cofradías.* In some instances, the king suspended tributary requirements or restored tributes to the communities.

The Indians employed numerous and complex survival strategies. Without a doubt, they made the most of the Spanish reliance on Indigenous labor. Labor power, land, and water represented their greatest wealth, and they struggled mightily to control these. In the seventeenth century, the control of the Indigenous labor supply to Spanish *haciendas,* ranches, and mines, previously regulated jointly by the Spanish and Indian authorities, reverted exclusively to the latter. This change benefited the finances of Indian *cabildos* because part of every worker's compensation in money and goods was paid directly to the community.

The *Criollo* Elite

The dire condition of the Spanish empire under the Count Duke of Olivares had enormous repercussions in New Spain. The Indigenous population was strengthened by its new strategies. This and the rapid growth of the mestizo population forced change upon the Spaniards. With the disappearance of the *encomienda* system by order of the Crown, it was in-

---

3. Being legally regarded as minors, Indians had the right to petition for the reversal of any transfer of wealth or other alleged offense against them.

cumbent upon the descendants of the conquistadors to abandon their leisurely lifestyles and find some form of livelihood. Thus they became *ha-cendados* (plantation owners), merchants, royal or government officials, professionals, or ecclesiastics.

The transformation of the Spanish population from a semi-aristocracy to merely a prominent estate was facilitated by family ties and connections developed in the sixteenth and seventeenth centuries. Their condition as vassals of the king and the increasing Indigenous autonomy made them nobles without vassals, so to speak. At the same time, the arrival of Spanish immigrants who occupied business and other lucrative economic sectors forced them to compete for wealth.

Throughout the seventeenth century and at the beginning of the eighteenth century, the principal Spanish families grew intricately interconnected by various mechanisms, in particular two Castilian social institutions: the *vínculo*, which assigned rural and urban properties to particular descendant heirs, and the *mayorazgo*, which established inheritance by primogeniture. These two institutions preserved the wealth, prestige, and honor of distinguished households by insuring that poor financial management by patriarchs would not translate into poverty for their descendants. But their effects went much further than just the protection of family property. *Mayorazgo* incentivized complex family strategies. The oldest son, the individual beneficiary of *mayorazgo*, had to provide his sisters with the wherewithal to marry within their social class or, if they preferred, to take their vows in a prestigious convent where they would continue to enjoy the privileges associated with their social standing. Likewise, he was obliged to help each of his brothers find a worthy ecclesiastical position, a military or civilian place in the royal administration, or a share in a mining or commercial enterprise. Thus marriage was important as a social class mechanism. Members of traditionally elite families with limited material resources could acquire wealth with the value of their last names through marriage, and wealthy individuals could marry into important families. Marriage provided the social mobility through which new families could enter the ranks of or even replace the descendants of conquistadors.

Another route of upward mobility for a wealthy *criollo* was to join a military order, such as the Order of Calatrava or the Order of Santiago. The purchase of a Castilian title was even more prestigious, and the title could be passed on to following generations or resold. The first Castilian titles in New Spain were acquired in 1616, but the majority were bought in the last third of the seventeenth century. Only some twenty families in New Spain, mostly in the capital, held titles in that century. Their privileges were more limited than those of nobles in Castile, however, because they acquired their titles in a period when the king was not delegating administrative or judicial functions. Thus a title of nobility in New Spain did not entitle its holder to exercise any jurisdiction over the population, making him a noble without vassals. The advantage of any Castilian title was social, as the right of primogeniture was inherent in its possession.

In addition to the *criollos* with important family names, there were others with lesser-ranking qualities who were nonetheless distinguished by virtue of having performed a service to the king; belonging to a Church *cabildo;* exercising a "virtuous" profession such as lawyer, physician, or scribe; owning a mine or workshop; or engaging in commerce. The sphere of influence of both greater and lesser families was primarily local administration, where men of illustrious lineage vied with other notables for positions on the *cabildos.* The fact that these positions were so coveted illustrates the importance of government institutions with respect to the representation of local *vecinos* and the defense of provincial interests. In the first third of the seventeenth century, the monarchy recognized the value and desirability of *cabildo* seats and began to sell them to *criollos* in all its domains. The *criollo* holding the position could pass it to his direct descendants, or even to a second-degree relative for an additional payment.

The new stratum of prominent *criollos* stubbornly opposed this policy, which disfavored them to the advantage of the more established families. The policy had been devised by the monarchy for kingdoms throughout the empire, with the idea of winning the support of the highest ranking local nobles in return for according them extraordinary privileges. Other elite *criollos* maintained that government positions should be filled by election. The Crown responded evasively, stating that the king was concerned about justice, which was why the most important position, that of magistrate, could not be purchased.

The Marginalized Population

At the end of the sixteenth century, travelers, churchmen, and officials all lamented that the population of mestizos and mulattos—the people they called *plebeyos*—was growing throughout the viceroyalty. In addition, escaped slaves and other people of color were living outside the effective jurisdiction of the king's government, along the coasts in autonomous communities called *palenques.* The institutions of some of these communities were so well organized that alarmed officials compared them to Indigenous republics. In fact, the Indian population grew from 1.3 to 2.0 million between 1646 and 1746, and the combined mestizo, mulatto, and black population grew even more rapidly, from 270,000 to 700,000. Mestizos, mulattos, and blacks accounted for one-fourth of the total population by the middle of the eighteenth century.

The most distinguishing characteristic of the Mexican population is its *mestizaje,* its racial blending. It was, and is to this day, emblematic of an entirely new civilization. Yet despite the importance of *mestizaje* in Mexico's material and cultural history, it has not been deeply studied. The unique characteristics of the new population appeared in this period. Mestizos lived outside the rigid legal and cultural schema of Indian and Spanish population groups, being the product of unions outside of holy matrimony, an institution over which the Church held an absolute monopoly. They were born and lived with the stigma of religious and cultural illegitimacy. No mulatto or mestizo could enter the regular or secular clergy or study at the university; thus they were disqualified from any position in the royal or provincial administrations.

Spanish colonial rule was initially designed around an Indian and Spanish population, as African slavery was not yet a factor in the Americas. The mestizos, mulattos, and blacks were pejoratively known as *castas,* "half-breeds." Their nonacceptability and lack of gainful employment deprived them of recognition as *vecinos* or even as residents of any town, divesting them of all basic civil rights and driving them to live as vagabonds. Nevertheless, labor power was scarce, and their services were in demand. At the midpoint of the colonial period, they lived in the cities, particularly in the capital, in the central mining districts like Taxco, and on the frontiers. They found work in the mining centers as mule drivers, or on newly formed *haciendas* tending cattle. Many worked in the growing transport industry, moving livestock and related products.

By the eighteenth century, the mestizo population was a majority in the northern provinces of Nueva Vizcaya, Nuevo León, and Nuevo México. They played a crucial role in populating these regions and in the struggle against nomadic Indians. The growth of the mestizo population gave birth to an image identifiable today as one of Mexico's national icons, the man on horseback. The mestizo population of northern Mexico collectively invented the Western saddle and developed a new breed of horse suited to long-distance travel and the desert climate there.

The New Economic Geography

Maps 3.3a and 3.3b illustrate the new organization of the viceregal economy better than any words. First, it should be noted that productive areas

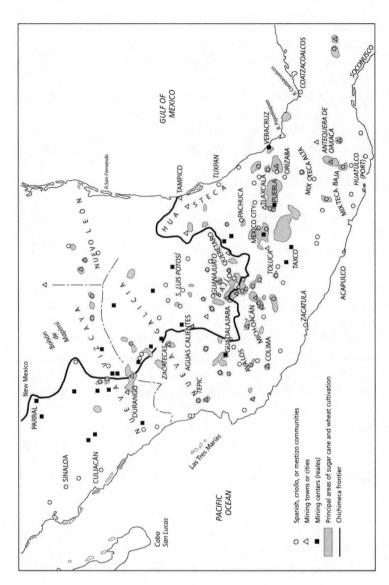

MAP 3:3A. Mining and agriculture in the seventeenth century. (Source: François Chevalier, *Land and Society in Colonial Mexico* [Berkeley and Los Angeles: University of California Press, 1963], n.p.)

Spanish, *criollo*, or mestizo communities
Mining towns or cities
Mining centers (*reales*)
Principal areas of sugar cane and wheat cultivation
Chichimeca frontier

GULF OF MEXICO

PACIFIC OCEAN

New Mexico
PARRAL
SINALOA
CULIACAN
Cabo San Lucas
Las Tres Marías
Bolsón de Mapimí
NUEVO LEON
R. San Fernando
TAMPICO
TUXPAN
HUASTECA
DURANGO
ZACATECAS
AGUAS CALIENTES
TEPIC
NUEVA GALICIA
NUEVA VIZCAYA
S. LUIS POTOSÍ
S. LUIS POTOSÍ
GUANAJUATO
QUERÉTARO
BAJIO
GUADALAJARA
AVALOS
COLIMA
MICHOACAN
ZACATULA
ACAPULCO
TAXCO
TOLUCA
MEXICO CITY
PACHUCA
ATLIXCO
PUEBLA
TLAXCALA
VERACRUZ
R. Papaloapan
R. Coatzacoalcos
COATZACOALCOS
SOCONUSCO
ORIZABA
MIXTECA ALTA
MIXTECA BAJA
ANTEQUERA DE OAXACA
HUATULCO (PORT)

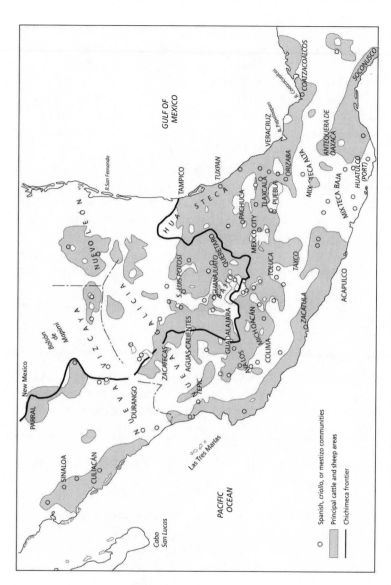

MAP 3.3B. Livestock in the seventeenth century. (Source: François Chevalier, *Land and Society in Colonial Mexico*, op. cit., n.p.)

Spanish, criollo, or mestizo communities

Principal cattle and sheep areas

Chichimeca frontier

were grouped around population centers; the more populous the urban area, the larger the agricultural, mining, and cattle areas. It seems that the population and the productive areas it created spun outward from the center of Mexico City. At the same time, people and goods from the north and west, where the frontiers between sedentary and hostile Indians persisted, were arriving in the viceregal capital. Silver extraction in the north ran along an axis connecting Parral with San Luis Potosí and the century's most productive mining center, Zacatecas, to converge on Mexico City. Southern products also streamed into Mexico City: cacao from Soconusco, textiles and cochineal from Oaxaca, sugar and Chinese products arriving from Asia by way of Acapulco. And of course imports from Spain and other European sources arrived in the capital: textiles, iron, mercury, paper, furniture, wine, and cooking oil.

Goods, including meat and agricultural products, were transported within regional circuits as well, since every demographic concentration also meant greater production and exchange. The circulation of goods through both Indian and Spanish productive areas was beneficial to both communities.

In addition to what we learn from these maps, we should mention the sea lanes that connected Yucatán, Tabasco, Coatzacoalcos, and Tuxtla with Veracruz on the Gulf Coast, and a great many ports and coves along the coastal routes to Acapulco on the Pacific. Sea transportation was a popular alternative to the expense of maintaining and using land routes, which were inevitably steep and dangerous and often further compromised by unfavorable weather conditions.

Map 3.4 illustrates the incorporation of the northern frontier into the new economy. Cattle led the way, reproducing and forming wild herds even before the Spaniards caught up with them. Abundant pasturelands and the cattle's own fecundity gave rise to large cattle ranches and made the development of silver mining possible. Sheep, goats, and pigs, on the other hand, were concentrated in the central south. They played an important role in the new economy developing in the traditionally sedentary Indian communities of the Mesoamerican area.

The cultivation of wheat closely followed the trail laid down by cattle and their cultivation. Corn, on the other hand, was the basic food grain grown and consumed throughout the territory. South of the twenty-first parallel, which stretches across the state of San Luis Potosí, it was the main food of the new mestizo population and of all the urban areas, including Mexico City.

We do not know very much about Mexican agriculture in this period.

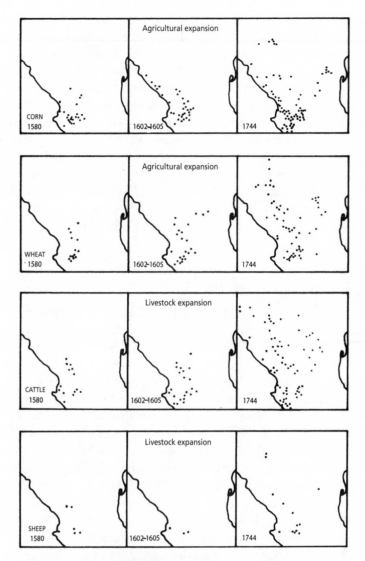

MAP 3.4. New products. (Source: Bernardo García Martínez et al., *Historia General de México,* vol. 1 [Mexico City: Instituciones a Cargo—El Colegio de México, 1976], pp. 395, 396, 407.)

Did it change? If so, how? Was production intensified? In what way? It seems that food was easy to obtain during most of the colonial era, even in the north. All evidence indicates that it was sufficient to free up enough labor to allow weaving, another important productive activity, to develop in workshops, or *obrajes*, and in people's homes. The same can be said of mining. Without the successful development of crop and livestock agriculture, mining could not have prospered as it did toward the end of the seventeenth century and at the beginning of the eighteenth century. Over the course of the eighteenth century, weaving spread in artisan workshops, homes, and among entire communities. The widespread weaving of wool, and even more widespread weaving of cotton, tells us that sheep herds and cotton agriculture were common and that enough food was being produced to free up labor for other activities.

Precious Metals and Trade

The principal wealth produced in colonial Mexico was in the form of precious metals bound for the international market, especially silver. Based on what has been reported, we see that there was a rapid increase in silver production after the opening of mines in Zacatecas and elsewhere, followed by a decline between 1630 and 1660. Production did not reach its earlier high levels again until after 1680–1700. However, Ruggiero Romano has questioned these figures. He argues that production did not decrease dramatically in the seventeenth century, that if there was a drop-off, it was minimal. The discrepancy is due to the fact that some account for the Mexican silver that arrived and was duly registered in Seville but do not account for silver extracted and sold illegally, of which there was a great deal. We know that the total amount of silver produced in Mexico, Peru, and Bolivia increased from 205 metric tons in 1576–1600 to 330 metric tons in 1651–1675, and that it reached 550 metric tons in 1701–1725. If we look at the figures for coins minted in Mexico City, we come to a similar conclusion. The production of silver did not decline at the end of the seventeenth century, nor at the beginning of the eighteenth. Romano asserts that growth in New Spain was uninterrupted for three centuries.[4]

If the silver coins or ingots did not arrive in Spain, it was because they were sent to other European destinations, usually Amsterdam, the prin-

---

4. Ruggiero Romano, *Monedas, Seudomonedas y Circulación Monetaria en las Economías de México* (Mexico City: El Colegio de México—Fondo de Cultura Económica, 1998).

e Panama Galleon and the Mexican t were scheduled return in January and February, respectively. They also had the option of joining forces in Havana.

e Spanish convoy system began under Charles V in response to French pirates' attacks and war ith France. It was institutionalized under Phillip II.

The Mexican fleet arrived in April or May. The Panama Galleon arrived in August.

Individuals and npanies managed trade between rtugal and Brazil until about 1650, when a convoy ystem like Spain's was instituted. lasted until 1766.

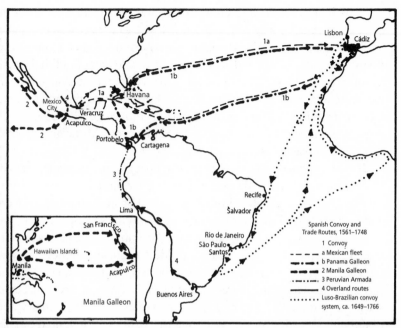

MAP 3.5. Trade routes, 1561–1766. (Source: Cathryn L. Lombardi and John V. Lombardi with K. Lynn Stoner, *Latin American Studies: A Teaching Atlas* [Madison: University of Wisconsin Press, 1983], p. 35.)

cipal financial center of the day. From there they would have been sold in the Eastern Mediterranean and Asia, including India. Mexican silver also circulated in other American territories around the Caribbean and on Pacific shores to pay for imports of contraband slaves and textiles, and for frequently illegal imports of cacao from Venezuela and Guayaquil. A large quantity of silver was exported to pay for Asian imports, mostly textiles and luxury goods, arriving on the Manila Galleon, a convoy that sailed annually between the Philippines and Acapulco. Another portion of the silver, impossible to quantify, remained in New Spain.

Map 3.5 illustrates how the system of convoys regularized at the end of the sixteenth century integrated New Spain into the commercial system of the empire. By the seventeenth century, Acapulco and Veracruz together functioned as a point of articulation between Spain's Atlantic and Pacific trade routes. The Mexican fleet was reinforced by the Panama Galleon, a fleet of ships that sailed from Spain to Portobelo and then to Havana, Spain's principal port in the Americas.

New Spain occupied an enormously strategic position, connecting Spain with Asia by way of the Atlantic and Pacific oceans. This is also what made it a rich target for ongoing contraband schemes. Contraband flourished because it offered very high profits, attracting English, Dutch, Spanish, and New World traders. Numerous coastal routes linked Mexican ports with each other and with other Caribbean destinations, where merchants found safe havens on the island colonies of all the European powers. Another set of routes connected numerous Mexican and other Spanish American ports on the Pacific.

The widespread tendency to engage in unauthorized trading practices was the response to a burdensome Spanish trade monopoly. In fact it was a double monopoly. Only a limited number of Spanish ship owners were authorized to conduct transatlantic trade. And in New Spain itself, another monopoly favored the small, closed group of principal merchants who belonged to the powerful Tribunal del Consulado, founded in 1592. Only members of the tribunal were authorized to do business with the Spanish ship owners and merchants at the Feria de Jalapa, a seasonal market for imported and exported goods in Veracruz, where mercury and iron required by the mining sector and the luxury goods desired by *criollos* were traded legally. As a consequence of this stifling double monopoly, legal trade grew only very slowly. Merchants, mine operators, *hacendados,* and even coastal Indian communities avoided the monopoly by making private arrangements with foreign traders. It was the prevalence of such agreements that broke the Spanish trade monopoly and hastened the decline of the monarchy, which had been the most powerful in Europe in the sixteenth century.

Political Activity

In the beginning, the colonial world was a mosaic of territories conjoined within an arrangement called the viceroyalty. I have described the colony's dynamism and its social, economic, geographic, and institutional development. And we have noted that between 1630 and 1690, the Spanish monarchy was in decline and the rest of western Europe, with the exception of the Netherlands, was in retreat. One may get the false impression that New Spain enjoyed a long period of tranquility thanks to the institutional arrangements that tied Spaniards and Indians alike to the monarchy and its local representatives. In fact, colonial society was anything but tranquil.

New Spain was negatively affected by the priority that Madrid placed on maintaining its dominant position in Europe, and by the monarchy's changing political and administrative strategies. Spain's fiscal demands were particularly burdensome, as were the confrontations between the royal administration and the recognized social groups of New Spain.

The Crown suffered one crisis between 1620 and 1664, and another as the seventeenth century came to a close. The first took place during the reign of Felipe IV, in the period of the Count Duke de Olivares's influence, and was the result of Portuguese resistance to the union of the Iberian monarchies, followed by rebellions in Catalonia and the kingdom of Naples. The second crisis was brought on by the struggle between the Hapsburgs and the Bourbons for succession to the throne. New Spain suffered the repercussions of these crises as the king increased taxes from 1621 to 1664 in order to compensate for the monarchy's growing expenditures.

In 1631, legal trade between New Spain and Peru was suppressed, which hurt Mexican merchants, particularly those who belonged to the Tribunal del Consulado. It also created a shortage of the mercury indispensable for the amalgamation of silver, which hurt mine operators and affected *hacendados* and food producers in general. It was a blow to the textile workshops of Puebla, too, who lost their best market.

The political instability of 1620–1660 forced every serving viceroy to resign in the face of fierce protests and uprisings. One of them, the Marqués de Gálvez, was deposed after a protracted popular insurrection stemming from a political crisis in 1623–1624. The unrest began among groups of Spaniards and *criollos* whose interests suffered as a result of increased taxes, and the discontent spread to officials whose opportunities to profit from their positions had diminished due to stricter controls. Spaniards, particularly *criollos,* were also angry that direct arrangements between Indigenous communities and the viceroyalty had made it impossible for them to appropriate Indian labor and resources. They were able to attract support from the mestizo and mulatto populations, and particularly from the secular clergy, who were interested in breaking the hold that the religious orders had upon Indian parishes.

This constellation of forces attracted the sympathies of *corregidores* and *alcaldes mayores,* who also objected to the autonomy that the Crown and the viceroy had granted Indian communities, putting a crimp in their economic relations. *Corregidores* and *alcaldes mayores* had been profiting from their role collecting royal tributes by disobeying royal and viceregal instructions about how to go about collecting them. Their greatest source of income was in trade with the Indians, as they forced them to sell their products in exchange for overpriced oxen, mules, and Spanish goods. Officials also profited from their role as suppliers of Indian labor, much in demand by Spaniards and *criollos*.

The struggle between the regular clergy and the secular clergy inflamed tensions, providing an ideological argument for the *criollos* and others who opposed policies protective of the Indians. The dispute polarized colonial society, with the viceroy, his magistrates and other high officials, the religious orders, and the Indians lining up as a bloc that confronted local and *criollo* interests.

In short, society was divided into two factions. At its core, it was a conflict between the viceroy and the *criollos,* especially those of Mexico City. By examining the *cabildo* records, one can deduce that these bodies represented *criollo* interests. They petitioned for the elimination of the Indian republics; the abolition of the *repartimiento,* under which the viceroyalty controlled the distribution and conditions of Indian labor;[5] a loosening of viceregal control over local officials; and the transfer of Indian parishes from the control of the regular clergy to that of the secular clergy. They consistently advocated for the mercantile interests of the Tribunal del Consulado.

The confrontation between the viceroyalty and *criollo* interests was sharpest between 1622 and 1640. After the middle of the century, the two groups reconciled somewhat in the face of a notable emboldening of the Indigenous population. An Indian rebellion in Tehuantepec in 1660–1661 was brought under control when one of its principal demands was met and the monopoly of Spanish magistrates over the lucrative trade with Indians was suppressed. The viceregal administration was able to channel *criollo* business interests toward local and regional commerce, diminishing if not eliminating the conflict. At the same time, the colonial administration pacified the *criollos* by transferring religious responsibilities toward the Indians from the religious orders to the predominantly *criollo* secular clergy.

An effort was made to pacify the *criollos* and calm the waters because in addition to the burgeoning Indigenous population, the menace of the *castas* was growing, and vigilance and unity were required. This concern grew as the seventeenth century progressed and Indians, mestizos, and

---

5. The *repartimiento* was an exchange mechanism that linked Indian communities to the market. Royal officers, profiting from their privileged position, advanced goods and means for production in exchange for future produce—a sort of trunk system.

blacks were involved in acts of violence and plunder. There were various attempted rebellions during the colonial period, but the uprising of 1692 was the most serious. A riot erupted at the very center of Mexico City in the Zócalo, the main plaza. Within a few hours, a mob of Indians, blacks, mulattos, mestizos, and some *criollos* and Spaniards had set fire to the main symbols of colonial power: the viceregal palace, the *cabildo,* the Audiencia, and the Royal Treasury. They also attacked and looted about three hundred businesses.

The 1692 uprising in Mexico City was duplicated on a smaller scale in other cities of the central region, notably in Tlaxcala. While the direct causes of the unrest were a series of poor harvests and a food shortage, the rebellions galvanized the viceroyalty to rethink the prevailing relations between the dominant social sectors—*criollos* and distinguished Spanish families, other Spaniards, and viceregal officials on the one hand, and the subaltern groups on the other. They were especially concerned about Indian participation in the disturbances. To them it meant that the institutional arrangements reached in the early seventeenth century, which had secured the support of leading Indian individuals, officials, and *caciques,* were no longer viable. The need for change was clear in the first third of the eighteenth century, when Charles II died without an heir and, after a conflict among the European powers, the throne was ceded to the Bourbons of Naples, relatives of the French ruling family.

The first reforms of the new Bourbon monarchy were immediately felt around the empire. A newly centralized administration disregarded the local autonomy of particular kingdoms and provinces. What had been the Kingdom of New Spain was now seen as a colony. What were known as the Ordinances of Intendants were enforced as of 1786 in New Spain. The provinces were reorganized into smaller administrative units called intendancies, and an executive officer called an intendant was assigned to rule each intendancy, much as was the case in France. The intendancy was further divided into districts headed by subdelegates. Attempts were made to impose royal prerogatives on the life of the Church. Substantial resources were allotted to the army, to the navy, and to the efforts of international diplomacy in order to redress the heavy losses suffered under the Treaty of Utrecht, when the empire lost most of its possessions in Italy and in northern Europe.

The first-ever relaxation of Spain's commercial monopoly got under way. While the convoy system was maintained, individual ships were also permitted to engage in trade. The new monarchy was more disposed than its predecessor to control the *castas* through police measures. This was also a moment for the *castas* to ease their way into the weave of society by enrolling in the recently formed colonial militia. Doing so provided them with new opportunities: they gained full *vecino* status and profited from opportunities for *composition*, the granting of land titles in return for a contribution to the Royal Treasury.

CHAPTER 4

The Twilight of the Colonial World

The second half of the eighteenth century was a time of material and cultural expansion for New Spain as a result of various internal and external factors: the changes imposed by the Bourbons, especially Charles III; advances by the European powers France and Great Britain; the speed with which the thirteen North American colonies achieved their independence; and the impact of the French Revolution in 1789.

During this half century, many of the political rivalries in Europe played themselves out in the Americas, giving New Spain and the other colonies of the Spanish empire much greater prominence in European power politics. Louisiana, as one example, went from being a French colony to a Spanish territory and was then restored to France, making possible its acquisition by the United States in 1802.

In this chapter I analyze the vitality of New Spain during this period, expressed not only in population growth but also in demographic transformation, producing a strongly regionalized multiethnic society in what was Spain's wealthiest American colony. This had significant political, cultural, and economic repercussions, but its greatest effect was on the colony's relations with Spain.

More than one hundred years had passed since the politically effervescent seventeenth century, and the changes begun at that time had matured. New regions were now settled and became populated much more rapidly. Demographic, social, cultural, and economic change came swiftly both to these areas and to the traditional centers.

Although many things changed, some things nevertheless remained the same. The population doubled from three to 6.1 million between 1742 and 1810. In table 4.1 we see that three areas maintained the greatest population density. These were Mexico and Puebla in the center, Oaxaca in the south-central region, and Guanajuato and Michoacán (Valladolid) in the west. Population density decreased as one moved south toward Chiapas or Yucatán, or from Guadalajara in the west northeast to San Luis Potosí or Zacatecas. The area beyond Durango was only sparsely settled. This was the frontier during the eighteenth and much of the nineteenth centuries, much as the area north of San Luis Potosí had been one hundred years earlier. The Californias and all the eastern and western provinces of the northern interior were sparsely populated, with less than one inhabitant per square mile.

The hierarchical organization of settlement persisted. Table 4.1 illustrates that despite increasing population, the traditional settlement categories of city, *villa,* town *(pueblo),* and mining district (included here in "other settlements") were stable. Cities held foundation charters and had the right, although not the obligation, to name a *cabildo. Villas,* which were urban sites holding lesser privileges than fully chartered cities, were a common form of Spanish American settlement in central Mexico and in the north-central region. Towns elected a town council if they acted as the seat of an Indian republic, but no new settlement populated by mestizos, "vagrant" Indians, or mulattos had the privilege of *cabildo* self-government. Table 4.1 also reveals the continuing concentration of cities, *villas,* and towns in the intendancies of México, Puebla, and Oaxaca. There were about 4,785 Indian towns scattered over the core area of New Spain, and Indian villages were also found in the western noncoastal provinces of New Mexico, Durango, and Arizpe.

While traditional settlement patterns were stable, the population grew ever more multiethnic and also settled in sites such as ranches, *haciendas,* and mining districts—the "other settlements" referred to in table 4.1. Table 4.2 and the ethnic division of the population have much in common with table 4.1 and its settlement patterns. By the late eighteenth century, society was no longer principally divided between Spanish and Indian. A new population sector referred to as *castas* had emerged and now included some 1.3 million people, more than 20 percent of the population. Thus a significant portion of the population had no recognized rights, although they performed certain categories of work, played a defined social role, and were liable for personal obligations.

Regional variations in population density influenced the recognition of new ethnicities and the redefinition of the ethnically defined social

TABLE 4.1. Kingdom of New Spain, 1810
Population by Square League and Type of Settlement

Intendancy	Inhabitants per Square League	Cities	*Villas*	Towns	Other Settlements[a]
México	269	6	15	1,228	1,783
Guadalajara	54	2	7	326	2,032
Puebla	301	5	1	764	1,403
Veracruz	45	2	5	147	217
Mérida	88	2	2	276	1,631
Oaxaca	134	1	5	928	367
Guanajuato	633	3	4	62	900
Valladolid	114	2	3	309	1,152
San Luis Potosí	74	1	2	49	588
Zacatecas	60	1	2	28	581
Government of Tlaxcala	—	1	—	110	207
TOTAL	n/a[b]	26	46	4,227	10,861
Eastern Internal Provinces					
Government of Nuevo León	17	2	4	16	27
Government of Santander	11	—	18	11	—
Government of Coahuila	6	—	7	7	98
Government of Texas	—	—	1	2	10
TOTAL	n/a	2	30	36	135
Western Internal Provinces					
Durango	10	1	8	168	397
Arizpe	7	1	7	138	441
New Mexico	6	—	3	109	—
TOTAL	n/a	2	18	415	838
Californias					
Government of Baja California	—	—	—	2	—
Government of Alta California	10	—	1	2	—
TOTAL	n/a	—	1	4	—
OVERALL TOTAL	n/a	30	95	4,682	11,834

[a]Includes mining camps, *haciendas*, cattle ranches, and other ranches.

[b]n/a = Total not applicable to inhabitants per square league.

SOURCE: Fernando Navarro y Noriega, *Memoria sobre la Población del Reino de Nueva España Escrita en el Año de 1814* (Llanes, Spain: J. Porrúa Turanzas, 1954).

TABLE 4.2. Kingdom of New Spain, 1810
Population by Ethnicity

Intendancy	Spanish (%)	Indians (%)	*Castas* (%)	Total Population
México	17.0	66.2	16.8	1,591,844
Guadalajara	31.8	33.4	34.8	517,674
Puebla	10.2	74.4	15.4	811,285
Veracruz	10.5	74.2	15.3	185,935
Mérida	14.9	72.7	12.4	528,700
Oaxaca	6.4	88.3	5.3	596,326
Guanajuato	25.9	44.1	30.0	576,600
Valladolid	27.7	42.6	29.7	394,689
San Luis Potosí	13.0	51.3	35.7	173,651
Zacatecas	15.9	29.0	55.1	140,723
Government of Tlaxcala	13.6	72.5	13.9	85,845
TOTAL	17.3	62.4	20.3	5,603,272
Eastern Internal Provinces				
Government of Nuevo León	62.7	5.6	31.7	43,739
Government of Santander	25.8	23.4	50.8	56,715
Government of Coahuila	30.0	28.9	40.2	42,937
Government of Texas	39.9	27.5	32.6	3,334
TOTAL	39.2	18.7	42.1	146,725
Western Internal Provinces				
Durango	20.3	36.1	43.6	177,400
Arizpe	28.6	45.0	26.4	135,385
New Mexico	—	30.9	69.1	34,205
TOTAL	21.5	39.0	39.5	346,990
Californias				
Government of Baja California	—	51.7	48.3	4,496
Government of Alta California	—	90.0	10.0	20,871
TOTAL	—	83.3	16.7	25,367
OVERALL TOTAL	18.0	60.1	21.9	6,122,354

SOURCE: Fernando Navarro y Noriega, *Memoria sobre la Población del Reino de Nueva España Escrita en el Año de 1814,* op. cit.

strata. An analysis of the data illustrates this demographic regionalization, and once again the south of New Spain stands out in contrast to the center and the north. In the columns representing ethnicities, we see that the Spanish population was distributed in somewhat similar proportions to that of the *castas*. Both of these groups tended to be less well represented in regions with Indian majorities, such as the intendancies of México, Puebla, Veracruz, Mérida, Oaxaca, and Tlaxcala. As one moved west, on the other hand, or north of San Luis Potosí, near the twenty-first parallel, the Indigenous population sector decreased relative to the others. There, Spaniards and *castas* combined to form a non-Indian majority.

Spaniards and *Criollos*

The colonial world was being transformed by these population changes. By the second half of the eighteenth century, the traditional Spanish and Indian population sectors were on the defensive, pressuring royal authorities to maintain their privileges and responsibilities and to grant them new ones. The *castas* were demanding a status of some kind in the ethnically and culturally hierarchized society of the viceroyalty. There were at least five political actors after 1750: Spaniards, Indians, royal authorities, *castas,* and the ecclesiastics who played a mediating role among them all.

The complexity of the social dynamics went far beyond straightforward confrontation. While each ethnosocial group sought to differentiate itself from the others, individuals sought to differentiate themselves within their group as well. This produced greater social competition and zeal, which tended to obscure strictly group-based distinctions. To be a member of the "Spanish" ethnosocial group could have different meanings. One could be a member of a distinguished family and a member of one of the important corporations such as the Tribunal del Consulado, which regulated international trade; the Tribunal de Minería, the guild that regulated mining; or the Tribunal de la Universidad, a university guild. A Spaniard from a prestigious traditional family could be a magistrate, an official of the Royal Treasury, or a member of the upper clergy serving on a church council or as a bishop. These men's prestige could be further enhanced if their family possessed a Castilian title or they belonged to a religious or military order. Other Spaniards were shopkeepers, artisans, and the like, mostly the so-called *gachupines,* those recently arrived from Spain who were in competition with older families. These included the new subdelegates, who held intermediate-level official positions created in the course of the political-administrative reforms of the last third of the eighteenth century. When the commercial monopoly was abolished, many people in Spain were attracted to the possibility of making their fortune in America, and a wave of immigration ensued. The latest immigrants took up positions in the newly strengthened royal and ecclesiastical administrations. Finally, there were Spaniards among the impoverished masses, difficult to distinguish from the others who shared their abysmal condition.

One division among the Spaniards that was insignificant at the beginning of the eighteenth century had become fundamental by its midpoint. This was the distinction of either having been born on the Iberian Peninsula and emigrated to America, or being a *criollo,* an ethnically Spanish native of America. What had once been a single, clearly defined ethnosocial group was transformed into two. The transition from an essentially Hispanic identity to identification with the land of New Spain counterposed these groups. The Spaniards had an unusual sense of belonging to the broad Iberian tradition that included the Catholic religion and the special position of the king, a sense that went beyond any territorial identity and even beyond the idea of "homeland." *Criollo* patriotism, while based on identification with the land where one had been born and where one lived, did not exclude a sense of universal belonging to the Crown, the monarchy, and the Catholic religion. While territorial identity set American-born and Spanish-born inhabitants of New Spain apart, the broader Iberian tradition continued to be shared by both, at least in this period.

The new identification with New Spain was a conceptual innovation that joined the provincial "homeland" with the universal "empire." This cultural and ideological identity allowed individuals and families of different ethnic identities—mulattos and mestizos—to also shed their status as *castas* and become *criollos.* In this way the concept of *criollo* lost some of its ethnic basis and became more socially inclusive. This inclusivity was reinforced when the monarchy made it possible for an individual *casta* and his descendants to obtain a certificate declaring their "purity of blood" and to be considered Spanish in return for a onetime payment to the king.

The change from a purely ethnic to a social definition of the population strata owed much to the dynamics within each sector. In the Spanish sector, for instance, the source of a family's wealth, its prestige, and the degree of respect its name commanded all contributed to the status it enjoyed. A family could be prestigious without possessing great wealth, based on the social position that went along with its name. Another, newly wealthy family might be considered unrefined and merit lesser overall status. All of these values reveal the importance of the family, including the mechanisms of extended family ties and *compadrazgo,* the culturally salient godparenting relationship.[1]

The *criollo* sector also included lower, middle, and upper strata. Relations among families played a key role in upward mobility. The new policies of the Crown in controlling the composition of *cabildos* also played an important role. When members of *cabildos* could no longer sell or transfer their positions to others of their own choosing, members of new families gained access to these important local institutions. Another mechanism for mobility was the purchase of certificates or titles. The king could grant a document to an individual or family certifying their purity of blood. A wealthy mestizo, Indian, or mulatto could become a property owner through the process of *composition,* whereby in exchange for a payment to the Crown, the lands he possessed without title could be recognized and fully titled in his name. Finally, the Bourbon reforms at the end of the eighteenth century reorganized New Spain into districts, and mestizos and mulattos were granted the right to serve as assistants to the district subdelegates and, as militia members, acquire *vecino* status.

The Modernization of the Indian Republics

As the colonial era drew to a close, the most important demographic shift was the recovery of growth by the Indian population as compared to overall population growth. All the population sectors—Indian, mestizo, *criollo,* Spanish, and so on—responded similarly to the epidemics, pandemics, and famines, that is, they lost ground but recovered once the crisis had passed. This indicates that the Indigenous population had attained the same resistance as the other groups to the biological causes of demographic crises: measles, smallpox, typhus, and a still-unidentified disease known as *matlazahuatl.* The Indigenous population, only two million at

---

1. *Compadrazgo* is a religiously based godparenting relationship established through co-participation in an event such as baptism, religious confirmation, marriage, the presentation to society of a girl on her fifteenth birthday *(la quinceañera),* or consecration of a religious image. The ties of friendship and fidelity that are established also entail political and social commitments, including bonds of solidarity and an implicit obligation to mutual protection.

the end of the seventeenth century, had reached 3.6 million by the end of the colonial period in the early nineteenth century. This was significant because as the population grew, the Spanish demand for Indian labor decreased in relation to available supply. This undermined Spanish control of the Indigenous communities, whereupon the Crown ceased to see them as the weakest and neediest population sector and therefore deserving the special protection they had been accorded.

Labor was now being provided by *castas* as well as Indian communities. As *hacendados* and ranchers were no longer dependent on Indian labor, Indian authorities lost their bargaining power as suppliers. At this point, the Crown's Indian policy focused on controlling the growing conflicts among communities. Controls were put on the demand for new republics, which were increasing with the spread of "irregular settlements." The circulation of Indigenous products was regulated and more *tianguis,* or open-air Indian markets, were established. The proliferation of markets was a problem for Hispanic beneficiaries of Indian *repartimiento,* since they were used to paying little and charging much for Indian products, and were not accustomed to competition. For the Indian *pueblos* and families, though, its abolition was a positive change.

The growing Indian population increased the pace of settlement in the Indian republics. At this point, each republic consisted of territories organized around an administrative center, the seat of the Indian *cabildo,* whose main function was to organize the land, water, and forest rights of the villages under its jurisdiction. In the outlying territories, the Indians established politically secondary *pueblos* with their own local authority, and smaller settlements called *barrios* or *estancias.* By the close of the eighteenth century the secondary *pueblos* had begun to call for an increased role in public administration of the republics. This was in keeping with other developments, such as evolving Indian hierarchies and the need to provide land to the growing population, land which in times of scarcity had been rented or sold under dubious terms. A nascent leadership within the ranks of the *macehualtin* profited from such discontent to become community leaders, some by providing services to the republics and others by becoming wealthy and making strategic donations to the communities or their principal *caciques.* The demand of secondary *pueblos* to be recognized as autonomous republics implied the formation of new *cabildos* and the distribution of additional government positions among their leaders. It also meant expansion into new lands, and the redemption of existing land grants.

This quick summary of internal changes in the Indian republics helps us to understand the features that they shared with the *criollo* sector. Both were hierarchically organized, struggling to maintain the distinction between commoners and elites, each with its defined privileges and obligations. Both hierarchies provided for a set of recognized positions that endowed their occupants with defined social roles accompanied by rituals and elaborate garments specific to a certain status and occasion. When *criollo* families took on Castilian titles, the king recognized their nobility, and they achieved privileged positions. The process of recognizing the aristocratic status of Indigenous leaders was analogous. Indigenous *caciques*, officials, and nobles established their identity in relation to the land or the region where they lived and where they acquired the status of *vecinos*. It may be that for leading Indians, homeland also had sacred meaning as a territory consecrated in ancestral and pre-Hispanic times.

The social and cultural cohesion of the Indians at this time matched the degree of self-determination and self-government they exercised within the republics. They sought to obtain resources, to improve and increase production and sale of their products, and to raise educational levels. In the first half of the eighteenth century, Indian parishes were removed from the jurisdiction of the religious orders and put under the tutelage of the secular clergy. The religious control exercised over them diminished for the first time since the conquest. The regular clergy had saddled the Indians with endless collections for charity and had charged them exorbitantly for religious festivals, weddings, baptisms, and funerals. With the secularization of the parishes, the Indians gained autonomy and were able to devote more of their time and effort to fulfilling their own needs.

Another factor in the increased autonomy of Indian communities was the fact that outside authorities tended to close their eyes to certain practices in return for Indigenous cooperation. For example, priests and subdelegates overlooked certain syncretic religious practices, as viceregal magistrates had done before, which allowed Indian authorities to freely exercise the control associated with their special religious authority over the population, especially over the *macehualtin*. At the same time, once the villagers felt freer to engage in these practices, the revival of traditional customs helped to consolidate the ethnic reconstitution that had begun in the previous century. The villagers who had full *vecino* status reinforced community bonds. Their plots of land were within the community's area of jurisdiction, and as *vecinos* they had rights to the use of community water, pasture, and forest resources, as regulated by local authorities. The *cofradías* and other religious *hermandades*, or brotherhoods, maintained additional resources in the name of their patron saints.

Indian communities began to accumulate wealth, which was kept under triple lock and key in chests called *cajas,* guarded by local magistrates. These *cajas de comunidad* served as savings funds for the community. They also began to accumulate other property in the form of land, livestock, and cash, rather astutely consecrated to their brotherhoods, where it was protected as property of the saints. Being free from Spanish government control and Church authority in the eighteenth century, the brotherhoods spread rapidly. In the early nineteenth century, however, the Crown seized the Indian *cajas* to use them in some ill-fated financial ventures, including the first royal bank, the Bank of San Carlos, founded in 1782. The loss of so much unprotected community wealth encouraged the widespread consecration of even more property to saints.

Several simultaneous changes contributed to the thoroughgoing reorganization of the Indian republics. Above all, family bonds were reinforced on the basis of neighborhoods, or *barrios*—a spatial form of organization that was then interwoven with the system of municipal coffers and religious *cofradías* and other brotherhoods. In the first third of the eighteenth century this structure was consolidated as positions of responsibility within the *cofradías,* other brotherhoods, and the secondary *pueblos* were linked to the hierarchy of the Indian *cabildo:* the governor, magistrates, and local councilors. The Indians' ability to tie particular family lines to institutional positions and their associated economic resources, and to link specific urban quarters and secondary *pueblos* to the leadership ranks of the *cabildo,* were completely innovative. The town that was the seat of the republic retained symbolic value, for the *cabildo* safeguarded the republic's titles, land grants, population registers, and all its historical rights. By the eighteenth century, Indian populations living in the central plateau and in the south, comprising the intendancies of México, Michoacán, Oaxaca, Chiapas, and Yucatán, had reconstituted an identity based on land, water, and forest rights with the power to govern and to regulate the use of natural resources. Autonomy sustained by self-government enabled the Indian republics to interact on more equal terms with Spaniards and *criollos.*

These developments explain the rarity and low visibility of Indian rebellions in the later colonial period, in contrast to those that had occurred earlier. In the north the situation was different, though. The majority of rebellions occurred there, perhaps because the government offered Indians in that region little in the way of protection. Indian wars raged openly on the northern frontier, especially north of Durango and in Coahuila and Chihuahua. Campaigns of persecution and extermination against nomadic Indians were accompanied by pillaging and the taking of "specimens" as slaves—a Spanish practice that the Indians quickly took up in imitation. New groups of Apaches frequently crossed the Río Grande and pillaged settlements in Coahuila and Chihuahua. In Chihuahua alone they killed or captured 154 people and stole 70,000 head of cattle and 200,000 sheep between 1771 and 1776.

The *Castas*

If we consider the number of evocative racial terms that arose in the eighteenth century—*coyotes, lobos, mestizos, castizos,* and many others, each with a distinct image and meaning—we realize that the word *mestizaje* does not begin to do justice to what had taken place.

People of combined Indian, black, mestizo, Spanish, or mulatto origin were collectively known as *castas,* although within this general classification there was continued differentiation based on status, wealth, and social recognition. The outstanding characteristic of the racially mixed population was its high birth rate in relation to that of the Spanish or the Indians, a phenomenon for which we have no explanation. The mixed race population was concentrated in the north-central region: in Mexico City, in mining districts, and around ranches, *haciendas,* and cattle ranches, which operated on the *hacienda* system but were devoted entirely to cattle raising.

The *castas* were already numerous in the seventeenth century but became even more so in the eighteenth, at which time they became a significant alternative to the Indians as a source of labor. In a hierarchical society strongly conditioned by Catholic doctrine and social convention, children born out of wedlock were considered illegitimate and often grew up without knowing a home or family. Some referred to themselves as *Indios trotamundos,* or "wandering Indians," due to their lack of *vecino* status and fixed income. They wandered in search of work in cities and mines, around ranch country, and in Indian pueblos. Sometimes they worked as muleteers. To colonial society, they were a dangerous class. In response to the social problems that these vagrants allegedly created, the authorities reinforced the Real Acordada, a police body assembled to patrol the outskirts of large cities, especially the capital, that became a regular police force in 1760. It does not seem to have been the royal policy to make the *castas* vassals of the king, but viceregal and local laws were enacted to control them. Vagrancy was defined as a crime, so that persons lacking a craft, profession, income, salary, occupation, fixed employment, or known residence were subject to arrest.

The new intendancies, empowered to centralize governmental procedures or rule in their jurisdictions, were unpopular and encountered strong provincial resistance. The intendants and subdelegates applied their mercantilist approach to social control by requiring all persons to carry a kind of domestic travel document. Any individual apprehended without a document could be labeled a vagabond and handed over to royal authorities for labor service.

The requirement to carry these passports had very negative consequences in the eighteenth and nineteenth centuries. The enforcement of the regulation soon led to the justification and eventual legalization of debt peonage, a practice already present at the end of the sixteenth century. Under the pretext of "civilizing" the *castas* by requiring them to stay in one place and work, landowners would advance them their pay in the form of goods, almost never in money, and hold them against their will to work at *haciendas, estancias,* mines, or workshops.

Seizing and holding itinerant labor had been common since the seventeenth century, but legalized debt peonage institutionalized the practice. Spanish and *criollo* mine operators, *hacendados,* and manufacturers used the practice to secure an alternative to Indian labor, and it spread throughout Mexico. It was most onerous, however, in the central region—the Valley of Mexico and Puebla—and in the west, in the Bajío. Forced labor was extracted not only by establishing indebtedness on the part of the worker but also at times by allowing wages owed him to accumulate. Either of the two forms of nonpayment resulted in servitude. The tyranny of debt provoked worker rebellions and escapes on many occasions.

By no means, on the other hand, was all labor forced. Free labor was employed in all types of workplaces to fill specialized positions, such as sugar mill supervisors, foremen, purging room workers, sharecroppers, and paymasters.

The new population of *castas* found unclaimed land available in the north, where they could herd livestock—often wandering or feral animals they had rounded up. Elsewhere they gathered on the outskirts of cities and towns to offer domestic services, shear sheep if there was a local wool industry, or work on ranches as muleteers or cowhands. It was difficult for them to alter their extralegal status. If they had work, it was itinerant. If not, they were treated as vagrants.

In cases of *compadrazgo* or of intermarriage, or if a *casta* somehow became wealthy and contributed to the community's welfare, he could leave behind his vagabond or itinerant status, move into town, and become a *vecino.* Those who did not establish these kinds of connections, though, remained marginalized and were the object of continuous hostile pressures, representing as they did a drain on community resources or simply members of a "dangerous class" according to social convention.

Economic Change and Reform

In chapter 3 we saw that one of the changes in productive technology in the sixteenth and seventeenth centuries was the replacement of human labor with animal power, which was important in view of the drastic decline in population. The use of animal power facilitated the development of agricultural areas devoted to commercial and highly profitable crops such as cotton, sugar, tobacco, and cochineal. As the population increased during the long colonial period and into the early nineteenth century, this new agriculture was intermingled with and sometimes replaced traditional Indian and *hispano-criollo* crops. (See map 4.1.)

Table 4.3 presents some of the changes that had come about by the first decade of the nineteenth century. We notice a predominance of working ranches over extensive landholdings, or *haciendas*. This was a departure from the sixteenth and seventeenth centuries, although the absolute number of *haciendas* grew as well. *Haciendas* and working ranches were the dominant productive units, but they varied in nature. The most sophisticated among them were productive complexes that included manufacturing and repair workshops, sugar mills, sawmills, and tanneries. This kind of agricultural-livestock unit was first consolidated in the eighteenth century and became dominant on the central plateau and in the west, the areas that had seen the most extensive settlement in the previous century.

In the north, on the other hand, settlements were widely dispersed. This changed in the period between 1750 and 1820, when advances in mining technology revolutionized that industry, creating a synergy that stimulated commerce and increased agricultural and livestock production. Mining districts sprang up all around the center and in the north. Zacatecas, Guadalajara, Guanajuato, San Luis Potosí, Chihuahua, Coahuila, Durango, and Nuevo León were all important producers. Even on the plateau, there were various mining areas in the intendancy of México, the silver center of Taxco prominent among them.

Two things stand out about this change: specialized production became possible only in the context of increasing commerce, and mining was the stimulus that accelerated all the other factors in the process. Finally, the centrality of these productive areas was not only economic but also social and political. They would later play a decisive role in the 1824

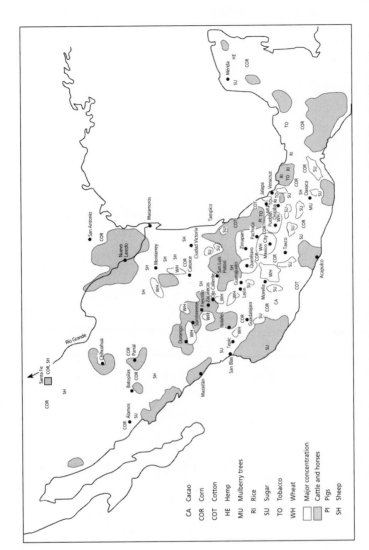

MAP 4.1. Agriculture and livestock in the eighteenth century. (Source: Colin M. MacLachlan and Jaime E. Rodríguez, *The Forging of the Cosmic Race: A Reinterpretation of Colonial Mexico* [Berkeley: University of California Press, 1980], p. 163.)

TABLE 4.3. Kingdom of New Spain, 1810
Numbers of Mining Districts and Agricultural Units

Intendancy	Mining Districts	Agricultural Haciendas	Ranches	Cattle Ranches
México	31	824	871	57
Guadalajara	33	370	1,511	118
Puebla	—	478	911	14
Veracruz	—	60	157	—
Mérida	—	563	312	756
Oaxaca	10	83	269	5
Guanajuato	10	445	416	29
Valladolid	18	311	708	115
San Luis Potosí	15	124	431	18
Zacatecas	19	108	438	16
Government of Tlaxcala	—	139	68	—
TOTAL	136	3,505	6,092	1,128
Eastern Internal Provinces				
Government of Nuevo León	4	23	—	—
Government of Santander	—	—	—	—
Government of Coahuila	—	32	44	22
Government of Texas	—	—	8	2
TOTAL	4	55	52	24
Western Internal Provinces				
Durango	26	155	184	32
Arizpe	40	34	356	11
New Mexico	—	—	—	—
TOTAL	66	189	540	43
Californias				
Government of Baja California	—	—	—	—
Government of Alta California	—	—	—	—
TOTAL	—	—	—	—
OVERALL TOTAL	206	3,749	6,684	1,195

SOURCE: Fernando Navarro y Noriega, *Memoria sobre la Población del Reino de Nueva España Escrita en el Año de 1814*, op. cit.

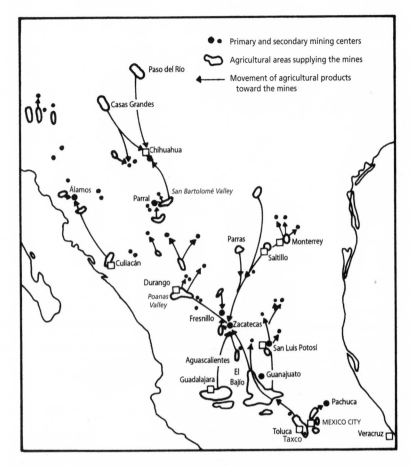

Primary and secondary mining centers

Agricultural areas supplying the mines

Movement of agricultural products toward the mines

Paso del Río

Casas Grandes

Chihuahua

Álamos

Parral

San Bartolomé Valley

Parras

Monterrey

Saltillo

Culiacán

Durango

Poanas Valley

Fresnillo

Zacatecas

San Luis Potosí

Aguascalientes

Guadalajara

El Bajío

Guanajuato

Pachuca

MEXICO CITY

Toluca

Taxco

Veracruz

MAP 4.2. Mining and agriculture in northern New Spain. (Source: *Historia General de México,* vol. 1 [Mexico City: El Colegio de México, 1996], p. 556.)

political confrontation between the individual states and the independent Mexican State.

In general terms, the production of precious metals grew from 65.7 million pesos between 1755 and 1759 to 122 million pesos between 1805 and 1809, representing 8.2 percent of New Spain's gross domestic product (GDP). The GDP itself is estimated to have reached 211 million pesos by 1800, equal to some 438 million 1950 U.S. dollars.

While mining itself was producing only 8.2 percent of the GDP, its impact was nonetheless enormous. It stimulated the much larger areas of raw materials and manufactured goods, believed to represent 70 percent of the GDP in 1800. The commercial sector also took on new importance beginning in 1750. By 1800 it comprised 16.7 percent of the GDP, twice that of mining.

These changes were due in large part to the commercial growth and dynamism that resulted from the breakdown of the monopoly on trade between Spain and Spanish America that the monarchy had exercised through the Casa de Contratación and the convoy system. All commerce had been channeled through this exclusive "corporation," a merchant guild located first in Seville and later in Cádiz, to the equally exclusive group of merchants in New Spain's Tribunal del Consulado. The point of contact was the Feria de Jalapa, near Veracruz, where the silver dealers of New Spain arrived loaded with newly minted coins to do business with Spanish shipowners bearing Iberian and other European merchandise. The double monopoly created strong incentives for contraband trade. Other sectors of society, especially *criollos* but also recently arrived Spaniards, were able to acquire lower-priced merchandise thanks to the development of illegal trade routes. This accounts for the extraordinary competition for the position of chief councilor in Huatulco, on the Pacific coast south of Acapulco, and for the importance of San Blas, another port farther north in Nayarit.

Eventually, the monarchy acknowledged that the monopoly was most beneficial to a handful of merchants in Spain and New Spain and to foreign powers, especially England. The Crown itself was incurring substantial losses, since those engaged in contraband, which was the larger proportion of trade, paid no taxes at all. In fact, the monopoly was detrimental to not only the Crown but also the manufacturing interests that supported it.

As a first step in the freeing of trade between Spain and New Spain, the flow of goods and supplies from the viceroyalty was stepped up by allowing individual ships to make the journey beginning in 1757. In 1774, direct trade was restored between New Spain and Peru. The process of change was complete by 1789, when all restrictions on shipping in or out of Spanish and Spanish American ports were lifted. Veracruz quickly became a major port. The number of ships docking there doubled from one hundred to two hundred per year between 1790 and 1810, half of them arriving from Spain. In 1797, the Spanish Crown authorized merchants of Spain and New Spain to use neutral shipping during the war against Napoleon.

In 1805–1810, one half of the vessels arriving in Veracruz were from other ports in the Americas, the number of such ships increasing from forty in 1805 to one hundred in 1810. U.S. ships sailed from New Orleans, and others came from French colonies like Trinidad and from Venezuela, Portobelo, and Cartagena in the Spanish colony of Nueva Granada. They formed a quadrangular trading system between Veracruz, New Orleans, the Caribbean ports of Trinidad and Cuba, and Spanish ports of Andalusia or Catalonia.

The Crown's decision to liberalize trade had two objectives: to better supply the viceroyalty, and to increase its own income stream by eliminating contraband trade. At the same time that trade within the empire was being invigorated, the Spanish also increased their military presence in port cities and improved their defenses. They made progress in all of these areas, particularly in increasing their income, which doubled between 1790 and 1810 despite the Napoleonic wars.

The first effect of this new policy was an increase in imports to New Spain. New Spain exported only agricultural goods and precious metals, mainly silver, so its trade imbalance worsened as its new demands for black slave labor and for foreign products, such as iron, steel, and mercury required for mining and agriculture, increased. There was an outflow of 426 million pesos between 1766 and 1791—about 16 million pesos per year. This does not include trade in contraband, which also remained high. During the same period, 450 million pesos in gold and silver coins were minted, and 419 million of these pesos left the country in legal transactions alone.

In conformity with mercantilist economic theory of the period, the outflow of coins and precious metals was a negative factor. Accordingly, precious metals were to remain inside their own national economies, on condition that foreign trade was not hindered. Silver and gold coins circulated within the economy of New Spain before they were exported in exchange for local products and for imports such as textiles, mercury, and luxury goods, thereby increasing the volume of regional commerce. If we measure this effect in relation to the proportion of the GDP that passed through the market, we can easily appreciate its importance. Alexander von Humboldt (1769–1859), a German scientist and explorer who traveled in Latin America,[2] estimated that between 90 and 100 million 1800 pesos were bought and sold in the market (in plazas, *tianguis,* and ports of export), while the proportion of total production that did not pass through the market could be valued at some 100 to 110 million pesos.

---

2. Humboldt's writings, such as his *Political Essay on the Kingdom of New Spain* and *Tablas Geográfico-Políticas del Reino de la Nueva España* (1803), reflected his optimistic view of the immense wealth of New Spain.

The free-trade reforms also led to the end of the monopoly exercised by the Tribunal del Consulado. In less than a decade, two new mercantile corporations were formed, one in Veracruz and another in Guadalajara. This increased the competition in both legal and illegal foreign trade among corporations and among and within regions.

Map 4.3 illustrates another structural change. Products now circulated regionally, and other cities developed alongside Mexico City as distribution hubs. The Veracruz–Puebla–Mexico City axis continued to be central, but many other important trading patterns emerged: Oaxaca–Guatemala; Acapulco–Tehuantepec; Morelia–Guadalajara and the port of San Blas; Colima–Morelia; Zacatecas–Charcas–San Luis Potosí, with export by way of the Gulf; and Durango, with export from the port of Mazatlán. In the north-central region, trade circulated through Durango, Parral, and Chihuahua as far as Santa Fe.

Although Mexico City had lost its monopoly position, the production of mining centers like Taxco, Pachuca, and Real del Monte, as well as some others farther away, continued to flow there.

Reforms and Anticolonial Opposition

The informal arrangement among the Spanish Crown, conquistadors, Spanish Americans, and Indian *caciques* was an ingenious feature of the colonial system. In chapter 3 we saw that this unwritten agreement made it possible for the different provinces of the viceroyalty to enjoy significant autonomy during the first two centuries of colonial rule, in effect governed only indirectly by the monarchy.

The absolute monarchy of France and Spain under the Bourbons in the second half of the eighteenth century never fully established itself in the American territories. In the Iberian kingdoms, the process of centralization limited the power of the *cabildos* and turned *alcaldes mayores* into royal functionaries. In the American territories, however, centralization ran up against the obstacles of distance, time, and internal resistance. Attempts to implement such changes lagged and their effectiveness suffered. The process began late in New Spain, in the final third of the eighteenth century, and produced effects unanticipated by the monarchy that benefited the *criollos* and the population of New Spain in general.

The goal of the Bourbon monarchy with regard to New Spain was identical to its goal in the Iberian kingdoms: to centralize under a single Crown what had been a compound monarchy of separate kingdoms. A unitary and absolute monarchy would be better able to control the

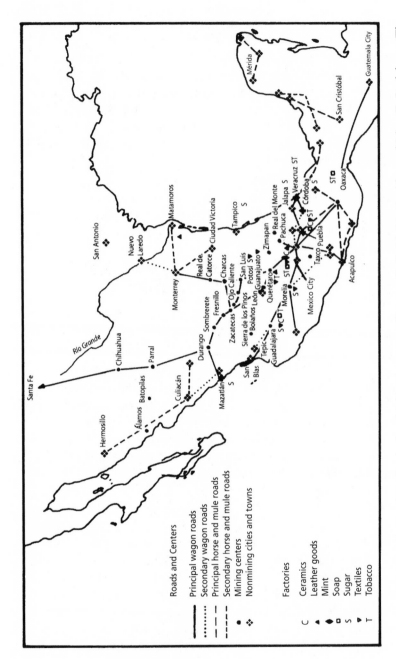

MAP 4.3. Mining and manufacturing in the eighteenth century. (Source: Colin M. MacLachlan and Jaime E. Rodríguez, *The Forging of the Cosmic Race*, op. cit., p. 178.)

divergent interests of the kingdoms, provinces, and colonies, and their administration could be centralized in the hands of royal functionaries. This goal was more evident when new relations were imposed on the Church and the regular orders. Jesuits had become the power within the power of the State through both their teachings and their close relationship with the rich and powerful in New Spain and in all Spanish dominions. The monarchy, however, had the upper hand as it attempted to gain control of the Church and reinforce its authority; the Jesuit order was expelled from its dominions in 1767.

France and other European powers had imposed thoroughgoing changes, and the Spanish Bourbons intended to do the same. The authority of collective bodies such as the Consejo de Indias and the Casa de Contratación were drastically reduced and eventually eliminated, and their responsibilities were reassigned to royal ministers. The positions of prime minister, minister of the Indies, and minister of war were introduced. José de Gálvez, the king's representative in New Spain from 1765 to 1771, was named minister of the Indies.

The ministers were responsible for the faithful and effective execution of all instructions issued by the king's government. We must remember that these were worrisome times for the monarchies. In 1776, thirteen of the eighteen British colonies in North America had declared their independence and by 1789 had constituted themselves as the United States of America. Then a revolution burst forth in France in 1789. The kingdoms of France, Naples, and Spain, in their antagonism to England—and in spite of the 1733 family pact that bound the Bourbon royalty—supported the independence of the thirteen North American colonies because it was in France's interest, if not to ruin the British in North America, to regain Quebec.

The reorganization of the monarchies was intended to improve order and control, and the creation of the new ministries and the new ministerial positions was a central aspect of that task. The minister was appointed by the king and served at his pleasure. He, in turn, appointed the ministerial officials responsible to him. The prerogatives and administrative structures of the ministries were designed to subordinate the interests of the guilds and corporations as much as possible to the general policies of the monarchy. Even the *cabildos,* largely autonomous institutions operating in the interests of the most prominent *vecinos,* were obliged to surrender the exclusivity of their position when the Crown provided for the *síndico del común,* a new magistrate to represent all residents, not only those with *vecino* status.

During the Enlightenment, the ideal was to construct a rational and efficient centralized State. In the name of reason, administrative norms were imposed on the American bureaucracy, providing for an efficient government with explicitly defined and operative rules in order to free all political actors from various constraints. This concept was summed up in an adage: ["A useful vassal is one who defends his own interests by defending those of the king."]

The set of reforms that culminated with the Ordinances of Intendants in 1786 had begun decades earlier. The system of tax and tribute collection was improved in 1750 when the old practice of contracting out the task to individuals acting for their own benefit was eliminated and the responsibility was placed under the direct control of royal officials. In the same decade, the sale of public office was eliminated, and tentative steps were taken to end the monopoly that magistrates and chief councilors had exercised over Indigenous commerce.

The reformers turned to military affairs beginning in 1765. Regular regiments were brought under tighter control and the traditional militias were reorganized. *Castas* were admitted to the militias' ranks for the first time, increasing their social mobility and imposing a degree of social discipline upon them, for now the *castas* could attain a status previously denied them, the prestige of military service and the privileges associated with it.

The 1765–1771 visit of José de Gálvez to New Spain had culminated in the Ordinances of Intendants of 1786. Now Bourbon reforms sought to weaken the *criollo* monopoly over local government and stimulate the participation of new social groups that had arisen along with the growth of production and commerce. Two measures were adopted for this purpose: The position of *síndico del común* was created to represent the general public in the municipalities, and the cities were divided into quarters, the residents of each quarter electing a representative to the municipal government. These measures were intended to favor the less-privileged population sectors, but they were inadequately implemented.

In the 1780s, the power of the viceroy was reduced, measures were taken to protect municipal finances and community property, and a unified military command was established to improve New Spain's defense posture with regard to foreign powers. Free trade was established and the *repartimiento*, the coercive trade mechanism for the sale of Indian products to Spaniards, was abolished. The reforms were strengthened with the increased control of the territory by the Ministry of the Indies through the creation of the administrative divisions called intendancies.

A comparison of map 2.1b (on page 35) with map 4.4 illustrates the significant changes in territorial organization that were made between the end of the 1600s and 1810. While the original political division of New Spain had followed upon the progress of Spanish conquest, the new intendancies were organized in relation to the cities that would become their capitals, their economic activities, and their corresponding importance at the end of the eighteenth century. The 1786 Ordinance of Intendants dictated political-administrative structures and procedures for governing the intendancies and established the position of intendant (the political and financial administrator of each province), who reported directly to the minister of the Indies. Secondary districts were governed in turn by subdelegates, who reported to an intendant. For the first time, a coherent hierarchical structure was created across the region, and officials responsible to the ministry were expected to operate on the basis of uniform administrative principles.

The reforms broke with traditional political practices. The intendants took on powers formerly exercised by the viceroy, which affected local and provincial interests and benefited newer social actors. For example, locally influential individuals became subdelegates. Provincial circles were favored in the creation of the new Tribunal del Consulado in Veracruz and new delegations elsewhere. Newly formed trade networks linked agricultural and mining areas with provincial capitals. The reorganization of the militias gave a social boost to their members, particularly those of modest birth, and provided the *castas* with a means of social mobility, since they could become vassals of the king by serving in his militia.

Seeing their political and commercial positions in the *cabildos* and in the royal administration compromised, prominent *criollos* reacted against the Crown's recently enacted policies. Their resistance only increased when they detected anti-Americanism in another royal policy that prohibited a native of America from holding official office in the province of his birth—a measure intended as a blow against nepotism and traditional patron-client relations. This combination of circumstances gave rise to anti-Spanish sentiment and to Spanish American resentment of the royal administration for its perceived errors and failures.

The *criollos'* rejection of the reforms was in keeping with their growing sense of cultural identity and willingness to defend their homeland, a land both American and Spanish. To a growing extent, members of the *criollo* sector represented the sentiment of the nation as a whole in their attachment to the land. Ultimately, they demanded the same rights of

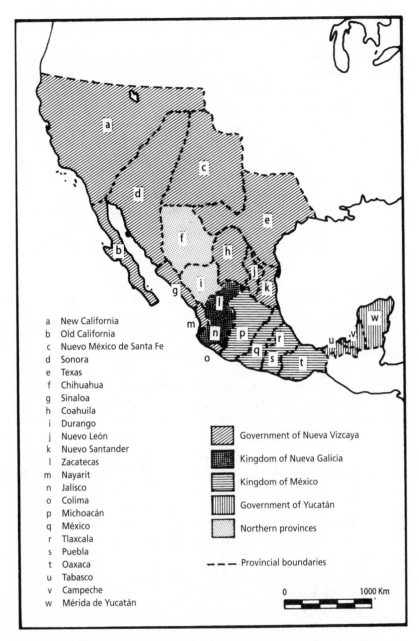

a	New California
b	Old California
c	Nuevo México de Santa Fe
d	Sonora
e	Texas
f	Chihuahua
g	Sinaloa
h	Coahuila
i	Durango
j	Nuevo León
k	Nuevo Santander
l	Zacatecas
m	Nayarit
n	Jalisco
o	Colima
p	Michoacán
q	México
r	Tlaxcala
s	Puebla
t	Oaxaca
u	Tabasco
v	Campeche
w	Mérida de Yucatán

Government of Nueva Vizcaya

Kingdom of Nueva Galicia

Kingdom of México

Government of Yucatán

Northern provinces

--- Provincial boundaries

0   1000 Km

MAP 4.4. Political divisions of New Spain, 1810. (Source: Edmundo O'Gorman, *Historia de las Divisiones Políticas Territoriales de México* [Mexico City: Porrúa, 1985], pp. 14–15.)

self-government under the monarchy as those granted to the different estates in Spain.

The oldest *criollo* families rejected the reforms even more resolutely than the others. As the original settlers of American lands, they said, they had earned the right to rule them. In 1792, fray Servando Teresa de Mier preached in a sermon that America had been evangelized before the arrival of the Spanish. He was rewarded with exile. Around 1780, the students of Father Miguel Hidalgo in the San Nicolás seminary of Valladolid, the city now called Morelia, began to proclaim the revolutionary Jansenist ideas that Hidalgo had picked up under the influence of Bishop Joseph Pérez Calama. Ecclesiastic reforms at the university also provided fertile ground for new ideas of autonomy and self-government. On his trip through New Spain, Alexander von Humboldt reported, concerning not only *criollos* but also the sector of European-born Spaniards, that their hearts belonged to America. Together, these two groups declared ever more emphatically their rights as the legitimate representatives of the land of New Spain.

CHAPTER 5

Independent Mexico

The independence period of Mexico has usually been portrayed as a disorderly time, a series of disasters, a breakdown of local and central government. This negative viewpoint is ideologically motivated. Porfirian liberals attributed anarchy to the colonial past in order to claim credit for bringing order and progress to the country. The post-revolutionaries of 1910–1920 did the same, blaming all of the country's problems on the Porfiriato in order to emphasize their own positive role and that of the revolution.

If we view history as a process, though, we must understand both continuity and change, both the successful and the not-so-successful steps in the construction of a sovereign nation and a new State. I want to describe Mexico in its independence period by exploring its social evolution; its economic behavior; its political institutions, such as Congress, the executive wing, and municipal governments; all the social and political actors; and its citizens and elected officials.

In previous chapters I have tried to explain how the groundwork was laid for the independence movement. Over the course of three hundred years as a colony, strong cultural, political, and social traditions had been established. With the rupture of the colonial pact, the strongest components of these traditions were revitalized, and they developed even more rapidly throughout the nineteenth century. In some sense, republican civic values grew out of the Hispanic ideals of good government as fostered by the Spanish and wider European Enlightenment and by the Bourbon reforms. Indeed, the independence movement was nourished by all of these sources.

The independence movement has usually been portrayed as a reaction to the Napoleonic invasion of Spain and the unseating of Charles IV in favor of Napoleon's unpopular brother, José Bonaparte, known derisively as Pepe Botella, "Pepe the Bottle," for his drinking. The dramatic events in Spain did indeed affect New Spain and all the other Spanish colonies in America. In fact, the circumstances propelled the citizenry onto the stage as a new actor in the historical process, where they proceeded to throw off the shackles of vassalage and construct a new order.

Antecedents to Independence

The historical process speeds up in times of crisis, and the Napoleonic invasion of Spain was a catalyst for accelerated change. The necessary conditions for change, however, develop more slowly and less visibly. Taken together, these smaller steps provide the necessary context for dramatic events to follow. The Seven Years' War of 1756–1763 had led to a new European equilibrium and to a complete organization of the domains governed by Spain, France, and Britain in the Americas. Britain had acquired naval supremacy, and the focus of world imperialism shifted from maritime commerce toward continental colonial rule. This led to a change from indirect rule to direct central administration.

These changes are known with respect to the Spanish domains as the Bourbon reforms. Royal authorities from Spain were put in charge of the different territories, new taxes were levied, and statistics and geographical charts were drawn up in order to register and effectively manage people and resources. Repeated tax increases and constant demands from Spain for more remittances caused disruption and discontent in New Spain. The creation of the administrative intendancies focused on effective central government and jeopardized local rule, which had the effect of accentuating regionalism. American-born Spaniards resented being replaced by continentals. The new notions of constitutionalism and the "rights of man" revolutionized political thought as early as 1776, when the thirteen colonies of North America declared their independence, and again in 1783, when the new United States established the first modern constitution, leading to an elected president in 1789. These major events on American soil were immediately followed by the French Revolution of 1789–1793. The French Revolution was far more radical than the American one, deposing and executing a king. In New Spain, informed public opinion emerged as a political factor, while the ideas of the Enlightenment were debated at the university and in cafés and discussion circles. Diverse forms of printed matter appeared with regularity, while scientific expeditions and expositions revealed the American continent's potential wealth. Nevertheless, before the Napoleonic invasion there were few Mexicans who wanted to separate from Spain, and it was unheard of to consider a republican form of government. At the most, Spanish Americans wanted equal representation within the Spanish empire.

A heightened sense of equality was understandable. Mestizos and mulattos had acquired new status and a new sense of identity as a result of the political-administrative reforms of the second half of the eighteenth century, largely through participation in the militia and being able to acquire land, earn a regular income, and attain full *vecino* status. Yet the *criollos* felt discriminated against in provincial capitals and in the viceroyalty as a whole. Their increasing desire for self-government was an outgrowth of this resentment.

It has commonly been asserted that the examples of the United States' independence and the French Revolution led directly to the birth of an independent Mexico, but few would concur with this today. We now know that those revolutions provoked a conservative reaction that led to the resignation of two prime ministers of Spain who were illustrious reformers, the Count of Floridablanca and the Count of Aranda. Their successor between 1793 and 1808 was Manuel Godoy, who put the brakes on reform, allied himself with the European powers in opposition to the French Revolution, and ensured that every royal official sent to Mexico would unequivocally resist any change whatsoever.

The decade leading up to the Napoleonic invasion of Spain was a time of active repression and resistance to reform. Spain signed on to the international anti-French alliance not only in response to the revolution but also to avenge the beheading of the French king, a relative of the Spanish ruling family. The cost of a conflict that lasted nearly twenty years, from the 1790s to 1810, was enormous. The bleeding of Spain's American colonies in order to finance the European wars was painful, and the richest of the colonies, Mexico, was hardest hit. Tax collection increased from 47.7 million pesos annually between 1790 and 1799 to 67.5 million pesos annually between 1800 and 1809. Thus an inhabitant of Mexico who paid twelve pesos in taxes in 1790 paid seventeen pesos in 1808. Additional remittances from Mexico to the metropolis and to other colonies increased in the same period from 6.6 million pesos to 21.6 million pesos annually.

The two social sectors hardest hit by taxes were the Indians and the Church. To begin with, the Church was targeted for forced donations. Then in 1804, the Crown confiscated the Indians' *cajas de comunidad,* their communal treasuries, which totaled about one million pesos, and the Church's institutional treasury, the Cajas de la Iglesia, containing more than ten million pesos. The Indian communities were angered, but so were *hacendados,* merchants, and mine operators, all of whom were accustomed to financing their operations with Church loans.

These were the factors responsible for the anger of wealthy *criollos,* Indian communities, and *castas* alike at the end of the eighteenth and beginning of the nineteenth century. Periodicals such as the *Gaceta de México,* founded in 1722, had begun to give voice to widespread discontent by the turn of the century. After Napoleon invaded Spain in 1804, the publication of the *Gaceta* jumped from one hundred to six hundred copies in just the four years between 1804 and 1808. In all, there were six biweekly publications circulating in Mexico City and Veracruz. One might question the significance of the periodical press in a predominantly illiterate country, but reading was a collective, not an individual, activity throughout the eighteenth and almost the entire nineteenth centuries. News circulated among extended families, discussion circles, workplaces, clubs, and social networks.

Stirrings of public opinion began to spread orally from town to town and city to city. The message was the repudiation of the Bourbon reforms, the new taxes, and various colonial policies, and a call for fundamental change in the monarchy. Slowly the idea of independence began to spread as well. In 1808, political messages began to be circulated on handbills and cards with succinct phrases like "Freedom, cowardly *criollos,*" and "Long live our religion and independence."

The idea of a common homeland took root in this context. Early patriotism spoke of identification with the land where a people had been born and raised and had grown to adulthood—the inhabitants of Mexican villages, towns, and cities. While the Napoleonic invasion was still not seen from a national perspective, the conditions were created in the 1808–1821 period for an entirely revolutionary concept to develop: the idea of the nation. And with it, a far-reaching political project was born.

The interests of the *criollos,* mestizos, *castas,* and Indians converged in a process that incorporated all of these different actors, making the 1808–1821 movement an inclusive, cross-class, multiethnic national awakening. Only in this light can we explain the rapid spread of the movement, the formation of an army by the priest Miguel Hidalgo, the proliferation of secret societies and armed groups, and the formation of a second revolutionary army by another priest, José María Morelos. At the same time, Mexican deputies participated prominently at the Cortes de Cádiz in 1812, the first joint Spanish and Spanish-American parliament. Their presence and outspokenness contributed to the growing atmosphere in favor of political and cultural change in both Europe and the Americas, and the right of the American countries to self-government. If the fact that the independence movement was shaped by people of diverse ethnicities and social conditions is not given the attention it deserves, we will not appreciate the nature of Mexico's independence itself, nor the process that led to the idea of a Mexican nation that encompasses the social, ethnic, and cultural diversity of Mexico.

Autonomy and Independence

Dissatisfaction had accumulated among the majority in every social sector in New Spain, but actual movement toward Mexican independence began when Charles IV abdicated the throne in favor of his son Ferdinand VII, who stepped down and delivered the Spanish kingdoms to the invading French forces. At this point New Spain was faced with the question of who really represented Spanish authority.

News spread in New Spain of a popular uprising in Madrid, of the formation of local juntas, and of the royal abdication. "The people," understood to be the source of the government's authority, rejected the dynastic change, invoking the juridical principle that in the absence of the king, sovereignty reverts to the people. In opposition to such a stand were the absolutists, who believed that the king's power was absolute and that under no circumstance could sovereignty revert to the people. The first institutional break came when the *criollo*-dominated *cabildo* of Mexico City, the city council, declared its autonomy. Traditionally, the Mexico City council had represented the interests of the realm, that is, of the *cabildos*, or city councils, of all the main cities in the viceroyalty. On July 19, 1808, the council in Mexico City declared that the sitting viceroy should retain his position for the time being. The other *cabildos* in the viceroyalty ratified this decision and resolved to convene a congress in Spain with representation from all the major cities of New Spain. The congress would function as a provisional body until Ferdinand VII, the legitimate monarch, was restored to the throne.

These decisions were accepted by the viceroy, José de Iturrigaray, but they met with immediate disapproval at the highest levels of the bureaucracy, the so-called absolutists, or traditional monarchists, who held positions in the Audiencia and the Royal Treasury and jointly sat in the Real Acuerdo, another judicial body established by the monarchy. In order to counteract these forces, the viceroy convened a general junta with representatives from all the corporations in the capital, including the merchant, mining, and military guilds, the Church, the Indian *cabildos,* the titled nobility, and the university. The advocates for autonomy proposed that a local junta and the viceroy's council should govern until the restoration of the legitimate king. This was the majority position in Spain, where local committees were governing in the name of Ferdinand VII. But in Mexico the traditional monarchists opposed any autonomous self-government and so regarded the proposal as subversive; they organized a coup d'etat on September 16, 1808, arresting the viceroy and the autonomist leadership. A new viceroy arrived with the mandate to restrain any movement toward autonomy.

The coup exacerbated the divisions between the colonials who were demanding self-government and those who supported monarchical absolutism. The absolutists held onto power until 1810, while autonomist groups, who favored a constitutional monarchy with equal representation for Peninsulars and for those born in New Spain, seethed. The persecution of autonomists by the government of Spanish-born *gachupines,* headed by the intendant of Guanajuato, Juan Antonio Riaño, led the autonomists to organize antigovernment conspiracies in Guanajuato, Querétaro, San Miguel el Grande, and Guadalajara. Together with Indians and *castas,* they planned an armed uprising in order to seize power in the name of the legitimate government that had been approved by the *cabildos* in 1808. The *corregidor,* or chief magistrate, of Querétaro and his wife, María Josefa Ortiz de Domínguez, popularly known as la Corregidora, planned the uprising for 1810 along with Ignacio Allende, Mariano Abasolo, and Miguel Hidalgo, the Dolores town priest. They proposed to reestablish the provisional government in preparation for the reversion of sovereignty to Spain. All political groups would be represented in a council of cities governing in the name of Ferdinand VII.

Tensions ran high between autonomists and absolutists. Although beginning in 1808, the absolutists controlled important government positions, they gradually lost political strength. Between July 1808 and September 1810, various developments strengthened the autonomists' position. In 1809, when Mexican representatives were elected to the Central Governing Junta in Spain, the absolutists were unable to prevail over the representatives of the *cabildos,* who were mainly autonomists and *criollos.* In Mexico, the absolutist minority monopolized the principal political positions in the Audiencia but were outnumbered by autonomists on *cabildos* and in intermediate positions of the bureaucracy.

While the problems of political representation and corresponding political rights were being debated in the capitals of the American provinces and in the Spanish Cortes Generales, or parliament, agitation for self-government was gathering strength. What had begun as a movement for provisional structures to govern in the name of the king was transformed by the prevailing social dynamics into something very different. On September 15, 1810, Father Miguel Hidalgo pronounced the Grito de Dolores, the cry of independence, at Dolores, Guanajuato. He called upon those gathered in his parish that Sunday to defend the country from the Spanish, who, he said, wanted to deliver it to the French. He called upon his parishioners to establish a new government and to abolish personal tribute to the Crown, which had been a punishing burden upon Indians and *castas*. Hidalgo's movement gained immediate popularity because Indians, *castas, criollos,* and even some Spaniards were convinced of the benefits that would result from an independent government.

The insurgents took control of San Miguel el Grande, where they adopted the banner of the Virgin of Guadalupe as their symbol. Their ranks quickly swelled to twenty-five thousand men. Hidalgo was designated Captain General of America, Ignacio Allende was appointed his lieutenant, and numerous *criollos* took up leadership positions in the improvised army. The capital was flooded with both insurgent and Spanish propaganda. On October 28, barely six weeks after the movement began, a force of eighty thousand troops controlled Ixtlahuaca, thirty miles from Mexico City. Although a confrontation between the viceregal and rebel troops was inconclusive, the advance of Hidalgo's troops on Mexico City was halted and the royalist army was able to reorganize its forces under the command of Félix Calleja.

The tactical retreat of the insurgents cost them momentum in their move on the capital and deprived them of the surprise factor, allowing the Spanish army to prepare a plan of defense. Hidalgo was losing the support of the *criollos,* who feared anarchy and the pillaging of their properties. The two armies met again in January 1811 at the Calderón Bridge outside Guadalajara. After less than three months of conflict, the independence forces had been defeated by the royalists. Hidalgo was taken prisoner in the northern state of Coahuila and put before a firing squad on July 30, 1811, in Chihuahua's state capital.

The *criollos* had not actually gone over to the Spanish side, but they preferred a popularly supported reformist movement to an armed insurrection. Between 1810 and 1812, members of the *criollo* elite participated in conspiratorial activities. Just when the repression against the insurgents was most intense, the moderate reformers among them regrouped and

MAP 5.1. Hidalgo's route. (Source: Enrique Florescano, coordinator, *Atlas Histórico de México, Cultura,* September/Siglo XXI [Mexico City: Editores, 1983], p. 95.)

emerged as a liberal faction to oppose the absolutists. The liberal group took advantage of a political opening in Spain when ascendant reformist forces called for elected representatives of the overseas kingdoms and provinces of the empire to attend a general congress, or *cortes,* scheduled to convene in Cádiz, Spain, on September 24, 1810.

The Cortes de Cádiz

First Viceroy Francisco Xavier Venegas and later Félix Calleja, royal military commander and viceroy, undertook to reestablish a viceregal government, but they encountered two obstacles. The first, an essentially Mexican problem, was the insurgency to the south of Mexico City headed by José María Morelos, a priest and former student of Miguel Hidalgo, and by Vicente Guerrero, the son of a prominent landowner. The other, wider obstacle was the 1812 Constitution promulgated by the Cortes de Cádiz. Its application in New Spain seriously undercut the foundation of the existing colonial order.

In fact, the insurgents at home and the delegates from New Spain at

Cádiz complemented rather than hindered each other. They agreed on a series of essential points: It was absolutely necessary for an independent country to be founded on the basis of a written constitution. That constitution should be the fruit of a congress composed of elected deputies. And it should establish the rights and obligations of citizens, the form of government, the distribution of powers, and a manner of electing representatives.

Fifteen of the twenty elected representatives from New Spain arrived in Cádiz, where the Cortes met from 1810 to 1813. They had been chosen by the capital city of each province, from the northern frontier to Yucatán in the far south. Among the most vocal spokesmen for liberal and reformist ideals were José Miguel Ramos Arizpe from Coahuila; José Miguel Guridi y Alcocer, a priest representing Tlaxcala; and José María Couto from Veracruz, a priest and the former rector of the Colegio de San Ildefonso. The American deputies took every opportunity to denounce the despotic, exclusive, and anti-American attitude of viceregal authorities from the floor of the Cortes. They proposed radical reforms to transform the imperial system into a constitutional monarchy, a community of nations or independent kingdoms organized federally under a single Crown and as parties to a written constitution.

The Constitution of Cádiz was applied in America from 1812 to 1814, stimulating a political reorganization in New Spain that indirectly contributed to the independence process. In New Spain, as of 1813, representative government, proposed by Ramos Arizpe in Cádiz and approved by Spanish and American liberals in the Cortes, was established for the first time at the provincial and municipal levels. At the provincial level, a newly created institution, the provincial deputation, combined elected members with royal appointees: a prefect and an intendant acting in the name of the central government jointly governed the territory, and provincial deputies, locally elected from among members of the leading families, took charge of the governments.

The 1812 Constitution of Cádiz also provided for the establishment of elected councils called *ayuntamientos* in towns of at least one thousand inhabitants, as long as they had sufficient resources to sustain self-government. In the midst of a popular upsurge, most townspeople willingly accepted this orderly option as much more attractive than war. With this new disposition available, calls for rebellion were subordinated to what was a profound political and social restructuring process. This was Viceroy Calleja's intention when he promoted the recognition of *ayuntamientos*—to turn people's attention to local matters and contain the insurgency. In fact, the people requested that fugitive insurgents be allowed to return and participate in the organization of local governments. The effort required to bring together and register one thousand residents must have been a powerful force for pacification. Individuals who had until that time held only transient residential rights were given the opportunity to acquire full *vecino* status, including the rights to full citizenship, to vote, to hold public office, and to use the land, water, and forest resources pertaining to a particular local jurisdiction. In return, they were obliged to pay certain fees and taxes, and to perform community service.

The right to an *ayuntamiento*—to elect authorities with jurisdiction over a municipality comprising a region and its settlements—meant the recognition of local authority and the right to community control of resources. The new municipality was also able to establish the status of *vecino* for all residents, integrating outlying populations in either longstanding or newly established towns. It is difficult to determine the number of *ayuntamientos* on the basis of population figures, as the requirements changed over time.[1] Given that the Indian population accounted for 60.1 percent of the total, it is important that most of the Indian republics readily adopted the elective municipal town council. In 1810, the Indian population was about 3,700,000, living in 4,682 towns. Each secondary town, or *barrio,* was subordinate to the seat of an Indian republic and its *cabildo.* Given the fact that Indian republics were abolished in 1812 and around a thousand constitutional *ayuntamientos* were organized between 1812 and 1814, it appears that of an estimated 962 constitutional *ayuntamientos* in 1821, the majority were formerly primary towns and seats of Indian republics. This means that there were probably at least five or six minor villages under the jurisdiction of each *ayuntamiento,* each with its own auxiliary town council. Many *ayuntamientos* developed in regions where non-Indians were dominant, but as time passed the ethnic criterion was superceded by the population factor.

The *ayuntamiento* evolved into an inclusive and complex municipal system, organizing the population and a huge number of secondary settlements. This expansion is impressive in itself, given that there had previously been no more than thirty Spanish *cabildos,* or city councils, in New Spain. Of course there had also been Indian *cabildos,* which by the end of the colonial period may have numbered in the hundreds. So, as the former Indian republics reorganized themselves under the new system, we see a much greater number of *ayuntamientos* in areas with large Indige-

1. Estimates of the number of *ayuntamientos* for the years 1812–1814 are not available. While in 1812 the population requirement for an *ayuntamiento* was one thousand, this number varied, increasing to four thousand by 1821. In that year, there were 962 *ayuntamientos.*

nous populations, such as in the intendancies of México, Puebla, Oaxaca, and Yucatán. These four intendancies alone accounted for 783 of the 962 *ayuntamientos* existing in 1821.

The establishment of *ayuntamientos* was well received by communities of all ethnicities, since it responded to one of their most heartfelt demands: for a local government coherent and strong enough to conduct effective and autonomous administration. In many regions, the longest-lasting effect of the reorganization into *ayuntamientos* was the breakdown of old ethnic barriers, to a great extent eliminating the existing divisions between Indian and Spanish *cabildos* and giving rise to the melting pot of Mexico as we know it. The fundamental change was the birth of the interethnic *ayuntamiento,* particularly in the regions where social, economic, and demographic evolution in the last stages of the colonial era had promoted social integration.

The establishment of provincial deputations also produced a political and administrative reorganization of the territory as the old intendancies governed by royal officials came to be governed as of 1812 by elected councils. Provincial deputies, elected from among the prominent residents of the province, were influential in local politics and occupied important public posts throughout the first half of the nineteenth century. Among the responsibilities of these councilors was to legislate for the province and to ensure the constitutionality of newly forming *ayuntamientos.*

The provincial deputation and the municipality with its town council turned out to be revolutionary institutions of enormous historical importance. Nettie Lee Benson, a renowned historian, called our attention to the fact that the provincial deputations' jurisdiction turned out to be the basis for the Mexican states of 1824. As can be seen in map 5.2, the provincial deputations corresponded to the regional diversity within Mexico, a set of divisions that continued beyond the establishment of the federal Mexican United States in 1824. To this day, the *municipio* is the basic institution of the federalist structure and the political arena of democratic change. The constitutional amendment of the 1980s that accorded greater autonomy to municipalities is a sign of their continuing political vitality.

These two institutions, the constitutional *ayuntamiento* and the provincial deputation, were critical in the move toward independence. Both of them grew out of a constitutional framework that gradually supplanted the conditions of royal vassalage and hereditary rule with the concepts of citizenship and electoral choice. The substitution of elected officials for royal representatives was revolutionary. Elected bodies played an

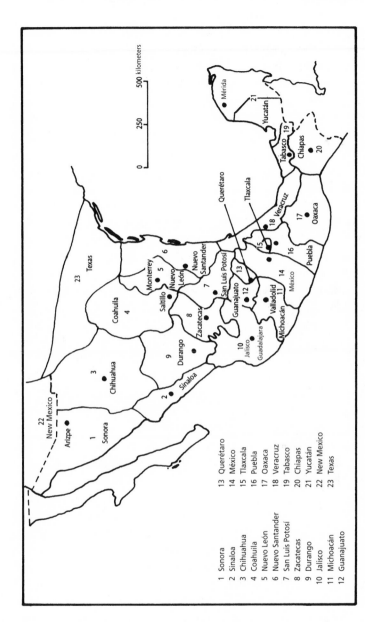

MAP 5.2. Provincial deputations of Mexico, December 1823. (Source: Nettie Lee Benson, *The Provincial Deputation in Mexico* [Austin: University of Texas Press, 1992], p. 51.)

1 Sonora
2 Sinaloa
3 Chihuahua
4 Coahuila
5 Nuevo León
6 Nuevo Santander
7 San Luis Potosí
8 Zacatecas
9 Durango
10 Jalisco
11 Michoacán
12 Guanajuato
13 Querétaro
14 México
15 Tlaxcala
16 Puebla
17 Oaxaca
18 Veracruz
19 Tabasco
20 Chiapas
21 Yucatán
22 New Mexico
23 Texas

important role in superseding the power of the intendants and the absolute power of the viceroy. Men elected to *ayuntamientos* replaced subdelegates, and others elected to provincial councils replaced intendants. The two new institutions provided links between local government and provincial problems, and provided channels for the peaceful transition from one political system to another.

Morelos and the Birth of Mexican Constitutionalism

When a local government was elected in Mexico City in 1813, it was called a constitutional *ayuntamiento* to distinguish it from the old *cabildo*. This was a victory for the reformist *criollos*, many of whom sympathized with the insurgency. Viceroy Calleja, a die-hard absolutist, understood the links between those advocating autonomy and those favoring independence and decided to implement the liberal Constitution of 1812 as slowly as possible.

Upon the death of Hidalgo, José María Morelos took up the leadership of the insurgency. He understood the need to reorganize the movement and strengthen its ties with the reformists. In keeping with his mestizo-*criollo* origins, Morelos was educated in Michoacán at the Colegio de San Nicolás and had served as parish priest at Carécuaro. He was politically astute, skillful at forming political alliances and choosing competent military leaders such as Guadalupe Victoria, Vicente Guerrero, and Mariano Matamoros. He sought to establish ties with reformist elements in Mexico City among midlevel politicians, local political bosses, and regional notables. The insurgents isolated Mexico City, then occupied the rich mining center of Taxco and other key points on the road to Acapulco. They occupied Oaxaca, established positions between the capital and Puebla, and hampered access to Veracruz by laying siege to Cuautla. Finally, they besieged the port of Acapulco for several months.

The military successes of the insurgency were counterbalanced by the institutional alternatives provided by the Constitution of 1812. Part of the reform movement dedicated itself to the election of representatives to the Cortes and the autonomous governments of each provincial deputation and its *ayuntamientos*. But Morelos and other independence leaders recognized the weakness of the Cortes at Cádiz as an instrument of progress, since many Spanish deputies did not wish to accord the Americans equal legal status.

The independence forces sought to Americanize the constitutionalism

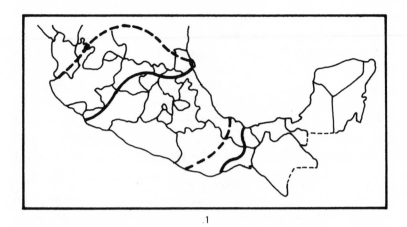

.1

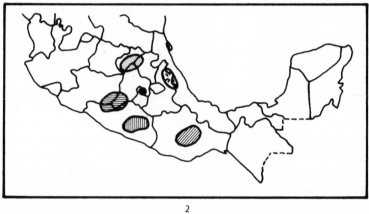

2

1 Territory controlled by Morelos	2 Centers of guerrilla resistance,
— — — 1811	1815–1817
▬▬▬ 1812	

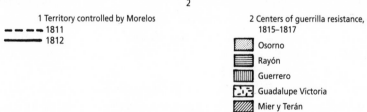

Osorno

Rayón

Guerrero

Guadalupe Victoria

Mier y Terán

MAP 5.3. The regions of the independence struggle. (Source: Enrique Florescano, *Atlas Histórico de México*, op. cit., p. 99.)

undertaken at Cádiz. In June 1813, Morelos called upon "the sovereign power of the people" in the provinces to elect their representatives to a "Supreme National American Congress." With Ignacio López Rayón, Morelos prepared a new constitution for "America, free and independent of Spain or any other Nation." Morelos proceeded to convene a Constituent Congress in Chilpancingo, Guerrero, in September 1813. Eight deputies attended, some designated by Morelos and others elected in their provinces. The Congress opened with the reading of an address by Morelos called "Sentiments of the Nation," which began by declaring:

> That America is free and independent of Spain and of any other Nation, Government, or Monarchy, and its sovereignty proceeds directly from the people, who willingly deposit this trust in its representatives elected by the provinces in equal numbers. That the legislative, executive, and judicial branches shall be divided into compatible bodies for the execution of their powers. . . . Because good laws are above every man, the laws that our Congress dictate should be such that oblige fidelity and patriotism, that moderate opulence and misery, and laws of such nature that increase the wages of the poor, that improve their standard of living, banishing ignorance, violence and theft.[2]

Morelos exhorted the Congress to enact legislation guaranteeing the equality of all before the law, equitable taxation, and respect for property. He assumed responsibility as chief executive under the title Servant of the Nation and Generalissimo of North American Armies. Despite conflicts between the Congress and Morelos, Mexico's independence was officially declared by the Morelos faction on November 6, 1813. The insurgent Congress confirmed this on October 22, 1814, at Apatzingán, when it approved the Constitutional Decree for the Freedom of Mexican America. The concept of a Spanish nation composed of all Spaniards in both hemispheres had provoked a heated controversy in Cádiz, and the citizenship of most Mexicans had been contested. The Apatzingán Constitution recognized all people born in America as citizens regardless of ethnicity. It stated that sovereignty resided in the people, in the citizenry, and that it was to be exercised through the election of national representatives. This sovereignty was inviolable, inalienable, and indivisible. Thus no nation had the right to impede the unfettered exercise of autonomy by any other. This was a momentous step forward.

---

2. José María Morelos, "Sentimientos de la Nación, o 23 puntos dados por Morelos para la Constitución," in Felipe Tena Ramírez, *Leyes Fundamentales de México 1808–1994* (Mexico City: Editorial Porrúa, 1994), pp. 29–30.

Due to the military situation and the capture and execution of Morelos, the Constitution of Apatzingán was never put into practice. Nevertheless, in the course of just two years, the demand of a major national movement had been transformed from autonomy under the Spanish monarchy to complete independence. In the process, it had appropriated those aspects of the 1812 Constitution of Cádiz that were pertinent to both continents: the Catholic religion, the national representation of provinces assembled in a general congress (the Cortes), the division of powers, equality before the law, individual rights, and respect for property. The new Spanish constitutionalism spread rapidly in Mexico and was quickly Americanized.

The transformation of the population from vassalage to citizenry with equal rights before the law was the most dramatic and substantial feature of the nineteenth and twentieth centuries not only in Mexico but in all western societies following the French Revolution. This transformation had scarcely begun in Mexico, however, before it was suspended by the restoration of Bourbon absolutism. Ferdinand VII returned to the throne in 1814, but rather than governing as a constitutional monarch, he abolished the Constitution of 1812 and imprisoned leading liberals. In Mexico, Viceroy Calleja immediately militarized the country, repressed the insurgents, and employed the iron fist in response to any advocacy of independence.

In what is called the period of pacification, from 1814 to 1816, all constitutional rights arising from the 1812 Constitution were suppressed, as were its institutional expressions: the Cortes, the provincial deputations, and the constitutional *ayuntamientos*. At the same time, new and punitive taxes were imposed, alienating even conservative *criollos* and some Spanish monarchists. Discontent grew among the common people. The arbitrary manner in which the old order was restored found few sympathizers, and the replacement of Calleja by a new viceroy, Apodaca, did little to stem popular anger. The scant legitimacy of absolutist rule and the weakened colonial administration allowed for the de facto preservation of some local constitutionalist reforms through informal political practices and understandings among the local gentry.

Independence

In 1820, courageous liberals in Spain organized an insurrection, openly defying both the king and the 1815 Congress of Vienna, where the combined European monarchies had signed a mutual assistance pact to turn back the liberal tide. However, the king was forced to reinstate the Constitution of Cádiz in 1820 over all the dominions of the monarchy.

Once that constitutional order was reinstated in Mexico, both provincial deputies and constitutional *ayuntamientos* assumed the functions of home rule. Liberal leaders emerged from secrecy and resumed their duties. Unlike previous viceroys, Apodaca was willing to exercise constitutionally defined powers. He probably underestimated the extent to which both the elite and the nascent Mexican citizenry were imbued with the ideals of constitutionalism and the extent to which the return to constitutional order would revive the zeal for full independence.

As civilian political factions emerged, the absolutist groups that had supported former Viceroy Calleja began to feel threatened. The most radical among them were the military officers, whose power had grown in the course of the wars between 1810 and 1820. Thanks to the special privileges and immunities accorded them in the late colonial period, they had come to represent a discrete political force. Their influence had grown with the substantial autonomy granted them by the Constitution of 1812, which had eliminated intermediate levels of civilian control and left the king as the only superior authority to which they were obliged to respond. As a gulf opened between civilian and military authority, the officer corps developed strong regional bases. In 1820, the armed forces in Mexico included some forty thousand troops in the regular army and as many in the militias, operating under nine commands completely independent of civilian control.

The Church was resentful that the king did not recognize its loyalty and had not compensated it for its assistance during the insurgency. It also felt threatened by hostile liberal reforms, accusing the proponents of those reforms of being atheists or Masons. The Spaniards, now known as "Europeans," were virtually alone in supporting the viceroy and the Bourbon monarchs, and they were uneasy with the level of hostility directed at them. The military command, the Church hierarchy, and the Europeans felt the political backlash from the restoration of constitutional institutions. The Cortes approved an additional set of reforms in October 1820 that Europeans interpreted as a direct attack on their interests. The reforms abolished primogeniture and related practices, secularized the property of religious communities, and stripped military officers of special privileges and immunities, thus undermining the three pillars of support for absolutism.

The new situation also worried Mexican *criollos* and liberals, who recognized the precariousness of self-government under the monarchy.

They remembered 1814, when the constitution was abolished, and they felt that the constitutional monarchy was a facade for absolutism. In fact, Fernando VII unsuccessfully tried to reestablish absolutism in 1823 with military support from the French king Louis XVIII.

After ten years of profound political change that involved large sectors of Mexican society, the foundations of the old colonial order were weak. The unquestioned fealty of royal subjects was a thing of the past, as was the notion that the king's authority was of divine origin. The spirit of the day was embodied in the desire to exercise citizenship by electing governing authorities and establishing constitutional institutions. Each of these ideological and cultural changes hastened the advent of Mexican independence.

Some histories of Mexico have asserted that independence was adopted as a lesser evil for the protection of society from economically powerful individuals and corporations opposed to liberal reforms. But this view ignores the possibility that republican and liberal values had become widespread, especially among lower and middle socioeconomic sectors, and it minimizes the degree of genuine opposition to the Spanish monarchy.

No, the independence of Mexico was not a conservative or counter-revolutionary option. It was necessary in order to preserve national unity and to incorporate the plurality of interests that found expression before 1810 and burst forth in the following decade. The level of unity necessary for the creation of a new political system was reached in 1820 and 1821. The Plan de Iguala was proclaimed on February 24 of the latter year. It was designed by Agustín de Iturbide, a prominent landowner from Michoacán, and was widely accepted because it provided for a peaceful transition guaranteed by Congress and a written constitution. Iturbide was able to muster a broad coalition of insurgents, constitutionalists, republicans, and monarchists around a single objective, the peaceful and orderly separation of Mexico from Spain.

The Plan de Iguala established the principles of Mexico's independence: a constitutional monarchy with a special role for the Roman Catholic Church. The throne was offered to Ferdinand VII or, in his place, to one of his princes. If no member of the royal family arrived to accept the offer, a sovereign provincial council would govern and would name a regent, leading to the convening of a Constitutional Congress. The Trigarante Army, or Army of Three Guarantees, would defend the independence of the country, its domestic peace and unity, and the Catholic religion.

The Plan de Iguala was widely supported. In their respective capacities as general commander of the Trigarante Army and newly arrived viceroy, Agustín de Iturbide and Juan O'Donojú signed a treaty in Córdoba, Veracruz, declaring the independence of the Sovereign Mexican Empire on August 24, 1821. Iturbide and the Trigarante Army triumphantly entered Mexico City on September 27. The proclamation of independence was by no means the end of the political agitation. But everyone, even those closest to Iturbide, understood that a new era had begun when the Constitutional Congress was installed in February 1822 and, in its first session, declared itself the embodiment of national sovereignty. Mexico had established its own national variant of the monarchy.

CHAPTER 6

The First Republic

It is a mistake to characterize the period from 1821 to 1850 as primarily a time of anarchy, social disorder, and economic crisis. It is often recalled that there were fifty changes of government, with Santa Anna presiding over eleven of them, and that the military dominated the political scene, overthrowing presidents and governors. Political anarchy, is it is said, gave rise to social chaos, criminal gangsterism, and banditry in central Mexico, along with Indian uprisings elsewhere, particularly in the Mayan area. There were repeated Apache raids in the north. We have been taught that the economy declined and collapsed, that the standard of living deteriorated for most people. As result of this turbulence, Mexico was independent but poor and battered, sorely lacking in social cohesiveness and peace.

Thanks to new research, Mexico's early independence can no longer be portrayed solely as a time of strife and disorder, as though nothing constructive had also occurred. In fact the disorder was more apparent than real. Circumstances imposed the kind of new and unforeseen challenges that all national groups, in North America, South America, Europe, and elsewhere, have had to confront at some point in their history.

The New Regionalism

In 1821, newly independent Mexico was faced with the need for political reconstruction and recovery from economic setbacks caused by internal war and the disruptions in international relations caused by wars in Europe. The cost of internal war damage was considerable, but the wealth that had been exported to Europe to fund the Napoleonic wars was even greater. José María Quiroz, secretary of the Veracruz Tribunal del Consulado and a founder of Mexican econometrics, estimated in 1817 that the money supply decreased by 31 million pesos annually, for a total of about 300 million pesos, in the 1810–1821 period—approximately the equivalent of one year's gross national product.

This dramatic loss of cash produced the impression that it took Mexico half a century to recover the levels of production reached at the end of the colonial period. According to one estimate, the 1800 gross domestic product (at 1900 prices) was 333 million pesos, which dropped to 326 million pesos by 1845 and to 314 million pesos by 1860. These figures, however, are based on data that do not take into account the regional diversification of the Mexican economy, which began in the last third of the eighteenth century and grew more pronounced between 1800 and 1830.

In the process of diversification—and given the weakness of the central government—each of the country's nineteen states and five territories acquired its own strengths in production, trade, and regional and interregional organization. This characteristic of the Mexican economy lasted throughout most of the nineteenth century, until railway development revolutionized transportation and communication. The isolation of the regions is illustrated in map 6.1, which outlines the time that was required for a letter to travel back and forth between Mexico City and Querétaro, Veracruz, and Zacatecas, as well as other locations.

The administrative disorder that followed the breakdown of the colonial system also contributed to regionalism. As the risks and uncertainties of doing business increased, producers and merchants opted to restrict themselves to local markets to ensure the safety of their transactions. As a result, much of their economic activity is not reflected in the macroeconomic figures that are available to us, making it impossible to accurately measure economic activity for this period as we can for the late nineteenth and twentieth centuries.

The loose confederal arrangement and the weakness of the central government led to political and administrative changes that also obscured the statistical record. Governmental authority and responsibilities were transferred to state administrations, which reduced the categories of economic data that they collected. Under the new system, for example, the federal government collected data on foreign trade and on economic activity in the Federal District (recently established within the limits of Mexico

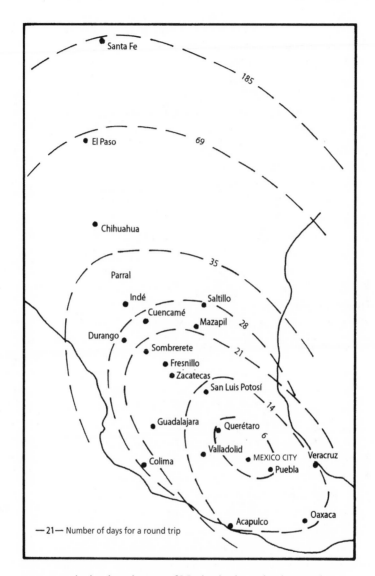

Santa Fe

185

El Paso

69

Chihuahua

Parral

35

Indé   Saltillo

Cuencamé

Mazapil   28

Durango

Sombrerete   21

Fresnillo

Zacatecas

San Luis Potosí

14

Guadalajara   Querétaro

6

Valladolid

MEXICO CITY   Veracruz

Colima

Puebla

Oaxaca

Acapulco

—21— Number of days for a round trip

MAP 6.1. An isochronic map of Mexico in the early nineteenth century. The isochronic lines represent the time necessary for a letter from Mexico City to arrive at its destination and return to Mexico City. (Source: Richard J. Salvucci, *Textiles and Capitalism in Mexico: An Economic History of the Obrajes, 1539–1840* [Princeton: Princeton University Press, 1987], p. 95.)

City), while the states recorded their own figures on production, domestic commerce, property taxes, and other data independently. Wealth was increasingly concealed for fear of confiscation. Government officials complained that people tended to migrate from their villages or hide their wealth when authorities ordered an inquiry. As a result of all these changes, the statistical record is not only less inclusive than that of the late colonial period but also follows different criteria, which makes it extremely difficult to assert that there was an economic depression between 1820 and 1860.

Studies of local and regional economic behavior indicate that if the value of local production in 1830 were added to the national data, the overall total would be similar to that at the end of the colonial period, and that the figures for the 1850s would probably be higher than those for 1800. One could argue, then, that the economy expanded very slowly between 1820 and 1850, and that real per capita income grew only slightly, at 0.2 to 0.3 percent per annum. Yet it did not contract. If we consider macroeconomic data such as mining production measured by the minting of coins in the 1790–1865 period (see figures 6.1 and 6.2), we observe two things: minting increased in the regions as it decreased in Mexico City, and the total amount of coinage minted in both the regions and Mexico City, as shown in figure 6.2, increased for the remainder of the period after a twenty-year slump between 1810 and 1830.

Mexico's estimated total population was 6.2 million in 1820 and 8.3 million by 1860, for an estimated growth rate of 0.83 percent over the period. If we break down these numbers by states, we find that people were moving toward the northern and north-central states, whereas migration toward the most established population centers of the central plateau ceased and out-migration from the south increased.

This regionally differentiated pattern of population growth reflected the increased internal migration of the late colonial period, when people had already begun to spread out from the traditional center and along the axis connecting Mexico City with the port of Veracruz. In the beginning of the nineteenth century these movements of people continued, but new patterns soon evolved to include newly developing areas as well. Population in these areas more than doubled between 1793 and 1842 period. For example, Veracruz grew from 120,000 to 288,000, Zacatecas from 118,000 to 225,000, and Nuevo León from 43,000 to 101,000.

National estimates for the gross domestic product are misleading for the 1800 to 1860 period. Yet they do tell us that agriculture and livestock were responsible for 42 to 44 percent of the total, mining for 8 to 9

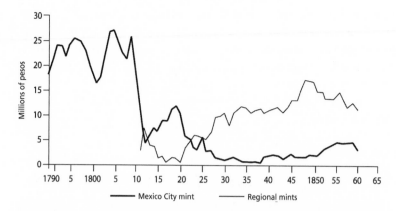

FIGURE 6.1. The minting of coins in Mexico, 1790–1865 (nominal value). (Source: Pedro Pérez Herrero, " 'Crecimiento' Colonial vs. 'Crisis' Nacional en México, 1765–1854," in Virginia Guedea and Jaime E. Rodríguez, compilers, *Cinco Siglos de Historia en México*, vol. 2 [Mexico City: Instituto José María Luis Mora, 1992], p. 96.)

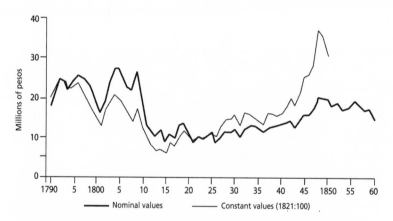

FIGURE 6.2. Total minting of coins in Mexico, 1790–1860 (nominal and constant values). (Source: Pedro Pérez Herrero, " 'Crecimiento' Colonial vs. 'Crisis' Nacional en México, 1765–1854," op. cit., p. 97.)

percent, manufacturing and construction for 20 to 22 percent, and commerce and transport for 19 to 20 percent. It is striking that these relative numbers hardly changed over a period of sixty years. But this only underscores the regional variation, because it means that the weak overall growth was truly anemic in some places and strong in others, such as Zacatecas and Nuevo León.

Economic Performance

The blurriness of the available statistics has led me to seek other sources, such as the reports coordinated by military engineers in each of the Mexican states. The statistical notes made available to Congress by the states are equally important. Again, the phenomenon of economic regionalism stands out, as does the organizational capacity of local economic actors. Once freed from the constraints of the old colonial order, and in the absence of a regular central government, local entrepreneurs took responsibility for public works. In 1822, Ortiz de Ayala claimed that private capital was abundant but well concealed for reasons of security. Backed up by municipal authorities, these entrepreneurs organized transportation and mail delivery. Charitable foundations funded hospitals and schools, and the traditional *cofradías* provided for the most basic community needs. Utilizing the same resources as previously but operating under a new system, rural production and society were transformed.

Between 1810 and 1854 the number of ranches expanded from 6,684 to 15,085, the number of *haciendas* increased from 3,749 to 6,090, and the number of towns and Indian *pueblos* grew from 4,682 to 5,000. What does this tell us? The greater number of ranches, *haciendas,* towns, and *pueblos* is a sign of a rural world in motion, growing in relative proportion to the dynamism of its protagonists: the Indigenous and mestizo communities, tenant farmers, sharecroppers, ranchers, and *hacendados.* Agricultural production must have increased in order to feed the growing populations of cities, towns, and mining centers. Little attention has been paid to the opening of previously untilled agricultural lands, mostly in the north but also in other states such as Michoacán, where both *haciendas* and ranches doubled in number between 1820 and 1850. A similar growth occurred in the state of Mexico. Owners of small and medium-sized plots of land were now selling their products directly in regional markets, as were tenant farmers and former sharecroppers, some of whom had become independent ranchers. In short, the image of an agricultural economy based exclusively on rich *haciendas* and poor smallholders simply does not mesh with the available information. It seems rather that agricultural production and distribution in the first half of the nineteenth century were organized around the market needs of cities like Mexico City, Puebla, Guadalajara, Veracruz, and Oaxaca. A similar situation prevailed in the north—in urban areas and mining centers of Nuevo León, Chihuahua, and San Luis Potosí, for example. While large land holdings predominated in regions where population was scarce and land abundant, the opposite was true in other areas, where there were three ranches for each *hacienda*. Tenants and sharecroppers were to be found everywhere. Changes in the rural world were related not only to land ownership but also to more direct economic links to urban consumption. Merchants provided credit in the form of cash advances based on the agreed-upon value of future harvests. This was in contrast to the colonial system, under which consumer products but not cash had been provided in advance to agricultural producers.

As pointed out above, figure 6.1 illustrates a slight recovery of mining activity beginning in 1825, thanks to the rehabilitation of mines in various regions. The heightened expectations of British and German prospectors for Spanish American mineral wealth particularly affected mines in the north and west. These mines were not controlled by royal officers in Mexico City, as they had been during the colonial period. As a British consul wrote, mine operators in Guanajuato could now send their silver directly to Veracruz through business arrangements with British merchant houses.

Figure 6.2 illustrates the crisis in mining that began around 1810 as the colonial period ended and lasted through the wars of independence and the European economic contraction, up to the 1840s. A weak recovery began in 1825 and only accelerated ten years later, as reflected in the line representing constant value in this figure. However, eighteenth-century production levels, which had been the highest until that time, were not matched until 1850. Although not illustrated in the figure, contemporary reports indicate that thirty to fifty centavos were illegally exported for every peso that was minted.

Domestic industry, comprised of mining, manufacturing, and agriculture, was affected by an influx of imported products. Imports of English cottons and wool textiles grew between 1820 and 1825, but then quickly shrank, and domestic production recovered, especially between 1830 and 1845.

The recovery in the mining sector, notably in the 1830s, was due to the discovery of new deposits—in Chihuahua, for example—and to the positive results of costly drainage and other engineering projects in the existing mines of Zacatecas, Fresnillo, Sombrerete, Guanajuato, and Mineral del Monte, in Hidalgo. This was the only sector to attract capital investment, both Mexican and from England, the United States, and Germany. In fact, the mine at Fresnillo, which accounted for 10 percent of the entire mining production of Zacatecas, was put into operation with state resources. These facts call into question the meager 9 percent of the GDP attributed to mining, compared with the following percentages of the GDP credited to manufacturing (defined as the production of cotton, jute, and woolen textiles, cast iron, carriages, sails, and rope): 22 percent in 1800, 18.3 percent in 1845, and 21 percent in 1860. These figures suggest that the mining percentage was much less than the manufacturing percentage because the GDP was determined on the basis of official documents that did not record trade in contraband silver. Other period sources, however, indicate that illegal trade was substantial and even increased due to war conditions.

Like other productive sectors, manufacturing activity varied among the regions and according to differences among consumer groups. The rich had their favorite textiles, the military demanded a certain quality of cloth, and the general population resorted to plain cotton and wool fabrics produced by local weavers who thrived in the absence of colonial constraints.

Mexican businessmen, who by late colonial times were well informed about the new steel mechanical looms, had substituted mechanical power for human and animal power by the 1840s. There were four modern textile mills by 1837 and forty-two by 1854, employing some ten thousand workers. These mills would supply the country's needs until the end of the century, when a new generation of textile mills came into production. By the 1840s, major cotton textile centers were located in the following states, in order of importance: Puebla, Mexico, Veracruz, Jalisco, Querétaro, Guanajuato, Durango, Sonora, Coahuila, and Colima. The data indicate that between 1843 and 1854 the number of active spindles increased from 106,708 to 126,186, mechanical looms increased from 2,609 to 3,493, and the amount of cotton produced jumped from 11,135 to 13,781 tons. Regional variation is again significant with regard to these figures, as mills and manufacturing facilities were established based on the regional or local availability of raw materials and proximity to a consumer market. The limited investment made in the textile and foundry sectors originated with the Banco de Avío, a state industrial development bank. Between 1830 and 1842, the bank dispersed loans of 1.3 million pesos for investment in the textile industry, iron foundries, glassworks, and paper mills, of which 243,000 pesos were used to import new industrial machinery.

Changes and Obstacles

With independence, the economic development process took on a new complexity, as the nascent Mexican State needed to regulate, guarantee, and defend its autonomy in relation to other countries. The economic reorganization was facilitated by the Mexican government's adherence to the principle of free trade. Agreement to the principles of free trade—demanded by Europe and especially by Britain—was a prerequisite for admission to the community of "civilized nations," all of which enjoyed the same rights and played by the same rules. In order to gain acceptance to this "club" of mostly European countries, Mexico signed friendship, commerce, and navigation treaties that regulated the free exchange of imports and exports.

The existence of these treaties was only a limited recognition of Mexico's sovereignty, in the sense that Mexican courts had no jurisdiction over British subjects and consular officers could oppose Mexican customs tariffs. The treaties established norms of reciprocity in commercial and maritime relations, and they protected the economic activities and property of merchants, landowners, and individuals in each of the signatory states. In their treatment of tariffs, the treaties held the signatories to equitable import policies and prohibited any restriction on the free circulation of goods.

Mexico had already liberalized its trade practices before signing these treaties—in fact, even before independence. A fixed import duty of 25 percent was established in 1821, eliminating import barriers and almost halving the colonial tariff of 40 percent. Similar measures to stimulate trade followed in subsequent decades, and export duties were regularized on gold, silver, and *palo de tinte,* the valuable wood of the *campeche* tree, which was used in Europe to produce a purple dye.

The benefit of free trade was that it offered guarantees to domestic and foreign investors with respect to their property and marketable products. This provided them with broad flexibility, and it signaled the beginning of the end for the monopolistic corporate trading system of colonial times. The competition among numerous merchants of different nationalities favored a greater number of producers, who could now negotiate more favorable prices for their products. It also benefited consumers, since the option of buying imported products put limits on the characteristic overpricing of domestic goods.

A number of regional ports profited when the port of Veracruz lost its monopoly in the middle of 1820. These included Alvarado, Campeche,

Tabasco, Tampico, Matamoros, Isla del Carmen, Huatulco, San Blas, Mazatlán, and Guaymas. These port cities handled both imports and exports—which also meant increased opportunities for contraband trade.

Nevertheless, both the structure of the economy and the precariousness of the public treasury presented obstacles to economic activity. Imports were constrained by the availability of cash, which was tied to the levels of silver production. Economic activity was also constricted by the meagerness of the public treasury. Between 1825 and 1840, annual federal income grew from 10.6 to 21.2 million pesos. Borrowing became a significant source of funds, reaching 6 to 8 million pesos annually by 1840. After 1850, total revenues fell from 21.2 to 14.7 million pesos; however, only 5 million pesos of this amount came in the form of loans.

A number of reasons were responsible for the limited federal treasury, including the collapse of central government institutions. The situation was exacerbated by the government's inability to maintain good financial relations with other countries, particularly with England. In 1824–1825, Britain authorized two credits to Mexico amounting to a total of 6.4 million pounds sterling. They were issued at a price of seventy-two pounds per one hundred nominal pounds, under conditions identical to those granted to other Latin American countries and to European countries such as Greece, Spain, and Denmark. But Mexico did not keep up with its interest payments, sorely damaging its credit profile for several decades.

One may rightfully ask why the new federal republic did not fulfill its financial obligations. One possible explanation is that tariffs were its only source of income. Another is that the states were not fulfilling their constitutional obligations to consign revenues to the central government. The fact is that when external credit was insufficient, the government became indebted to lenders on very unfavorable terms. In addition, merchants were compelled to lend money to the State, special taxes were decreed, and the Church was pressured to make its liquid assets available to the public treasury.

Between 1825 and 1850, the government obtained some eighty million pesos by coercive means, creating a time bomb of debt. Merchants became greedy when they saw that lending money to the government was highly profitable and entailed little risk. After all, they were collecting thirty centavos up front for every peso that they lent. The government's coercive economic demands on the middle and upper economic sectors also had very negative political repercussions, as these sectors then withdrew their political support at critical times. Forced contributions and loans created a negative climate that ended up suffocating the growing social energy that the independence movement had released.

In any case, the government was unable to construct either a system of public credit or the conditions for a banking system, which was indispensable for capital investment. Lacking investment, the Mexican economy did not progress from a narrow regional economy to one more closely tied to the market, international finance, and intensive production. This was the negative side of the regionalism that sprang up in the late eighteenth century and accelerated between 1820 and 1860; it hindered the development of a national market. The available data may be insufficient to draw any firm conclusion, but questions and hypotheses are inevitable. Could it be that a rigid traditional order was responsible for the relative underdevelopment of Mexico despite all these positive changes? Was Mexico's economy stymied by the negative conditions of a worldwide recession that began in the 1820s and ended only in the 1840s?

The Breakdown of Social Hierarchies

Political regionalism was more pronounced than ever. Beginning with the confederation of 1824, Mexico struggled with different forms of government, all of them highly decentralized. The dominant feature of them all was a low level of institutionalization. The municipalities and their town councils were the stabilizing institutions of the period; their electoral procedures were mechanisms for the resolution of conflicts. After the 1820s, new and vital political practices emerged at the municipal level, reflecting the republican principles upon which the new State had been founded.

It is difficult to generalize about local political institutions, since the broad diversity of populations was reflected in the variety of political forms. One prominent nineteenth-century liberal characterized Mexico as a "society of societies," an idea that is supported by what we know of the multiplicity of voting mechanisms used in the first electoral processes. The organization of biannual elections had the salutary result of establishing the first consensus among society's differing status groups, social sectors, and interest groups. The cultural practices of a given locality were reflected in the voting procedures adopted there. This was common not only in Mexico but also in other Western countries where the right of suffrage was being put into practice—though both suffrage and citizenship rights were still very limited by modern standards.

The institution of elections had the virtue of, among other things, breaking old molds. Access to positions of responsibility through kinship relations was made more difficult. To the extent that the electoral process led to a periodic turnover in leadership positions, it stimulated social mobility within communities, undermining traditional power bases and the privileges enjoyed by traditional *caciques* and their political heirs.

The wars of independence had mobilized large numbers of people, patriots who demanded new rights after the victory. At the municipal level, any resident could aspire to office, though the criteria were more rigorous at higher levels. Early liberals like José María Luis Mora referred to the *ayuntamientos* as schools of good citizenship where the public spirit was generated. The first sets of elections led to a certain consensus among different status groups, social sectors, and interest groups, and contributed to one of the country's most important transformations, the establishment of governability at the municipal level. Municipal organization affirmed the republican principle of government by elected authorities whose actions could be approved or reprimanded by their constituencies.

While some municipalities participated in the modernization process, other municipalities and some traditional authorities acted upon their historical memory of pre-Hispanic ancestral rights that the Spanish king had recognized during the colonial period through the granting of titles and special dispensations. Their insistence on autonomy and sovereignty gave rise to the so-called *casta* movements, or movements demanding municipal sovereignty. I discuss this phenomenon in my book *La Tradición Republicana del Buen Gobierno* (The Republican Tradition of Good Government).

The New Levels of Government

The Mexican republic as we know it today, with its central State apparatus, was construed and constructed over the course of most of the nineteenth century, actually taking shape only after the midcentury. The process of nation-building took place as the different levels of government were established, commencing with the towns and their seats of government. These small but important polities then drew together into a series of networks that began to define the modern states. The social organization of each new state was woven around towns and municipal government centers, each linked to a main city. Like the tendrils of a vine holding the different territories together, municipalities were the basis of political organization and the nodes of a social network based on kinship ties, *compadrazgo,* and business and trade relations. The recently acquired notion of citizenry was built around specific institutions. Close relations among towns facilitated parallel cooperation among elite groups within the municipality. Thus the municipality provided the social and political basis for the formation of coherent federal states. Once the federal republic was established in 1824, the municipality provided the essential mechanisms for the election of the representatives to the federal Congress, the president, and the Supreme Court justices. In fact elections were held under the scrutiny of the *ayuntamientos* throughout the century.

Under the first republican Constitution of 1824, each state was free, independent, and sovereign with regard to internal administration. The states retained significant constitutional powers, inhibiting the consolidation of the central government. Regional political groups agreed to delegate certain limited powers to the Congress, producing a confederal assembly of deputies who operated in the interests of their states rather than the nation. In this early period, the state and federal congresses held more authority than their corresponding executive branches.

Thus a new relationship was established between local and regional elites, one that would evolve through the different historical phases that would define independent Mexico. The strength of the regional elite derived to a great extent from their ties to the *pueblos* and *municipios* in their respective zones. They came to realize that room for maneuver depended on their autonomy, which would guarantee their independence from the political and economic elite in Mexico City.

Citizens and *Vecinos*

The constitution of each state established the internal mechanisms of its government and laid down the conditions for citizenship and *vecino* status. Most state constitutions shared the same general characteristics, which were reflected in the common political processes and social initiatives they introduced. We can begin with the *ayuntamiento* and the parish, which were the basic cells of the entire political structure, and with the key actor within them, the *vecino.* The head of each family could qualify as a *vecino* as long as he was able to provide for his household, contribute to community welfare by paying his taxes, and live within the law. Economic and political autonomy went hand in hand. One who was judged worthy was also said to be a man of reason, *un hombre de razón.* With citizenry came the obligation of permanent residency and the requirement that his household be economically active in the *pueblo, villa,* or community. Since each municipality was free to define such criteria, a wide array of arbitrary definitions was produced. In all cases, the granting of citizenship to a wider sector of the population was antithetical to the old hierarchical structure, which had concentrated wealth, honor, prestige, and social and political privilege in the hands of a very few notables.

The press in Michoacán in 1830 described the *vecino* as a property owner. Property owners are those who own real estate or practice a profession, such as attorneys, notaries, military officers, scribes, scholars, manufacturers, bankers, merchants, currency agents, artisans, or any persons with a fixed income and capable of bearing the burden of both personal and indirect taxation, so that their interests are intimately tied to the survival of the government. If we apply these criteria to an 1845 occupational census taken in the state of Querétaro, we find that 10,636, or 29.4 percent, of the 36,216 individuals then employed were considered property owners. If, on the other hand, if we were to apply colonial standards of citizenship, only 2,736, or 7.6 percent, would qualify as notables.

How did the *vecinos* exercise their voting rights? The *vecinos* voted for primary electors, who selected secondary electors, who in turn designated third-level electors, who appointed deputies to the state and federal congresses. The respective congresses elected state governors and a federal president. Only at the municipal level did *vecinos* vote directly for their representatives, who served in various capacities within the *ayuntamiento*. According to an 1861 electoral census, there were an estimated 1.5 million qualified voters from among a total population of 8.2 million. They included active citizens (those who voted and were eligible for public office) and passive citizens (those *vecinos* eligible only to vote).

The large number of males voting at the municipal level may be explained by the dynamics of war mobilization. Militia and National Guard troops were recruited in the villages and towns in return for full citizenship rights, which had historically been tied to property and income. This could also explain a difference between Mexican and North American and European electoral practices. In Mexico, many voters participated at the municipal level, but beyond that level, they were distinguished along a hierarchical continuum based on income, literacy, and other indices of power. A smaller number of individuals participated at the higher steps of the electoral process, that is, in the selection of primary and secondary electors. Those eligible to serve as a deputies or senators constituted the smallest group and occupied the top of the hierarchy.

Presidents, Congress, and the Military

Having described the three-step electoral procedure that linked the different levels of society, I will continue with the basic institutions that gave life to the republic. The first half of the nineteenth century has been described as a period of struggle between federalists and centralists, between liberals and conservatives—and, I would add, between republicans and monarchists. But things were more complicated than that. There was a wide range of political actors who sometimes acted together and at other times opposed each other. They all shared one ideal, however: the construction of constitutionally based republican legitimacy and the exercise of power through public institutions. The political elite were well aware that a country lacking a constitution was in what they called a natural state, *en estado natural,* and therefore defenseless against foreign invasion and occupation. Under international law, sovereignty could be established through the adoption of a constitution written by "the people," that is, their elected representatives.

Traditionalist and corporatist forces within institutions such as the army and the Church were active on the political scene, as were their opponents, who represented newer regional or urban pressure groups. Despite the presence of these old and new forces, however, there was surprising continuity in the overall composition of legislative bodies. Antagonistic forces formed alliances at critical times, making it difficult to delimit the political positions of the various forces very precisely. They tended to take positions that changed along with the historical circumstances and, given the decentralized nature of the country, with the needs of their respective states.

The construction of the Mexican State was a multistaged process that saw successes and failures. Mexico experienced the 1823 empire, the 1824 confederal republic, the centralist republic of 1834–1846, and the federalist republic of 1846–1854. Each was based on a constitution. Today we can see that the split between centralists and federalists did not always coincide with liberal and conservative political positions. Liberalism itself was never monolithic. Different kinds of "liberalism" appealed to republicans and to monarchists. Lucas Alamán was both a monarchist and a moderate liberal.

The search for an adequate form of government presented the political elite with its first dilemma. Powerful opposition to Agustín de Iturbide's nationalized version of the imperial monarchy eliminated the option of a unitary and centralized government. The possibility of an effective unitary government was compromised by the strongly regional nature of congressional representation. The number of provincial deputations grew from six to fifteen in 1820; by 1822 there were eighteen, and in 1823 there were twenty-three. These strong regional forces quickly organized themselves into what would become the sovereign states that ratified the confederal Constitution of 1824. The second problem was that as representatives of the states gathered in Congress to constitute and organize the "Mexican nation," the state deputies conceived of themselves as the repositories of popular sovereignty. This conception of the road to national unity was very strong in this first period of independence.

Given the obstacles to a unitary government and the strong pressures from the states, Congress approved the Constitution of 1824, establishing a federal republic. This constitution produced a highly imbalanced federal system, actually more of a confederation. Sovereignty resided in the states, which were independent entities that delegated to the federation only those powers that related to international relations, the military defense of the nation, and the maintenance of domestic peace and tranquility.

In his December 1823 *Profecías* (Prophecies), a deputy from Nuevo León named Servando Teresa de Mier described the absurdity of a federal Congress and national deputies whose powers were strictly limited by the provinces that they represented, and he warned that the continuing existence of multiple sovereignties would lead to fragmentation, division, and failure.

By 1836, due to the dispersal of power, the political elites radically reformed the 1824 Constitution in an effort to unify and centralize the government of the republic. The Constitutional Bases of 1835 and the Constitutional Laws of 1836 provided for a radical reduction of regional autonomy. The states were downgraded to departments, each run by a governor appointed by the central government. Power was centralized both because the departmental governors were subordinate to the central government and because the elimination of state legislative bodies enhanced the powers of the national Congress.

Under both the 1824 and the 1836 constitutions, the executive branch was subject to Congress and the limitations it imposed. In the case of the 1824 document, the state congresses elected the president, who was then responsible to the legislative branch. The prerogatives of the executive were limited, since Congress retained most powers over economic and budgetary matters, public works, and education. The Laws of 1836 added to Congress's powers and increased its annual sessions to two. Under this

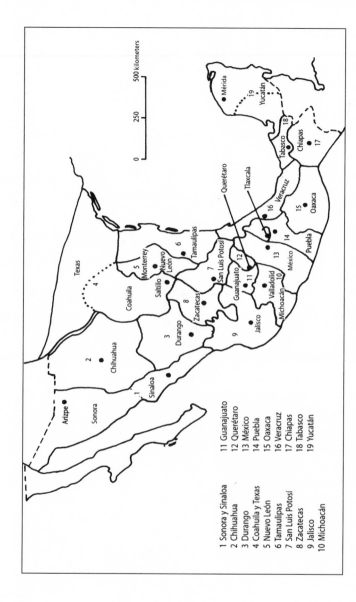

500 kilometers

250

0

Mérida

19
Yucatán

18
Tabasco

Chiapas
17

Querétaro

Tlaxcala

Veracruz
16

15
Oaxaca

Tamaulipas

San Luis Potosí

6

12

7

13

14

Monterrey

Nuevo
León

5

Saltillo

Guanajuato
11

México

Puebla

Texas

4

Coahuila

8
Zacatecas

Valladolid
10

Michoacán

9
Jalisco

Durango

3

Chihuahua

2

Sinaloa

1

Sonora

Arizpe

1 Sonora y Sinaloa
2 Chihuahua
3 Durango
4 Coahuila y Texas
5 Nuevo León
6 Tamaulipas
7 San Luis Potosí
8 Zacatecas
9 Jalisco
10 Michoacán

11 Guanajuato
12 Querétaro
13 México
14 Puebla
15 Oaxaca
16 Veracruz
17 Chiapas
18 Tabasco
19 Yucatán

MAP 6.2. The Mexican United States, 1824. (Source: Edmundo O'Gorman, *Historia de las Divisiones Políticas Territoriales de México* [Mexico City: Porrúa, 1985], pp. 74–75.)

system, the legislative and executive branches were subject to a fourth branch called the Supremo Poder Conservador, the Supreme Conservative Power, composed of five members and thirteen counselors elected by the departmental councils. The Supremo Poder had wide authority, even over the president, whose decisions it could annul and whom it could sanction or even remove from office.

This quick review of constitutional history should illustrate the fragmentation of power and the overlapping or contradictory mandates of the political institutions in this period. Throughout much of the nineteenth century, there was an exaggerated fear that a powerful chief executive would monopolize power, so various constitutional structures were devised to limit and distribute the prerogatives otherwise pertaining to that office. Another significant factor was the jealously guarded autonomy of municipalities and states as opposed to a central administration. Some municipal authorities went so far as to conceal information from their own state governments, such as the number of *vecinos* in their census or their wealth and productivity statistics. At first, governors struggled to control problematic municipalities, but in the absence of effective administrative mechanisms at the state level, they came to depend on municipal authorities in order to govern.

These conditions gave rise to frequent insurrections and rebellions, often coinciding with important political changes, such as the advent of federalism in 1824, centralism in 1836–1838, and once again a return to federalism in the 1850s following the United States' invasion of Mexico in 1846–1848. But while general insurrections coincided with other dramatic events, short-lived local uprisings and outbreaks of lawlessness were more frequent.

Instability was most acute at the highest level of government, as presidents and their cabinets came to power elected by state legislatures and supported by regional coalitions. They ruled for as long as those coalitions supported them. Faced with strong regionalism, central institutions were economically and politically weak. Fluctuations in the structure of the central government reflected a search for political institutions through which the State could govern effectively but not tyrannically. Political plans, as they were called, guided the interaction of government bodies and established a place for the military on the political scene, avoiding the anarchy that could have led to a constitutional rupture between the central government and the states and municipalities.

In the absence of a stable executive, and given the local and regional dispersion of powers, the army was the only national institution other than the Church. As defined in the Plan de Iguala, which led to the independence of Mexico, the armed forces were a national body that guaranteed public order and national unity, and defended national sovereignty at times of foreign invasion. The army had command centers and garrisons distributed throughout the country. When faced with uprisings, they would mobilize, integrate, and engage in joint operations. If an uprising took on unusually large proportions, additional troops and officers would be assigned to an operational force, temporarily bringing together officers from widely dispersed command centers, which led to the formation of political-military factions and alliances.

We should take a moment to examine the political mechanisms operative during much of the nineteenth century, before constitutional powers were sorted out among governmental institutions and before these political institutions were stabilized. If we accept the idea that the coordination between general constitutional powers and the authority of states and municipalities was weak, then it becomes necessary to explain how the multiple interfaces among Mexican political spaces and groups were first constructed. It seems that an element of the army or other armed forces would mediate in a federal-state or a state-municipal political conflict by intervening and imposing an agreement based on a coalition of forces. This would last until new internal conflicts required additional intervention. I do not hold to the traditional analysis of the *pronunciamiento* as a kind of coup d'etat. I see the phenomenon more as a form of political expression and participation stemming from the particular circumstances in Mexico. In a *pronunciamiento,* a *caudillo,* or strongman, intervened in events in order to establish and guarantee a new consensus that would restore governability, be it within a centralist or federalist framework. Antonio López de Santa Anna repeatedly played this role. He has been described as a federalist until 1834, and then a centralist, even a monarchist. Santa Anna certainly recognized political opportunity and knew how to make the most of it. In his role as commander-in-chief, he seized multiple opportunities to enter the national arena and mediate the recurrent conflicts between national and regional power spheres in order to restore political agreement.

Operating through *pronunciamientos* and political plans, the military mediated among the institutions at all levels of government to balance their constitutional powers. A *pronunciamiento* by a military faction could bring down a president and produce a new pact, which would itself be provisional, as illustrated in figure 6.3.

Not every political plan had a national impact. Sometimes a military

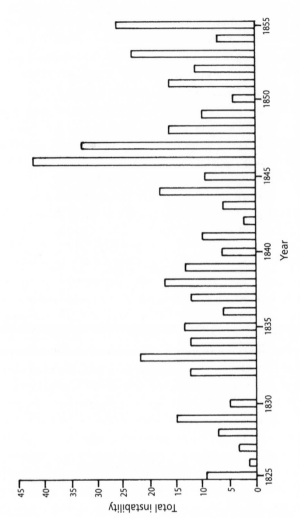

FIGURE 6.3. Total changes in national executive posts, 1825–1855. Instability is measured in this figure by the rapid turnover of the central executive power as represented by presidents and ministers of war, the interior, finance, and foreign affairs. (Source: Donald Fithian Stevens, *Origins of Instability in Early Republican Mexico* [Durham, NC, and London: Duke University Press, 1991], p. 12.)

faction would declare itself in support of a plan emerging at the level of the *ayuntamiento* and circulate it among state National Guard commanders, but it would not attract the support of more than a few municipalities or a faction of one state congress. If a political plan did garner more than municipal or statewide support, however—if it found support in several states and if it was backed by a significant number of important military officers—then a high-ranking commander or one of the plan's leading military backers would issue a *pronunciamiento*. With success, a *pronunciamiento* launched at the *ayuntamiento* level would circulate among the citizen-electors, who would pass it on to the state congress. At the same time, the *ayuntamiento* would communicate with its citizens in arms, those elements of the National Guard under local jurisdiction. Local officers of the Guard would deliberate as to whether they wished to strengthen the plan by affiliating themselves with it and passing it along to other sectors of the army. Since these circles of communication were quite active, the news of the plan would spread quickly. But its success ultimately depended on support from significant military factions. If that support was forthcoming, a prestigious and high-ranking officer would lend his weight to the plan and become its chief advocate in negotiations between the authors of the *pronunciamiento* and the president. If the president rejected their petitions, this officer, or *caudillo,* might confront him—and by extension, his executive power. A military confrontation could be avoided, however, if multiple members of Congress took joint action against the executive, whose autonomy was limited.

A successful *pronunciamiento* returned the nation to what at that time was called its natural state. This meant that power had been returned to the citizenry, who, through the electoral process, would "reconstitute the nation" by changing the makeup of the Congress, the executive branch, or both. This was the process by which a consensus incorporating the new demands was established and national unity was restored.

The Crisis of the First Republic: Domestic and International Issues

The vulnerability of the country and the extreme fragility of its political system, already unmistakable in the 1840s, became even more striking as a result of the 1846–1848 United States invasion. Large segments of society were shocked and appalled, probably for the first time, by the violation of Mexican territory.

When Mexico was invaded by the United States, municipal and state militias acted upon their rejection of an oligarchic republic by redefining military forces along political lines. Liberal commanders reorganized locally based militias, federalizing the National Guard and integrating it into the command structure of the standing army. This decision enabled all males living in a municipality to acquire the status of citizen and *vecino* by serving under arms. Diverse social sectors united in the common cause of defending the nation. Once they returned to civilian life, they demanded the rapid concession of citizenship rights and the establishment of direct elections.

Specific events triggered the sentiment for political reform, but other factors intervened, such as the presence of a new generation of people who had grown up in an independent Mexico and who by the 1830s occupied political and professional positions or worked as salaried employees in business or manufacturing enterprises. This new generation belonged to families that had achieved a certain social standing on their own merits. They favored reform and opposed the traditional practice of dispensing favors to all political factions. They had acquired a certain degree of political experience and wisdom, and they understood the reasons for the failure of federalist reforms in the 1830s. They conceived of a different kind of Mexico, a liberal and federal State that was more than a set of regional identities united only by limited common interests.

The new liberal generation criticized the political class for making careers out of public office based on the rule of *caudillismo* and clientalism in order to hold onto power indefinitely. These practices were particularly common in Congress, where many members had begun as state legislators, moved into various federal jobs, and capped off their careers as long-term federal deputies. This generation of liberals did their job so well that succeeding liberals accused them of being too moderate, or even called them conservative.

Political tensions worsened when the centralist faction was unable to form a government, and army interventions occurred with increasing frequency. In the last decade of centralist dominance, the republic survived thanks only to a continuous dependence on the army and the preeminent role of the *caudillo*.

In its struggle for a federal republic, the new liberal generation repudiated the *caudillos* and their influence on the standing army. They envisioned the National Guard as the army of the new republic. This was a more open body, composed of the armed citizenry and responding to the authority of the state or the municipality. National Guard troops elected their commanders by direct and secret vote.

The elitist first republic was thus eroded by continuous and increasing social antagonism and by the conflicts generated by its own exclusionary nature. The idea of a nation with territorial sovereignty and inviolable borders would develop over a period of nearly half a century, strengthened by recurrent foreign threats and invasions.

The Mexican struggle for international recognition provided its people with a basis for unity, which grew throughout the century. In 1822, the Spanish Cortes had declared the Treaty of Córdoba null and void. Because Spain refused to recognize Mexican independence, other European powers also declined to do so, and the country's participation in international affairs remained marginal. When a treaty was negotiated, as one was with Britain, it was a limited recognition of the republic's de facto existence but not of its de jure sovereignty. The refusal to fully recognize the international rights of Mexico and the other Latin American countries was mandated by the Holy Alliance, an agreement among the European monarchies signed at the 1814–1815 Congress of Vienna and reaffirmed at the 1822 Congress of Verona. In accord with the principle of mutual support entailed by these treaties, the refusal of Spain to recognize the newly independent American republics discouraged their recognition by the other monarchies. This legal obstacle was maintained until the end of 1830.

The other reason for Mexico's international marginalization was its inability to build a federal treasury adequate to meet debt commitments like those it contracted in London's capital markets. Mexico's noncompliance with debt payments and the complaints of European traders about the risks of doing business in the country sorely detracted from international confidence in Mexico. In this negative climate, Spain launched an expedition from Cuba to reconquer its former colony in 1828, and in 1838 France occupied the port of Veracruz under the pretext that it was only demanding payment on debts owed to French citizens.

Continuing European hostility fed United States interest in Mexico, which dated from its 1803 purchase of Louisiana from the French monarch. The Mexican state of Texas declared itself an independent republic in 1835, and Mexico found itself ever more exposed to U.S. expansionism.

The secession of Texas pointed up the weak link between the first republic and the states. When the Mexican republic was born, Texas was already occupied by foreign colonists who had responded to the colonization-friendly policies of the Spanish crown. The new Mexican republic had proceeded to authorize new concessions to those willing to colonize unpopulated regions, with the result that only 3,500 of the

25,000 inhabitants of Texas claimed Hispanic roots. The rest neither spoke Spanish nor practiced Catholicism. The de facto absence of a central State apparatus effectively granted Texan residents a level of autonomy bordering on independence, to the extent that colonists kept slaves—a practice that had been outlawed throughout the republic in 1829. They also used the territory as a base for trade in contraband. In short, there was a vacuum of authority in the least culturally Mexican territory of the republic.

In 1830, the Mexican government banned all further colonization by U.S. citizens. Texans reacted immediately. They met in assembly in March of that year and declared the Independent Republic of Texas. That July, they sent a request to Washington for annexation to the Union. The United States government at first rejected their petition as incompatible with its own internal political problems. Political stability in the United States was dependent on maintaining equilibrium between its "slave" and "free" states, which made the admission of new states and territories a politically volatile issue. But the future of North America was at stake, since without annexation England was likely to ally itself with the Independent Republic of Texas and reassert a role for itself on the continent. On the other hand, annexation could lead to a confrontation between the United States and Mexico. Hoping to reach an accord, England, Mexico, and the Republic of Texas initiated conversations in 1843. Concerned with this development, elements in Washington began a successful lobbying campaign that enabled them to assure Texas leader Sam Houston of a large majority of Southern votes in Congress in favor of annexation.

A wave of expansionism was sweeping through the United States, carrying James K. Polk to the presidency in 1844. In Mexico, business forces faced the prospect of losing the profits associated with established commercial networks, and nascent public opinion resented the virtual annexation of Texas by the United States as an assault on Mexican national sovereignty. At the same time, it began to be clear that the United States also had designs on other territories under Mexican rule, stretching from California to parts of Colorado and Wyoming.

Negotiations between the two countries broke down when Mexico refused to sell these territories. The Americans could not or did not want to understand that although Mexico was faring poorly and its finances were exhausted, it was not money but the idea of national unity that lay at the heart of the problem.

In January 1846, U.S. forces occupied the area located between the Río Nueces and the Río Grande—or the Río Bravo, as it is called in Mexico.

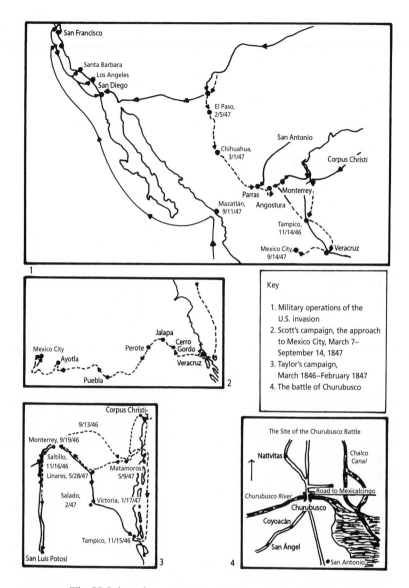

MAP 6.3. The U.S. invasion, 1846–1847. (Source: Enrique Florescano, co-ordinator, *Atlas Histórico de México, Cultura,* September/Siglo XXI [Mexico City: Editores, 1983], p. 109.)

TABLE 6.1. The Relation of Forces and Casualties in Three Key
Battles against the U.S. Army

	Troops in Combat	Dead and Injured
Battle of Churubusco		
USA	n/a[a]	1,014
Mexico	n/a	4,297
Battle of Molino del Rey		
USA	7,000	780
Mexico	12,000	2,000
Battle of Chapultepec		
USA	n/a	836
Mexico	n/a	1,800

[a]n/a = Information not available.
SOURCE: Archives of the Secretariat of National Defense, Mexico City.

In May of that year, President James Polk signed a congressional declaration of war on Mexico. Antiexpansionist voices were raised in the U.S.
Congress, but they were too few in number to prevent a majority vote to
declare war. The United States invaded Mexico in March 1846 by land
and sea in the north, at the ports of Tampico and Veracruz on the Gulf
Coast, and at the Pacific port of Mazatlán. U.S. troops took control of (or
occupied) the seat of government in Mexico City eighteen months later,
on September 14, 1847.

Map 6.3 illustrates the routes taken by U.S. forces, the armed opposition to their advances, and the resistance they met with in the different
Mexican regions. It is true that only seven governors sent out their National Guard units to defend the country against invasion. Some governors refused to leave their states unprotected by dispatching the National
Guard to defend the capital or other states. But the defense of the Mexican nation went beyond the states' tepid first response. The U.S. Army
was soon confronted with guerrilla resisters who were less vulnerable
than the regular forces.

According to the reports of U.S. officers, they did not fear con-
fronting regular Mexican troops but did live in constant apprehension of
an invisible enemy, the volunteer militias and semiregular National
Guard battalions that harassed the invaders. U.S. military reports chron-

icle the resistance in the north by six thousand regular forces under General Mariano Arista, in which one thousand Mexicans died while General Winfield Scott lost two hundred men. Once war was declared, the invading army was reinforced, reaching a strength of twelve thousand. Six thousand of them confronted the troops of General Pedro Ampudia in Monterrey, composed of seven thousand regular army troops and three thousand militiamen. Each side had over four hundred dead and wounded. Tampico was invaded by an army of ten thousand troops, who were met by fifteen thousand Mexican troops commanded by Santa Anna. The Americans lost about one thousand and the Mexicans fifteen hundred. Eight thousand five hundred U.S. soldiers landed at Veracruz and advanced on Mexico City. The invaders approaching the capital reached a total of eleven thousand men, including reinforcements, and some three thousand men incapacitated by illness. Santa Anna reconcentrated his forces, which now numbered thirty thousand men. The defense of the capital was the bloodiest confrontation of the war. The defeat of Mexican forces in the battles of Churubusco, Molino del Rey, and Chapultepec left the capital city defenseless.

The Mexican military did not defeat the invading army, nor did Mexican society or the armed citizenry, not to speak of the political class. On the other hand, they clearly demonstrated the will to resist and to defend Mexico's national sovereignty. Although internal political divisions, inadequate financial resources, and the inability to defend the coasts made defeat inevitable, the enormous loss of territory was shocking and made an indelible mark on the national consciousness nonetheless. A peace treaty was signed in the village of Guadalupe on February 2, 1848. It established a new international boundary at the southern border of Texas, the United States winning possession of what are today California, Nevada, Utah, most of Arizona and New Mexico, and parts of Colorado and Wyoming. The United States government paid Mexico fifteen million dollars for half its territory.

CHAPTER 7

Liberalism and National Reconstruction

In the second half of the nineteenth century, Mexico confronted the challenge that Octavio Paz called the reconformation of the nation by means of a triple negation: the negation of its colonial heritage, of its ethnic differences, and of the Catholic religion. Disavowing these legacies became unavoidable when the old corporative regime, which had survived the struggle for independence and the first republic, entered into crisis. The incompatibility of corporate privileges and immunities with the needs of the new liberal republic produced deep contradictions. There was also a crucial generational succession. The youths who had experienced the 1846–1848 United States invasion and confronted French imperial troops in 1862–1867 supplanted their elders to reestablish the republic in 1867.

The generation of 1846 and the generation of 1867 bore all the marks of a civil war and an anticolonial war that had lasted two decades. The internal war pitted Mexican against Mexican over the nature of their state and government: unitary republic, federal republic, or monarchy. In international and anticolonial conflicts, Mexicans defended their sovereignty and territorial integrity from United States invaders, and defended the republic from Europeans attempting to reinstate the monarchy.

In the two decades between 1846 and 1867, the country was financially and morally devastated. The unstable political system and the physical danger to life and property were profoundly discouraging. The population cried out for peace and order. It fell to the liberal republican generation to rebuild the nation, reestablish order, renew constitutional guarantees, construct a new financial architecture, and promote social, economic, and cultural progress. The years from 1867 to 1890 stand out for the efforts of Mexicans dedicated to peace and reconstruction that made social coexistence possible.

War, Foreign Interventions, and Internal Conflict

A brief chronological overview shows us that Mexico was at relative peace for only three of the twenty years between 1846 and 1867. During the remaining war-filled years, foreign troops occupied Mexican soil almost half the time. The United States army was present from 1846 to 1848, and between 1862 and 1867, English and Spanish forces occupied coastal areas and a French army penetrated the interior, establishing an imperial regime under Maximilian of Hapsburg. The dispute over the nature of the state and government—whether it should be federal or unitary, republican or monarchical—was sorely aggravated by the foreign presence, producing explosive social tensions. These questions had plagued the nation for many years, but polarization became acute as each contending force found supporters among the foreign powers. The resulting civil war was the most dramatic and painful conflict that the country had known—the war for independence included.

It was a chaotic period. Rebellions and wars within wars swept the nation without respite. Liberals went to unprecedented extremes, while conservatives and supporters of the old order seemed to surrender to self-destructive impulses. The Church's tooth-and-nail defense of its riches and privileges enraged many Mexicans, despite their continued Catholicism. Local notables and the army were despised for allying themselves with the forces of political reaction. In this extremely antagonistic atmosphere, every political tendency came to be intimately associated with one or more of the forces in conflict.

Rather than providing the dates of important events and enumerating the *pronunciamientos,* or extraconstitutional regime changes, I will begin by describing the domestic situation at the time of the United States' declaration of war against Mexico in 1846. When the Americans invaded, broad sectors of society reacted to reject this outrage and defend Mexican sovereignty. It was probably the first time that so many sectors united around the idea of a shared national identity. These forces included moderate and extreme liberals, local notables and prominent individuals, politicians, and businessmen, as well as the grassroots population. They set aside their differences for the time being, but the dispute over the best form of government for Mexico was still unresolved. Supporters of a stronger central government, advocates of having powerful states with a weak federal government, and champions of all possible variations on these basic positions could be found at both the elite and popular levels of Mexican society.

Despite internal divisions, stability and equilibrium among political factions had been maintained within Congress. Surprisingly, there was continuity of between 15 and 40 percent of the members of the legislative body from the 1820s until the mid-1850s. This equilibrium was lost, however, when citizen pressure to eliminate the system of indirect election increased, as reflected in the constitutional debates of 1842 and 1847. This demand grew out of a spreading constitutionalism and increased citizen awareness as a result of service in the National Guard, where the direct election of commanders was a common practice and full citizenship was obtainable in exchange for active service. New social groups demanded that individual rights and citizenship rights be made explicit in the constitution, and that they be respected. Significantly, the 1824 Constitution did not have a section on individual or citizenship rights, but they were spelled out in the Laws of 1836, viewed as fundamental texts of centralism. The movement for individual rights got its start in the regions outside central Mexico. The state assemblies of Yucatán, Puebla, Mexico, Zacatecas, Durango, and Sonora all took up the popular demand and in 1841 asked the centralist government for a clear recognition of individual rights.

The dynamic between popular demands and their expression in constitutional guarantees developed under the protection of liberal federalism. In the absence of organized parties, a movement for federalist liberalism sprang up in various social spaces and governmental bodies. The federal and liberal movement was advanced in the 1842 Congress, and reached its climax in response to the 1846 invasion by the United States and the 1853–1855 dictatorship of General Santa Anna. The U.S. occupation shone a light on the weakness of the central government and the need to strengthen the federation. Imperiled by the U.S. occupation of Mexico City, Congress, before it dissolved in 1846, provided for the reversion of constitutional powers to the states, and in order to guarantee strong liberal federalist representation, it instructed its deputies to prepare for new elections once the appropriate conditions were reestablished.

Newly converted liberals loudly demanded that equality before the law be extended and guaranteed to all Mexicans, and their demands gathered social momentum. The Santa Anna dictatorship was repudiated when it reversed this process and even annulled certain already established rights. In one such instance, an 1853 decree reduced the number of municipalities and suppressed municipal autonomy by imposing top-down and uniform national criteria. Not only did most municipal bodies reject the decree, but most state governors refused to impose the rule within their states.

Federalist liberals established ties with the grassroots liberals of the *pueblos* then engaged in resistance to the United States invaders. Their common position, also shared by liberal landowners, was opposition to the authoritarianism of the Santa Anna dictatorship. The U.S. invasion and the Santa Anna dictatorship had convinced these sectors of the need for a more stable government and for a redefinition of the balance of powers between states and the union.

By midcentury, society was divided. The people's war had brought together popular forces and liberal middle classes. On the other hand, some blamed republicanism and democracy for instability, continuous warfare, and the concessions made to unruly popular sectors. Monarchical rule was still very much favored in those sectors of society who believed that hereditary rule was the only answer to the existing chaos, and they proposed a constitutional monarchy as a solution. Although these conservatives were marginalized and labeled reactionaries, the idea gained some popularity among landowners in various parts of the country, especially among the hierarchy of the Church, the only coherent national institution left standing.

Eventually, both the option of a liberal federal republic and that of a constitutional monarchy with strong central powers found wide support in Mexican society. Both were responses to the urgent need to organize new forms of political practice and to find economic and cultural options that would restore social peace and national unity, but they were diametrically opposed positions. When the liberal federalists triumphed in 1854 with the Plan de Ayutla, monarchist military factions rebelled and were defeated. The federalists were clearly dominant, especially in the Constituent Congress, which proclaimed the new liberal and federal republic under the Constitution of 1857.

The new constitution was expected to incorporate the "Juárez Law" of 1855, which abolished both military and ecclesiastical immunity and the special privileges that the Church had enjoyed since colonial times. The religious hierarchy knew that this would open the way to further State appropriation of Church wealth. In addition, they feared the spreading influence of liberal ideology, which emphasized individual rights and promoted lay attitudes, thereby diminishing ecclesiastical authority. In response, the Church lent its full institutional weight to the forces of reaction.

The civil war between liberals and conservatives resumed with great fury for two years, from 1858 to 1860. While the conservatives controlled Mexico City, liberal forces regrouped around Benito Juárez, a politician of impeccable reputation. As governor of Oaxaca, Juárez had demonstrated the ability to establish links with liberal groups around the country, most importantly with the liberal forces in Veracruz under the leadership of Miguel Lerdo de Tejada. Juárez had also demonstrated an admirable modesty and personal austerity in keeping with the ideals of republicanism. He was faithful to his liberal ideals, politically skillful, and an adept administrator. Even his bitterest enemies were forced to recognize his unusual and absolute incorruptibility. There was no question of Juárez's legitimacy as the leader of the new republican, liberal, and federalist Mexico.

Juárez understood how to delegate appropriate authority to the military, and he defined Mexico's foreign policy in collaboration with Melchor Ocampo, another great figure of Mexican liberalism. Official recognition by the United States came quickly, on April 6, 1859. The Reform Laws of the same year attracted the sympathies of nascent middle sectors in cities and towns. The concept of the lay State, and the principle of the separation of Church and State, were introduced. Specific laws established freedom of religion, the nationalization of Church properties, and the secularization of hospitals, charitable institutions, and cemeteries. The creation of the Civil Registry had an enormous impact. With this law, the maintenance of vital population statistics was removed from the purview of the Church and placed under the jurisdiction of the lay State. The Church had not adequately considered the consequences of its support of reactionary and unpopular forces on its attempt to shake off its subordination to civil authorities. The population reacted positively to the effective separation of Church and State, which freed rural areas and the poor in general from the fees imposed by parish priests for birth, baptism, marriage, and death ceremonies and documents. In addition, small plots of land owned by the parishes became available for purchase.

Juárez's personal prestige and the support for him from the military, the people, and different political groups led to the recovery of the capital and the installation of constitutionally mandated governmental bodies. What had not been anticipated, however, were the repercussions of the reforms on Mexico's international relations, beginning with the Vatican. This, along with political developments in Europe, provided the opportunity for a revival of Mexican conservatism in concert with powerful European counterparts. The spread of liberalism in Europe, which the Vatican associated with anticlericalism, and the revolutionary movements of 1848 had provoked a strong backlash, which strengthened the alliance of conservatives in Mexico with their counterparts in Europe.

On October 31, 1861, Britain, France, and Spain, with the indirect support of Austria and perhaps of the Vatican, agreed on a military intervention in Mexico. Their pretext was the liberal Mexican government's moratorium on debt payments. The European expeditionary force arrived on the Gulf coast of Mexico with two goals: to collect the debt and to establish a French protectorate in Mexico. The goal of France's Napoleon III was to form an empire in Mexico based on Latin and Catholic traditions that would serve as a barrier and counterweight to Anglo-American power in the Western Hemisphere. The French and their conservative Mexican collaborators chose the Austrian Archduke Maximilian as emperor of Mexico, which prompted Britain to withdraw from the alliance.

But first a combined force of French, English, Spanish, and Mexican troops invaded Mexican territory at Veracruz on December 17, 1861, advancing toward Orizaba. The English and Spanish contingents withdrew four months later, but Napoleon III considered the project viable nonetheless. He did not believe that the United States, then preoccupied with a civil war between its liberal North and slaveholding South, would intervene in support of Juárez's government.

On May 5, 1862, the eyes of the republican world were turned toward Mexico. In the words of French poet Victor Hugo, "The future of the Republic is being decided in Mexico." Republican troops commanded by Ignacio Zaragoza and Porfirio Díaz defeated the invaders in the Battle of Puebla. France immediately sent new commanders and thirty thousand reinforcements, taking Puebla and advancing toward the capital despite incessant guerrilla attacks. The liberal government of Juárez, with the fate of the republic on its shoulders, moved north to began a period of rule from the hinterland. The Second Empire was declared on June 12, 1862, to the jubilation of the Church and Mexican conservatives.

Maps 7.1 to 7.5 illustrate some of the aspects of this long period of war (1857–1866) between Mexican liberals and conservatives. Maps 7.1 and 7.2 portray the division of territory between 1857 and 1860. Map 7.3 shows the penetration of imperial armies in 1863–1865, and maps 7.4 and 7.5 delineate the principal republican enclaves under the presidency of Benito Juárez, and his retreat to Paso del Norte, now known as Ciudad Juárez.

Several forces combined to compel the withdrawal of the French

MAP 7.1. Territory under liberal control, 1857–1860. (Source: Enrique Florescano, coordinator, *Atlas Histórico de México, Cultura,* September/Siglo XXI [Mexico City: Editores, 1983], p. III.)

MAP 7.2. Territory under conservative control and the last pockets of resistance, 1857–1860. (Source: Enrique Florescano, *Atlas Histórico de México,* op. cit., p. III.)

MAP 7.3. Offensive movements of the invasion forces, 1863–1865. (Source: Enrique Florescano, *Atlas Histórico de México,* op. cit., p. III.)

MAP 7.4. Principal Mexican resistance groups, 1865–1866. (Source: Enrique Florescano, *Atlas Histórico de México,* op. cit., p. III.)

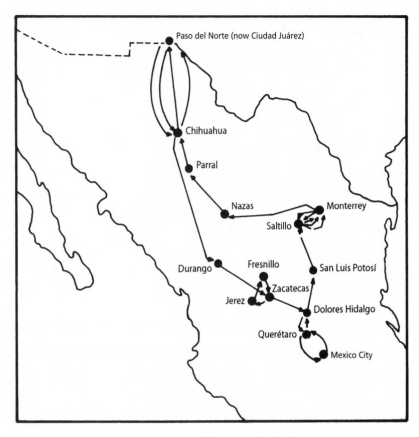

MAP 7.5. Juárez's movements, 1863–1866. (Source: Enrique Florescano, *Atlas Histórico de México,* op. cit., p. 113.)

troops, among them the resistance of the republican forces under Juárez, the efforts of guerrilla forces, and the open support of the United States. In 1866, after the end of the U.S. Civil War, fifty thousand battle-hardened U.S. troops were moved to the Texas-Mexico border on the Río Bravo, known in the United States as the Rio Grande. President Juárez returned to the capital, and the republican government was definitively reinstalled.

This synthesis of events calls for a certain amount of explanation. Map 7.3 shows the greatest extent of imperial control. Juárez commented that the imperial forces took advantage of the prestige associated with their novelty and also enjoyed the collaboration and good will of the clerical party, to whom the emperor was deeply indebted. In return for Vatican support, Maximilian promised to annul the Reform Laws, restore

Catholicism as the official religion of the empire, and return all responsibility for education to the Church. In fact, none of this came to pass, as Maximilian opted to establish instead a constitutional monarchy with a moderately liberal and religiously tolerant government.

Nevertheless, the empire was losing support in Mexico and in Europe, and the prestige of the liberal republicans grew as the effectiveness of their resistance increased. Public opinion in Europe and in the United States saw President Juárez as a noble and indomitable symbol of the anticolonial, republican, and liberal cause. Most importantly, the United States categorically rejected the presence of a French protectorate on its southern border.

Resistance was more intense and extensive than it appears in map 7.4. All across the country, the social mobilization that had first formed during the United States' invasion reached its greatest expression. It was a people's war, and the armed citizenry was decisive in the defeat of the imperial army. Constituted into National Guard units, they organized effective resistance in villages, towns, and cities.

The Republic Restored: Its Organization and Its Institutions

Calamities of all kinds assailed Mexico at midcentury, ranging from battles, wars, and political transformations to the collapse of institutions, the loss of the northern territories, the partial application of the Reform Laws, the nonenforcement of the Constitution of 1857, and occupation by wide-ranging foreign armies. More than two decades of violent conflict produced a clamoring for peace and order, and for the establishment of institutions that would prevent future internal war. The idea, and even the conviction, matured among Mexicans of all ethnicities and conditions that they constituted one nation and that it was imperative to reach a political consensus for national unification. This is not to say that there was complete accord, for varying interpretations of liberalism persisted. Those favoring a strong central authority did not disappear, nor did those who resisted change, but with the defeat of the monarchy the idea of the federal republic had definitively triumphed.

After two decades of fierce struggles, an entirely new phenomenon emerged: the idea of the nation as defined by the State's new political, social, and economic institutions. This concept put flesh on the liberalism and federal republicanism expressed in the 1857 Constitution.

The essential difference between the 1857 Constitution and those that had preceded it was that the former conformed to the fundamental liberal principle of the constitution as a programmatic text describing the direction to be taken by the nation-state. It was a flexible document, as all modern constitutions are, that defined the powers of each branch of government, assigned Congress a crucial role, and established limits to government power in order to protect the rights of the individual, whether Mexican or foreign. It provided mechanisms for constitutional change. The concept of individual rights was an essential component of the document, and these rights were spelled out for the first time. It was clearly stated that the economic, political, and social rights of all Mexican and foreign inhabitants of the republic were guaranteed. The protection of these rights was the basis and purpose of all social institutions, and governments should respect and sustain the guaranties expressed in this constitution.[1] The new constitutional framework required some fundamental changes, however. Equality before the law could be guaranteed only by granting citizenship to all. This would entail the right to vote and the right to political representation. The states would be deprived of the right to define citizenship based on residency in a particular jurisdiction, thus eliminating the category of citizen-*vecino* and establishing universal manhood suffrage, or voting rights for all males. As we shall see, the states resisted this change, which they considered a violation of their sovereignty. They took the position that the constitutional guarantees of freedom and equality before the law protected their own powers from federal intervention.

The Mexican State established under the 1857 Constitution was based on new principles. The sociopolitical system was opened to all, irrespective of ethnicity or origin, on the basis of merit, talent, and individual ability. The elimination of special privileges granted to corporations, and of privileges and immunities for the Church and the army, was an important first step toward channeling individual loyalties toward the secular State and weakening loyalties to mediating individuals and institutions such as the Church, local *caciques,* regional economic interests, and the military, all of which presented obstacles to the development of a national consciousness.

The speed with which President Juárez was able to reconstitute the republic can be explained only by the fact that relations between federal and

---

1. Further information is provided in Francisco Zarco, *Congreso Extraordinario Constituyente, 1856–1857* (Mexico City: El Colegio de México, 1957), and Richard N. Sinkin, *The Mexican Reform, 1855–1876: A Study in Liberal Nation-Building* (Austin: Institute of Latin American Studies, University of Texas at Austin, 1979).

state, as well as state and local, government institutions had been strengthened in the preceding years. Juárez's power as president from 1867 to 1872 stemmed from his capacity to establish political space in Congress for all the branches of liberalism without simply imposing his will. He learned to establish consensus among all the liberal factions represented in the body. This was fortunate, for the constitution had once more given the executive only limited official powers.

It should not be forgotten that there were no political parties in this period, just different political "clubs" that attracted the followers of liberals Juárez, Porfirio Díaz, or Sebastián Lerdo de Tejada. Each liberal faction had its own concept of how to exercise power and establish the foundations of State financial administration within the context of federalism. These factions were sustained by the electoral system, which had changed dramatically during the civil war. It was now based on the single-level indirect vote, which favored the election of individuals based on personal merit and leadership qualities. New leaders from among the commanders of the National Guard and from the world of elective politics arose to displace the traditional *caciques,* notables, and other elites. These men had distinguished themselves by their military exploits or by their ability to reconcile the different needs of states and municipalities and to maneuver them onto the federal agenda. Over the course of a few decades, wealth ceased to be a prerequisite to political office, and increased social mobility enabled new actors to play important roles on the national political scene.

Yet these changes were incomplete. A new leadership arose thanks to the electoral process, in particular the direct vote in the municipalities. But this leadership was still interwoven with the traditional structures of power composed of extended families, *compadrazgo* relationships, and shared interests and loyalties. The National Guard undoubtedly helped to reformulate political relations among different popular sectors, and between these sectors and traditional leaders. In the process, ties among municipalities grew stronger as well. Yet this is not to say that the new political class did not, like the more traditional players, develop arbitrary forms of exercising power.

Suffrage practices continued to evolve within states and local districts, and within their sphere of sovereignty the states retained the power to define the concept of citizenship. Nonetheless, the national mobilization had produced an expanded electorate. Between 800,000 and 1,000,000 voters went to the municipal polls in the 1856 congressional election. They chose a body of 10,420 primary electors, who selected 521 secondary electors, who were responsible for the final designation of congressional representatives. These data tell us that at the municipal level about 20 percent of the male population enjoyed political rights, which was high for the period compared to other countries. The numbers were similar in 1856, in the last doubly indirect electoral process.

The elimination of secondary electors in 1857 was another significant reform, establishing a once-removed (rather than twice-removed) indirect electoral process. This change was adopted unevenly among the states, though. Between 1860 and 1870, twenty-seven states promulgated new constitutions. Of these, thirteen introduced the direct popular vote for both legislative and executive offices. In four states, either the governor or the deputies were elected directly, and in ten the indirect vote was maintained across the board. These different forms of suffrage corresponded to the characteristics of the regions. The direct popular vote was instituted in the sparsely populated northern states of Coahuila, Chihuahua, Nuevo León, Sonora, Sinaloa, Durango, and Tamaulipas. But demography was not always the deciding factor. The direct vote also prevailed in central, Gulf Coast, and Pacific Coast states such as Jalisco, Guanajuato, Hidalgo, Guerrero, and Veracruz. Mixed direct and indirect voting systems were concentrated in the center and south, in states such as Zacatecas, San Luis Potosí, Colima, Querétaro, Morelos, Puebla, Oaxaca, Chiapas, Tabasco, and Yucatán.

The manner in which the different levels of government interacted, in keeping with the different voting systems, benefited local rather than national interests. This prevented provincial elites from adapting to the interests of the federation. The executive branch of the federal government took advantage of this situation to acquire extraordinary powers supposedly intended to provide the country with a more unified government.

The federal constitution had empowered Congress at the expense of the executive branch, an arrangement that kept the government off balance. Juárez and his successor, Lerdo de Tejada, were preoccupied with the need to establish a balance of powers between the branches, as were their ministers Matías Romero, Ignacio Vallarta, Guillermo Prieto, and José María Velasco. All agreed on the need for constitutional reforms in order to strengthen the hand of the executive branch by granting it veto power over congressional legislation, among other things, and by reestablishing the Senate. In addition, they wanted to give the federal government a role in the conducting of elections and to settle the struggle over the balance of federal and state sovereignty, which was essential in order to avoid the recurrent usurpation of state powers through federal intervention. The overwhelming power of Congress thus induced the executive branch to exercise insidious political tactics. Rather than be faced with a permanently confrontational Congress, the executive manipulated the electoral process, not by buying votes or stealing ballot boxes, but by controlling the selection of candidates to both houses of the legislature.

The Senate had been eliminated in 1857 but was reestablished in 1874, and with it the parity of state representation in one house of Congress. Prominent voices within liberal factions, in the press, among the public, and in Congress had favored this direct and equal representation of every state, in contrast to the situation in the Chamber of Deputies, where representation was proportional to population. The debates around constitutional reform and the reestablishment of the Senate shed light on the various interpretations of federalism and the political practices that were developing. It was argued that the excessive power of the Chamber of Deputies had stemmed from the elimination of the Senate, a move that had left the Chamber with no counterweight. By restoring the Senate, state representation at the federal level was recalibrated, with two senators from each state, while federal powers were augmented. If the branches of government in any state came into conflict with each other, the parties in dispute would petition the federal Senate to resolve the problem, which was within the scope of its new powers. The Senate would also collaborate with the president to name a provisional state governor in the eventuality that an intrastate conflict resulted in a vacuum of executive power. The Senate was additionally granted the authority to deploy National Guard units outside their state boundaries, and to place them under direct presidential command.

Some congressional voices were raised against increased federal powers and in favor of a more confederal arrangement. Nevertheless, the reforms quickly led to a lessening of the conflicts that had flared up repeatedly in the states between 1867 and 1874, a period that had seen twenty-four uprisings led by local *caudillos* and supported by one or another of the branches of state government. The new authority of the federal government to mediate conflicts, and the power of Congress to authorize military intervention, provided for an institutional response to such disputes.

The uprisings died down as tensions decreased between liberal military commanders and defeated conservatives. At the same time, however, some liberals felt marginalized and objected to Benito Juárez's reelection to the presidency. Under the leadership of General Porfirio Díaz, they attempted to seize power in 1871. The manifesto of their Plan de la Noria denounced the reelection and continued presidency of Juárez. The group lacked coherent leadership, and while the plan accurately identified some problems in legislative and judicial institutions, it was extemporaneous and inconsistent. The government of interim president Sebastián Lerdo de Tejada was able to crush the rebels before their movement could develop much momentum.

The 1876 Plan de Tuxtepec, also backed by General Porfirio Díaz and his Army of Regeneration, came at a more propitious moment and met with success. Juárez had passed away four years earlier. This time Díaz was able to solidify his *pronunciamiento* around the principles of no reelection, limits to state and federal executive powers, and guarantees of municipal autonomy. Díaz had enjoyed considerable prestige as a victorious liberal officer in the anti-French war, and he maintained connections with municipal authorities, political bosses, and the upper and middle officer corps around the country. These groups made up the foundation of his movement. Díaz's military exploits led to his triumph in the presidential election of 1877, when he attracted an absolute majority of the votes. This pointed to the participation of midlevel functionaries in the political process and the strength of thousands of electors who represented the interests of districts and municipalities. With his accession to the presidency now legitimized by an electoral victory, two of Díaz's primary political objectives were to make peace with the other existing factions and to attract the support of interim president Lerdo's following. Thus he decided to respect the freedom of his opponents. In 1878, the constitution was amended by Congress in order to eliminate the possibility of reelection, a change that would stimulate political mobility at all levels.

The national climate of reconciliation never extended to a general agreement over the future of the presidency. Nevertheless, it was constructive. Discontented military commanders were placated without recourse to violence, and the alternation in office of different power groups in the states brought a measure of stability. Federal intervention in electoral matters decreased. This is not to say that opposition ceased to exist. On the contrary, political factions were energized and engaged in strongly contested electoral contests in some states, such as Coahuila, Nuevo León, Jalisco, and Tabasco. In these cases, the central government intervened to balance factional interests. For example, Porfirio Díaz dispatched General Bernardo Reyes to reestablish political equilibrium in the northeastern states of Coahuila and Nuevo León. The important thing about this new kind of intervention was that for the first time, the federal government had placed itself above the fray among the contending political factions in state-based disputes and exerted an authority of its own.

Administrative Organization

The republican administration required institutional means to exercise State functions, to establish a national treasury, and to implement State reforms. Institutional structures were also needed to strengthen the judiciary and guarantee commercial, financial, and mining rights, as well as individual property and constitutional rights. These goals were accomplished within the flexible programmatic guidelines of the 1857 Constitution. The new government replaced the colonial-era legal code with a new set of laws that made it possible to implement constitutional guarantees.

Finally stable enough to serve out their legal terms, the republican governments laid the foundations of the new Mexican State. Never before had a government of independent Mexico enjoyed the prerequisite conditions for such a huge and ambitious project. They needed to construct a solid financial basis for governance on the federal level that would not compromise the individual states' finances or autonomy. It was important not to depress foreign trade and not to endanger the well-being of the citizenry through arbitrary or excessive taxation.

The architect of the new Treasury Department and of the federal budget was the treasury secretary, Matías Romero. Ignacio Manuel Altamirano summed up the importance of these matters to a generation of liberals: "Without a treasury there is no government; without taxes there is no treasury; without the rule of law there is no obligation to pay taxes. Thus without a legislated financial framework there is no possible organization of the Nation."[2]

Figure 7.1 illustrates the success of the new financial policies. The deficit was eliminated, while spending and investment grew. Federal revenues increased overall, as a tax on consumption compensated for reduced taxes on foreign trade, freeing the treasury from its dependence on international commerce.

Treasury Secretary Matías Romero not only designed the new finan-

2. Ignacio Manuel Altamirano, "La Votación de los Presupuestos," in *Obras Completas* (Mexico City: Conaculta, 1989), vol. 19, p. 99, cited in Marcello Carmagnani, *Estado y Mercado: La Economía Pública del Liberalismo Mexicano, 1850–1911* (Mexico City: Fideicomiso Historia de las Américas—El Colegio de México—Fondo de Cultura Económica, 1994), p. 37.

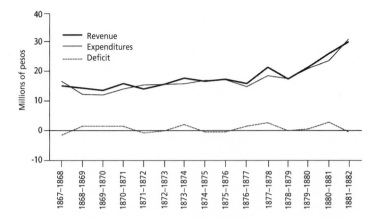

FIGURE 7.1. Federal revenues and expenditures, 1867–1868 to 1881–1882, in millions of pesos. (Source: Marcello Carmagnani, *Estado y Mercado: La Economía Pública del Liberalismo Mexicano, 1850–1911* [Mexico City: Fideicomiso Historia de las Américas—El Colegio de México—Fondo de Cultura Económica, 1994], p. 198.)

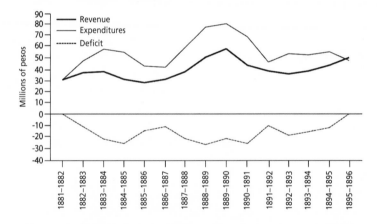

FIGURE 7.2. Federal revenues and expenditures, 1881–1882 to 1895–1896, in millions of pesos. (Source: Marcello Carmagnani, *Estado y Mercado: La Economía Pública del Liberalismo Mexicano, 1850–1911,* op. cit., p. 237.)

cial regime but skillfully managed its performance as well, achieving previously unimaginable budgetary goals. For example, between 1867–1868 and 1881–1882, federal spending rose at an annual rate of 3.5 percent, and spending on education and services such as mail, telegraphy, ports, and roads grew two to five times as fast as spending overall. Romero also reduced the public debt from 142 to 127 million pesos, which gave Mexico domestic and international financial credibility for the first time.

The first blow to federal finances came in 1883–1884, as illustrated in figure 7.2. Mexico ran continuous budget deficits in the fourteen years between 1881–1882 and 1895–1896. The deficit was not fully eliminated until the end of the century, when the domestic and foreign public debt was consolidated and reduced from 181 to 134 million pesos. The measures adopted at that time attracted new investment from the United States and Europe and allowed for the immediate availability of new loans.

Nevertheless, Mexico's financial credibility was solid throughout the period, even during the deficit years. High government spending sustained the first significant wave of foreign investment—in railway construction—without the need to cut spending on education or urban social services. The continuity of Mexico's financial policies was a positive factor between 1867 and 1890. Military spending was held constant at 10 million pesos annually throughout Juárez's presidency and in the first period of the Porfiriato. Expenditures on domestic programs, on the other hand, quadrupled from 2.5 to 10 million pesos between 1877 and 1892 alone.

The nascent middle class prospered under these policies, as did the civil administration and private businesses, including the transportation sector. Federal funds flowed to the states. The central administration established a public presence through the provision of services and the opening of government offices, making federalism visible. This combination of factors gave birth to what was celebrated as "organic peace," the new ideology of political harmony.

The governments of Juárez and Lerdo de Tejada (1860–1870) are notable for having resolved the persistent conflicts between Congress and the executive branch, and between the federal government and the states. The next decade, the 1870s, was a period of institutionalization. The constitution was put into practice through the passage of legislation such as the 1870 Civil Code, initially applicable only to the Federal District (Mexico City) and the territories, but adopted ten years later by all the states as federal law. Property rights were concretized in the 1880s, for example, with the transfer of untitled lands to private owners, as originally prescribed by law in 1863. The Code of Business Procedures was passed in 1883, implementing the constitutional guarantee of free trade, and the Code of Civil Procedures was approved in 1884. In 1887, the Mining Code established regulations for that industry. The governments of Díaz and González reaped the benefits of the political efforts made by Juárez and Lerdo de Tejada between 1867 and 1876.

The Reestablishment of International Relations

The victory of the Mexican republic over the empire had international repercussions that benefited other Latin American countries. All of them, Mexico included, had participated in only a limited and conditional way in the international arena since their independence. The European monarchies had refused to grant Mexico official recognition, which would have acknowledged the country's unconditional sovereignty, regardless of its form of government. Mexico's international image improved with the 1857 Constitution, which established equality before the law to all its inhabitants, foreign nationals included. The codification of business and mining rights also created a new framework for international business relations.

The decision of the Mexican government to execute Archduke Maximilian, despite significant pressure not to do so, was well received by European proponents of republicanism and democracy. It was a clear expression of Mexico's diplomatic posture that no further aggression would be tolerated. To reinforce this position, Mexico demanded that all countries that had recognized Maximilian's empire, including France, should petition the legitimate government for a renewal of diplomatic relations. The new republic also renounced all the limited friendship and trade agreements previously signed with the European powers. Any future relations would require the formal recognition of Mexico as a fully sovereign nation and the recognition of its republican government.

With the restoration of the republic, this new international doctrine was immediately put into practice, despite an unfavorable international context in which stronger states often resorted to force on the basis of financial claims. The European powers were also engaged in a new wave of colonialism, seeking to assure themselves access to foreign markets and investment opportunities. At the Berlin Conference (1884–1885), Africa had been divided among not only the leading European nations of France, England, Spain, and Portugal but also the emerging nations of Germany and Italy. Russia and other powers struggled over Eastern Europe and Central Asia. The Western powers scrambled for trade concessions and the control of territories in East Asia, Southeast Asia, and India. The international system was undergoing a dramatic realignment along with the new expansion of the industrial powers. Under these circumstances, the Mexican government renounced all foreign debts acquired by Maximilian's empire and made it clear that the reestablishment of foreign relations would be conditional upon the renegotiation of only those debts incurred by the first republic at the beginning of the nineteenth century.

The first European countries to sign trade and friendship treaties with Mexico under the new terms were the newly emerging midsized industrial powers, Germany and Italy, reluctantly followed by Spain and Britain. A treaty with the French republic was signed in 1880, after France renounced all financial claims against Mexico.

A renewal of relations with Britain was more difficult for various reasons. English bankers had extended loans to Maximilian's empire and also had outstanding loans dating from 1824 and 1825, during the first republic. But a treaty was signed with Britain in 1884, opening the door to debt renegotiation and new credits in 1885. With these accomplishments, the governments of Manuel González, and of Porfirio Díaz in his second term, were able to take full advantage of the international context in Europe and the Americas.

A Growing Society, a New Economy, a Strong State

Any consolidation of a federated, internationally recognized nation-state must be examined in the context of the relationship between its federal government, its states, and its population. As of the 1870s the relationship between the Mexican government and the people was improving, despite the slow pace of social change and scant improvements in living standards. The federal justice system, including the Supreme Court, was gaining in efficiency, providing an alternative to the state courts, which were considered by many to be unacceptably arbitrary. Many factors contributed to improved relations between the government and society, including new guarantees on property rights, the reduced regulation of business activity, new technologies such as rail transportation, and the first appearance of a domestic financial system. Business prosperity enabled economic actors to diversify and move beyond the limitations of mere subsistence activity outside the cash economy.

We can indirectly draw some conclusions about social change on the basis of various figures available to us. The population grew from an estimated 7.5 to 9 million between 1850 and 1869, despite the civil war, reaching 11.5 million by 1890. The 1890 figure is the most reliable, and that for 1850 is the shakiest. Even so, we can estimate an annual growth rate close to 1 percent, about double that of the first republic. Ongoing demographic dispersion was notable, especially in the sparsely populated northern states. Between 1857 and 1877, the number of *pueblos* grew from 4,709 to 5,052; medium-sized cities increased from 193 to 374, and the number of major cities grew to 57. It seems that the number of ranches and *haciendas* remained relatively stable. However, by 1877 the number of unincorporated settlements with populations under five thousand had grown to 27,899. Sixty percent of the people now lived in these new population centers near railway construction or mining districts, close to cities and villages, or at new town sites. These new settlement patterns reflected the new ways that people lived and worked.

The economic data do not support the image of a socially stagnant Mexico. The estimated gross domestic product grew substantially, although it is not clear if the figures represent only market commodities or also include products intended for self-consumption. According to estimates, the GDP increased from 326 million to 456 million pesos (at their 1900 value) between 1845 and 1877, showing its strongest growth between 1860 and 1877, when it increased from 315 to 456 million (1900) pesos.

The relation between population growth, new demographic patterns, and economic expansion may be explained by the fact that subsistence economic activity began to expand and become integrated into the market under the second republic. Between 1850 and 1870, imports were valued at 25 million to 27 million pesos annually, while exports grew from 12 million to 28 million pesos. Figures for 1877 to 1890 are more reliable. Imports grew from 30 million to 93 million pesos, and exports grew from 33 million to 91 million pesos. These estimates indicate that Mexico achieved balanced trade in this period. Thus the country was able to reduce the export of silver coinage as a compensation for a negative balance of trade, and it became possible to increase the supply of currency in circulation, overcoming what had been a persistent weakness in the domestic cash supply.

Exports also became more diversified. Between 1885 and 1890, precious metals, silver in particular, represented 60 percent of total exports, agricultural products making up the remaining 40 percent. The first signs of change in the character of imports appeared during this time. One-third of the total came in the form of machinery, iron, steel, tin, lead, yarns, and other products—the raw and intermediate materials necessary for domestic manufacturing.

These changes were the positive results of business deregulation and newly defined property and mining rights, all of which facilitated corporate transactions and land transfers, as well as the sale of unused public lands called *baldíos*. Mineral rights, considered a part of the national patrimony under colonial era legislation, were now made commercially available. With these changes, owners of small-, medium-, and large-sized landholdings began to invest in new properties and explore the income-producing potential of open lands and mineral deposits.

Dramatic changes became possible following the implementation of the 1856 Lerdo Law, which nationalized the properties of ecclesiastical and public corporations, and the 1863 Ley de Baldíos (Law on the Occupation and Transfer of Public Lands). The first law established the sale of ecclesiastic properties and corporative property to private parties at values calculated on the basis of their income-producing potential. The law covered the property of all Church-based and public corporations, including those of religious orders and congregations, bishoprics, parishes, *cofradías,* and brotherhoods, as well as *ayuntamientos,* towns, and Church school properties. The Ley de Baldíos established norms for the sale of lands unoccupied and untitled, and therefore in the federal public domain, to private owners. The law authorized the Treasury Department to negotiate prices on these lands and established reduced prices for buyers already in uncontested possession of the property in question.

These laws were harshly criticized by their detractors, who argued that they favored large-property owners and the holders of great fortunes. But these critics did not take into consideration that owners of small- and medium-sized rural and urban property also prospered under the new rules. The data are difficult to interpret because they do not account for everything that was sold. With regard to Church property, for example—said to have been worth fifty million pesos at the time—we have records of only those sales recorded by public deed, which was required for any transaction over ten thousand pesos, an enormous sum in those days. The Church properties sold under public deed were valued at a total of twenty-three million pesos, which leads us to think that many of them fell into the hands of the rich, both old and new; others were bought as *condueñazgos,* which are joint property owners' associations, and the remainder went to small- and medium-scale buyers. In previous works I have described how the government sold properties valued at two hundred pesos or less to private parties, free of taxes or title fees. These buyers would preferably have been the tenants of the property in question, and the sale would proceed as long as the district political authority known as the prefect approved the transaction.

It has also been said that the disentailment law of 1856 and similar laws in following years were contrary to the tradition of collective and indivisible community property, leading various *pueblos* to repudiate their implementation. While acknowledging the idealistic objections of disen-

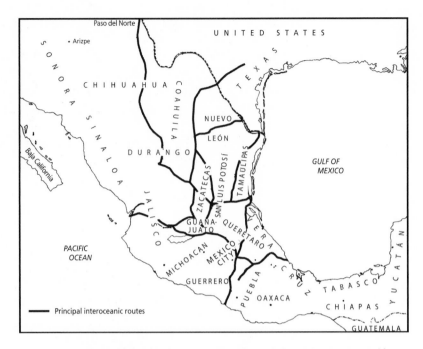

MAP 7.6. Roads and other land routes, 1853. (Source: Juan Nepomuceno Almonte, *Guía de Forasteros y Repertorio de Conocimientos Útiles* [Mexico City: Imprenta de I. Cumplido, 1852], Facsimile Collection, Instituto Mora, pp. iv–v.)

tailment's critics, who opposed it in all good faith, it must be said that these critics conceived of "the people" in an overly monolithic sense. In fact, internal social differentiation was already pronounced and had been so for quite some time. While liberal legislation did strengthen the hand of large-property owners, it also created conditions that encouraged small- and medium-sized individual holdings.

Regulatory mechanisms were established six months after the passage of the 1856 disentailment law. They illustrate the benefits to small- and medium-sized property. The law established that renters would have the first right to retain lands in the form of private property, and that unrented lands and lands forsworn by their renters would revert to the *ayuntamiento* for auction. These properties were usually valued at under two hundred pesos. Their values were determined on the basis of the rent being paid for them either in cash or in the estimated cash equivalent of goods or personal services provided as rent. Thus the privatization regime benefited those who worked the land, including those who farmed small rented plots.

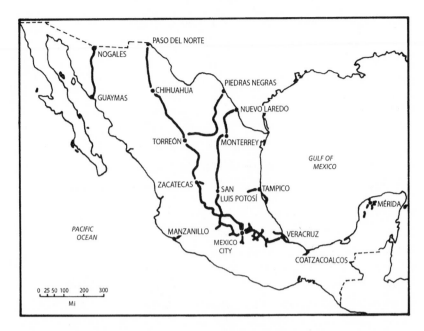

MAP 7.7. Railroad lines, 1884. (Source: Francisco Calderón, "Los Ferrocarri-
les," in Daniel Cosío Villegas, ed., *Historia Moderna de México,* vol. 7, part I
[Mexico City: Hermes, 1965], pp. 540–41.)

Because the law empowered district prefects to grant titles or register
properties but did not mandate formal procedures, much of the movement of land into the hands of holders of small- and medium-sized plots
was accomplished without the benefit of careful record-keeping. Let us
look at a representative example. In 1856, Mexico was the largest and most
populous state in the republic, home to 30 percent of the total population.
In addition to today's state of Mexico, it included today's states of Morelos, Hidalgo, and part of Guerrero. In 1856 and 1857, ownership of half of
the collective properties belonging to the state's communities were transferred to their tenants, while half remained in the hands of the *ayuntamientos.* Of the latter, 60 percent were made available to renters of
small- and medium-sized plots, while 40 percent were divided among the
community's Indigenous inhabitants and resident citizens. Similar disentailment of lands in favor of those holding small- and medium-sized
plots took place in the states of Puebla, Michoacán, Querétaro, Veracruz,
Zacatecas, and Yucatán. The government promoted the transfer of municipal and community lands into private hands in an attempt to end in-

stability around the land question. The security provided to landowners through the titling process was enhanced by the amended Constitution of 1879, which prohibited state occupation of land without consent, and only by means of eminent domain and the previous indemnification of the owner. Landowners were additionally protected from legal challenges to their titles by public or ecclesiastic corporations.

The law on untitled public lands had beneficial effects similar to the effects of the law on disentailment, helping to create a rural sector open to the cash economy and the market. While only 600,000 hectares were bought and occupied by new owners in 1867–1877, 15 *million* hectares of public land were sold to 5,266 people in 1878–1890. Of these 15 million hectares, 6 million were productive lands already in the hands of private parties, who simply went through the titling process in order to formalize possession.

The figures and their interpretation outlined above lead us to the conclusion that in the process of property transfers, a portion of the available productive resources came into the hands of a new social sector. Ranchers, owners of small and large holdings, and *hacendados* invested in new land for productive and commercial purposes once their property rights were guaranteed. But the transfer of agricultural and mineral resources to new sectors more intimately associated with production and commerce would not have produced nearly so much wealth had it not been for the transportation and communications revolution that had begun in the 1870s. The main regional economies within Mexico were integrated into the national economy by means of the railroad, the telegraph, and maritime transport.

Maps 7.6 and 7.7 illustrate the scale of change brought about by railway construction in a single generation. When the 355-mile Mexican Railroad between Mexico City and the port of Veracruz was inaugurated in 1873, sixty million pesos had been invested in its construction by the states through which it passed. By 1880, the rail network had expanded to 621 miles, and 5,282 more miles of track would be laid in the following decade (see map 7.7). Between 1873 and 1890, total freight carried by rail grew from 165,000 to 2.75 million tons yearly. Nearly 27,000 miles of telegraph wire were strung by 1890, including 21,750 miles along federal, state, and private railway lines, and 5,128 miles along independent rights-of-way.

The railroad, telegraph, and telephone all shrank time and distance, so that people, goods, and ideas circulated much more freely than before. Maritime connections improved dramatically, and with the technological advances in ship construction, the introduction of the internal combustion engine, and the reduced costs these developments offered, Mexico became more integrated into world markets. As late as 1870, Mexico had needed to subsidize the port calls of foreign merchant ships in order to attract them to its shores. Two decades later, British, French, German, U.S., and domestic vessels were regularly docking at Mexico's Pacific and Gulf Coast ports.

CHAPTER 8

The Decline of the Liberal Order

Chapter 7 was concerned with the construction of a new order and the consolidation of the republic. I described how the idea of a Mexican national State gained acceptance, with an emphasis on the process leading to establishment of citizenship rights without distinction by ethnicity or social position and on the meaning of political representation in the process of national consolidation. This chapter describes the historical period traditionally known as the Porfiriato, acknowledging the repeated re-election of President Porfirio Díaz, from the constitutional reform of 1887 to his resignation in 1911.

The importance that has been accorded to the figure of Díaz and his authoritarian style of governance has overshadowed other historical points that I will try to rescue here, as I believe they can help clarify the nature of the period. In chapter 7, we saw how in the nineteenth century the consolidated Mexican nation and State were able to integrate themselves diplomatically and commercially into the Atlantic world. When the Mexican revolution exploded onto the stage in 1910, however, it revealed a country deeply divided by social class. In addition, the Mexican economy was moving toward or beginning to operate in the context of a national market, which made it more vulnerable to international economic fluctuations. Political conditions threatened to erode regional autonomy and to undermine the very bases of the liberal and federal system. How and why had Mexico come to such a pass?

A Society in Transition

Seen through modern eyes, Mexican society of the late nineteenth and early twentieth centuries seems highly self-contradictory. We see traditional social forms based on the hierarchical ideology of earlier times, especially in those areas more removed from the market economy, from commercial routes, and from railroad transportation. In other areas, we see a society in keeping with the times and organized by economic class around specialized forms of productive activities where the market economy prospered, such as mining, manufacturing, and export agriculture. All were tied to the market and to the needs of the cities, where the wealthy population dressed, behaved, and consumed in the European style.

The new society, while maintaining certain archaic traditions such as arbitrary local rule by *caciques,* also had new forms of social organization. There were middle-class liberal clubs opposed to the regime; the so-called socialist and anarchist organizations of the nascent working class; mutual aid and Catholic societies; and artisans, family workshops, and manufacturing guilds. In general, society was secular and placed more importance on the individual and individual rights of expression and organization than before. Modernity had not been imposed by the State, yet it was by no means a fiction, as one historian has called it. Modernity was constructed through the efforts of many social actors, including those who risked their fortunes to migrate to new zones that offered economic opportunities on a national and international scale. It was in this period that modernization produced new disparities and a new kind of poverty appeared. The fruits of the new economy were distributed very unequally, and peasant society was uprooted in the process.

Social inequality was more a function of class, and thus of work and production, than of the urban-rural distinction. In 1890, the total population was estimated at 11.5 million and the annual population growth rate exceeded 1 percent for the first time. At that rate, the population would double every thirty years. This higher rate of growth can be attributed to improved public health, which, along with education, was the highest priority of federal, state, and municipal governments. The separation of Church and State also led to the availability of more reliable population data through civil registries.

Between 1890 and 1910, 60 percent or more of the economically active population was engaged in agriculture. Internal migration increased the population of agriculturally modernizing areas in the north, such as

Coahuila, Chihuahua, Durango, Nuevo León, and Tamaulipas. The number of wage earners grew by 38 percent in these states—almost double the national average of 20.6 percent. In contrast, the wage-earning population grew by only 9 percent in the agricultural regions of central Mexico—less than half the national average. Employment in manufacturing and services grew even more in 1895–1900, although its growth slowed in 1900–1910. Manufacturing employed 5.4 percent of the economically active population, a proportion that grew rapidly in the northern states of Coahuila and Nuevo León, and in Veracruz, Puebla, and the Federal District. In these last three areas, manufacturing continued an expansion that had begun in the 1850s. As trade was liberalized, the north took the lead and the three traditional areas in the center also regained their status as industrial leaders.

In table 8.1 and figure 8.1, we can see the growth of the service industries, which benefited the middle-income sectors, providing private-sector employment to teachers and other professionals, a group that grew at an impressive rate of 9.1 percent annually. People employed in what we now consider middle-class occupations and the modern working class were new social groups that would play key roles in the evolution of the country in the two decades between 1890 and 1910.

At the same time, limits were placed on the number of army officers and troops in keeping with the political master plan of the Díaz government. Past experience had shown that direct challenges to U.S. power were unproductive, so a military buildup was a strategically futile form of resistance. In order to avoid domination by any one power, Mexico maintained a broad base of international investors (British, German, French, and the United States). In contrast to some other Latin American countries, Mexico has kept military forces small and expenditures low since this period and up to the present day. Surprising as it may seem, this was the Porfirian policy from the very beginning in 1896, when 20.7 percent of the regular army officer corps and 76.5 percent of the auxiliary army officers corps were moved to the reserve or put on leave. Between 1884 and 1910, the strength of the armed forces was reduced by 25 percent. Even in the midst of civil war in 1910, the aging president resigned rather than expand the military.

Social Mobility:
The New Characteristics

The structure of the workforce and occupational mobility at the end of the nineteenth century were quite different from the internal migration

Its Sectoral Evolution from 1895 to 1910 in Thousands and in Percentages

	1895		1900		1910		Annual Growth Rate (%)		
	Number	%	Number	%	Number	%	1895–1900	1900–1910	Overall (1895–1910)
Total population	12,632.4	—	13,607.3	—	15,160.4	—	1.5	1.1	1.2
Labor force:	4,441.9	100.0	4,819.2	100.0	5,272.1	100.0	1.6	0.9	1.2
Agricultural sector	2,977.8	67.0	3,182.6	66.0	3,592.1	68.1	1.3	1.2	1.2
Industrial and artisanal:	691.1	15.5	798.5	16.6	795.4	15.1	2.9	-0.1	0.9
Extractive	88.5	2.0	107.3	2.2	104.1	2.0	3.9	-0.1	1.1
Manufacture	553.0	12.4	619.3	12.9	606.0	11.5	2.3	-0.2	0.6
Construction	49.6	1.2	63.0	1.3	74.7	1.4	4.9	1.7	3.0
Energy	n/a[a]	n/a	8.9	0.2	10.6	0.2	n/a	1.8	1.8
Services:	773.0	17.4	838.1	17.4	884.6	16.8	1.6	0.5	0.9
Commerce	249.6	5.6	261.5	5.4	293.8	5.6	0.9	1.2	1.1
Transport	55.7	1.3	59.7	1.2	55.1	1.0	1.4	-0.8	-0.1
Technical and professional:	99.5	2.2	121.7	2.5	125.6	2.3	4.4	0.3	1.7
Medical doctors	2.2	0.04	2.6	0.05	3.0	0.05	3.6	1.5	2.4
Attorneys	3.3	0.07	3.6	0.07	3.9	0.07	1.8	0.8	1.2
Private office and clerical employees	22.7	0.5	33.9	0.7	83.4	1.6	8.4	9.4	9.1
Public office and clerical employees	26.3	0.6	25.2	0.5	27.7	0.5	0.1	0.9	0.3
Schoolteachers[b]	12.7	0.2	15.5	0.3	21.0	0.4	4.4	3.5	4.3
Armed forces	33.2	0.7	38.6	0.8	36.7	0.7	2.2	-0.5	0.7
Household employees	273.3	6.2	282.0	5.9	241.3	4.6	0.6	-1.5	-0.9

[a] n/a = Not applicable; there was no energy industry before 1900.

[b] The teachers classified as technical workers by Rosenzweig have been extracted from that category, since some were public employees and others were private.

SOURCES: This table reflects information found in *Estadísticas Económicas del Porfiriato* (Mexico City: El Colegio de México, 1960), pp. 38–66; Fernando Rosenzweig, *El Desarrollo Económico de México, 1800–1910* (Toluca: El Colegio Mexiquense, 1989), p. 236; and Donald B. Keesing, "Structural Change Early in Development: Mexico's Changing Industrial and Occupational Structure from 1895 to 1950," *Journal of Economic History* 34.4 (December 1969): 716–38.

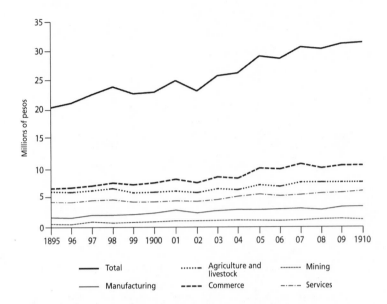

FIGURE 8.1. Gross domestic product, 1895–1910, in millions of 1960 pesos. (Source: Bank of Mexico, *Indicadores Económicos: Monetarios, Financieros y de Finanzas Públicas* [Mexico City: Banco de México, 1991].)

and population changes at the end of the colonial period. People were moving from the south, primarily from Chiapas, Yucatán, Oaxaca, and Michoacán, to central and northern Mexico and the Gulf states, in particular to Veracruz. These were the states where new industries were developing and job opportunities were available. This migration is evidence of significant ruptures and changes, such as the breaking of traditional community ties and the weakening of social domination through traditional mechanisms such as debt peonage and personal tribute—practices that prevailed in certain states in spite of their illegality. The migration speaks to the formation of a national labor market and of structures that freed individuals from coercive relations of usury, forced labor, and exploitative sharecropping and tenant farming practices.

New work opportunities mobilized enormous numbers of people, who then relayed information to their home areas about salaries, working conditions, and the cost of living in their new locations. The tendency was to liberalize labor contracting and to monetize salaries, to construct a free labor market based on supply and demand. Migrants quickly established what we call migratory chains: the first to leave a *pueblo* would later send word to others back home, "pulling" his relatives and friends after him, perhaps even financing their journey to the region where he had found work.

The new social mobility is primarily measured by examining occupational categories, economic class, and wealth. By *social mobility*, we refer to changes in the occupational level of individuals and in their family income. The particular geographic location where this occurred is significant. Map 8.1 illustrates the location and growth of settlements of five thousand or more people, the minimum number then required for a settlement to be considered a city. The role of these small cities was to regulate and provide marketing infrastructure and other services to surrounding agricultural, mining, and manufacturing activities. Those that grew and successfully mediated social and economic relations came to serve as seats of municipal government.

A few examples of cities that were established and flourished within the span of a single decade are Torreón, in Coahuila, in 1895; Gómez Palacio, in Durango, just across the river from Torreón, in 1900; Dinamita, in Durango, founded in 1903; Ensenada, in Baja California; and Cananea, in Sonora, as of 1900. The growth of such new urban centers was a significant phenomenon, mostly due to the new railroad system that linked these productive centers to national and international markets.[1] Their total population came to more than two million, or 14.5 percent of the national total. This was an impressive development in what was still considered a rural country. We can see on map 8.1 that the new urban centers ranged from the north to the center and from the center to both coasts, counterbalancing the traditional power of the Mexico City–Veracruz axis.

Up to this point, the reader might suppose that the growth of small population centers of more or less five thousand people was the motor that drove social transformation. In fact, the most rapid growth occurred in urban centers with populations of over 20,000. In 1900, there were seventeen such cities, with a total population of a little over 500,000. By 1910, there were twenty-two of them, with a total population of 700,000—an increase from 3.8 percent to 4.7 percent of the total population. At the other extreme were old as well as new towns and settlements of under 2,500 people. These communities numbered 53,252 in 1900, and 70,342 in 1910—an increase of 32 percent in a period when the population itself grew by only 15 percent. If we break down these data,

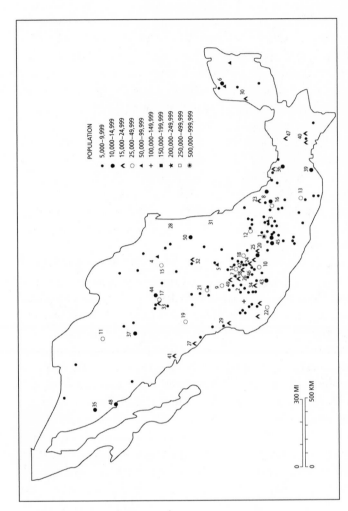

MAP 8.1. Population distribution in concentrations of over five thousand inhabitants, 1910. Cities and towns are numbered in terms of size, with 1 being the largest. (Source: Dirección General de Estadística, *Tercer Censo General de Población*, 1910; François-Xavier Guerra, *México: Del Antiguo Régimen a la Revolución*, vol. 1 [Mexico City: Fondo de Cultura Económica, 1988], p. 349.)

however, we see that there were not many new *pueblos*. In 1900 there were 5,010, and in 1910, 5,042—just thirty-two more. On the other hand, informal settlements with no legal status grew up around farms, cattle ranches, villages, industrial and mining centers, construction sites, and railway stations. While their number decreased from 8,011 in 1900 to 7,070 in 1910, they may have accounted for 20 percent of the total population. Unlike the established *pueblos,* these settlements had no municipal administrations and lacked most public services. They were mostly located in central Mexico: in Puebla, Hidalgo, the state of Mexico, Veracruz, and Yucatán. Many of these states were on the receiving end of labor migration from less prosperous regions.

The informal settlements were important because they reflected one of the many obstacles that the force of social change was bumping up against at the beginning of the twentieth century. People living in settlements along railroad lines, in mining centers, and on *haciendas* and ranches probably demanded better living conditions, regular salaries, and payment in cash, as well as new social organizations. Had they obtained some of these demands, they could have become a kind of transmission belt of modernity from urban to rural Mexico. But municipal bosses and district political prefects resisted granting them official town status, with the corresponding schools, services, and self-government.

In addition to the demographic dynamism, education no doubt played an important role in the spread of the Spanish language and the shaping of new generations of Mexicans. The number of primary schools increased from 9,200 in 1878 to 12,010 in 1900, 12,310 in 1907, and 12,510 in 1910. The number of students increased even more impressively, from 227,000 in 1878, to 821,000 in 1907, and 901,000 in 1910.

The number of students enrolled in public schools more than tripled between 1878 and 1910, from 204,000 to 733,000. Private schools educated 23,000 students in 1878 and 168,000 in 1910. The successful spread of primary education can be gauged by the fact that of the 2.1 million children between the ages of six and ten in 1910, 42 percent were attending school. Between 1895 and 1910, the literacy rate increased from 14 percent to 19.7 percent of the total population. The political leadership and other social sectors understood that an educated population was the prerequisite to all progress, and education expenditures were increased at the federal, state, and municipal levels. Benito Juárez, in his day, had proposed mass education as a liberal ideal, and it was now taken up in earnest, with the knowledge that only the provision and the defense of education could produce the necessary consciousness and will to construct a liberal social

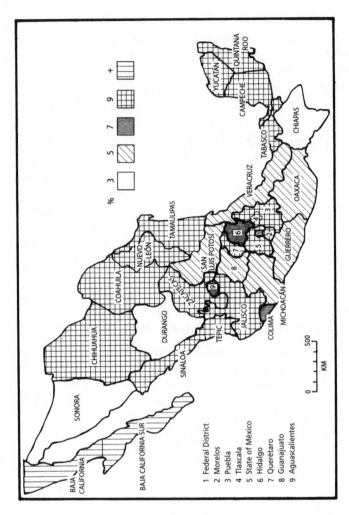

MAP 8.2. School enrollment (at all educational levels) as a percentage of the general population, 1910. (Source: Moisés González Navarro, *Estadísticas Sociales del Porfiriato, 1877–1910* [Mexico City: El Colegio de México, 1960], pp. 233–34.)

order. Unlike in some other countries, though, the development of education was deficient when it came to secondary and technical schools, which were still limited in number. Nevertheless, the National School of Engineering graduated a total of 444 engineers between 1876 and 1910.

Public education was the greatest promoter of the secular and republican values that were driving social change. The spread of these values was slow, but by the beginning of the twentieth century, large sectors of Mexican society were secularized. The process had begun in earnest when the republic under Juárez made the separation of Church and State a reality, and it had deepened through a century of educational efforts.

The diffusion of secular values was important because they encouraged individuals to conceive of the world as a set of material circumstances that can be modified through the exercise of free will. With this worldview, the social actor was inclined to actively forge his or her own destiny rather than passively wait for other forces to define what was possible. It ushered in a new era in which merit, ability, and intelligence became the building blocks of social mobility.

International Economic Growth

The Porfiriato is said to have been distinguished by economic growth and the rigidity of its political system, and its economic growth is attributed to the success of the export sector, from which a small nucleus of powerful producers, investors, and speculators reaped enormous returns. But Mexican economic performance during that time was less spectacular than all that. While open and modern behavior on the part of social actors was responsible for the demographic and social dynamism described in the preceding sections, the same cannot always be said of the country's principal economic groups.

Table 8.2 compares the economic performance of Mexico with that of four other countries. Notably, Mexico's per capita income in 1870 was 2.5 times lower than that of the United States and 3.5 times lower than that of Great Britain, and not much more than half that of Argentina. The data also indicate that Mexico's growth rate was far from outstanding compared with the growth rate of a similar economy such as that of Argentina, yet it was higher than Brazil's. In Mexico, per capita income increased rapidly, over 2 percent annually, between 1870 and 1900, but growth slowed to 1.7 percent after 1900.

Unlike in the period between 1820 and 1870, the international econ-

TABLE 8.2. Mexican Economic Growth in a Comparative Context, 1870–1913
(Per Capita GDP in 1990 U.S. Dollars)

Country	1870	1900	1913	Annual Growth Rate, 1870–1913 (%)
Mexico	$710	$1,157	$1,467	1.7
Argentina	1,311	2,756	3,797	2.5
Brazil	740	704	839	0.3
United States	2,457	4,096	5,307	1.8
Great Britain	3,263	4,593	5,032	1.0

SOURCE: Angus Maddison, *Monitoring the World Economy, 1820–1992* (Paris: Development Centre of the Organization for Economic Cooperation and Development; Washington, D.C.: OECD Publications and Information Center [distributor], 1995), tables 1-3, 3-2.

omy expanded between 1870 and 1913 as a result of free-trade policies and the free movement of ideas and capital. International capital markets, along with banks and other financial intermediaries, helped to account for the rapid development of an international financial system, and the widespread acceptance of the gold standard facilitated international payments and transfers. This development of the financial system sustained international trade and the real economies of Europe and the Americas. International trade grew 3.3 percent annually between 1873 and 1913, thanks to a dramatic reduction in the cost of maritime transport, lower insurance costs, and the construction of rail connections between productive areas and their corresponding ports. Thus one of the elements responsible for Mexico's economic growth in this period was the expansion of its international trade, which increased from 5 percent of the world's combined GDPs in 1870 to 8.7 percent in 1913.

If the international context was so favorable to national economies, why was Mexico unable to fully exploit the comparative advantages that it enjoyed? In 1870, western Europe exported 10 percent of its GDP, but Mexico exported only 3.7 percent of its GDP. By 1913, Europe exported 16.3 percent of GDP and Mexico only 8.7 percent of its GDP. Yet despite Mexico's reduced participation in international trade, Mexico's exports grew 4.4 percent annually between 1870 and 1890, which contributed to a 5.9 percent annual increase in the purchasing power of imported goods that improved a balance of payments surplus. Between 1890 and 1912, however, purchasing power fell by 3.9 percent annually despite a 5.2 percent annual increase in exports. The result was higher-priced imports, in particular the machinery and other supplies needed to improve industrial productivity. In other words, falling purchasing power undermined the modernization of production for export.

Mexico's process of development presented a paradox in the last thirty years of the nineteenth century and the first decade of the twentieth. The society was dynamic and receptive to new ideas. There was significant investment in brewing, textiles, communications, mining, smelting, explosives, rubber, sisal hemp, cotton fiber, cottonseed, and sugar refining, but with only a limited domestic market, these industries were not motivated to seek investment to increase productivity. The liberal model dictated that government and industry should collaborate to increase productivity, but in Mexico their relations were less harmonious than was to be desired. As a result of these incongruities, products made in Mexico were uncompetitive, in both domestic and international markets, with similar or identical goods made in other Latin American countries or elsewhere.

A look at monetized salaries may help to explain the lack of progress in productivity. According to available statistics, overall salaries were stagnant nationwide during the entire period between 1877 and 1913. In those thirty-six years, agricultural wages fluctuated between a low of twenty-eight centavos and a high of thirty-nine centavos per day, calculated in 1900 pesos. Recent research on the textile industry between 1900 and 1913 shows that real salaries increased by 12.6 percent from 1900 to 1907, but then decreased by 17.9 percent in the following five years, losing more than what had been gained. Thus employers were motivated to—and apparently did—hire more workers rather than invest in new technology.

Figure 8.1 (see page 174) illustrates economic performance in terms of number of participants in different sectors in the fifteen years leading up to the 1910 Revolution. This performance was not always positive or evenly distributed. The GDP rose from 20.5 to 31.4 million (1960) pesos, but discounting population growth, the real GDP grew by only 1.4 percent annually. Commerce was among the important sectors in terms of volume, growing rapidly between 1895 and 1902.

Mining was the most dynamic sector, despite its limited contribution to the GDP. Mining productivity increased in the 1890s thanks to technological innovations in the production of silver and nonferrous metals such as copper, zinc, lead, and nickel. Activity in this sector was also stimulated by the extraction of new energy sources such as coal and, after 1904, petroleum. The petroleum boom itself, however, would not begin until 1910.

The profitability of mining and the guarantees on investment provided by the mining law of 1892 attracted domestic, and above all foreign, investment. The latter came to a total of 817 million pesos in 1910, half originating in the United States and the other half in England and France. Although silver mining was beginning to decline, overall mining production grew thanks to the mining of coal and industrial metals such as copper, lead, nickel, and zinc.

The mining of industrial metals, mostly in the northern part of the country, grew continuously from 1890 to 1907, increasing in value ten times over, from nine million to ninety million pesos. This fabulous growth was a response to the second Industrial Revolution taking place in Europe, the United States, and Japan. New metals and energy resources were in demand for the production and operation of maritime and rail transportation equipment and for telegraph and telephone wire. Coal and petroleum were required to fuel the new engines. Lead was needed in the new steel plants. Raw materials such as copper, lead, zinc, and antimony also underwent initial processing in Mexico before being exported. Toward the end of the nineteenth century, the establishment of coal mining produced an industrial synergy among mines, foundries, and the first coal-powered electric generating plants. The first production of explosives was put into operation in 1903 by the French Nobel company in association with a Mexican glycerin plant. This gave birth to the factory town named Dinamita, in the state of Durango. Its products were used in mining as well as road and railroad construction.

The construction industry was another important source of prosperity. Numerous roads, bridges, tunnels, railways, trolley systems, electric lines, artificial harbors, industrial facilities, and surface drainage systems, plus the extensive storm sewers of Mexico City, were all built in this period.

Industrial modernization, technological innovation, and constant infusions of capital at first brought higher productivity and a more skilled labor force, without increasing the number of industrial workers, which stabilized at around 120,000 between 1897 and 1907. Investment in industry increased the role of industrial production in the GDP, rising from 3.0 percent to 4.7 percent between 1890 and 1903, although it later stagnated. Around the turn of the century, however, the Mexican economy began to send out negative signals as growth slowed in some sectors—services among them. The agricultural sector was doing poorly, growing by only 2 percent annually—barely more than the rate of population growth of 1.4 percent. Manufacturing grew until 1900 and then stagnated. These problems of economic growth may be attributed to the fact that the general economic model of 1850–1890 was still being followed, a model based on population growth and extensive, rather than intensive, expansion. The fact that technological change was constrained and capital investment slackened could explain why productivity increases were forestalled, salaries stayed low, and profits did not increase significantly. In other words, demographic growth discouraged technological innovation except in mining, textiles, and distilling, and the technological and productivity advances in these sectors were insufficient to increase overall productivity, profitability, or real salaries.

The technological revolution had begun well enough in Mexico. Rail transport underpinned the economic transformation of 1870–1890. The basic structure of the national rail system and the initial laying of track were basically completed by 1890. Important branch lines were added later, such as the line connecting Torreón and Monterrey, which stimulated the industrial development of the northeast. Nonetheless, the Pacific line connecting Nogales and the U.S. border in the north with southern and central Mexico across the Sierra Madre Occidental was left incomplete, due to the difficulties of crossing the mountain chain. The interoceanic rail line across the Isthmus of Tehuantepec also ran into major technical difficulties and did not live up to expectations. In the absence of additional investment, the entire railroad infrastructure amounted to just one complete single-track route with a system of inefficient freight yards, which made transportation cumbersome and deliveries slow. In addition, railroad policies did not allow for partial loads. Freight cars were required to be fully loaded and booked for long-distance transport. This inhibited the formation of intermediate markets and small producers.

The expansion of the electrical infrastructure had been a critical factor in industrialization in the United States and Canada. In Mexico, the expansion of electrical infrastructure was slow and inadequate, and the production of electrical power suffered, rising from 7 million 1960 pesos' worth of electrical energy in 1895 to 15 million in 1900, 18 million in 1901, and only 41 million in 1905.[2] This level of production was clearly insufficient, given the requirements of new industrial plants and mining companies. The power supply consisted of a series of small generating plants dedicated to specific mines, mills, and factories. Rarely was electrical energy generated for use in a wider industrial area, and only the largest cities, such as the capital, could boast of an urban electrical grid.

---

2. Figures from Bank of Mexico, *Indicadores Económicos: Monetarios, Financieros y de Finanzas Públicas* (Mexico City: Banco de México, 1991).

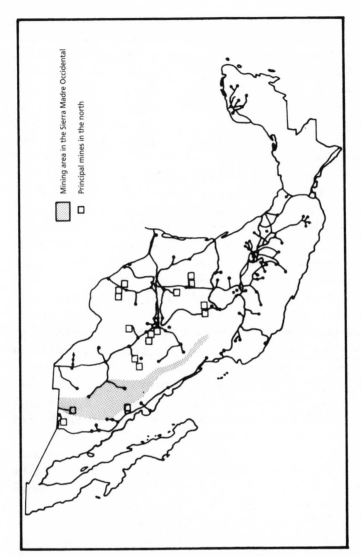

MAP 8.3. Railroads (represented by black lines) and mines, 1910. (Source: François-Xavier Guerra, *México: Del Antiguo Régimen a la Revolución*, vol. 1, op. cit., p. 327.)

Mining area in the Sierra Madre Occidental

Principal mines in the north

Obstacles to Growth

Three areas of growth crucial to the development of the United States after 1870 were relatively neglected in Mexico. First, a modern transportation system had been developed in the United States that could move large volumes of merchandise and supplies—an indispensable precondition to the building of a modern industrial economy. Second, electricity replaced steam power in the United States by about 1880 as the source of energy in factories, urban transportation, chemical processing, and metal industries. Third, skilled workers and technicians were accommodated in laboratories and workshops where they could experiment and develop new technologies on a full-time basis. No equivalent opportunity was available in Mexico, where there were only limited and isolated programs for the education of midlevel technicians and specialists in some fields. The prestigious Ateneo Fuente de Saltillo stands out as an atypical preparatory school that served this function.

A summary review of Mexican economic performance from 1890 to 1910 points up the gaps, deficiencies, and obstacles that went beyond the question of human capital, which was the problem when it came to the need for professionals, technicians, and specialized workers. Mexico's overall backwardness, however, stemmed from a political economy that tended to reproduce what already existed, a feeble judicial system with a high level of uncertainty in business transactions, and a poorly integrated market and trading system.

The government stuck to the silver exchange rate and resisted adopting an exchange rate based on gold. The declining value of silver was an economic deterrent, because "by increasing import prices in domestic currency, depreciation erected a barrier favoring domestic producers, whose prices tended to be higher than world prices."[3]

A few among the powerful Mexican business class understood how to exploit the opportunities presented by international markets, which explains their investment in some of the most modern industrial plants in the world. The great majority of people, however, as well as the government itself, were insufficiently imaginative to appreciate what was taking place in front of their eyes: the birth of a new international economic, financial, and trading system.

3. See Jaime E. Zabludovsky, "La Depreciación de la Plata y las Exportaciones," in Enrique Cárdenas, compiler, *Historia Económica de México* (Mexico City: Fondo de Cultura Económica, 1992), vol. 3, pp. 290–326.

A 2003 study by Victor Bulmer-Thomas asserts that in order to take advantage of the growth in world trade, Mexico's economy would have had to expand by at least 4.5 percent annually between 1850 and 1912. In fact, because it was not as open as the British or Dutch economies, and because it was closed in the wrong ways, its average growth rate in those years was only 3 percent. Some have blamed Mexico's failure to keep pace on the continued preponderance of the traditional minerals, livestock, and agricultural goods in its exports, rather than new industrial products. Even in 1910, Mexico was still importing industrial machinery and inputs, which led to deteriorating terms of trade. At that point, the government attempted to address the problem by promoting diversification of both imports and exports.

Another important factor in Mexico's industrial development was its dependence on the export of silver, a product that had been losing value since 1880, as the industrialized countries adopted the gold standard. Between 1890 and 1905, the value of an ounce of silver dropped from forty-eight to only twenty-two British pence. Silver made up much of Mexico's exports, but it lost considerable comparative value when exchanged for gold. This deterioration in export value would be addressed only when Mexico began to export industrial minerals in 1901.

Mexico's dependence on silver and rather late conversion to the gold standard discouraged direct foreign investment. Mexican capitalists also encountered more impediments than incentives to domestic investment and often invested their profits in London instead. The situation was not helped by the delay in approval of the Banking Law until 1897 or the slow development of a banking and credit system. The combined effect of all these factors discouraged individual initiative and impeded the formation of an entrepreneurial class with the vision and skill to promote the new productive and service sectors that Mexico needed for its industrial modernization.

Among the obstacles to Mexican economic development were the fiscal and economic policies of Porfirio Díaz's government and much of the political class that then supported it. It has often been said that José Y. Limantour's management of the national treasury was one positive aspect of the Porfiriato. In his book *Estado y Mercado* (State and Market), Marcello Carmagnani demonstrates that the sole merit of Limantour's treasury policies was that they did not generate a deficit. However, guided by that single goal, he abandoned what had not long before been considered important national priorities. Government appropriations were no longer used as a tool to stimulate the new economic activities that the country needed. The growth of spending on the justice system, public education, health, and sanitation ground to a halt. At a time when Mexico required public investment to accelerate its industrial and economic transformation, Limantour maintained a budget surplus and starved development. Under Limantour, treasury policy took on economistic and even statist characteristics, as in the purchase of a part of the rail system. Tax policy, on the other hand, punished the low-income consumer more than any other sector. The average tax paid between 1895 and 1910 rose from 4.4 to 6.8 pesos. Protests against tax inequity grew in volume from 1892 onward, adding to the discontent that led to the 1910 Revolution.

It is routinely stated that the public debt was a tremendous burden and an obstacle to Mexico's economic transformation. This is questionable. Mexico was less indebted in 1910 than it had been in 1870. Expressed as a multiple of annual federal government revenues, the debt actually decreased from 9.4 times revenue in 1870 to only 3.9 times revenue in 1910.

Political Life and Elections

I have described Mexico's economic performance as weak in comparison to both the economic activity in other countries and the dynamism of Mexican society. Unfortunately, the political system at this stage of Mexico's history was equally fossilized.

At the beginning of the 1880s, numerous political forms coexisted in Mexico. There were direct elections of local authorities in almost every municipality of the nation—impressive evidence of a grassroots democracy. The different social and economic interests within each jurisdiction interacted on the municipal level, and the electoral process was the vehicle for that interaction. This was the progressive face of Mexican politics. But more traditional and conservative forms of suffrage were maintained at the other levels of government. There were direct elections for governors and state congressional seats in some states, and indirect elections elsewhere. The Mexican states still differed over the concepts of citizenship and political representation, according to regional socioeconomic characteristics.

At the national level, there was a third form of suffrage, also indirect. The 1857 Constitution and federal election law established the indirect election of deputies, senators, Supreme Court justices, and the president. This electoral procedure, at that time called "direct in the first degree," was considered necessary so the work of federal authorities would not be excessively affected by local interests.

Together with this diversity of electoral practices, there had been attempts to define citizenship and to set qualifications for suffrage: having "an honest means of earning a living" or a minimum level of wealth would guarantee individual political autonomy. In the second half of the nineteenth century, however, there was an increasing demand for political and social rights, and the earlier qualifications gave way to other values such as literacy, personal merit, and having served in the military. The quality of patriotism, demonstrated by having risked one's life, family, and property in order to defend the nation from foreign invaders, became a powerful qualification for political participation.

Research in the military archives indicates that the protests and proclamations of 1883–1893, though usually described as rebellions or *pronunciamientos,* were of little military significance. Rather, they were demands for the full reestablishment of the 1857 Constitution, for voting rights, for government noninterference in the electoral process, and for municipal autonomy. Intermediate sectors such as merchants and renters of small and middle-sized plots demanded greater rights, as did smallholders and industrial workers. They complained that taxation so onerous that it inhibited consumption was a violation of economic rights. They were clearly demanding a balance between rights and obligations—the typically liberal idea that those who directly support the State through their taxes should enjoy full political rights. Protests over increased taxes, especially common beginning in 1892, were not really about taxes alone but concerned the lack of corresponding State services such as schools, passable roads, and fair prices on basic goods. The continuing clamor for more freedom of action for the municipality, which was constantly threatened by higher authorities, was expressed in the demand for free elections and autonomy. In an example of historical parallelism, Mexico and other countries that had expanded suffrage in the late nineteenth century experienced parallel movements to make that suffrage a genuine and effective right of citizenship.

The historical trend was in favor of direct elections, but only Hidalgo and Tlaxcala introduced the direct vote into their state constitutions, also mandating consultations with their municipalities in formulating state policy. The practice of indirect voting continued to be the norm when it came to midlevel and higher offices, and the tendency to maintain limitations on suffrage only increased.

After the first liberal governments, and from 1887 onward, limits on political participation and representation were increased. The gap between the government and the governed, which had been narrowed by the liberal revolution, began to widen once again. Organized communities and *pueblos* pulled back from state and national politics to focus more exclusively on matters within the local and municipal spheres. As they distanced themselves from national life, a historical memory of autonomous communalism came to the fore. It is a mistake to characterize this tradition as socialist, though some have done so. *Caciques*, local notables, and other authorities reinvoked their traditional and hereditary rights to manage political, social, and material resources in the name of the community. Yet what appeared to be manifestations of historical memory at the end of the nineteenth century were in fact new codifications of various elements. They combined the legacy of colonial legislation, which recognized the prerogatives of the *pueblo,* with the political rights stemming from the liberal revolution, such as freedom of association, the right to petition for redress of grievances, and the right to elect political representatives.

Municipal Retreat and the Increased Power of the Oligarchy in State Government

A political change began to be seen in the 1890s when government spending on public services lessened nationwide, rule became increasingly authoritarian, and elections were rigged. Political ties between higher authorities and townspeople were becoming practically nonexistent. Because the political class was more interested in material progress and in the administrative control of their states than in the development of democracy, public politics reverted almost entirely to the municipal sphere. However, the retreat to the municipal sphere was not just a return to the past. It was a legally based strategy pursued by different *pueblos* in the state and federal courts, a defense of both newly established administrative prerogatives and historical rights in relation to resources, especially land and water. The municipalities sought to codify their rights to hold indivisible property in common, to rent community properties to individual users in order to generate resources for municipal economic needs, and even to title and definitively transfer properties to individual smallholders. This represented an expansion of community rights beyond the traditionally established concept of patrimony, which held sway exclusively over community property used collectively. Owning land was not the same as renting or tilling an otherwise indivisible property owned either communally or jointly. The municipalities sought to legislate these new rights based on judicial decisions and common law. They understood that the existence of different roles within the community gave new meaning to the rights granted by the liberal revolution. New economic obligations in the form of municipal, state, and federal taxes were based on the ownership of property and the consumption of goods and services. It was precisely this blend of individual and municipal resources, taxes and public services, that entitled townspeople to political representation. The universal application of taxes opened up the possibility that all the members of the community, *vecinos* and non-*vecinos,* could demand equal citizenship rights.

Given the disconnect between the governing elite and the rural population, these two groups drifted further apart. The social and political response of the communities was to reject the new impositions, and all external authority along with them. They argued that their political rights were being continually eroded. As a result, there were new demands to reactivate the National Guard and abolish the federal army. In essence, there was political sympathy for a renewal of confederalism, based now on the primacy of the municipality.

The tenuous reach of the federal and state justice systems diminished municipal confidence in both of these superior levels of government and encouraged municipalities to distance themselves from them. The existence of this divide is probably responsible for the concentration of powers in the hands of federal authorities, either de jure or de facto, and in particular for the increased powers of the president.

The political value of elections diminished toward the end of the 1880s, due to the 1887 reform on the issue of reelection and the rigidity of the indirect representation system. It was also difficult as well as costly to participate in every general election. However, the participation rate remained high when it came to municipal elections, for the simple reason that in direct elections every single vote counted. In addition, the effects of the election would be felt on a daily basis for the following two years.

The indirect federal elections were largely discredited. Following from the abstentionism and apathy generated by the divide between municipal voters and the members of the electoral colleges, the latter tended to abuse the power conferred upon them. The electors, popularly chosen in order to select representatives to federal bodies, no longer felt answerable to municipal voters for their performance, and they began to be chosen based on the preferences of higher authorities. The resulting complacency and malleability of the electoral colleges further enhanced the power of the states and the federal government.

The decreased political accountability of the political class and its distancing from the population consolidated the formation of a political oligarchy that had begun in the states. At the beginning of the 1890s, all the states except those in the north amended their constitutions to institute the indirect election of governors and deputies. This was a definite regression in the system of political representation.

In the face of municipal resistance to political control and subordination, the central authorities resorted to an indirect mechanism. They strengthened the role of the political authority known as the district chief, or *jefe político*. Traditionally, the district chief was popularly chosen—by direct election in the northern states and from a short list proposed by the municipality elsewhere. Thus district chiefs had to be attentive to the needs of the municipalities under their jurisdiction and maintain contact with their constituents, especially with the president of the municipal council. In the south-central states, however, district chiefs were state officials appointed by the governor. Within a few years the governors were appointing district chiefs in every state, and the relationship between the chiefs and their municipalities was rendered moot. They became enforcers of the governor's policy priorities and were responsible to him alone. The image of the Porfirian district chief as an arbitrary and odious political boss comes from this period late in the Porfiriato.

In a parallel process, the relationship between the municipality and the national State was effectively made moot as well. Federal elections were indirect, and electors regularly colluded with senators and deputies in return for their votes. Eventually, this subordinated the electors to federal power. Perhaps this slow degeneration of political democracy, and of the relationship between the political class and the rest of society, puts the 1887 constitutional reforms in a new light. It has been said that these reforms were imposed by President Díaz's authoritarianism and that they brought back the reelection of officials. However, let us examine what happened in detail.

Beginning in 1887, the institution of reelection meant that electors no longer needed popular support. The understanding and commitment between them and the population broke down entirely, and state authorities provided them with positions of power and privilege. District chiefs abandoned their commitments to their municipality and their constituents and became protégés of higher political authorities. The political class's condescension and its effective divorce from the citizenry crippled Mexican republicanism in one of its most vigorous moments. Not only did the national movement for individual rights under the law suffer a setback, but informal, arbitrary, and inconsistent political practices reappeared at the district level. The rupture between local concerns and the broader context was quite complete. Citizens active in local government distanced themselves from regional and state affairs. Among the lasting negative effects was the fact that state affairs were now conducted by an intermediate layer of officials who also managed state relations with federal authorities. This provided the context for arbitrary and self-serving political deals to be concluded behind closed doors.

The political demobilization of Mexican society took other forms as well. The National Guard, which had been the principal organized citizen network on the local, state, and federal levels, was essentially disbanded in 1880. Only its officers were integrated into the permanent federal army reserve, and only if they met certain criteria. This initiative of the federal government met with serious resistance from the municipal battalions of the National Guard, which were composed of peasants, workers, and artisans from each *pueblo*. They demanded the Guard's reconstitution and repudiated the regular army as an institution, demanding that it be reduced in strength. The federal government made some concessions in response to the outcry. State National Guard units would be maintained intact but under the explicit control of the state government. National Guard officers could maintain their positions but only if they met certain federally mandated criteria. In other words, the ties between the state and federal executive branches were strengthened at the expense of the organized citizenry and its nationwide, municipally based participation. The armed forces were formalized as a hierarchical and professional institution under federal jurisdiction alone. Governors continued to command state forces, but the municipalities lost all their input in the matter.

The effective disappearance of the National Guard as the armed body of the citizenry eliminated the only secular organization with a national presence. It was not immediately replaced, but its memory persevered on the local level and nurtured the political "plans" that would later emerge from the municipalities. The historical memory of an armed citizenry endured as a potent instrument of political expression, playing a role in the rapid establishment in 1901 of the Second Reserve, composed of citizens from around the country.

Elite Politics

Political regression had distanced the government from the citizenry. The political class itself, however, was far from homogeneous or compact. It was more of a coalition of different elements in the Congress, the army, and the state and federal bureaucracies. The business class, meanwhile, worked very successfully in Congress and in the government to acquire subsidies as they developed the land and sea transportation infrastructure for their own benefit. These subsidies and the other conditions that they acquired guaranteed them high rates of profit. Economic and political regionalization and the political nature of industrial development tended to create closed markets with only limited interaction among them, reinforcing the power of regional elites without promoting national integration.

Although some state constitutions already allowed for reelection (though not for consecutive terms), the legalization of constitutional reform allowing for reelection on the federal level guaranteed continuity in power for whichever political circles came out ahead in the state elections that year. The victory of one faction would debilitate its competitors and break the customary cycle of alternation in power. In other words, the winner would be in power to stay. This would inhibit the development of alternative circles and political interests and would put a halt to any coalition-building or competition for elective office.

The electoral reform of 1887, which nurtured the formation of closed political circles, may have been a response to the need to develop new organizational forms in order to avoid recurrent political conflicts among interest groups. In fact, these political circles strengthened the connections between local notables and their respective municipal seats, between the municipalities and their district capitals, and between the states and the federal government. In other words, the reform created channels for national political ties and avoided conflicts within the political class.

What came to be known as the government party grew out of these circles. Established in 1892 at the initiative of one of the larger political factions and inspired by the ideology of liberal positivism, the party was founded specifically to support the reelection of Díaz. The Gran Círculo Porfirista, or Greater Porfirian Circle, including most government bureaucrats, decided to constitute itself as a political party to contest the 1892 elections. The Gran Círculo was a liberal faction with circles in the capital and around the country. The capital-city circles founded the Liberal Union and announced its program. The government bodies themselves were to be its organizing network, and what was called "the party of the State" would parallel the structure of existing official entities. On January 25, 1892, a confidential letter was sent to each governor with instructions to forward copies to each of his district chiefs. The latter were enjoined to organize a party committee in each municipal seat. This municipal committee would then organize a local committee in each *pueblo* under its jurisdiction. Together, the district and local committees would constitute "branches" of the state body, which would itself be called the Liberal Convention. Each state convention would send one delegate to the National Convention in Mexico City.

While the organizing letters sent to the district chiefs indicate that the Liberal Union was conceived of as the "party of the State," their confidential character also indicates that this was not to be declared openly. Each district chief was instructed to "make use of your numerous friends" to recruit party members, but the involvement of state officials was to be strictly behind the scenes. The committees were told not to declare their support for any presidential candidate, for the official candidate would be designated in April at the National Convention.

The Liberal Convention was a short-lived organization. It did not succeed in its goal of uniting elite factions, despite its origins in one of the most important of them, the Científicos. This faction counted among its adherents intellectuals of the stature of Justo Sierra, business leaders such as Enrique Creel, and professionals such as Pablo Macedo and Joaquín Casasús. It was led by José Y. Limantour, best known as the long-standing treasury secretary during the Porfiriato who hoped to succeed Díaz in the presidency. The group came to be known as the Científicos for their interest in and attempts to promote economic and technological progress and for their inclination to place new restrictions on suffrage. The very idea of a return to a social and legal system based on considerations of material wealth met with the opposition of both regional elites and the government itself, aborting the consolidation of the party under Científico leadership. It seems that no further attempt was made to establish a national party at this time. Municipal and state politics found expression in political, literary, and spiritualist circles instead. Between 1892 and 1901, the political reorganization of the citizenry took place primarily within the *ayuntamiento* and the municipality, to reemerge on the national stage in 1901–1902.

Another movement was taking shape at the beginning of the 1890s as well, led by Bernardo Reyes, a former National Guard general, and supported by elements of the army general command and the non-Científico factions of the government and armed forces. It would be incorrect to call this a military movement, though. In fact, it had a strong civilian component, which led to the establishment of the Second Reserve in 1901. Like the old National Guard, the Second Reserve mobilized contingents of citizens by municipality. It eventually included twenty thousand citizens under arms, led by reserve officers who by then had gained the confidence of Secretary of War Bernardo Reyes.

Both Reyes's movement and the Liberal Convention were eventually condemned and repressed by President Díaz, undermining Reyes's and Limantour's aspirations to national power. In any case, neither of the two had made progress in reconciling the interests of crucial but disparate elements in governing circles. Lower- and middle-ranking local notables balanced out the power of the most wealthy and prominent political families, and without meeting the needs of both groups, no political project was viable.

In this politically active period, the Roman Catholic Church defined its own political position with the 1892 encyclical *Rerum Novarum*. The Mexican hierarchy disregarded it, however. A social Catholicism was slowly beginning to spread through the parishes and within lay Catholic circles. Social Catholics founded community mutual aid societies and social clubs—very successful cross-class associations that held their first national conventions in 1901. Protestants also began to organize their first churches at this time. These became real citizenship schools, dedicated to the modern civic spirit.

Opposition to the Regime

Between 1903 and 1907, there was clearly a qualitative shift in the organized oppositional political networks, which provided a platform for the new social and political demands arising among the citizenry. What had happened? First, the political shift initiated by the Porfiriato in 1890 had deepened at the turn of the century. Second, although the worldwide crisis of 1906–1907 does not in itself explain the shift, the inability of the Díaz regime to satisfy the material needs and political demands of the populace led people to look elsewhere for relief. By this time, workers, middle-class social clubs, liberal constitutionalists, progressives, social Catholics, and Protestants—some of the latter with a European orientation but mostly with ties to the United States—had all consolidated their organizational networks.

The social changes underway accelerated with each presidential succession. The first organized group to take advantage of the historical opportunity was the liberal constitutionalist network. Still fragmented at the beginning of the century, this group now developed a well-articulated network and built a national leadership. Their success was largely due to the work of the liberal constitutionalist group of San Luis Potosí, led by Camilo Arriaga, grandson of the great liberal of 1857, Ponciano Arriaga. Once again came the call for a full implementation of the secular State envisioned in the 1857 Constitution, in clear counterposition to the growing social Catholic movement. The popular mythology associated with Juárez and his movement was revived in order to add strength to the voices of liberal republicanism.

In 1900, Camilo Arriaga invited all the Mexican liberal clubs to meet the following year in San Luis Potosí. The proposed national convention was intended to promote democratic reform and transform the separate initiatives of liberal clubs around the country into collective action. It was important that a convention was chosen as the mechanism to accomplish this. The first sign of success was that more than fifty delegates met at the convention, out of about one hundred liberal clubs around the country. In addition, the clubs quickly united around a common program to oppose the national regime and the authorities in their own states. The convention offered the various liberalisms in the country a common denominator to unite around; it also acknowledged the autonomy of the different clubs, and it provided a forum for the discussion of a minimum common program.

The success of this formula and the appearance of the first national organization representing liberal constitutionalism were abruptly terminated by the government. The virulence of the repression against urban middle-class sectors was unprecedented. There had been government hostility toward liberal constitutionalists before 1901, but not like this. This time their leaders were jailed and more than forty liberal periodicals were shut down.

The liberal constitutionalist movement did not die, however. It grew and regrouped nationally in 1903 as the Confederation of Liberal Clubs of the Republic. As the word *confederation* indicates, this was an alliance of forces with different ideas about the best route to social and political renovation. In this sense it was like all Mexican liberal democratic movements. The complexity of the coalition makes it difficult to explain the different positions within the 1906–1907 liberal constitutionalist movement. It is too simplistic, however, to just say that Arriaga was a liberal and Ricardo Flores Magón was an anarcho-syndicalist. In my judgment, the split between the two leaders developed out of their different conceptions of the best organizational form for the movement at that conjuncture, Arriaga preferring a confederation and Flores Magón a political party.

This difference deepened during the exile of the two leaders in the United States. Arriaga was attracted to progressivism, the liberal democratic current that also influenced Francisco I. Madero. Beginning in 1906, on the other hand, Flores Magón turned wholeheartedly to anarcho-syndicalism. When the Liberal Party program appeared in June of that year, some followers of Flores Magón rejected its moderate stance, reorganizing themselves into clandestine clubs and armed cells.

The 1906 program proposed the formal establishment of a liberal party and stressed that constitutional reform would prohibit reelection and concentrate on guaranteeing freedom of association and freedom of opinion. It emphasized the civilian character of the State, demanding the reestablishment of the National Guard. It also reiterated the liberal demand to promote and improve education, and proposed a set of labor laws and greater tax equity through the abolition of the "head tax," or capitation.

Flores Magón assumed the leadership of the liberal constitutionalist movement under this program. Functioning as the Mexican Liberal Party in 1906–1907, it managed to hold onto every one of the existing liberal clubs around the country and to add new ones in most states. The democratic program attracted progressive individuals of the lower and middle strata, both rural and urban. Its growing number of adherents included teachers, students, wealthy farmers, and poor peasants. By 1909, liberal constitutionalism was a national movement for the democratic renewal of society. As in every movement, minority currents began to form. In this case they were often anarcho-syndicalist in orientation. As a result, the Mexican Liberal Party split apart.

The Catholic movement evolved in a similar fashion. In the last decade of the nineteenth century and the beginning of the twentieth, Catholics had their own social-political organizations in the states of Jalisco, Guanajuato, Puebla, Michoacán, and Mexico, with subsidiary branches in other states. Unlike the liberal network, the Catholic movement was stronger in the center and west than in the north. It also had substantial strength in Oaxaca and Yucatán. Like the liberal clubs, however, local Catholic social groups were cross-class organizations. Beginning in 1903, these local groups came together in Catholic congresses, culminating in the agrarian congresses of 1909. Clerical and lay representatives met in these congresses to ask the government to address social problems. Simply by meeting and expressing themselves on the social question, they demonstrated the important division within Catholicism between the Church hierarchy and the rest of the clergy, with repercussions in society as a whole. Supported by a broadly defined middle class, the rank-and-file clergy stepped forward to speak up for the voiceless on social questions and in favor of social renewal. The clergy's interest in social issues and the wide dissemination of Catholic periodicals help explain the spread of Catholicism among workers, artisans, and independent professionals.

Unlike the liberal movement, however, the growing number of Catholic organizations in 1906–1907 did not make the qualitative leap to a national organization or a party. For this the Catholic movement would have to await the galvanizing moment of 1909–1910, when the general social crisis and the political crisis of the Díaz regime would combine to split the governing elite and open the door to new possibilities.

In secular society, however, the liberal constitutionalist citizens' movement continued to grow in numbers and broaden its constituency. A wave of militant strikes in 1906–1907 brought the workers' movement to the fore and into a convergence of interests with the Mexican Liberal Party. By 1905, workers' circles had evolved in much the same way as liberal clubs had done. Local organizations had transcended the status of mutual aid societies and acquired explicitly liberal positions, as illustrated by the names given to some of the workers' political clubs: Benito Juárez, Ignacio de la Llave, Sebastián Lerdo de Tejada, Mariano Escobedo, Ignacio Zaragoza, and Guillermo Prieto. Others evoked independence heroes such as Miguel Hidalgo and José María Morelos, and several recalled the indigenous past with the name Cuauhtémoc. There were those that commemorated positivism, with names such as Enlightenment and Progress, or constitutionalism, by calling themselves Constitutional Liberty. However, many workers' groups did not participate in political circles, preferring to consolidate themselves as labor unions.

The growth of these multiple liberalisms was not the work of just a few enlightened groups. It counted on the participation of broad social elements, including working-class sectors, as evidenced by the liberal program of 1906. Thus the prestigious anarcho-syndicalist leaders may have formed a bridge between the workers' movement and the Mexican Liberal Party. Liberals and anarcho-syndicalists seem to have parted company after 1906, the former strengthening their democratic program and the latter their revolutionary program based on land occupations, strikes, direct action, and the revolutionary uprising of the poor against the rich. The two groups were divided over the desirability of direct action, armed insurrection, and the strike weapon.

As a result, the influence of the anarcho-syndicalists was largely restricted to their social base, concentrated in the Gulf area of Veracruz, Tabasco, and Tampico, and on the border with the United States, principally in Sonora and Coahuila, where they had significant support. The interchange of ideas and organizational experiences between Mexican and American workers on railroads in the United States and in mine-related employment on both sides of the border was a significant stimulus for radical labor agitation. Liberals, on the other hand, were strongest in urban areas; in the villages and cities of the northern states of Sonora, Chihuahua, Coahuila, and Nuevo León; and in the mining areas of Zacatecas, Coahuila, and San Luis Potosí—areas from which they would extend their reach throughout rural central Mexico and win the wide support of small-town notables.

The increasing citizen demands were expressed in many ways, from the publication of newspapers and pamphlets to protests and strikes, and in popular theater and satire and in the public square. The clamor for change could not be ignored. Luis Méndez, the president of the Mexican Central Academy of Jurisprudence, advocated the passage of new labor legislation in 1908, and President Díaz himself agreed to mediate in a labor dispute in Puebla. He also arbitrated in several other conflicts, in particular, conflicts concerning railroad labor. Despite the opposition of U.S. mining interests, the government favored the passage of legislation demanded by workers to compensate them for accidents suffered in the mining industry.

All the evidence indicates that by 1907, the social and political demands expressed in workers' circles, liberal clubs, Catholic associations, and anarcho-syndicalist organizations had pushed their way to the center of Mexican public discourse.

The Fragmentation of the Porfirian Elite

There was considerable political bickering among government liberals, divided as they were into various factions such as the Científicos, led by the powerful treasury secretary José Y. Limantour, and the faction headed by Bernardo Reyes, the ex-secretary of war and now governor of Nuevo León. Factional strife within the government sharpened every time there was to be a presidential election, for these were opportunities for various groups within the government to maneuver for comparative advantage. But of course the struggle always ended with the reelection of Porfirio Díaz.

The position of vice president had been established as a result of a constitutional amendment in 1904. It was an important office, given the advanced age of Porfirio Díaz and the possibility that whoever occupied the position might ascend to the presidency. Díaz's appointment of Reyes as secretary of war and of the navy in 1900 had strengthened Reyes's position as a possible heir to the presidency. His performance as a cabinet secretary reinforced this idea, as he focused his efforts on a major reorganization of the armed forces. Most importantly, he organized the Second Reserve in just a few months' time, a body of twenty thousand citizens in arms, all of them volunteers, and many of them representing the growing middle class. These men joined the reserve not necessarily because they were followers of Reyes but because it was a form of social and political participation at both the local and national levels. The memory of the National Guard was so compelling that people of all social circumstances enlisted. Every Sunday they would participate in exercises as citizen-soldiers, a practice that in itself recalled the republican years.

The high point of Reyes's organization was certainly on September 16, 1902, when a parade of six thousand reservists was reviewed by the president and his cabinet secretaries in Mexico City. From that point on, the Científico faction and Díaz himself realized the threat represented by that force, and its potential use by Reyes as a springboard to power. Subsequent attacks on Reyes resulted in his resignation as secretary of war, the abolition of the Second Reserve, and the nomination of Ramón Corral as vice president.

Although the Second Reserve was eliminated as an institution, its members regrouped in a municipally and state-based network, and remained almost as numerous as the liberal constitutionalists. In 1909, the movement inspired by Reyes was still evident in every state of the republic with the exception of those in the south-central region (Oaxaca, Chiapas, and Tabasco) and the southeast (Yucatán and Campeche). The Reyes movement was resilient and survived because it was attractive to the upper, middle, and popular social classes, although the more powerful sectors did predominate. Numerous governors, senators, deputies, judges, and military officers affiliated themselves with it. The Científicos, on the other hand, were unable to sustain that kind of organizational structure after the 1892 failure of the Liberal Union, although they did continue to enjoy support within the state bureaucracy.

As the opposition grew, the government became increasingly divided. In 1908, Díaz granted an interview to James Creelman of *Pearson's Magazine*, which was reprinted in *El Imparcial*. This interview shook the Mexican political class to its roots. Díaz stated that he would not be a candidate for reelection in 1910, that Mexico was mature enough for democracy, and that he thought the formation of an opposition party would be a good thing.

Every history of Mexico, and in particular that of Daniel Cosío Villegas, has pointed out that Díaz's statements in this interview were ambiguous and represented a political time bomb. All agree that the interview caused a furor that extended to the Porfirian political class. In December 1908, nine months after the interview, a Porfirian group formed the Democratic Party, a political vehicle for the regime that was supposedly a "neutral pole" between Reyistas and Científicos. This group intended that the new presidential candidate would be chosen from among its ranks, and under the right circumstances, this neo-Porfirian party could certainly have carved out a political space as a conservative force. However, the splits in the central government reverberated through the states, breaking apart arrangements that since the elections of the 1890s had served to coalesce diverse factions around common gubernatorial candidates. The first state to see a complete breakdown of the elite Porfirian coalition was Morelos, where Pablo Escandón, the official candidate for governor, was opposed by Patricio Leyva, son of the first state governor, Francisco Leyva. Leyva stood for republicanism in the style of Juárez and for state sovereignty. As it happened, the turbulence of this confrontation coincided with a struggle over the vice presidency, and the gubernatorial election in Morelos became a proxy battle for national Reyistas, Científicos, and liberal constitutionalists to measure their relative strength. Leyva's campaign became something of a popular movement, and his supporters organized themselves into twenty-five local clubs around the state. While the Leyva campaign did not prevent the election of the official candidate, his supporters had established an ongoing organizational network that we will consider when we analyze the Maderista and Zapatista movements—the followers of Madero and Zapata.

A similar phenomenon followed the death of the aged governor in Sinaloa. General Francisco Cañedo had held the post since 1877. As in Morelos, the time was ripe for a reordering of political factions. Three candidates sought the support of the government, but the candidate of the new Democratic Party was the winner. The party proceeded to organize Democratic Clubs in agricultural areas and town centers, in collaboration with *hacendados* and merchants who had long been excluded from the spoils under Cañedo. In 1909, gubernatorial elections divided the elite coalition in Yucatán and Coahuila. In Yucatán, the struggle began among powerful Porfirian factions, but José María Pino Suárez, running on an anti-reelectionist platform, won in the end. In Coahuila, there were two candidates. Venustiano Carranza was sympathetic to Reyes but was a longtime constitutionalist and carried a lot of weight in state politics. He faced the favorite of the three most powerful groups in the state, Francisco I. Madero. Coahuila became the bastion of liberal constitutionalism as Madero and Carranza joined forces, attracting the popular support to elect Carranza governor.

The gradual splintering of the old system encouraged the Reyes movement, which returned to the political fray and met with some success. In 1909, a Reyista club launched the joint candidacy of Díaz for president and Reyes for vice president. This was a clever move that attracted public support, but ensuing Reyista demonstrations were repressed by the government and a section of the group broke away to join the broad anti-reelectionist coalition.

Factional strife among government forces noticeably weakened the regime in 1908–1909, but they attempted to regroup themselves into a reelectionist coalition. The Porfirian elite was faced with the spread of popular movements, however, to which their own disunity had contributed. As the 1910 presidential election drew near, there was no power vacuum, no opening for any factional takeover. Instead, Mexican society and its political organizations became polarized in terms of two positions on the presidency: reelectionist and anti-reelectionist.

CHAPTER 9

The Revolution

The traditional interpretation of the Mexican revolution tends to describe it as an unprecedented social and political phenomenon having only tenuous continuity with the republican and liberal nineteenth century. Recent historiography, however, puts more emphasis on its nineteenth-century roots and on the role played by the ideas, social groups, and organizations of that century's last decade. These studies also question the monolithic view of the revolution. They endeavor instead to recapture its pluralistic nature and its specific characteristics in different states and regions.

For these reasons, it is useful to remember what was said in the previous chapter about the incongruence at the end of the century between an evident social dynamism and the ossified politics, which were inadequate to the needs of the new social actors who were recognizable some fifteen years before the revolutionary convulsion. More concretely, liberal republicanism retreated in the 1890s as the regime it had spawned proved incapable of regeneration and unable to develop policies that could give voice to the new forms of liberal opposition. At this stage we can begin to discern a growing plurality of social actors in Mexico, the precondition for what today we call the revolution. The new society of the day, born under the republic in the most robust period of liberalism, found its way through a thicket of difficulties to establish new social networks and to transform underlying organizational forms, responding to new demands and extending itself throughout the country.

In this chapter we will examine the efforts of thousands of social actors to coordinate their own demands and wherever possible to piggy-back them onto the demands of the local and national elites. We will begin by discussing how the 1910 Revolution was born from the entrails of the Porfiriato, and how the revolution's social actors, the citizenry, arrived at new demands, organized them within the framework of preexisting ones, and established priorities.

The Mexican revolution was not, in this view, just a large pluralist popular movement. It was also a confluence of regionally based movements sustained by a strong federalist tradition that never lost control of its territories.

The Social Question

The large-scale social question that drove the movement toward revolution was more than a simple peasant demand for land; it incorporated the new citizen demand throughout the Western world for social and political rights, such as the right for assistance in the case of sickness or accident, the right to universal suffrage, to social peace, to have work and to be paid fairly. However, the situation has not always been understood in these terms. One often-repeated and reductionist interpretation goes like this: The social question behind the revolution has its roots in the agrarian question—the instability of the *pueblos'* traditional properties and the lack of guarantees for small property in general. These conditions, along with threats to property rights by political bosses and state authorities, provoked rural protest between 1890 and 1910. There is truth to this argument, yet these factors cannot be considered in isolation from political demands for free elections, tax justice, definitive land titling, and strict enforcement of the 1857 Constitution. These demands were already contributing to the development of the social question in the decade of the 1890s.

Nonetheless, the traditional land-question explanation of things does have its value. Migrants to new rural, urban, and mining population centers brought rural social problems with them as the demands of day laborers, sharecroppers, and owners of small land holdings were superimposed on the uncertainty over property rights and concrete political rights. In fact these demands were even more visible in the new population centers, lacking as they did the political status of municipalities. The states' refusal to give political recognition to new settlements crystallized the migrants' situation and linked their new problems to those they had faced in their old *pueblos.*

There is not sufficient historical evidence to determine the extent to which prior demands directly influenced events in the new population centers. There were continuities in social organization, however. Migration was not an individual phenomenon. Families and other groups left their *pueblos* together or separately and reproduced their organizational forms in new towns. They established *cofradías* and celebrated their *pueblos'* festival days. In the new setting, the *cofradías* and other traditional groups worked to strengthen community spirit, and they practiced solidarity through mutual aid.

We have more evidence for events in the year 1902, from which we know that new demands had permeated the traditional organizations. There were demands for land rights, voting rights, equal justice, municipal autonomy, the just remuneration of labor, education and training, productive business and agricultural policies, freedom of expression, privacy rights, the inviolability of human life, the protection of social peace, and the privileging of honest work over capital and manipulation. And there were protests against preferential treatment for foreigners.

The demands were clearly numerous. While some were more important in specific regions, all of them were spontaneous and reflected the general wishes of the society. They did not stem from any doctrine. The existence of many common problems explains the spread of citizen organizations—a phenomenon that only subsequently was interpreted in the light of specific theories or ideologies. Later, when the rigidity of government bodies suffocated the new social demands, they found fertile ground in numerous ideologies such as socialism, communalism, anarcho-syndicalism, democratic liberalism, the social Christian movement, Protestantism, and Catholicism.

Modern Industry and New Directions

The arrival in Mexico of new currents of thought being discussed in Europe and elsewhere in the Americas provided context for the public debate. Ships arriving at Mexican ports brought news of strikes and other struggles of stevedores, longshoremen, and other workers in Europe, Cuba, Venezuela, and the United States, as well as other places in Mexico. The Industrial Revolution introduced a new division of labor and a reorganization of the labor force in the new railroad, telegraph, textile, brewing, and metalworking industries. Now the affinities or connections among workers were based upon their positions within the segmented labor force. Workers in a specific position had more in common with their fellow workers in similar work positions, whether in a generating plant, machine shop, or maintenance facility. Work was carried out in co-ordination with other industrial facilities in Mexico or even abroad. Each industrial facility and every industry has a role to play in an extensive, complex, and coordinated industrial division of labor. The primary nexus between an individual worker and organized labor was now his work position. The new mobility in work life and the affinity between workers despite different locations and industries helped those with common problems to come together. Workers in new specializations, such as mechanics, machinists, boilermakers, and drivers, communicated closely with their colleagues both inside and outside of the country, stimulating the organization of workers.

Despite the growing importance of modern industry and relations between workers in different industrial sectors, the rural areas, both new and old, continued to carry the most weight in the country. The new social vitality introduced additional tensions into the countryside. A new regionalism arose, which, as in the past, preserved some ethnic characteristics but also incorporated the current social demands.

Social or popular Catholicism was one of the principal interpreters of regional demands. After a long period of profound conservatism after the liberal revolution and an adjustment to its new relation with the State, the Church began to play a political role and diplomatic relations with the Vatican were reestablished. A commitment to social involvement arose within the Church itself, as a consequence of a new doctrine, proclaimed in the encyclical *Rerum Novarum,* that opposed lay liberalism. A similar process took place in other Latin American and European countries, where the new social doctrine gained strong acceptance among the local clergy, parish priests, and, in general, those of the Church faithful who witnessed the people's needs on a daily basis.

The engagement of the Church in the social question, especially the involvement of local clergy and lay Catholics, led to the creation of Catholic circles in old and new rural areas where cooperatives had been formed, sometimes with the support of landowners and the political elite. The Catholic movement was diverse and at times contradictory. New religious orders committed to more profound social engagement, like the Salesians and the Sisters of the Sacred Heart, were arriving in Mexico. For its part, a lay Catholic network was deeply involved in organizing around popular demands, first in Jalisco and the Bajío, and later in the entire country.

The Catholic renovation was expressed in Chiapas through Bishop Orozco, who sharpened the social action of the Church in 1902 by reinforcing the authority of the hierarchy and the clergy. Bishop Gillow did the same in Oaxaca. The so-called reconquest of Catholic souls spread rapidly in Indian areas, where the Church tried to destroy the unauthorized religious hierarchy that in the absence of clergy had given the religion a strong vernacular component.

The penetration of social Catholicism in the Mexican regions was simultaneous with the renewal of liberalism. The new liberalism stemmed from opposition to recent Church-State relations and to Porfirio Díaz's policy, beginning in 1890, of reconciliation and cooperation between state-based elites and government authorities and their counterparts on the federal level. This policy, which was discussed in chapter 8, created divisions both between the authorities and the population and within the government itself.

Díaz's policy of establishing special arrangements with the Church and with the traditional large social and economic interests led to a deep split between "official" liberalism, that is, the liberalism in power, and liberal constitutionalism. The latter took on a strong lay and anticlerical connotation and became the leading voice for the ideals of "the glorious Constitution of 1857," the guarantor of "the happiness of the peoples." This view advocated the strict enforcement of the constitution as the only sure way to provide order, the rule of law, and freedom.

Liberal constitutionalism, or democratic liberalism, began to spread slowly as a generation of liberals strongly criticized violations of the constitution in 1877–1879. Thanks to pressure from them during those years, Congress passed an electoral reform that opened the way for electoral circles to participate in organized political activity. Electoral clubs and political discussion groups spread the new ideas, which were then translated into concrete action in various political arenas. By 1896, liberal constitutionalism had a presence in practically every state in the republic with the exception of Oaxaca and was particularly strong in the northern states, the states of the central plateau, and on the Gulf Coast. Some data report as many as 113 formal circles of liberal constitutionalism around the country.

In addition to these liberal constitutionalist clubs, we would have to add social Catholic circles, Protestant schools, and other political and civic education clubs. None of these formations had any national structure, however; they were organized within municipalities or town centers. At times they counted on statewide links, but rarely interstate ones.

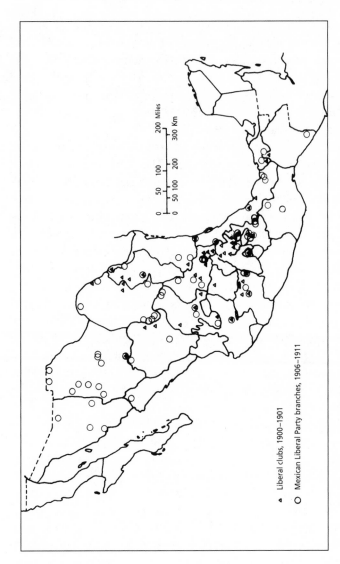

MAP 9.1. Distribution of liberal clubs and Mexican Liberal Party branches. (Source: François-Xavier Guerra, *México: Del Antiguo Régimen a la Revolución*, vol. 2 [Mexico City: Fondo de Cultura Económica, 1988], p. 18.)

▲ Liberal clubs, 1900–1901

○ Mexican Liberal Party branches, 1906–1911

200 Miles

300 Km

0 50 100 200

0 50 100 200

Unfortunately, there are no studies of these spontaneous forms of organization, nor of the public opinion, citizenship education, or daily political activities they would have represented. If we consider, however, that daily political events were discussed and decided at the municipal level, we can imagine that there may have been as many, or more, such circles as there were municipalities in the country.

The spread and influence of democratic liberals has been underestimated, and when they are mentioned, they tend to be linked to the elite or to the comfortable, educated urban middle class that repudiated the Díaz regime more for political than for social reasons. This is a false image. Among the new democratic liberals were people from other economic sectors and with worldviews that were not necessarily representative of the middle class.

It is an exaggeration to say that democratic liberalism was a strictly urban phenomenon. The fact that democratic liberal clubs operated out of cities and towns does not mean that all their members lived there. It could be that clubs met in towns because that was where people who lived in villages and settlements went to do their business and shopping. In this sense, the diverse expressions of liberal constitutionalism reproduced the tradition, born of the liberal revolution, of bringing together people of different sectors and social classes.

New Demands

As the nineteenth century drew to a close, the new ideologies that filtered into Mexico were being picked up and reformulated within the social collectivity, influencing social and political groupings. By 1890, these culturally motivated reconstructions were producing changes in traditional organizations. The new ideologies permeated society from the municipalities to the political elites. Some groups referred to the historical liberal tradition, the 1857 Constitution, and the liberal republican revolution, others to Church social doctrine, and still others to anarchist, communalist, and socialist ideas.

As the twentieth century began, democratic liberals, Catholics, and socialists were forming organizations to oppose the government, but without any formal relations among them. Their opposition was not yet capable of influencing public opinion, so it constituted no real threat to the regime, and the government made no effort to restrict any of them other than the socialists and anarchists. After 1900, though, the strength of these networks became clear.

As has been stated, liberal groups were demanding full compliance with the 1857 Constitution, and lay Catholics were appealing for a reordering of the social collectivity. At first, Catholic workers' circles competed and even clashed among themselves in the attempt to gain adherents. At the same time, the new liberals clashed with anarchists and socialists. In the first years of the new century, these divisions hardened, and more militant groups appeared calling for direct action. Working conditions had worsened by 1907, and, in a break from the previous decade, the demand for labor generally slackened outside the newest economic sectors of oil and textiles around the Gulf of Mexico, harbor construction in Veracruz, and the light and power infrastructure of Mexico City. The number of Mexicans living in the United States grew from less than 78,000 in 1900 to more than 250,000 in 1910.

The lack of work had its first impact on the rural labor market, where sharecroppers, renters, and seasonal workers lost access to land or found that the conditions of access had become more stringent. *Haciendas* erected walls in order to protect their harvests and water supplies, cutting off resources and reducing the mobility of villagers who farmed their own plots or raised livestock on communal grazing lands. Real wages decreased, and peasant servitude reverted to its harshest forms in the entire southeast.

The reduction in demand for labor, probably a part of the business cycle, struck hard at mining, transportation, and services, while construction was the sector least affected. The growth of employment in construction and energy provided work for younger workers, despite the drawbacks of more difficult working conditions and employment insecurity. Labor migration can be measured in the population growth of new towns and, beginning in 1900, the number of migrants to the United States.

All these circumstances, almost unknown until this time, changed the world of work and the human geography associated with it. In 1880, liberal legislation protected artisans, laborers, and skilled and semiskilled workers, enforcing their rights of freedom of association and free labor through individual contractual employment. By the beginning of the twentieth century, however, a new demand for social rights was being heard. This is understandable. Before, small business owners and tradespeople could still collaborate through *pueblo*-based guilds. They could found mutual-aid societies and cooperative assistance funds as compensatory mechanisms to redress economic disparities. Under the new circumstances posed by the modern division of labor, workers in the service,

TABLE 9.1. Population Distribution in Traditional and New Economic Sectors, 1900–1910

	1900		1910		Annual Rate of Growth (%)
	(Millions)	%	*(Millions)*	%	
Total population	13.60	—	15.10	—	1.1
Economically active population	5.24	—	5.71	—	0.9
	Traditional Sector				
Agriculture	3.18	60.7	3.60	63.0	1.2
Manufacturing	0.61	11.6	0.60	10.5	−0.1
Mining	0.10	1.9	0.10	1.8	−0.1
Construction	0.06	1.1	0.08	1.4	1.7
Commerce	0.26	4.9	0.30	5.3	0.5
Services	0.83	15.9	0.40	14.0	−0.1
	"New" Sector				
Fuel and energy	0.01	0.3	0.02	0.4	1.8
Transportation	0.06	1.1	0.06	1.0	−0.8
Technical and professional	0.13	2.5	0.15	2.6	0.6

SOURCES: *Estadísticas Económicas del Porfiriato* (Mexico City: El Colegio de México, 1956), pp. 38–60; Fernando Rosenzweig, *El Desarrollo Económico de México, 1800–1910* (Toluca: El Colegio Mexiquense, 1989), p. 236.

industrial, and technical sectors had yet to reorganize and find their points of leverage. New realities had to be considered. Unlike rural and artisanal labor, modern industrial and mining workers sell only their labor power. Consequently, the remuneration for labor performed is the worker's principal and almost sole means of subsistence. What is more, working conditions in the period we are discussing, universally described as hellish, were subject to no legislative supervision whatsoever, leaving the workers utterly unprotected.

The available data tell us that salaries stagnated between 1890 and 1900, increased by 12.6 percent between 1900 and 1907, and then fell 17.9 percent from 1907 to 1911, more than canceling the previous gain. This is a gross generalization, however, because in any newly industrializing country there are extreme wage differences across industries and even among different employers in a given city. The scanty data on working-class family budgets are not very helpful either, but one significant factor is worth noting: about 70 or 75 percent of salaries was used for food, the purchase of corn alone accounting for over 20 percent of income.

The reality of deteriorating living conditions and the nascent workers movement, on the other hand, are statistically well attested. Between 1900 and 1905, there were twenty-nine strikes, but between 1906 and 1910, the number shot up to 106. Most probably the heightened organization of work had led to more modern and effective workers' organizations. In this sense, the number of strikes in the textile industry is important to note, since this was the most developed manufacturing sector. This industry was the object of 10 strikes between 1900 and 1905 (34 percent of the total strikes) and 77 between 1906 and 1910 (72 percent of a total 106). A similar pattern may have played out among railroad and energy-sector workers, but that information is not available.

It has often been presented as incontrovertible fact that 1906 saw a tremendous mobilization of textile workers in Río Blanco and Orizaba in the state of Veracruz, as well as in Puebla and Tlaxcala; of copper miners in Cananea, Sonora; and of mechanics on the main rail lines. They all protested low salaries, poor conditions, and the favoritism shown foreign workers. If we examine the strike cycle, however, it can be seen that the most intense activity was in fact in the textile sector. Of a total of eight strikes in the first half of 1906, five were in textiles. In the second half of the year, textiles accounted for seventeen out of nineteen strikes. In the first half of 1907, fourteen out of twenty were in the same industry. In all, there were twelve textile strikes in Puebla, sixteen in Veracruz, thirty-seven in Mexico City, one in Jalisco, two in Tlaxcala, three in Querétaro, and three in the state of Mexico. The qualitative importance of the miners' strike in Cananea, Sonora, is not to be underestimated, but the critical working-class mobilization was in the textile industry because of the number of workers it employed (some thirty-one thousand), its geographical dispersion in seven states, and its location in numerous urban centers, where strikes had a dramatic effect on social and economic life and on other social groups.

Textile workers in multiple factories acted together for the first time in the 1906–1907 movement. In December 1906, workers in thirty Puebla mills collaborated to defend their salaries and to demand a reduction in hours, regular Saturday payment, the standardization of fines for poorly executed work, the end of mistreatment by supervising master workers, no employment of children under fourteen, the right to a minimum pension, increased pay for the night shift, and the elimination of company stores, *tiendas de raya,* where workers were effectively paid in kind.

The workers also demanded respect for their political rights. In concrete terms this meant the recognition of the constitutional guarantees to free expression and freedom of association, and the employers' full respect for Article 13 of the 1857 Constitution, which asserted full equality before the law for all citizens, workers and industrialists alike, and prohibited the trial of any citizen by a special court. The workers' demands were not only social and economic but also political and institutional. They demanded social justice and political equality.

The Democracy Movement

The sixth reelection of Porfirio Díaz, in June and July of 1910, drove a wedge in society between the democratic anti-reelectionist movement and the conservative reelectionist movement. The anti-reelectionists were also demanding expanded political and economic prospects for the new generation of Mexicans, which were beyond the capacity of the existing system to provide. Within a few months, what had begun as a peaceful democracy movement became a national insurrection with the participation of large numbers of *hacendados* and entrepreneurs, opposition politicians, merchants, white-collar workers and professionals, ranch hands and administrators, miners, industrial workers, railroad employees, muleteers, cattle herders, and peasants, among others. An anti-reelectionist movement of such magnitude had until then seemed inconceivable. Porfirio Díaz was celebrating his eightieth birthday and had been reelected half a dozen times in his thirty-five years of power.

Francisco I. Madero belonged to one of the most prominent landowning and entrepreneurial families of northern Mexico. He had studied both in Europe and in the United States and was a strong advocate of progressivism. He began a nationwide campaign for the presidency in 1909 with the support of his powerful family group—an unusual step that enabled him to reach out to the general public. His basic constituency was the middle class, and his great innovation was to establish connections between worker and peasant demands and between social and political ones, crystallized in the calls for free town councils, the elimination of political bosses, effective suffrage, and no reelection. Madero was the beneficiary of a long tradition of political opposition in the northeast and in other regions of the country. Since 1892, this opposition had been kept alive through years of vicissitudes by liberal constitutionalists, Catholic modernizers, Protestant groups, anarcho-syndicalists, and followers of

Ricardo Flores Magón and Bernardo Reyes. Throughout the country, the movement was coordinated and spread by organizations that sponsored congresses, tours, and conventions. The dimensions of the 1909–1911 anti-reelectionist movement would have been inconceivable without this history (see map 9.2).

Porfirio Díaz was well aware that the anti-reelectionist movement was a national force, and in June 1910, before the elections, he ordered Madero's arrest. Several uncertain weeks followed, but the elections produced a resounding victory for the government, and with the success of this fraud, the electoral route for political action was closed.

Through his Plan de San Luis, Madero called upon the nation to rise up in arms. The insurrectional plan—logical and seemingly feasible—called for the capture of several important state capitals, which was expected to attract the support of a significant nucleus of federal army officers. Operations would be coordinated by a revolutionary junta, and it was expected that other rebel circles would join the movement. The goal was for a handful of state capitals and railroad centers to fall into Maderista hands, which would put them in a position of strength from which to enter into negotiations with the government. But the government repressed the uprising, the Maderistas did not take any cities, and the insurrection took on new characteristics. The movement burst out of its initial organizational confines and into regions where the leadership and social composition of rebel circles fell to ranchers, small business owners, muleteers, miners, white- and blue-collar workers, professionals, railway employees, *hacienda* administrators, and peasants in general. From December 1910 until the end of March 1911, rebel bands wreaked destruction on a daily basis, targeting bridges, railroads, telegraph lines, and small towns with only local defenses. The spontaneity and broad diffusion of the insurrection forced the government to employ its garrisons in defense of the principal cities, at the cost of mobility and flexibility. The insurrection was so effective and widespread that the political-military crisis of the Porfirista regime became unmanageable.

The government could not last more than a few months under these circumstances. Díaz publicly acknowledged his defeat and resigned in an attempt to salvage the regime. The two parties signed the Treaty of Ciudad Juárez in May 1911, which stipulated that in return for Díaz's resignation, the Maderistas would advance the electoral and political proposals they had advocated in 1909–1910.

The democratic insurrection, like any other, created and strengthened new organizations and promoted demands for social and political

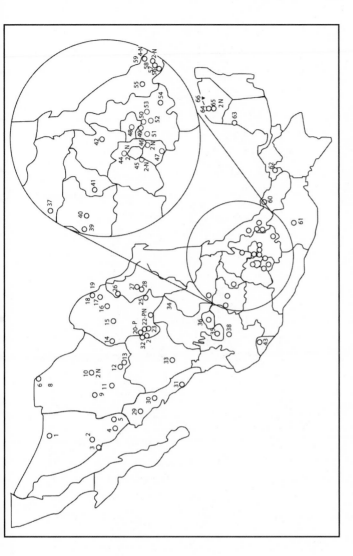

MAP 9.2. The anti-reelectionist election campaign: anti-reelectionist clubs founded in 1909 and 1910. The points numbered 1–66 are places where there are records of anti-reelectionist clubs or, in the cases of Guadalajara and Mexico City, clubs affiliated with the Independent or the Democratic Nationalist parties, which aligned themselves with the National Anti-Reelection Party, endorsing its principles and candidates. In the cases of Chihuahua, Nuevo León, Zacatecas, Puebla, and Yucatán, the references are general in the sense that there were a great many clubs, but more detailed information is unavailable. A number followed by "N" indicates the number of clubs or similar groups in the indicated location; otherwise, there was just one club in that place. A numbered location followed by "P" indicates the probable site of a club. All locations are approximate. (Source: Santiago Portilla, *Una Sociedad en Armas* [Mexico City: El Colegio de México, 1995], p. 116.)

change. This process was accelerated by the fact that many of these organizations had also developed their military capacity by 1911. At its peak, the democratic insurrection mobilized sixty to eighty thousand armed combatants, many more than in the federal army.

The insurrection was a national phenomenon, although its intensity differed from region to region, and some areas were untouched by the conflict. The location of rebel activities coincided with the centers of political opposition in 1884, 1892, 1895, 1901, and 1906, illustrating the insurrection's continuity with the political past.

The leadership of the democratic movement headed by Francisco Madero was fundamentally a coordinating body for many strongly autonomous regional revolutionary organizations that all agreed upon one national goal: to liquidate the Porfiriato and transform the old social and political order. The result was the resounding defeat of the Porfiriato with the triumph of Madero in the election of October 1911. Held under the old system of single indirect elections by means of electors, Madero received 98 percent of the vote. In the vice presidential results, however, there was a notable split among the Maderistas and between Maderistas and Catholics. José María Pino Suárez, a moderate Maderista, received 53 percent of the vote, the conservative Francisco León de la Barra received 29 percent, and Vázquez Gómez, a more radical Maderista, received 17 percent. The democratic coalition and the conservative coalition were each supported by about half of the public.

With the introduction of universal male suffrage on May 22, 1912, the first democratic Congress was elected, as was a partially reconstituted Senate. It should be noted that the new electoral law not only promoted broad participation in voting for all male citizens but also recognized all parties and political groups with at least 150 members and guaranteed the broadest possible freedom of opinion and public expression to all parties and political circles.

The 1912 electoral campaign further mobilized the public opinion already engaged at the national level by the presidential election of 1911. It was a major opportunity to bring some coherence to the multitude of political demands being made by disparate groups. But we know little about this first democratic electoral process in Mexico—the campaign, how candidates were registered, how coalitions were formed. We do know that many candidates received votes—there were more than ten candidates in some districts. This tells us that there were multiple electoral options within the democratic and conservative blocs.

The essential fact is that in only five years, and especially between 1910

and 1912, society had taken a qualitative leap forward in political organization. The National Catholic Party participated in this first democratic
election in Mexico, and its participation defined the electoral alliances:
two large blocs formed to reflect the polarization of forces, the Conservative Bloc and the Liberal Renewal Bloc, which included the Progressive
Constitutionalist Party of Gustavo Madero, the president's brother. The
fluidity of political life in those years did not allow for categorical divisions, however. The liberal renewal bloc also included some members of
the National Catholic Party, and some independent groups attempted to
promote and capitalize upon the discontent of conservative urban sectors.

It is difficult to interpret the 1912 congressional election results. Some
newspapers reported that 130 deputies were *gobiernistas*, supporters of the
group in power. This would have given the Maderistas 50.9 percent of the
seats in Congress. Another fifty deputies (19.6 percent) were in the opposition, and the remaining seventy-five (29.4 percent) identified themselves as independents. It appears that the elections provided a valuable
opportunity to set a new direction for the country and were a corrective
to the political fragmentation that resulted from the armed conflict. This
is not an unusual phenomenon and had previously occurred in Mexico
between 1867 and 1880. The electoral results spoke to a new democratic
option in the form of coalition politics that pointed the country toward
a new governability.

We attribute the crisis of the reform movement to the inability of the
democratic elite to understand the speed and extent to which the armed
insurrection had changed society and accelerated popular demands. The
elite had attempted to overcome the political impasse from the top down.
Gustavo Madero and the Progressive Constitutionalist Party intended to
gain a majority in the Chamber of Deputies and to capture the open seats
in the Senate, assuming that it would be possible to organize a new government by eliminating or quashing the conservative bench. The
Maderista elite did not recognize that the election results clearly indicated
a society divided three ways, and that no one of the three forces had the
strength to dominate the political process. Concluding that with 51 percent of the deputies it did not need to work in a broader coalition, the
government gave the conservatives the opportunity to reach an agreement with a not entirely conservative grouping, the Catholics. Together
the conservatives and the Catholics held a majority of the seats in the Senate, though not in the Chamber of Deputies.

The reformers' control of the Chamber of Deputies under the leadership of Gustavo Madero and Luis Cabrera, a lawyer and staunch

Maderista, led to constant friction with the Senate. While the deputies seriously took up the need for policies to restore lands to the communities, conservative and Catholic senators concentrated on hobbling the government at every turn. The intolerance and inflexibility of both blocs produced a gridlock that extended to the highest levels of state authority, producing a growing power vacuum.

Under the circumstances, it was no surprise that the conservative forces appealed to the only well-organized state body, the federal army, to organize a coup. They failed twice. The first attempt was in October 1912, instigated by the Científicos and led by General Félix Díaz, nephew of the exiled president. The second was in February 1913, led by General Manuel Mondragón and Bernardo Reyes, former minister of war and organizer of the Second Reserve in 1902. They finally succeeded later that month, when a group of Reyista officers joined the conspiracy along with General Victoriano Huerta, a hard-liner with a strong following in the officer corps.

The violence of the military coup, the assassinations of the president and vice president, and the formation of a Catholic and conservative government led the democratic forces to organize in opposition. Some leaders of the Casa del Obrero Mundial, a radical workers' movement, began to circulate among existing revolutionary garrisons; others remained in Mexico City. The social Catholic movement distanced itself from the Catholic hierarchy and the illegitimate government. Most important, protests and rebellions against the takeover broke out in the states, especially in Sonora, Chihuahua, and Coahuila. Álvaro Obregón, a farmer, schoolteacher, and recently elected mayor, was given command of the militias in his state of Sonora; the figure of Francisco Villa emerged in Chihuahua; and the constitutionally elected governor Venustiano Carranza, twice elected mayor and an avowed anti-Porfirian and anti-reelectionist, headed up the resistance in Coahuila.

The Plan de Guadalupe of March 27, 1913, is considered the foundation of the constitutionalist movement, but insufficient attention has been paid to the fact that with the assassination of the constitutionally elected President Madero and his vice president, the federal compact was ruptured for the first time in Mexican history, in the sense that sovereign state authorities determined the federal government to be illegitimate and unconstitutional. History vindicates the durability of Mexican federalism, for when the federal compact was broken, a constitutionalist movement arose to return sovereignty to the states. Both the constitutionalists and then Emiliano Zapata, a village authority from southern

Morelos, expressed this idea. Zapata's manifesto of March 4, 1913, included these words: "With the victory of the Felicista [led by Félix Díaz] uprising, a spurious and illegitimate government holds power . . . [one] which can never represent our national sovereignty, nor that of the states, in accordance with the 1857 Constitution." The Plan de Ayala was reformulated on May 30, 1913, to characterize Victoriano Huerta as "a usurper of authority."

While in 1910 Madero had appealed to the army to join his movement, Carranza in 1913 had used his position as governor of Coahuila to decree, along with the legislature, the rupture of the federal compact, the withdrawal of recognition from the federal army, and the recognition of the Constitutionalist Army as the only legitimate military force. No doubt the recentness of the state elections had facilitated this process. Officeholders had just taken up their positions, and a significant number of antireelectionists had won municipal posts. They proceeded to integrate Maderista rebel groups into the irregular forces of their states.

The 1913–1914 *pronunciamientos* against the Huerta dictatorship closely paralleled the map of the highly regional 1911 insurgency. A strong northern center radiated toward Coahuila, Durango, and Zacatecas; the states of Morelos and Guerrero formed the core of a central zone; a moderately strong zone ran through the north-central states of San Luis Potosí and Tamaulipas; and, in Sonora, Álvaro Obregón headed the state militia. Once again there was only a weak presence in the far south.

While the 1911 power shifts and organizational changes had primarily been accomplished by political means, the corresponding events in 1913–1914 were the result of military action. As a result, society was ever more militarized—a phenomenon that paralleled the growth of the federal army, which Victoriano Huerta tried to increase to a force of 200,000 troops.

The Huerta regime collapsed after fifteen months of being in power, from March 1913 to August 1914. The federal army was defeated not in large-scale battles but in a war that resembled the events of 1911, including surprise attacks and the frequent defection of garrisons. The army was hampered by its own slowness, lack of logistical support, and lack of trust among its officers and between them and the population. Widespread demoralization led to the army's surrender and dissolution. The military institution's disappearance from the scene left the country in the hands of the victorious political-military factions and provided an unusual opportunity for political reorganization on a national scale. Within Latin America this disbanding of a regular army is unique to Mexico and accounts for the stable evolution of the country's political system. The armed forces that fought in the conflicts of 1914 to 1920 were civilians in arms upholding the tradition of the National Guard. A professional modern army was developed only as of the 1950s, once a civilian political framework had been set in place.

From 1914 onward, peace was one of the most important demands of the citizenry. All agreed on one thing: without peace, other demands could not be satisfied. Without peace and stability there was no possibility of national reconstruction or renewal, and only peace could bring the local and regional pieces of the national mosaic back together.

The Revolutionary Groups

Unlike in 1911, political groups in 1914 tried to respond to the demand for peace, knowing that if it were not reestablished, social and political reforms would not be realized and the revolutionary struggle would have been for naught. Each demand received a different response from the various revolutionary groups, according to their strength, the territorial control they exercised, the relationship between their urban and rural components, and their own interests. The Constitutionalist Army, headed by Venustiano Carranza, represented a segment of society that came to hold governorships and mayoralties as a result of the revolution. The positions of these men as military commanders deepened their control over the regions, enabling them to secure most of the available business contracts. The Carrancistas, for example, occupied strategic zones and benefited from an effective political-military and administrative apparatus. Venustiano Carranza, as Primer Jefe of a movement that favored an immediate return to constitutional order, developed a centralized political leadership with a fairly powerful civilian component more disposed to restoring order than negotiating with popular sectors. Constitutionalist cohesion did not mean complete unity for at least one of its factions, however, that of Álvaro Obregón. While Obregón's forces depended on Carranza for supply, they tended to assert a certain autonomy when it came to military policy. This was partly because they were cut off from their territorial base in Sonora and needed to form alliances with the lower- and middle-class population sectors of the areas they occupied.

The followers of Francisco Villa were markedly heterogeneous, both socially and politically. Villa's Division of the North was composed of ranch hands; muleteers; agricultural, mining, and railroad workers; and former soldiers of the Porfirian army. Its higher officers included federal army deserters, Catholic Maderistas, and former ranch foremen and supervisors. The relationship of the officer corps with social Catholics, Protestants, and former federals provided a means for Villismo to build bridges to people in other states and even internationally. The funds necessary to maintain the division were raised from confiscated *haciendas* and from compulsory taxes levied on commercial agriculture. The operation was administered from a headquarters in Chihuahua that provisioned both the Division of the North and the needy among the population. Villa's agrarian program of 1915 proposed to distribute land to veterans, widows, and orphans when hostilities ended.

In 1914–1915, Zapatismo represented the interests of the municipalities and *pueblos* with strong communitarian traditions based on the defense of their historical right to manage both private and collective patrimony over water, forests, pasture, and cropland. To these ends, the movement relied upon an extensive network of local notables and organic leaders who personified the long-standing defense of the right to self-government and municipal autonomy. In this sense, Zapatismo was more than a regional movement. By taking up the demands for self-government and municipal autonomy that resonated throughout the country, it came to extend its influence over *pueblos* and municipalities in other regions.

Would three large social sectors with apparently incompatible bases and interests be able to find a way to live and work together to define a direction for the nascent State? The first effort in this regard was an attempt to reach unity among the constitutionalists gathered in Mexico City on October 1, 1914; this meeting led to a new recognition of the Primer Jefe, Carranza. In addition, all the revolutionary groups agreed to meet at a convention in Aguascalientes on October 10, 1914. The differences among the armed factions represented there were a reflection of the general social upheaval taking place. Constitutionalism itself was by no means homogeneous. Obregón, for example, was disposed to advance worker-peasant social organization and to develop the growing call of the middle classes for greater political and economic rights. The Villistas and Zapatistas, inclined to advance the social movement by producing tangible gains in the areas of social rights and land reform, seemed to be potential allies of Obregón. The most strictly constitutionalist grouping, centered around the forces of Carranza, was convinced that the key to peace would be reforms to the 1857 Constitution in order to reliably and unambiguously codify newly won social and political rights. Carranza believed that in the absence of the legal instruments necessary to guarantee a state of law, pressure from the popular movement would lead to a long civil war.

The differences and deep hostility between the different factional leaders ended up producing a wider split. The constitutionalist faction pulled out, and the convention selected Francisco Villa as military chief. When the forces under Villa's command entered Mexico City in December 1914, they obliged the constitutionalists to withdraw to their stronghold in Veracruz, where they reaffirmed the authority of the provisional government under Carranza. The convention delegates had not been able to reach any major agreements, and as a result the conventionist government lost the support of Villa and with it the authority to enforce its will. The provisional president of the convention, Eulalio Gutiérrez, and other former delegates deplored Villista outrages, saying that homes had been violated daily and the right to life and property had been violated, sowing fear and apprehension in Mexican society. Gutiérrez declared the limits of the revolution: "We cannot conceive of it in an alliance with theft and murder. . . . It must be remembered that Mexico has struggled not just for bread, but also for freedom, for a government that respects and guarantees the rights of all against whomever may violate them, and a system of law that applies equally to all and is the firm basis of our progress and well-being."

The relative power and momentum among the various factions began to shift in September 1915. The Villistas were defeated in the Bajío region and failed in a campaign to take the petroleum-rich area around Tampico, forcing them to retreat to their old base in Chihuahua. The constitutionalists turned back Zapatista forays into Guerrero and Puebla, and the latter retreated to their own territory in Morelos. The United States' recognition of the Carranza government in October 1915 established the definitive claim of power by the constitutionalists. From this moment on, Carranza exercised extraordinary powers as Primer Jefe, acting upon the widespread desire for order and for work. He attempted to establish a central bank, promoted the normalization of agricultural property, and sought to devise mechanisms for the resolution of disputes between workers and employers. With the eventual victory of the movement, he intended to explicitly incorporate the reforms brought to bear by his provisional government into the constitution.

One goal of Carranza's provisional government was to curtail food riots and protests against the devaluation of paper money, which enriched speculators and further impoverished the poor. Carranza's preconstitutional government from 1915 to 1917 coincided with increased exports because of the world war. The government used the proceeds from the export of strategic goods and food staples to stabilize regions falling under its control and to generate income. It operated in a strongly statist fashion that included military control of the railroads, regulation of business and of grain production, and the seizure of banks.

Carranza and constitutionalism had gained so much power that the Obregonistas, Villistas, and Zapatistas intensified their collaboration in an effort to counter them. When Obregón occupied Mexico City in March 1915, his improved ties with the Casa del Obrero Mundial led to an agreement in which its leadership made a commitment to organize the workers throughout the constitutionalist-occupied area. In return, the Red Battalions were formed to operate on various fronts. Carranza and the most conservative constitutionalists thought that the agreement was but a maneuver by Obregón to increase his personal power. But Obregón's policy of forming coalitions with popular sectors led him to hand over management of the telephone and telegraph company to the workers. This seems to have been the beginning of Obregón's relationship with the working-class leader Luis N. Morones. In 1918, the two men would sign a secret mutual assistance pact, and Morones would later help Obregón reach the presidency.

Relations between the workers' movement and the Zapatistas solidified when the conventionist government came under Zapatista control between July 1914 and May 1915. During the Zapatista administration, Mexico City was more orderly than ever before, partly due to the cooperation between Zapatistas and workers, which put an end to strike movements. In addition, the Federal District's judiciary was reestablished and the free circulation of all the currencies distributed by the revolutionary factions was accepted, so that the flow of goods was unimpeded. They reconciled with the Church, in particular with the new vicar general, Pedro Benavides. Collaboration between Zapatistas and workers led to the founding in those months of the Sindicato Mexicano de Electricistas, the Mexican Electricians Union, an organization whose members seem to have collaborated with the Zapatista city administration. When the convention moved its government to Morelos, south of Mexico City, the original Zapatista project was enhanced, as the provisional government took on a formal structure that included the Executive Council of the Mexican Republic, with a president and a governing council.

Zapatismo spread beyond Morelos; in the April 1916 Manifesto to the Nation, signed by the civilian representatives of thirty-eight generals of different regions, it was agreed that a parliamentary republic would be established (Article 33), municipal autonomy would be recognized (Article 32), and the Senate, considered an aristocratic and conservative body, would be eliminated. Congress would be unicameral (Articles 34 and 35), and the judiciary would be autonomous and independent (Article 36). All of the above was in accordance with the Plan de Ayala and the revolution's program of social and political reforms.

Social groups outside the ranks of constitutionalism, including significant anarchist forces, supported and joined the process of social and political organization. The provisional executive council in Morelos legislated the establishment of small-property rights at the expense of the rich sugar-producing *haciendas;* the direct vote and no reelection; municipal autonomy, including a municipal judiciary and municipal cooperatives for agricultural and industrial producers; the right to work, with guarantees for the freedom of association, the right to strike, and the right to engage in boycotts; unemployment insurance; an eight-hour workday; salaries indexed to the regional cost of living; the abolition of scrip and payment in kind through company stores; and the right to free enterprise by means of antimonopoly legislation and regulated expropriation in the name of the public good. Taxes were made equitable through the imposition of a progressive tax regime and the elimination of consumption taxes.

The Birth of a New Order

Carranza mobilized rapidly in mid-1916, alarmed by popular support for the new coalition and the possible defection of constitutionalist generals, particularly Obregón. Ten days after the Carrancistas occupied Mexico City, the city's workers launched the offensive that they had promised the Zapatistas. The United Federation of the Federal District called a general strike, and the electricians took the lead in bringing it to bear. Carranza immediately decreed the death penalty for strikers and jailed their leadership.

Obregón made no decisive move but threatened to resign from the Secretariat of War. Carranza forced him to choose between staying at the head of the secretariat or going to Spain, and he agreed to stay on, but with the proviso that after the elections he would step down and return to Sonora. Thus Carranza managed to neutralize the one general with the greatest potential to solidify the emerging coalition. At the same time, he understood that the strikes were one aspect of a more general political plan, and he launched a two-part offensive. On the military front, he set fire to the harvests and concentrated civilians in hamlets in order to cut off popular aid to the Zapatistas. Politically, he attacked the autonomy of the *pueblos* of Morelos. In addition, he established the Constitutionalist Railroad System and put its workers under military discipline, and he dissolved the Casa del Obrero Mundial and ordered the arrest of all "agitators."

The rapid response to the nascent anti-Carranza coalition owed a lot to the nature of constitutionalism as the embryo of a new State. Although the divisions of the Constitutionalist Army enjoyed significant autonomy, the Primer Jefe was in a position to coordinate their activities. This applied to the Sonoran army of Álvaro Obregón, to Francisco Villa's Northern Division, and to the Army of the East, commanded by Carranza's nephew Pablo González. But the role of the Primer Jefe went beyond coordination. At the beginning of 1915, Carranza was in a position not only to coordinate but also to act as administrative, political, and military chief of all the main components of the Constitutionalist Army.

The ever more centralized organization of the Constitutionalist Army was due in a large part to the ability of Luis Cabrera, who was in charge of finances, to consolidate control over key cities and to dominate the periphery of the country in order to administer sea and land customs. Since the provisional government was based in Veracruz, two-thirds of all import income was within its immediate grasp. The strategy for the other third was simple and easy: maintain strategic control over transportation through the Constitutionalist Railroad System under military command, and free up forces from the occupation and administration of the interior in order to capture the Pacific and Gulf ports and the areas along the United States–Mexican border. The duties collected would generate hard currency and would provide hard cash to pay the army and the civil administration and keep the constitutionalist territories supplied.

Without sacrificing its regional bases, the Constitutionalist Army established a general command in the person of the Primer Jefe, and being a citizen army, it was able to project both its military and administrative policies on a national level. Its organizational complexity was greater than that of the Zapatistas. In order to maintain military mobility, it managed to name civil authorities and establish governmental functions in its territories very quickly. The immediate establishment of civil administration prevented the militarization of social and political demands or their subordination to military needs. The evidence tells us that the constitutionalists' application of social and political reforms kept pace with their military defeats of the dictatorship. One example is the March 4, 1913, executive law on land distribution. It proclaimed "the urgent need to solve the agrarian problem, the distribution of lands, that is, through the expropriation of rural and urban properties of the Porfiristas and of Huerta's henchmen." The same law established that all inhabitants had the right "to gather in every small or large town and name their leader."

The December 1914 reformulation of the Plan de Guadalupe points in the same direction. The reformed plan exemplified the civil side of constitutionalism, which picked up the demands of the 1911–1915 period and set out to satisfy them through government action. Equality was construed as more than just formal "equality before the law" and integrated broader social components. Thus agrarian laws were instituted, as were laws against the monopolization of natural resources and laws to guarantee the social rights of all workers. Equality meant the direct vote and the strengthening of freedom of expression, freedom of opinion, freedom of the press, and freedom of association. The interesting thing about the reformulated Plan de Guadalupe is that it laid the basis for all the manifestos and plans that came after 1915.

The specific challenge for constitutionalism at the beginning of 1916 was to consolidate its victory over its principal armed adversaries so it could devote maximal energy and resources to governing the country. Ending the civil war was an urgent matter. The constitutionalist military was given carte blanche, while Carranza and the central bodies of the government concentrated on setting a viable political direction, responding to a minimal number of popular demands, and liquidating the anti-Carranza coalition that was coming together between 1914 and 1916.

The Economic Effort

The country had gone through economic difficulties from 1907 until the First World War, when wartime demand for agricultural products, minerals, oil, cotton, and other products skyrocketed. Before the war, the extraction of copper, gold, and especially silver had decreased. The 2,663 tons of silver produced in 1910 had dropped to 785 tons by 1915, which is to say that almost 70 percent of capacity was nonproductive. Harvests of commercial crops like sugar and cotton had dropped to 50 percent of capacity. Basic food crops like corn and wheat fared somewhat better, perhaps due to the increased cultivation of marginal lands. Production levels did not drop for petroleum or for henequen because Yucatán saw little military activity during the revolution.

The decreased production was reflected in the level of international trade. Between 1910 and 1915, exports were stagnant at about 140 million dollars, and imports remained at about 90 million dollars. However, these stable dollar values reflected not the quantity of goods traded, but increased prices on international markets leading up to and during the First World War.

The economic indicators cited above are so general that they obscure the important fact that the 1911–1916 war seriously damaged the domestic transportation system, particularly the railroads. According to the Secretariat of War, national transport capacity as measured in rolling stock decreased almost 60 percent. The breakdown of the railroad system devastated the patterns of domestic commerce that had gradually developed in the last third of the nineteenth century, and trade reverted to regional markets. Since 74 percent of the freight stock connecting the north and the center of the country was out of circulation, it became more practical to export northern agricultural products to the United States than to sell them domestically.

Production and marketing were now regional or local, and since military commanders enjoyed considerable autonomy, they were able to appropriate resources in their zones to finance the war, and sometimes for personal enrichment. The insecurity and arbitrariness of economic life was another burden for the citizenry. Newly formed regulatory bodies were unable to protect the citizens adequately. Insecurity, famine, and disease were serious new problems that helped radicalize the various armed movements.

In addition to the degradation of transportation and communication, 1913 saw the destruction of the monetary system as each of the armed movements issued paper money and required its use in the area it occupied in order to raise funds for the war. By November 1914, the constitutionalists had issued almost 50 billion pesos. The Villistas issued their own paper money and required businesses in their zone to accept it. Many counterfeit bills circulated as well. It must be said that the Zapatistas printed less paper money and opted instead to pay their bills in highly valued hard pesos. All together, the various groups must have issued the startling sum of 1.5 billion pesos in paper money.

The result of the uncontrolled printing of money was rapid currency depreciation. The 150 million pesos in circulation in 1912 had been multiplied by a factor of 10. A people accustomed to the use of coinage and convertible banknotes was forced to accommodate overnight to the use of overabundant paper money whose value could hardly, if at all, be guaranteed. Silver and gold coins disappeared from circulation, but the new bills were rejected by working-class wage earners. Their unease can be understood if we note that bills issued at par by Carranza in April 1913 had lost 30 percent of their value that December, 50 percent by August 1914, and 90 percent by the end of the year.

The monetary situation accelerated inflation in the price of basic goods, affecting economic life in general, especially in the cities, where all transactions, including salaries and wages, were in paper money. The urban poor and workers were undoubtedly the most affected. In addition to unemployment due to decreased production, they suffered great economic difficulties because they had no option but to use paper money to address all their basic needs.

Economic recovery was at first the result of an international event, the outbreak of the First World War. Exports took off beginning in 1916, and they had nearly doubled in value by 1920, from 242 to 426 million dollars. Imports began to increase in 1917, and they too had increased dramatically by 1920, growing in value from 105 to 180 million dollars. Growth was rapid in the mining sector, in commercial agriculture, and in internal consumption. The warring countries favored neutral Latin American countries like Mexico as suppliers of raw materials and agricultural goods. The international situation benefited the Mexican economy in two ways: the increased demand not only raised prices on export commodities but stimulated increased production. This made it possible to recover unused capacity.

Petroleum production jumped from 3.6 to 32.9 million barrels between 1911 and 1918. Pumping was restricted to certain geographical areas, which were guarded and defended by the oil companies. Owners of petroleum-rich properties received royalties from the petroleum companies and actively participated in the armed defense of their land. Most importantly to the security of petroleum operations, however, no political-military group wanted to kill the goose that laid the golden egg, since petroleum companies regularly paid all required export royalties. The data for 1921 tell us that, compared with the same results for 1910, the gross domestic product (measured at 1960 prices) was 7.6 percent higher, the mining and petroleum sector had increased 181 percent, and cattle ranching had increased 5.8 percent. The agricultural sector, internal commerce, and manufacturing, on the other hand, did not recover their 1910 levels until 1921.

The international situation provided incentive for national reconstruction, which in its way created a contradiction within liberalism due
to the then-current statist tendencies. A new current of thinking arose
among government ranks as officials proposed the implementation of
some new social programs without abandoning their basic liberal orientation. Perhaps the world war could be exploited to reactivate the economy, stimulate investment, and address social needs. The new political-
economic approach was to contain imports by increasing import duties,
thus hopefully benefiting Mexican industry, which, according to John
Womack, "[had] emerged intact from the struggle; it was not destroyed."[1] What hampered industry however, was the difficult problem
of distribution in light of the degraded transportation system and the
monetary collapse. Nationalization of the railroad and currency controls
benefited manufacturing, especially beginning in 1917, and contributed to
its recovery as well as to the expansion of consumer-oriented manufacturing and medium-scale industry.

The protectionist customs regime provided a powerful stimulus to the
recovery. Beginning in 1916, customs duties were again paid in gold and
silver. Salaries, too, were paid in coins or their equivalent in paper money
according to the daily exchange rate. These measures made it possible to
collect all taxes in coin or its equivalent in paper currency. The next step
was to reestablish parity between paper money and gold coins, and finally,
to regularize the payment of taxes in the paper money equivalent of gold.
The government's rejection of unbacked paper money brought about a
definitive return to the gold standard, in particular after January 1, 1917,
when all salaries were to be paid either in Mexican gold coins or their
equivalent value in silver coins.

The return to stability was no small matter, considering that monetary
inflation had stirred up tremendous popular discontent and precipitated
widespread urban protests. The government's success certainly generated
a wider consensus in its favor.

The government's neoconservative policies limited social and political
participation. Nevertheless, it would be a mistake to see the Constitutionalist Army as an army of occupation outside of Morelos, Oaxaca, Chiapas, and perhaps Yucatán and Tabasco. In the areas where local politicians and Carrancista military commanders could work together, the

1. See John Womack Jr., "The Mexican Revolution 1910–1920," in Leslie Bethell, ed., *The Cambridge History of Latin America* (Cambridge: Cambridge University Press, 1984), vol. 5, pp. 79–154.

Constitutionalist Army promoted the renewal of political life. At first, this renovation was influenced by "northern ideas," but when over one hundred thousand soldiers were mobilized and sent outside their own regions, they intermingled with and were exposed to the experiences of others from all around the country. We should remember that in 1915, the government depended on the Constitutionalist Army to govern the many states where it was the only authoritative presence. It was also the principal body to which the middle and upper social groups within pacified areas could address their needs.

Without a doubt, northern military commanders and troops were present in the center and south of the country. Many of them arbitrarily appropriated goods to themselves or operated personal businesses with the benefit of their military authority. Their negative practices were more spectacular than their positive ones, though, and tend to obscure the cooperation between the Constitutionalist Army and some civilians. They cooperated on the reestablishment of order through joint action against guerrillas and on the reactivation of municipal politics, in keeping with Carranza's December 15, 1915, decree that municipal governments should be chosen by direct popular election.

The 1916 municipal elections returned local government to civilians, an important step in the reestablishment of institutional order. Once again, as in 1812—although over one hundred years had passed and the historical circumstances were new—the municipal election process contributed to the reestablishment of order and of local institutions. The municipality reemerged showing new strengths. The electoral process brought about a new correlation of local forces with the Constitutionalist Army. Political clubs and electoral groupings were reconstituted and even strengthened through new organizations such as labor unions; farmers', peasants', and renters' leagues; and urban tenant associations. Between 10 and 30 percent of enrolled voters participated in the municipal elections of 1916, an impressive number given the state of war. Yet the process was not free of irregularities. As a result of political and military fragmentation and factionalism, the election was manipulated to put civilian allies of the Carrancistas in positions of power. Nevertheless, it marked the return of civilians to political life as rule by military decree yielded to the decisions of civilian bodies.

Carranza's intent to return confiscated property should be seen as part of his strategy to reorganize the country by handing properties back to their lawful owners. He transferred the land that had been confiscated from Porfiristas, Huertistas, and Convencionistas to a federal agency.

This centralized their management and generated additional government revenue. Thanks to this decision, Church real estate, which by itself represented 90 percent of all that had been confiscated in Puebla, was never returned. The State also retained the properties confiscated from Convencionistas and Huertistas. In some regions and localities, however, the return of confiscated property to its previous owners was not universal. Some governors redistributed land to needy peasants and returned *haciendas* and other lands only if they were abandoned or if their evacuation by the Constitutionalist Army would have caused new problems.

The policy on property restitution was somewhat balanced by the distribution of land to peasants and by bringing day laborers into the cash economy. Although the amount of land distributed was insignificant—only 180,000 hectares distributed to 48,000 families in 190 pueblos between 1915 and 1920—significant expectations were created when the government enforced labor laws and demanded that rural day laborers be paid in cash. More importantly, *hacienda*-based company stores—the use of which amounted to payment in kind—were abolished. Together with the mandate to pay workers in cash, this benefited the entire rural population and began to erode the institutions that had maintained peasant servility, which was especially strong in the south-central states.

As can be seen, national reconstruction was multifaceted, having social, economic, and political dimensions. It was not a unidirectional, top-down process, but one in which a plurality of actors were set in motion. If we reflect for a moment on these social actors, we can discern similarities with those of 1892, 1895, 1901, 1906–1907, and 1909–1910. The difference is that in 1911–1920, as in the mid-nineteenth century, the primary dynamic was toward the consolidation of a new relation between the elites and the wider population. This was the outstanding characteristic of the revolutionary period. The 1915–1920 postwar social process does not seem to have been regressive, a "betrayal of the revolution," or a rejection of new social demands.

The 1917 Constitution and the Return to Legality

In 1914, Carranza decreed an important reform of the 1857 Constitution, granting autonomy to municipal governments, accompanied by their return to civilians. These directives were reinforced when he declared, in 1915, the need to convert the reforms decreed during the revolutionary struggle into constitutional principles. The reforms were to be institutionalized and incorporated into a new legal order guaranteed by a new federal constitution.

The delegates to the 1917 Constitutional Assembly carried out that task. Without abandoning the 1857 paradigm, they clarified and codified the fundamental meanings of the revolution in a new constitution. Politically, they reaffirmed the federalist State, its constitutional guarantees, and its separation from the Church. They developed political rights in the form of direct suffrage for all males. They gave form to the repeated social demands of society before and during the revolution for universal rights, the right to land, and the protection of the most vulnerable economic groups. The greatest contribution of Carranza and his constitutionalist followers was to give the country a legal instrument that provided for the rule of law, a progressive liberal-democratic constitution intended to apply the terms of the new liberalism to the reality of Mexican society.

In stating that the content of the new constitution was liberal-democratic, I am departing from previous interpretations in which the document has been called radical or pseudo-socialist on the basis of socioeconomic reforms introduced in Articles 27 and 123. Article 27 granted the nation the exclusive right of eminent domain, which provides for the expropriation of private property in the public interest. It also reserved underground mineral rights to the nation and authorized the government to grant mineral extraction contracts to individuals and to Mexican and foreign corporations duly constituted under Mexican law. Article 123 established the norms under which complex legislation would be passed that abolished debt peonage; regulated labor contracts, working conditions, and women's and children's labor; and established a minimum wage, an eight-hour workday, and the right to strike and to arbitration in disputes between labor and capital.

These two articles formally articulated the demands that had been made throughout two decades of social unrest. They provided the legal instruments to guide social, political, and economic progress. The federalism of the 1917 Constitution was much more than a mere carry over from that of 1857. It was a conceptual reformulation of the Mexican United States on the basis of a cooperative federalism. The constitution regulated the cooperation of the states in land distribution and labor law, but the application of the laws was the responsibility of each state. Article 115 guaranteed the political and economic autonomy of municipalities for the first time, thus affirming citizen rights. These rights were additionally reinforced at the political level by the direct vote and by requirements in

Article 3 for the provision of obligatory education, seen as necessary for establishing a real connection between political and social guarantees. A new balance between the executive and legislative branches was achieved. As memory of the parliamentary republic faded and disappeared, executive power was reinforced and the presidential republic was born.

If we are to be consistent and thus assess the revolutionary process in the light of historical evidence, we can say that the social norms enshrined in the 1917 Constitution are best evaluated in conjunction with the new freedom they guaranteed. In this sense, this constitution was more than a reform; it was a departure from the Constitution of 1857 to the extent that the union it established was not merely liberal but liberal-democratic. This constitution was the logical product of a process that began as a liberal revolution and became liberal-democratic along the way.

An appreciation of the 1917 Constitution helps us to understand how the governability it made possible led to an unprecedented equilibrium between the people and the elite. Without this understanding, we would be unable to interpret the post-1920 course of Mexican social and political history.

CHAPTER 10

The Foundations of the New State

Once the 1917 Constitution was approved and Venustiano Carranza was duly elected president, it was incumbent upon Mexico to rebuild and to stamp out the embers of violent conflict between the various factions. External pressure to complete the task was brought to bear by the Great Powers, for with the end of the First World War, they would no longer tolerate civil war in Mexico.

Between the two world wars, countries around the world were addressing various social needs, and Mexico was no exception. But unlike many other countries, Mexico lacked the means to respond to pent-up social demands in the immediate wake of revolution. Nor did Mexico have the institutional mechanisms in place to implement the recently approved constitution. On the other hand, there was no lack of energy and will to innovate. This is clear from the efforts made to rebuild the economy in a way that would promote social peace and general well-being—the foundation stones of a democratic system.

The modern Mexican State was successfully rebuilt between 1920 and 1940. Society at large and the political class worked together to ensure stability, avoid military uprisings, and face up to external pressures and threats.

The adoption of the 1917 Constitution was the most important outcome of the years of fratricidal war. The constitution defined the rights of new social groups, addressed the demands of workers and peasants, and definitively established a secular State with increased executive and regulatory powers. These fundamental characteristics of democratic liberalism marked the desire for a Mexico with freedom for all under the law, a balance of powers, and protection for society's weakest members.

Though such principles may have described the desired Mexican future, daily life still reflected the ravages of civil war. The gross domestic product had decreased by 10 percent. Famine and epidemics of typhus, yellow fever, and finally the deadly Spanish flu had killed far more people than had the war itself. The first order of business was to suppress the remnants of rebellion and reestablish the consistency and predictability of political functions.

The fragmentation of authority had deepened with the factional war of 1915–1916. Several factions had emerged from the convention at Aguascalientes. A radical wing included Zapatistas and Villistas, and constitutionalism, the expression of moderate reformists, was itself divided. Venustiano Carranza led a conservative faction unfriendly to popular sectors. Álvaro Obregón led progressive constitutionalism, tied to popular forces demanding liberal-democratic reforms. Factional tensions negatively affected political stability during the three years of Carranza's presidency. In addition, the new ruling class was faced with hostility from the United States over Article 27 of the constitution, which threatened U.S. mining and petroleum interests as well as agricultural properties. Above all, order was required in a fragmented and fragile country. Military commanders and the governing class were running their states as personal fiefdoms purely on the basis of their having played a role in the revolution. The richest states, such as Yucatán with its henequen and Veracruz and Tampico with their oil, were being economically bled to meet the financial needs of the federal government.

The presidency of Venustiano Carranza was hampered by divisions within the political-military command. Carranza never accepted a military rank, but from 1913 to 1917 he was the commander-in-chief of a confederation of armies under generals such as Obregón, Pablo González, and, at first, Francisco Villa. The first two were powerful and popular, the principal field commanders of the Constitutionalist Army. Each considered himself the ideal candidate to succeed Carranza. With this in mind, they proceeded to strengthen their respective power bases, selecting governors and military commanders as close allies. From 1917 to 1920, they hand-picked candidates for elective office in their zones, effectively crowding out political alternatives. They dominated elected governors by exercising their economic power and their control of the transportation system. The military began by controlling regional transportation and trade in close cooperation with local business interests but ended up deeply involved in business themselves.

Among the political-military groups, two stand out. The Sonoran group was personified by Álvaro Obregón and Salvador Alvarado from Sinaloa, and the northeastern group by Carranza's nephew Pablo González. The first represented northwestern agribusiness and the henequen interests of Yucatán, with strong ties to California and New York, respectively. The second faction, in the northeast, was made up of middle-class political forces that had taken shape at the peak of the Porfiriato and struggled against the regime but had fallen into disgrace together with Carranza. This generation was born and had reached adulthood under the Porfiriato. They had held elective posts, worked as schoolteachers, or owned farms or small businesses, and they came to form a widespread network with political and family ties.

At this juncture, political leaders tempered their ambitions in keeping with two constitutional principles: No government official who attained his position by force of arms would be recognized (Article 82), and there was to be no reelection (Article 83). These two precepts were the most powerful mechanisms in the difficult tasks of political institutionalization and the subordination of the military to civilian power. The latter was a major political task. When Obregón became president in 1920, Mexico had 679 generals, 4,463 senior officers (ranging from colonel to major), 15,421 field officers, and 98,000 soldiers. This meant that there was one member of the military for every 121 Mexicans, without counting the members of other armed groups.

Officers did not hold themselves apart as a military caste, or professional "corporation," however. They engaged in political activity as citizens in arms and established alliances with different social sectors and groups. Obregón is a good example. A respected farm owner, he was born in Sonora in 1880. He had been elected mayor of his home town in 1911, and organized a civilian armed force in defense of constitutional order at the time of the 1913 coup. By 1914 he was the commander of the Northwest Division of the Constitutionalist Army.

He surrounded himself with Sonoran troops and Yaqui Indians, and strongly supported first Madero and then Carranza. Once his army left Sonora for the central plateau, he realized that they were losing their ties to their isolated home base west of the Sierra Madre, and that for them to subsist and grow he would need to develop flexible political positions and establish alliances in the territories they won. This approach allowed Obregón's army maximum mobility. He was able to concentrate his forces on the campaign in which they were engaged by leaving the cities and territories he controlled under the rule of civilian allies.

Obregón employed a strategy of inclusiveness. In 1915 he forged an alliance with the leaders of the Casa del Obrero Mundial, helping them to organize the workers in the cities and industrial areas occupied by the Constitutionalist Army. In exchange, he insured that electricity and other public services operated regularly. His pragmatism would pay off when he began his presidential campaign. He gained the support of Emiliano Zapata in October 1918 by forging an agreement that included an endorsement of the Ayala Plan and a broader democratic vision. This was very important for both men, as it allowed them to show themselves capable of working with different social sectors in the interest of the national good. In particular, it allowed the Zapatistas to shed their strictly provincial image. Maximino Ávila Camacho acted as political intermediary in this agreement. Ávila Camacho sealed an agreement under similar circumstances with the railroad workers' union, and in 1919 a secret mutual-aid agreement was signed with the Mexican Regional Workers Confederation, known as the CROM for its initials in Spanish. These alliances were signs of a grand democratic coalition in the making, consisting of peasant, working-class, and middle-class forces, that Ávila Camacho and Benjamin Hill pulled together as they traveled around the country forming new liberal clubs.

Obregón also had bases of support in the army, where many recognized him as their commander. Jesús Agustín Castro, the undersecretary of war, assured him of the support of garrison commanders in many states. In February 1920, Carranza called a meeting of state governors to support Ignacio Bonilla, the Mexican ambassador in Washington and his designated candidate for the presidency, but a number of governors closed ranks around Obregón instead, including Pascual Ortiz Rubio of Michoacán and Francisco Figueroa of Guerrero. When Carranza ordered Obregón's arrest, railroad workers saved his life and spirited him out of Mexico City and through Zapatista territory to the state of Guerrero, under the protection of Governor Figueroa.

First Results

Obregón did not sign the April 1920 Agua Prieta Plan, because Article 82 of the 1917 Constitution disqualified from the presidency anyone who had participated directly or indirectly in a coup d'etat, mutiny, or insurrection. Other Sonorans signed the plan, which demanded full compliance with the 1917 Constitution, individual guarantees, and effective suffrage. It refused to recognize the Carranza presidency on the basis that sovereignty had reverted to the states with the rupture of the federal compact. A mechanism was designed to appoint a provisional president, Adolfo de la Huerta, who then prepared the coming elections. Obregón launched his candidacy in June 1919 without domestic or foreign commitments of any kind. He promised to purge the army of those State officials who had abandoned the honorable path and acted as if the only goal of the revolution was to enrich those who joined it. Soon thereafter, he was elected president for the 1920–1924 term.

During those four years, Obregón fulfilled his agreement with the Zapatistas, redistributing all the Morelos sugar cane *haciendas* in the form of *ejidos*. The *ejido* is a form of property under which certain lands may be used individually, collectively, or, in the case of pasture land, forest land, and water rights, in common. The *ejidatario* is a peasant who has individual use rights or shares in collective use rights of a piece of land that forms part of the *ejido*. The *ejidatario* also has rights to property held in common by the *ejido*.

Obregón went forward with agrarian reform. Between 1921 and 1924, 1.2 million hectares around the country were distributed to 132,969 families consisting of some 750,000 individuals. Being a practical and eclectic politician, Obregón was out to subdue rebelliousness. He extended guarantees to wealthy farm owners in Chiapas and on the Gulf Coast—landowners such as Manuel Peláez, for example, who collected royalties for access to the petroleum resources on his property—and to anti-Carranza forces who had laid down their arms. He was generous with the leaders of labor and peasant organizations. The CROM, founded in 1918, was led by Luis N. Morones. Morones, along with Ricardo Treviño of the IWW (Industrial Workers of the World), Jacinto Huitrón, Celestino Gasca, and other leaders of anarchist, socialist, working class, and union groups, formed the Action Group, based in Aguascalientes. Carranza had little influence in Aguascalientes, but it was an important railway junction and mining district and thus a stronghold of the railway workers and miners. The strength of these leaders, along with the support they received from the Obregón faction, explains the immense power they accumulated in just a few years. In 1919, they founded the Mexican Labor Party (PLM) and signed a secret agreement with Obregón to name a party member to fill the new position of minister of labor. As a result of the alliance between President Obregón and Morones, the secretary-general of the

CROM and leader of the PLM, working-class organizations and their leadership became a very powerful force.

The CROM was very heterogeneous. In addition to its five thousand industrial workers, it included small groups of artisans, machine operators, workers in traditional manufacturing activities, and a number of peasant organizations, but Morones always inflated the number of its affiliates in order to exaggerate his power. In the 1920s, the number of industrial workers in Mexico was slightly over one hundred thousand, of whom the CROM could claim the affiliation of about five to ten thousand. Most of the industrial proletariat stayed outside the federation. The railroad workers, for example, were traditional enemies of the CROM. They numbered around forty-seven thousand; there were a similar number of petroleum workers, and there were some three thousand electricians. All of these workers maintained strong independent unions. As president, Obregón supported the CROM with economic and organizational resources and significant wage increases for its membership. A worker who earned a nominal 1.90 pesos a day in 1912 was earning 4.21 pesos in 1926. Article 123 of the constitution was implemented in many other ways. Conciliation and Arbitration Boards were created. The right to strike was exercised and became a powerful mechanism in union organizing and for forcing improvements in working conditions. There were 778 strikes between 1921 and 1924. Because the federal system left labor relations largely under the jurisdiction of individual states, laws were more favorable to unions in some places than in others, leading to disparities in what the movement was able to accomplish.

When Obregón initiated his land distribution program, he also promoted peasant organization. The National Agrarian Party (PNA) was founded as a counterweight to the PLM and the CROM. Peasant leagues proliferated, the strongest among them being the National Peasant League, founded by Úrsulo Galván, a radical socialist leader from Veracruz. The Communist Party was founded in 1921 with the strong support of agrarian leagues in the southeast, bakers' organizations, and some industrial unions. This was the beginning of a period of radical agitation that received support from the Soviet Union. The leaders of this movement intended to steer Mexico toward socialism.

The singular thing about the 1920s was the strength and number of organizations, parties, and unions comprised of peasants and industrial, manufacturing, and artisanal workers. Some were autonomous, some were supported by the State, and others were sustained by affiliation with international movements. It was a decade when thousands of workers, armed peasants, and formerly unemployed were integrated into the workforce. The number and diversity of new organizational forms was unprecedented. The new unions, peasant organizations, union federations, and political parties represented the first efforts to create a nationwide network of social and economic organizations, which nevertheless still revolved around strong regional power centers.

Obregón instituted educational and cultural policies to channel the energy unleashed by ten years of revolution. These policies were intended to support social growth and enrichment, spread equality of opportunity, and forge an inclusive nation for the benefit of all its people, whatever their wealth, social condition, or ethnicity—one of the most heartfelt ideals of the revolution. The Secretariat of Public Education was established and charged with enormous tasks in a country 72 percent illiterate. Its initial budget was 300,000 pesos. This rose to six million pesos, however, increasing from 1.3 percent to 9.3 percent of the federal budget. José Vasconcelos, then rector of the University of Mexico, was put at the head of the secretariat. He began a cultural revolution, promoting a secular system of education accessible to all, regardless of race or class. Knowledge, equally available to everyone, would be the means to abolish social and economic disparities, and a shared culture would be an instrument for forging national unity. Teachers and bookmobiles crisscrossed the country with missionary zeal, imparting basic cultural knowledge and the Spanish language as passports to the broader world of ideas. The classics of world culture were introduced in the most remote schools, and attempts were made to establish lasting bonds between teachers and the communities where they worked. Teacher education, technical academies, and rural schools were strengthened. At the same time, Mexican anthropology and archeology were developed under the guidance of Manuel Gamio, who encouraged everything that promoted the Mexican national identity, such as pre-Hispanic studies and Mexican literature and art.

Vasconcelos called upon Mexican painters to express the ideals of the revolution and the future of the nation on the walls of public buildings. Diego Rivera, David Alfaro Siqueiros, and José Clemente Orozco turned away from easel art and gave birth to the Mexican muralist movement, which depicted the struggles of the masses. Novels about the revolution, poetry, short stories, and theater—both on stage and at fairs and festivals—all engaged a public anxious to read, see, and hear works concerning the new social actors. These activities led to the myth that so-called middle-class elements were the organizers and leaders of an army of workers and peasants. But this was a new middle class, a symbol of popular unity in the factories and the fields, "middle" not because it was situated between upper and lower social elements but because it was at the center of events, the fulcrum of a newly united and balanced society.

Vasconcelos forged an ethnocultural strategy: to create a Latin American "cosmic race" and a new experience of collective life, a fusion of universal and Latin American cultures. Social classes, too, were to be conflated as "the people." This idea, spread in Latin America by writers such as Alcides Arguedas *(Raza de Bronce)* and Américo de Almeida *(O Bagaceira),* seems to have been modeled on the Italy of Benito Mussolini, who, together with his Fascist Revolutionary Party, had taken power in 1922 to guide the country in the name of cross-class unity. The idea of a united body, "the people," produced a new sense of the nation and a new nationalism. Álvaro Obregón, Plutarco Elías Calles, Luis N. Morones, and many others found inspiration in existing fascist and nationalist movements as a supposed "third way" for Mexico—neither capitalist nor socialist, but simply the mobilization of all available social forces in support of government action.

The Return to the International System

The international revolutionary ideal of the 1920s resulted from a new correlation of forces in the post-war world, which was the most important impediment to the United States' imperialist foreign policy. The United States had demonstrated its expansionism in its incursions into Cuba in 1898 and Veracruz in 1914–1915. Through these experiences, the U.S. Department of War had learned that, in military terms, an invasion of Mexico would be costly and almost impossible to sustain. U.S. foreign policy in the 1920s shifted instead to what was known as dollar diplomacy, which consisted of extending U.S. economic interests into Latin America, Mexico in particular. According to the United States, the Mexican people would benefit from the resulting need to modernize their way of life and their way of thinking.

Experience had taught Mexico's northern neighbor that Mexico would seek allies to resist U.S. dominance. During the First World War, Venustiano Carranza, who seemed to fear that Francisco Villa was headed for victory in Mexico with the support of the United States, had sought the help of Germany to counteract U.S. attacks. During the decade of reconstruction, Mexico and Latin America developed a strong sense of identity and had no intention of being transformed into U.S. protectorates.

The Mexican experience was undoubtedly a lesson for the international community with regard to foreign intervention. The international adoption of the Calvo Doctrine during the Carranza period affirmed the principle that sovereignty is the principal attribute of the nation, and the world community came to agree upon the principle of nonintervention. Carlos Calvo was an Argentinean legal scholar who even before the First World War established certain principles of international law. The Calvo Doctrine states that the debt of a government cannot justify a violation of national sovereignty. Thanks to this doctrine, there is a basis in international law for national self-determination, the legal equality of States, and the prohibition of intervention by one State in the internal affairs of another.

Building on the Calvo Doctrine, the 1917 Mexican Constitution, still in effect today, states in Article 27: "Ownership of the lands and waters within the boundaries of the national territory is vested originally in the Nation. . . . In the Nation is vested the direct ownership of all . . . minerals or substances, which in veins, ledges, masses or ore pockets, form deposits of a nature distinct from the components of the earth itself." This constitutional principle is the foundation of the Carranza Doctrine, which is the guiding principle of Mexican foreign policy.

Based on these postulates, the Mexican State set a tax on petroleum production that became a principal source of federal income. In 1918, the State took direct control of all petroleum deposits included in legislation passed in 1887. Carranza astutely based Mexico's new international relations on access to petroleum, which interested all the Great Powers, especially businesses in the United States, Britain, the Netherlands, and even France.

The new direction of international relations was also a response to a changed U.S. foreign policy. President Woodrow Wilson wanted to exercise U.S. power through economic penetration rather than the force of arms. He saw the United States extending its leadership to free peoples and nations in defense of liberal principles, and proposed to create a world free of socialism and bourgeois or imperialist reaction. The U.S. Senate effectively rejected Wilsonian ideals, however, when isolationist forces defeated Wilson's proposal that the United States become a member of the League of Nations. Had the United States joined the League, it would have expended most of its energy on the political and economic reconstruction of Europe. As it was, the United States turned its attention to developing its dominance of the Americas.

The Mexican government and the presidency of Obregón were recognized by the main European powers, but not by the United States. In 1922, however, Mexico came to an agreement with the International Committee of Bondholders on Mexico and took responsibility for its foreign debt and the unpaid interest it had accumulated since 1914. This opened the way to a new set of conversations, known as the Bucareli Conference of 1923, between personal representatives of the U.S. president and the Mexican president. The agreement that they reached was informal in that no treaty was produced or sent to the Senate for ratification. However, they established mechanisms to indemnify U.S. citizens for war damages to their properties, losses resulting from agrarian reform, and the nationalization of petroleum deposits. The U.S. government finally recognized the Obregón government in September 1923. Two months later, Obregón faced a rebellion of the army general command, which wanted to replace him and prevent his selection of Plutarco Elías Calles, a Sonoran schoolteacher, as his successor. They preferred to see a more malleable civilian in the presidency, namely, Adolfo de la Huerta. The rebellion was defeated with the help of the United States, the mobilization of peasant leagues and the CROM labor federation, and the opposition of more than half of all active army officers.

Constraints on Calles's Presidency

When Plutarco Elías Calles assumed the presidency for the 1924–1928 term, there were several centralized bodies in place that could help maintain national unity: the various administrative apparatuses, labor organizations such as the CROM, peasant leagues, and the army. The railroad unions were the government's Achilles heel. They had supported Adolfo de la Huerta in his attempt to topple Obregón and prevent the succession of Calles. Calles was determined to undermine their power with the help of the CROM. In 1926, CROM occupied National Railways facilities in order to wear down the railroad workers' resistance and pressure them to affiliate with the confederation. Instead, railroad workers founded the new Transport and Communications Confederation, which called a general strike for the end of 1926, the largest and most dangerous strike that Mexican government and industry have ever had to confront. Having failed to destroy the railworkers' autonomy, the government further strengthened its resolve to eliminate independent unionism and federalized the Conciliation and Arbitration Boards in matters pertaining to interstate transportation or commerce.

The CROM was the most powerful labor organization when the struggle for presidential succession unfolded in 1926–1927. The PLM, which was its political wing, attempted to cash in on some of that power and proposed CROM leader Luis Morones for the position. With no new personalities of the stature of Calles or Obregón on the horizon, another constitutional change was suggested to once again allow reelection. These factors and others opened up a dispute over the course to be taken. It was not a matter of passing power from one *caudillo* to the next. The country was continuing to fragment on the basis of powerful regional interests, and a number of generals believed that they deserved the presidency. Peasant movements and workers in the modern industries seemed to be moving in the direction of social revolution.

Obregón had exercised the presidency as a prestigious *caudillo* with connections in many regions of the country. He had personally guided and coordinated different social movements but with some flexibility, attracting the sympathies of certain popular groups. Calles was a different kind of president. He was less charismatic and put more power into the hands of the central administration. He initiated the institutionalization of Mexican politics, designed mechanisms to inhibit *caudillismo* (the personal power of the strongman), and steered governmental policymaking into the sphere of State administrative organs.

The Calles presidency was statist insofar as he enhanced the power of the executive branch, and of the federal administration in general. In the first years of his administration he focused on the minimal infrastructure necessary to unify the country by linking together its productive areas. He began construction of a road network and a global irrigation infrastructure, and he established the National Road and National Irrigation Commissions. He began the process of modernizing the credit system, founding the National Bank of Agricultural Credit and the National Bank of Ejidal Credit. He laid the groundwork for what would become the Central Bank, the sole issuer of the national currency. The Bank of Mexico was also established during this period, in 1926. Calles created the General Pension Directorate, reorganized the federal treasury offices, and oriented agrarian policy toward the owners of small landholdings. The *ejido* was promoted as a formative stage for an agricultural system based on individually owned small holdings, preceding the acquisition of individually titled property.

Responding to certain events, Calles centralized not only the economy but other aspects of governance as well. Between 1926 and 1929, during and immediately following Calles's term in office, a large part of Mexican territory was the scene of the Cristero rebellion, a religiously inspired peasant war fought in the name of Christ the King. Under pressure from the CROM, Calles took an anticlerical stance. He supported CROM's propaganda campaigns, even endorsing the establishment of a national church, the Mexican Apostolic Catholic Church. The State and the Roman Catholic Church entered into a bitter struggle. The Church condemned and mobilized against constitutional provisions for secular education, prohibitions of monastic orders, and the disentailment of the Church's urban and rural properties. The government responded by ordering the immediate and universal application of the constitution. State governors ordered the expulsion of foreign priests, and local authorities closed Catholic schools, convents, and orphanages. A Catholic resistance took hold and formed the National League for the Defense of Religious Liberty. The government expelled the apostolic delegate, further hardening the bishops' opposition. Calles implemented a constitutional provision that gave the federal government authority to regulate religious practices.

The tension reached its climax when the government came to believe that the Catholic clergy was conspiring with the United States against Mexico and its revolution. In 1927, the U.S. ambassador protested the appropriation of American properties by Mexico, to which President Calles responded that Mexico's petroleum was the property of the Mexican nation, and that only Mexicans had the right to make use of it. He prohibited the purchase by foreign nationals of any land contiguous to Mexico's coasts or borders. Luckily, sanity prevailed and interventionist impulses were moderated by the exponents of dollar diplomacy within the U.S. government and among U.S. investors. This group preferred to draw Latin America into the U.S. sphere of influence by providing the investments and means to economic modernization that Mexico so desperately needed for its recovery and reconstruction. This meant calming the fears of investors and delinking the problem of petroleum rights from diplomatic relations with the United States and Britain. It is also possible that the radicalism of some Mexican organizations with roots among workers and peasants convinced the Great Powers, led by the United States, not to further inflame tensions with the Mexican government.

In 1928, a fanatical Catholic assassinated Álvaro Obregón, exacerbating the Cristero rebellion, which now spread to thirteen states. To make matters worse, there were two attempted coups d'etat in 1928–1929. At this point, U.S. Ambassador Dwight D. Morrow, who had gained the confidence of Calles through the successful renegotiation of the foreign debt, lent his good offices to the problem and helped end the religious-political conflict. Under agreements reached in 1929, the Church submitted to the secular State and Mexican law, and the government curtailed its intervention in Church affairs.

The Nationalization of Politics: Combating Regionalism

Forces disruptive to political institutionalization took longer to eliminate. In 1929, former president Calles called a closed meeting of all the leading generals of the revolution and had them promise, for the good of the country, that none of them would aspire to the presidency. Calles himself made the same promise. This closed group chose a civilian, Emilio Portes Gil, as interim president. Portes Gil was the governor of Tamaulipas and founder of the Socialist Borderland Party, doubtless one of the most powerful political organizations in the Gulf Coast region. Congress proclaimed him interim president and assigned him the task of organizing elections for the 1930–1934 presidential term.

The agreement among the revolution's political leaders and generals brought together numerous movements, currents, and parties, each exercising its own regional clientalism. The first attempt at building a national political organization had been made by the Communist Party, but in 1929 the party was declared illegal and its leaders were either jailed or forced underground. Other organizations that gained some prominence were the Socialist Borderland Party and the Socialist Party of the Southeast, but there was none with national reach. Calles decided to form a party representing the governments that had resulted from the revolution. The new party would be national and would be the sole political frame of reference for all "revolutionaries," both civilian and military. As such, it would implicitly be the government party.

The organization of the party would have to begin with the negotiated incorporation of the many organizations born out of almost two decades of social mobilization. Up until this time, Calles's personal qualities had been key to mediating among the diverse forces gathered under the political umbrella of the government, and he had been able to hold them together under his leadership. Given the international crisis of liberalism and the worldwide economic depression, ex-president Calles was faced with dominant political forces under the influence of new corporatist tendencies such as those espoused by Italian and Spanish fascism. The National Revolutionary Party (PNR) was founded in November 1928. It was intended to control political events on the national level while recognizing the autonomy of local parties.

The PNR brought into its confederal structure all the organizations claiming their origins in the revolution, absorbing both strong regional parties, such as the Socialist Borderland Party of Portes Gil and the Socialist Party of the Southeast, and other, smaller parties. As long as they agreed to adhere to the decisions of the PNR central executive committee in Mexico City when it came to national matters, they were allowed to preserve their local or regional autonomy and their own independent structure. The foundation of the PNR was the first step toward a single national party, created not only to contest elections but, as a cross-class national party, to guide the political destiny of the so-called revolutionary society and its components, including intellectuals, the bourgeoisie, and the proletariat. Calles, known by then as the Jefe Máximo, led the new party and guaranteed the military's nonintervention in political affairs. It was clear that the PNR would eventually absorb all the representatives of local authority, including governors, zonal military commanders, and national politicians. Being organized through government structures meant that the PNR could count on the five thousand municipalities that constituted the Republic—five thousand political springboards reinforced by two hundred and eighty subordinate district centers and thirty-one state parties that recognized but one central leadership: the PNR National Committee. The actual number of *municipios* is not believed to have exceeded two thousand, so the figure above must have included auxiliary town councils, or *ayuntamientos*, as well. This conception of the party based on the historic strength of the *municipio* helps to explain why despite certain corporatist features, the PNR maintained a markedly territorial orientation in the years immediately following its founding.

An attempted rebellion by José Gonzalo Escobar in 1929 marked a turning point. In its wake, the word went out that any rebellion would be considered treason and would lead to the purging of disloyal governors and generals. It was ordered that all other potential enemies of the revolution be eliminated. The message was clear: henceforth the struggle for power was not to be conducted by force of arms but institutionally, through the party.

The first national election was a trial by fire for the PNR. The party nominated Pascual Ortiz Rubio for the presidency. Since Ortiz Rubio had no political ties, he was exclusively dependent on the party. His opponents were Aarón Sáenz from the Callista faction, a sugar baron and profiteer who made his fortune after the revolution, and José Vasconcelos, the popular former secretary of education and representative of liberal society. With aid from the *municipios,* the PNR very efficiently organized a rural majority. Vasconcelos did best in the urban centers. His campaign was the final somewhat "Maderista" effort to achieve power by playing the democratic game. The overall vote was overwhelmingly in favor of Ortiz Rubio, who received 1,948,848 votes to Vasconcelos's 110,979. The PNR had demonstrated its electoral effectiveness—and Calles his ability to manage an orderly transition of power.

In 1930 and 1931, the political struggle was centered within the party organization, to which Calles had named a trusted general, Lázaro Cárdenas, as president. Born in 1895 as the power of the Porfiriato was diminishing, Cárdenas had joined the revolutionary forces in 1913 and served under General Calles until 1920, when he was named governor of his native state, Michoacán. Cárdenas was an advocate of agrarian and social reforms. He had a strong army following and a reputation as a serious and disciplined organizer. His main assignment was to manage the functioning of regional and intraparty factions within the structures of the party and in Congress.

The first test of political strength came when Calles returned from a European trip. At this time a certain eclecticism was noted in his directives to the party organization. It seemed that he was sometimes influenced by the internal workings of parties in the United States, sometimes by those in Europe, particularly the Fascist Party in Italy, and sometimes by the Soviet Communist Party. All of these influences were tempered by his own knowledge and understanding of Mexican politics and politicians.

It fell to Cárdenas, as president of the party, to complete the process of centralization and eliminate the undisciplined factions and those linked to outside forces. These elements were concentrated in the Senate, among some governors, in the army, and in the new and independent workers and peasants organizations. Juan Andrew Almazán, Saturnino Cedillo, and Lázaro Cárdenas himself were three of the four divisional generals who lent vital support to the regime. The fourth was General Joaquín Amaro, the secretary of war under President Ortiz Rubio. Ortiz Rubio was so dependent on his secretary of war that Amaro was said to be the real power behind the throne. The support of a powerful secretary of war for a president who had three more years to serve was contradictory to the concept of a national party that would dominate the government.

The scheme was for Generals Cárdenas, Almazán, and Cedillo to tender their resignations as the result of a ministerial crisis in October 1931. They did so, and General Amaro was obliged to do the same. President Ortiz Rubio stepped down a few months later, and Congress designated Abelardo L. Rodríguez as provisional president to serve until December 1, 1934.

From 1929 to 1934, Congress was the focus of the opposition by regional parties and internal factions to the centralization of power. Regionalist forces took control of the Permanent Commission and the Credentialing Commission of Congress, which would play key roles in confirming the validity of the next presidential election and approving reforms. The formal seating of deputies brought with it a showdown. Calles and Portes Gil, also a powerful party boss and then secretary of the interior, intervened with all the means at their disposal to assure a comfortable majority for the PNR.

A dispute over the reelection of deputies arose in 1932 and 1933. A major reform was proposed to make terms of office in the Chamber of Deputies coincide with the recently instituted six-year-long presidential term. This would mean changing the duration of congressional terms and disallowing reelection. Although reelectionists were strong in Congress, they were forced to yield after the national convention of the PNR, held in Aguascalientes, voted to prohibit the reelection of state and federal deputies and of senators. On April 29, 1933, Congress amended Article 83 of the constitution and instituted the terms and limits that are still in effect today. The presidential term is six years with no reelection, the senatorial term is six years, and the deputies serve for three years with no immediate reelection.

The years 1929 to 1934 were legislatively very active. The liberal federal Constitution of 1917 was significantly amended in order to create a stronger central State with authority over strategic production activities. As of 1929, Congress increased its legislative prerogatives with respect to mining, trade, and credit institutions, and the establishment of a bank with the exclusive power to issue currency. In 1933, federal authority was expanded in the area of labor law, which up until that time had been the sole prerogative of the states. Federal jurisdiction was established over work on the railroads and interstate transport, in mining and petroleum, and maritime and port labor. In 1934, this authority was extended to the textile sector. It was codified in the federal Labor Code, which was harshly criticized by opposition deputies for undermining the sovereignty of the states. They further characterized the law as fascist, and an affront to the autonomy of organized labor in that it subordinated labor relations to federal power, interposing the State between labor and industry.

Article 115 of the constitution was also amended, weakening munici-pal government in various ways, including the mandating of a govern-ment period of four years with no immediate reelection.

Each of these measures was undoubtedly intended to strengthen the central State and the power of the presidency in the context of a domi-nant PNR with an enormously powerful party president and a Congress peopled by disciplined party members.

At its December 1933 convention in Querétaro, the PNR transformed itself from a confederation of state parties into a unified structure corre-sponding to that of the reengineered State. It took on the characteristics of a genuine and modern political party. Membership was made individ-ual and party organs became vertically structured, with a presence at every level of government. There would be municipal and state party organi-zations everywhere in the country and a National Executive Committee (CEN). The CEN designated the party's presidential and legislative can-didates and was responsible for designing a national program that the presidential candidate would then adhere to. The party's Institute of So-cial, Political, and Economic Studies was responsible to the CEN and produced the legislation that the president was expected to submit to Congress, as well as the proposed laws that federal and state deputies sub-mitted to their respective bodies. The PNR approved its first six-year plan at the Querétaro convention and chose Lázaro Cárdenas as its presiden-tial candidate. In short, the party intended to strengthen the civilian char-acter of government institutions. However, it also created the framework for dual power, exercised by the president of the republic and the presi-dent of the party.

The Nationalization of Society

At the same time that national politics was undergoing this reorganiza-tion, unions and other social movements were centralizing on the na-tional level as well. One should keep in mind that while these develop-ments were taking place in Mexico, countries such as Italy and Spain were devising new corporatist structures under fascism, claiming to have found the way to effectively channel the collective energy of society. At the same time, socialist and communist movements were lauding their own accomplishments and pointing to the Soviet Union as the model for the future of the working class. Other social and labor movement lead-ers, however, wanted to liberate society from capitalism without resort-ing to a dictatorship of the proletariat. They were attracted to a political model under which the State would mediate in social conflicts, wield the power to regulate the competing interests of labor and capital, and guide society to national unity.

This was a period of profound reorganization for unions in Mexico, coinciding with the fragmentation of the CROM. The first cracks in CROM unity appeared in 1928, when Lombardo Toledano, a socialist labor lawyer and himself a member of the organization, led a movement in favor of a "purified" CROM. Fidel Velásquez began his ascent to national prominence by organizing milkmen, garbage collectors, and transport workers in Mexico City. He and four of his lieutenants, collectively known as "the five little wolves," separated from the CROM in 1929, when Portes Gil turned the Conciliation and Arbitration Boards over to them and provided them with the means to organize the Federal District Workers Union Federation. Other spin-offs, such as that led by Alfredo Pérez Medina, regrouped under the anarcho-syndicalist Chamber of Labor. With these losses, the CROM suffered a big setback, but it was not decimated.

Other groups, such as the railroad workers, electricians, miners, metalworkers, and the communist unions, increased their militancy and in late 1928 formed the Mexican Federation of Unions (CSUM, Confederación Sindical Unitaria de México), later a powerful organization. In 1933, Toledano broke with the CROM to form the General Confederation of Mexican Workers and Peasants (CGOCM). This confederation brought together a number of unions and peasant leagues that were unaffiliated, lacked unified leadership, and were outside governmental control. It was in this context that laws were passed giving the federation jurisdiction over the workforce in the major branches of industry. These laws had corporatist characteristics in that they authorized State administrative organs to codify and regulate labor relations.

The first federal labor law, passed in 1931, had empowered the Autonomous Department of Labor to function as a federal prosecutor in defense of labor rights, and had put the Federal Conciliation and Arbitration Boards under its authority. The boards were key in the resolution of salary and other labor-related disputes. The government's role as mediator put it in a position to name board members. Portes Gil put Fidel Velásquez and his "lieutenants" in charge of the boards, with very wide discretion in determining which strikes were legal and which were not. All unions were required to legalize their status with the Department of Labor and register with the Conciliation and Arbitration Boards. This provided the State with control over labor organization and gave Velásquez direct knowledge of all the unions in the country.

The fragmentation of peasant organizations and the dispersion of the rural population were accelerated by rising unemployment and a decrease in agricultural production—the effects of the economic depression. This was partly due to the fact that large landed estates and midsize agricultural properties were still predominant, and that landowners responded to poor market conditions by reducing their acreage under cultivation.

The Sonorans were inclined to promote the ownership of small properties, and they thought of the *ejido* as a transitory step toward private holdings. They preferred to distribute land to the *ejido* sector selectively, that is, in order to pacify certain regions, as Obregón had done during his presidency. Later on, during the Cristero war, land distribution was again used tactically to pacify rural areas and assure the loyalty of agrarian reformers. Between 1929 and 1933, land distribution increased once more in response to rising unemployment and the needs of Mexicans returning from the United States. While almost 4.6 million hectares of land were distributed to 468,000 peasants between 1915 and 1930, and another 2.6 million hectares were distributed to 133,000 peasants between 1930 and 1934, the distribution was concentrated in areas where the government wanted to see peasant settlement for political reasons. Except in the state of Morelos, it was accomplished without dismantling the *hacienda* production system. The distribution of small parcels was intended to provide an income supplement or a cushion for times of unemployment.

In 1934, steps were taken to bring order to rural Mexico. Agrarian reform ended and small agricultural properties, including all irrigated properties of 150 or fewer hectares, were protected under a newly passed Agrarian Code. Land distribution was legislatively codified, however, and *hacendados* organized in the National Chamber of Agriculture were turned down in a bid for broad immunity. The Autonomous Department of Agriculture—a department of the federal executive branch that successfully promoted additional agricultural legislation—began to function. Its policy was to promote agriculture by guaranteeing property rights, regardless of the size of the holding.

Cárdenas and the Demise of the Jefe Máximo

When Cárdenas took office as president on December 1, 1934, he was intimately familiar with ex-president Calles's arrangement of weak presidents who governed under his thumb, while he controlled national politics as head of the governing party, the PNR. Cárdenas made it his first task to transfer the loyalties of the National Revolutionary Party, the army, the unions, and the peasants to the presidency. He founded a political order that would be consolidated and endure for more than thirty years, based on the new power relations that he imposed on the leadership of the State, the party, and the mass organizations. He was also the first president to take office and complete a six-year term backed by a six-year plan supported by his party. In his first four years he built a progressive "national unity agreement" based on a corporatist model. The agreement, which some have called populist, was inclusive, providing a space for each social and economic group according to its political weight.

In the 1930s, the State faced a serious challenge in trying to restructure the way politics was conducted so as to fully include the demands of the urban and rural middle classes. The existence of two large social movements is testimony to the problem. One was the Cristada, the movement of the Cristero rebels. This was a messianic armed rural movement that attracted middle social sectors in towns and villages between 1926 and 1929. The second was an urban citizens' movement for democratization inspired by José Vasconcelos. Both movements were politically suffocated without being entirely eliminated. Social inequality was rampant, popular mobilization had produced meager material returns, unemployment was high, factory layoffs were frequent, and the ownership of agricultural land continued to be highly concentrated. Mexican society had barely changed as a result of the recent revolution, and social frustration had grown with the onset of the economic crisis. The working-class movement was desperately searching for a means to confront the depression. Peasants had benefited little from the revolution and were dispersed, reduced to cultivating marginal lands or working in servile conditions in the *hacienda* sector. As a result, they became radicalized and were organizing peasant unions under the leadership of the Communist Party.

Contrary to what historians have traditionally written, the policies of Lázaro Cárdenas's government were not merely responses to internal and external pressures. Cárdenas's political project differed from those of his predecessors, and upon taking office, he took three important steps. The first was to replace the commanders of the military zones in order to break the bonds between them and the Callista governors. Then, in 1935–1936, he vacated the powers of fourteen governors by obtaining legislative declarations of internal disorder, and replaced them with others more to his liking. This threw the federalist arrangement seriously out of balance, but it avoided potential coalitions between zonal commanders and governors, who might have collaborated in organizing a political-military coup. At the same time, Cárdenas curtailed the independence of Supreme Court justices by eliminating their permanent status on the bench and having their terms coincide with the six years of his government. New justices would be designated based on "their full and accurate interpretation of the new Government's revolutionary policies."[1]

The first significant removals of governors and operational commanders took place between December 1, 1934, and May 1935. This was before the first crisis between Cárdenas and Calles in June 1935 and Calles's expulsion from the country in April 1936. The dismissals and transfers were sweeping. They were accomplished with firmness, but they were highly risky. For this reason they were carried out over time and strategically, as can be seen in table 10.1. In addition to those generals expelled and those who found themselves on "forced leave" between the beginning of 1935 and February 1938, ninety-one of the 350 active service generals of the army, plus sixteen division commanders, all found themselves "temporarily without command responsibilities."[2] Most of the transfers were made in order to displace the Sonoran group from their positions of fifteen years' standing and replace them with either Cardenista officers or others who had been marginalized by the northerners. Continuing transfers uprooted officers from their zones of influence and cut them off from their established economic interests, accelerating the process of centralization and the subordination of the army to the executive branch. The new configuration of power within the military helps to explain Cárdenas's success in asserting presidential authority in his very first showdown with Calles.

The Social Pact

In the first three months of the Cárdenas presidency, work was begun on a revision of Article 27 of the constitution, with instructions to "reformulate the national project in order to give new meaning to federalism." The basic legal instrument was to be a law entailing "expropriation for reasons of public utility," or eminent domain. The urgency to spell out the contents of a new Paragraph 8 of Article 27, according to the president, was the lack of:

1. Correspondence between Lombardo Toledano and Labor Ministry, 1936, Fondo Francisco J. Múgica, vol. 49, doc. 27, *Recomendaciones de la CTM y Organizaciones Obreras y Campesinas al Presidente de la Republic*, Archivo Vicente Lombardo Toledano, Mexico City.

2. Alicia Hernández Chávez, *La Mecánica Cardenista*, vol. 16 of *Historia de la Revolución Mexicana* (Mexico City: El Colegio de México, 1979), p. 105.

TABLE 10.1. Changes of Command in the Military Zones
(Generals Only)

Year/Month	Number of Changes	Total to Date
1934		
December	36	
1935		
January	67	
February	5	
March	39	
April	21	
May	18	
June[a]	27	213
July	29	
August	44	
September	22	
October	32	
November	16	
December	14	370
1936		
January	27	
February	5	
March	36	
April[b]	6	444
May	2	
June	32	
July	28	
August	42	
September	11	
October	19	
November	30	
TOTAL		608

[a]First Calles-Cárdenas crisis.
[b]Expulsion of Calles.

SOURCE: Alicia Hernández Chávez, *La Mecánica Cardenista,* vol. 16 of *Historia de la Revolución Mexicana* (Mexico City: El Colegio de México, 1979), pp. 96–104.

a federal law authorizing expropriation for reasons of public utility, which is an enormously important omission considering modern demands pertaining to the collective interest. It impedes the federal government from responding in a timely, legal, and appropriate fashion to emergencies that call for a decisive response by the State authorities in the defense of interests that are often national in scope.[3]

This was a radical change. The amendment transformed the nation into a superior entity with interests situated over and above considerations of individual or group rights. It reformulated federalism in the sense that the State, in the name of the nation, was now empowered not only to balance the interests of the federated states but to intervene and direct society itself in the interest of the general good.

The next step was to immediately begin a profound economic restructuring in the name of the national interest. Beginning in 1935, proposals were put forward to expropriate properties in the petroleum, electrical, communications, and agricultural sectors. Each step was to be taken on a legal basis and with the approval of the Supreme Court when necessary. Large mobilizations were organized to demonstrate popular support for the reforms and to reactivate the populace as social actors. The first expropriations came in the area of commercial agriculture. Expropriated lands became the exclusive property of the State but were distributed to the *ejido* sector for cultivation. Figure 10.1 illustrates the intense pace of land distribution. In the six years between 1934 and 1940, 18.8 million hectares were distributed to nearly three-quarters of a million heads of families. In addition to expropriating the richest commercial agriculture lands, the State also took possession of the related agrobusinesses. Sugar, cotton, oilseed, and hemp mills were turned into peasant cooperatives. The railroads were nationalized in 1937, and the petroleum sector in 1938. The expropriation of the electrical infrastructure was proposed for 1938 but was suspended.

This would be a useful place to point out a general fact that was reinforced with each of the reforms. To the extent that the management and direction of the expropriations was concentrated in the presidency, neither the other branches of government nor the social actors themselves operated with much autonomy. The legislative and judicial branches had ceded their authority to the presidency in the name of a national project,

---

3. See Alicia Hernández Chávez, "El Estado Nacionalista, su Referente Histórico," in Jaime E. Rodriguez, ed., *The Evolution of the Mexican Political System* (Delaware: Scholarly Resources, 1984), pp. 203–13.

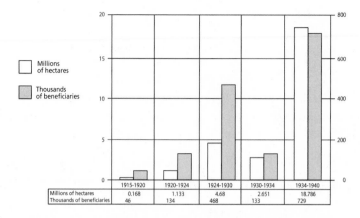

FIGURE 10.1. Land distribution, 1915–1940. (Source: *Estadísticas Históricas de México* [Mexico City: INEGI-SPP, 1985], p. 273.)

and the president's power to represent and guide the interests of the nation was correspondingly enhanced. Recognizing this strengthening of the executive branch by endowing the president with the power to oversee the well-being of the nation is essential to an understanding of Mexican presidentialism.

From its inception, the Cárdenas government's six-year plan contemplated the direct expropriation of major and highly concentrated economic sectors as part of a national economic strategy. To this end, the government enacted the law on expropriation and broadened its content by introducing the factor of general interest into the legal concept of property. This was a fundamental change in the nature and function of the State, which took on the power to intervene without delay if productive property was left idle or if a producer was operating so as to create a detrimental economic imbalance. In general, it could intervene whenever necessary to guarantee the well-being of society.

The six-year plan was conceived as a model to advance and even accelerate the social and economic development of the country. It did not propose to abolish the predominantly capitalist nature of the Mexican economy, much less transfer ownership of the means of production to the workers. The guiding economic principle was to strengthen and expand the internal market and create the conditions for industrial development. The political goal was to strategically position the State so it could guide what would be a mixed economy, redistributing income and otherwise operating in the interest of sociopolitical equilibrium. Furthermore, the

State would take control of the means of production in certain economic areas.

The basic assumption of the national plan was the direct intervention of the State in the centralized areas of the economy, including the energy sector (both electricity and petroleum), communications, transportation, and finance. Mining was viewed as requiring greater centralization; thus, a reorganization was proposed as a preliminary step to future nationalization. The distribution of consumer goods would be organized through the control or management of rail transport. In the case of basic foods, the market would be further regulated by agencies established for that purpose. Private industry under domestic or foreign ownership would operate freely as long as this was not harmful to the general interest. Thousands of small cooperatives, small-scale landowners, small industrial enterprises, artisans, retailers, and light manufacturers would be free to operate private businesses in open competition, while the State would help to organize a network of worker cooperatives in factories, mines, and fields. In theory, the power of the State to intervene would accelerate the process of economic transformation.

To the present day, the Cárdenas government is described as having focused primarily on land distribution. I believe that while the promotion of the *ejido* sector was central to Cardenismo, the government's strategy was substantially based on strengthening the internal market and expanding agricultural and manufacturing production. Still, the accelerated land distribution was particularly visible, with about 18.8 million hectares distributed to some 750,000 heads of families, as figure 10.1 shows. The result was that the peasants in the *ejido* sector came to represent 41.8 percent of the total population working in agriculture, and they farmed 47 percent of all cultivated land.

The agrarian reform and the massive redistribution of commercially viable land served various purposes. Economically, the expropriation of the great landed estates with the greatest productive potential displaced capital from the rural sector to industry, usually to be invested in the most dynamic sectors of the economy. This eliminated the economic drag that agriculture had placed on industrial investment. Land distribution also added nearly three-quarters of a million families—no less than one-third of the economically active population—to the consumer market.

For two essential reasons, the landowning oligarchy did not strongly resist the massive agrarian reform of 1936–1937. First, unlike in Brazil and Argentina, in Mexico there was no sector of the military to which they could turn for support, as the regular professional army had been disbanded in 1914. Second, international markets were so depressed and unstable that the oligarchy had no alternative but to quickly reinvest their capital in domestic industry and commerce, which were attractive in themselves due to increasing domestic demand.

The government's political and economic strategies meshed well. Land distribution created a massive client sector of *ejidatarios*. Thus the peasantry, the most volatile social sector, was politically co-opted, and the movement of agricultural workers into the most combative peasant unions was restrained. The State circumvented significant opposition from the potentially most dangerous sector and at the same time consolidated a reliable base of support, thus giving itself invaluable political latitude.

The definitive characteristic of this period was State intervention in strategic areas of the economy. This was accomplished through direct participation in productive activities and by means of legal reforms and structural changes, enabling the creation, expansion, and transformation of Mexico's productive and institutional infrastructure.

When the State designed and implemented a new model of domestic development, it became an agent of economic growth. First steps were taken to abandon the old export-oriented economic strategy. The new focus of growth was on agrobusiness and manufacturing, and substantive changes were made in the configuration of the national productive capacity as domestic demand increased. The four pillars of government policy were the use of public spending as an instrument for capital formation, the establishment of financial and banking institutions, strategic expropriations, and agrarian reform.

In a break with the thinking of Calles, the Cardenistas recognized the danger posed by the middle class. The middle class, defined as including small-scale landowners, artisans, industrialists, farmers, and *ejidatarios,* was assigned an important role in what was formally called the National Development Plan. The Cardenistas argued that the formulation of any development project should begin with the recognition that the middle class was "partisan to private property, economic independence, and free competition" and that its political ideology stemmed from this orientation. "They hate big capital, they condemn monopolies, and they reject imperialism. They know instinctively that these forces are responsible for their ruin as an autonomous class. But they hate socialism and the working class that advocates it even more, because they consider themselves superior to workers and they resist falling into their ranks."[4]

This social analysis had political, economic, and policy consequences.

4. *Plan Nacional de Desarrollo,* 1935–1936, Archivo Francisco J. Múgica, Michoacán.

According to the plan, the national economy would follow neither a capitalist nor a socialist model. It would be carried out "with the support of the middle class or not at all," and the middle class's support could be won only if the new national economy was based on the idea that the middle class would both limit the power of monopoly capital and guarantee free competition. If these two objectives were met, the plan argued, the middle class could even accept a "loss of political freedom and an antidemocratic regression, as long as respect for individual property was upheld absolutely." And if this could be accomplished, then the middle class "would support the government against socialism and the proletariat."[5]

By so characterizing middle-class interests, the government could project that in return for economic guarantees, it might win middle-class support for the new national economy, as well as middle-class acceptance of the goals and priorities established autonomously by the ruling class. The analysts who put forward the National Development Plan felt strongly that while the broadly construed middle classes were numerically the largest group, they were not developed enough, and lacked an organizational center coherent enough, to generate coordinated, sustained, and autonomous action on their own behalf.

According to the plan, the proletariat was a strategic sector whose small numbers obliged them to ally themselves with the State and depend on its support in the promotion of their interests. They were a strategically important class because they worked in the economic sectors where capital was most highly concentrated, but there were no more than 600,000 of them, of whom only 200,000 could really be considered industrial workers.

The workers' small numbers and dependence on the State led planners to believe that they could redirect the organized working-class movement into support for the goals established in the plan. In effect, the State would recognize and legitimate the economic demands of the unions, on the condition that the unions recognized that the national interest ultimately took precedence over the interests of their class. The result was a substantial change in working-class status. The nationalization of the railroads and the expropriation of the petroleum sector transformed the workers from "proletarians" to State-sector employees, working now in the interest of the nation.

In the course of the six-year Cárdenas era (1934–1940), tension between unions and the State sprang up when certain of the unions' economic demands were deemed incompatible with the interests of State-

5. *Plan Nacional de Desarrollo,* 1935–1936, Archivo Francisco J. Múgica, Michoacán.

sector industry. The State declined to accept the role of employer, always characterizing State-sector workers as public servants, beginning from the time of the railroad (1937) and petroleum (1938) nationalizations. The State came to categorically declare that its mission was to safeguard the interests of society as a whole, and that under certain circumstances, yielding to union demands would prejudice those interests, or even betray them. President Cárdenas expressed this idea succinctly in a 1940 letter to the Petroleum Workers Union rejecting their economic demands: "Some union leaders have not taken into account the change in circumstances that took place when the petroleum industry passed from the hands of foreign businesses into the control of the State. The workers and the government now have a shared responsibility and common interests."[6]

The New Party of the Mexican Revolution

Once Mexican society was organized by sectors, these sectors needed to be placed under the umbrella of a political body. The credibility of the PNR was almost nil, both in society in general and among its own members. The party was already outmoded, and the Cardenista reforms and popular mobilizations made it nearly unsustainable. A new party needed to be organized on a sectoral basis of the military, workers, peasants, and middle class.

Preparations for the new party began in 1937 with a certain sense of urgency, due to the fact that Lombardo Toledano was organizing the Socialist Party to be "the representative of the true left." As leader of the powerful Confederation of Mexican Workers (CTM), Toledano was in a position to unite the most radical forces, and nothing was impeding him from integrating the huge National Confederation of Peasants (CNC) and the energy of the peasant movement into his new party.

At the same time, opposition to the regime was growing daily. Sinarquismo, an ultraconservative and authoritarian Catholic movement, claimed to have a million followers. General Juan Andrew Almazán, the opposition presidential candidate, had the solid support of conservative army officers and politicians. Elements of the urban middle class had grown uncomfortable with the radical tone of the government and the nationalizations and were frankly anti-Cardenista.

The government had no intention of leaving these political problems unaddressed. Its plan was to reorganize the party to incorporate the pop-

6. Personal correspondence, Archivo Lázaro Cárdenas del Río, Michoacán.

ular sectors identified and promoted by the regime. At the beginning of 1938, the government put out the call for a March 30 founding convention of the new Party of the Mexican Revolution (PRM). This was the high point of Cardenismo. All of Cárdenas's enormous power and prestige was invested and channeled through the various social sectors into the new PRM and its political machinery.

The organized working class was represented at the founding convention by the CTM, the CROM, the CGT (the General Confederation of Workers), and the Union of Miners and Metalworkers—a total of ninety-six delegates, most of them from the CTM. The agrarian sector was represented by three delegates per state, elected from among the leadership of the Leagues of Agrarian Communities and the Unión Campesina either existing or established before March 29, 1938. Where there was no such league, the Mexican Confederation of Peasants and the executive committee of the PNR would oversee the election of delegates. The army chose forty delegates to represent thirty-three military zones, two naval zones, three command structures, and the leadership of the army secretariat.

With an official membership of 500,000, the National Confederation of Popular Organizations (CNOP) was a highly diverse organization. It included PNR members who did not belong to any of the other three sectors as well as women's and youth organizations, professionals, small-business owners, and workers and artisans who did not belong to any of the union federations.

Belonging to a union, an *ejido,* a corporatist body, a military command, or a constituent body of the CNOP automatically qualified one for membership in the PRM. The key was that these organizations were committed to collective, sectoral political activities within the framework of the party. Party membership jumped from less than one million in 1937 to more than four million, comprising 2.5 million in the peasant sector, 1.25 million in the worker sector, 500,000 in the popular sector, and 55,000 in the military sector.

The sectors, represented in proportion to their presence in society, had their own special characteristics. The peasants were the largest sector and the basis of the regime's popular legitimacy. The organized workers were important not so much for their numbers, but because they held the country's industrial production in their hands. They could either provide a solid foundation to development or create serious political and economic difficulties. The middle-class sector, organized as the CNOP, drew its membership from small entrepreneurs, professionals, public employees, and artisans who could otherwise fall into the hands of Juan An-

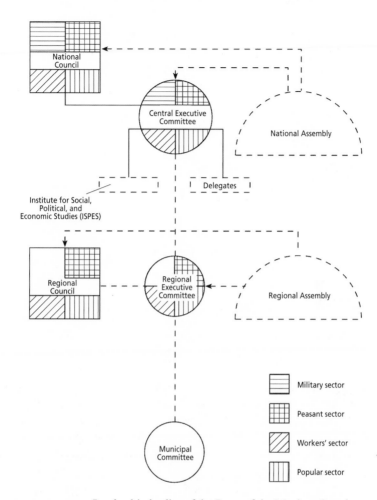

FIGURE 10.2. Leadership bodies of the Party of the Mexican Revolution according to its 1938 statutes. (Source: Luis Javier Garrido, *El Partido de la Revolución Institucionalizada. La Formación del Nuevo Estado en México, 1928–1945* [Mexico City: Siglo XXI, 1982], p. 249.)

drew Almazán's opposition movement or of the National Action Party (PAN), formed in 1939. Founded by Catholic groups in favor of social Catholicism as well as businessmen who promoted free enterprise, PAN had been organized in opposition to the government's corporatism, and its program drew members from the broad areas of society not organized sectorally by the regime.

CHAPTER II

Growth and Stability

During the presidency of Lázaro Cárdenas, Mexican society and its political system underwent transformations as dramatic as those that had taken place between 1911 and 1917. Events to come would radically change the face of Mexico. The nature and speed of what took place suggest that contemporary Mexico was in a sense fully configured in the 1930s and 1940s. I see the Mexico of today as the product of the changes made in those decades and of the challenges imposed on Mexico and the Mexicans by the new international context. The challenges faced were equal to those of the independence period or those of the mid-nineteenth century, with the distinction that the changes in the twentieth century took place during a period of peace. This important distinction explains how the new order born of the revolution laid the basis for the great transformations of the 1940s.

Economic Alternatives

The period from the Great Depression of 1929–1933 to 1945 and the end of the Second World War was a turning point for the whole world, Mexico and Latin America included. The economic transformations, which began in 1914 with the collapse of the self-regulated world market, were accentuated during the Depression. The total value of international trade in 1929 was some 50 billion dollars, dropping to 36.5 billion in 1932 and to about 30 billion in 1939, and further declining to 25 billion during the

Second World War. The halving of international commerce was due to reduced trade, the difficulty in obtaining gold and investment capital, reduced profits, and, for the first time, business insolvency—a symptom of
changed relations in the international system of payments. Governments
abandoned the gold standard, which before the First World War had been
the mechanism used to expand multilateral trade and develop the financial economy. During the Great Depression, the capital flow between
leading and secondary economies sputtered and then stopped.

For reasons that I will explain, the depression and the war had positive effects on the Mexican economy and perhaps on other Latin American economies as well. Trade between Latin America and the United
States, which had reached 3.2 billion dollars in 1929, fell to only 650 million dollars in 1934 but rose again to 1.4 billion dollars in 1940. Trade between the United States and Latin America grew to 2.8 billion dollars
during the war, but even so did not return to the levels of fifteen years earlier. Trade between Latin America and Europe also dropped steadily,
from 1.7 billion dollars in 1929 to 550 million in 1934, 500 million in 1940,
and 450 million in 1945.

All of this meant that, to a great extent, Latin American economies had
to fall back on their own resources to generate capital and solve problems
of production and distribution. It was a kind of forced economic isolation such as Latin America had previously experienced in 1914–1917, but
on this second occasion it lasted fifteen long years. In political terms it
meant that governments had more latitude to devise and adopt domestic
policies. Simply put, it was a period when the United States intervened
less in the internal affairs of Latin America countries. In his 1933 inaugu-
ral address, President Franklin Delano Roosevelt had announced a new
diplomatic posture of noninterference, a position that was further elabo-
rated by Secretary of State Cordell Hull at the Montevideo Pan-American
Conference of the same year. Hull declared that no State had the right to
interfere in the internal or external affairs of any other country in the
hemisphere. Therefore, he said, the United States would not intervene in
internal power struggles. It would maintain good relations with those
countries' governments.

Pressed to increase its economic self-sufficiency, Mexico responded
with a massive agrarian reform that injected new life into a depressed domestic market. Reduced imports of manufactured goods and increased
government subsidies stimulated Mexican industry to operate at full capacity. Activity increased in traditional industries such as food, textiles,
and footwear, increasing salaries and positively affecting the circulation

of goods. The cement industry and the Iron and Steel Foundry Company in Monterrey grew in pace with a wave of new construction. At subsidized prices, petroleum grew in importance as an energy source and as transportation fuel. Increased activity and prosperity in all of these industries stimulated the developing domestic market.

The three decades between 1940 and 1970 have been called the period of the Mexican miracle, when the country underwent the transformations that would give it its contemporary features. During this period Mexico changed from a predominantly rural country to one with urban and industrial characteristics, and the government responded to a demographic explosion with expanded educational and cultural programs. This unprecedented growth gave rise to unrestrained presidentialism and to an uncompensated federalism that tended to absorb and overshadow the powers assigned to the states.

The Domestic Market

I must emphasize once again that Cardenismo's accomplishment in the 1930s was the completion of a process begun in the late 1880s: the construction of a comprehensive domestic market. This was as revolutionary an achievement as the political transformations of 1911–1917. The general circulation of goods and services produced a wage and price structure based on supply and demand that tended to find its equilibrium throughout the diverse regions. Without this change and the unrestrained movement of labor, the rapid economic growth of 1940–1970 would not have been possible. Several important breaks with the past strongly stimulated overall demand: the evolution of agrarian reform, especially during Cárdenas's presidency; the 1926 establishment of the Bank of Mexico as a regulatory institution; the birth of a monetary system and the monetarization of salaries; and the definitive liberalization of the labor market.

The new economic institutions were accompanied by corresponding political and social institutions, especially with the formation of the corporatist system, which came to include large numbers of Mexicans—all of whom the State could organize and whose economic activities it could regulate.

The domestic market was built in stages, as can be seen in the growth of the gross domestic product between 1921 and 1940. It should be noted that the GDP estimates may not be absolutely accurate. They have been arrived at only indirectly by compiling the separate statistics for the differ-

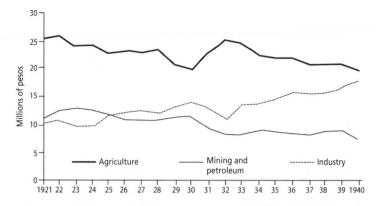

FIGURE 11.1. Economic performance, 1921–1940 (participation in GDP). (Source: Bank of Mexico, *Indicadores Económicos: Monetarios, Financieros y de Finanzas Públicas* [Mexico City: Banco de México, 1991].)

ent macroeconomic aggregates. Figure 11.1 illustrates the repercussions of the 1929 crisis in Mexico. Note the steadily increasing role of industry in the GDP and the slow but sure erosion of the agricultural component. These figures should be examined in the context of demographic change, however. Between 1920 and 1930, the population had recovered its pre-revolutionary levels and increased from 14.4 to 16.5 million, an annual growth rate of 1.4 percent. The urban population grew at a rate of 3.5 percent annually, double the overall rate, while the rural population grew at an annual rate of only 1 percent. As Mexico's transformation from a rural to an urban society accelerated, its domestic market was consolidated.

During the international economic crisis of the 1930s, Mexico's economic growth was sustained by industrial production. Output in the mining and petroleum sectors began to decline during the international crisis, and dropped sharply as a result of U.S. and European reprisals in response to the expropriation of the oil industry. Mexico would not benefit from the 1938 expropriations until the 1940s.

In 1940, very similar to previous years, the total population grew 1.7 percent and the urban population grew 3.1 percent. The total population reached 19.6 million, of whom 3.9 million, or 20 percent, lived in urban centers of over fifteen thousand inhabitants.

Table 11.1 illustrates the changing demographics. We can see that the population distribution was related to the expanding domestic market. The population of urban centers grew, and the population living in rural

TABLE 11.1. Urban and Rural Population Distribution by Percentage, 1920–1940

	1920	1930	1940
Urban:	14.2	17.4	20.0
A million or more inhabitants	—	6.4	7.9
100,000 to 999,999 inhabitants	5.7	2.1	2.9
50,000 to 99,999 inhabitants	3.2	3.2	3.6
15,000 to 49,999 inhabitants	5.3	5.7	5.6
Rural:	85.8	82.6	80.0
10,000 to 14,999 inhabitants	2.5	2.6	2.5
5,000 to 9,999 inhabitants	5.9	5.6	5.4
2,500 to 4,999 inhabitants	8.2	7.9	7.4
Fewer than 2,500 inhabitants	69.2	66.5	64.7

SOURCE: Alejandro Rodríguez y González, "De lo Rural a lo Urbano," in *México: 75 Años de Revolución,* vol. 2 (Mexico City: Fondo de Cultura Económica, 1988), p. 235.

towns and villages decreased, particularly in those with fewer than twenty-five hundred inhabitants. As explained in chapter 10, the relationship between these changes and the consolidation of the domestic market was due to the effects of agrarian reform.

With respect to the formation of the domestic market, in Mexico, unlike in other Latin American countries, agrarian reform stimulated production in various ways. Large agricultural properties were redistributed for use to *ejidatarios,* and in some cases were bought by small- and medium-scale landowners. Large agricultural entrepreneurs either kept their 150 hectares of irrigated land and produced for the market as ranchers or took the opportunity to invest in the more profitable and rapidly expanding industrial and commercial sectors. Producers in the huge network of towns observed the dynamism of the market and accelerated their integration into it. Every economic actor benefited: small-town producers, Indian communities, small-scale landowners, and individual and collective *ejidos.* The most important factor was that the rural world ceased to be simply a set of isolated producers drawing an income from the consumer market. Together with urban producers, they stimulated the process of industrial import substitution.

There were definitely two important pillars of the internal market. The first was investment in irrigation and roads in the 1930s and 1940s. Between 1935 and 1939, 18.6 percent of federal spending went to irrigation and 26.6 percent to roads, for a total 45.2 percent of spending. The second pillar of the market was the railroads. The feasibility of distribution on the network of federal highways, secondary roads, and rail transportation was a powerful stimulus to production for the domestic market.

Recent studies highlight the important participation of business, the *ejido* sector, agricultural landowners, and labor in the formation and growth of the domestic market. In the textile industry, for example, labor productivity, meaning the value of goods produced per worker, increased by 30 percent in the 1930s, equal to the increase at the beginning of the twentieth century, before the revolution. Total productivity increased 69 percent. This is a measure of goods produced per unit input of labor and capital, the joint input of workers and employers.

Mexico in the International System

After the worldwide depression and the Second World War, international politics and the world system had to be completely reorganized. The concept of sovereignty itself underwent changes as significant as those subsequently experienced at the end of the twentieth century. A bipolar world formed around the United States, the champion of liberal capitalism, and the Soviet Union, a socialist alternative. Countries everywhere aligned themselves with one or the other of these powers, and Latin America, including Mexico, fell into the U.S. sphere of influence.

The new set of international organizations formed in 1940–1970 were important to Mexico. Largely excluded from international forums by the United States and the European powers after the revolution, Mexico now entered into full participation in the new international system. The United Nations and the other organizations of the U.N. system, including the International Monetary Fund (IMF) and the General Agreement on Tariffs and Trade (GATT), were founded beginning in 1945. Regional organizations were established at the same time, including the Organization of American States (OAS), the Economic Commission for Latin America and the Caribbean (ECLAC), and the Inter-American Development Bank (IDB).

Thanks to the new international order, Mexico was relieved of the isolation it had suffered at the hands of the Great Powers between 1938 and the Second World War in response to its expropriation of the oil industry. At that time, the powerful companies whose investments had been compromised had mounted an intense campaign against Mexico when the country sought to break out of the boycott imposed upon it for doing business with Germany and Italy. If U.S. President Franklin Delano Roosevelt had not remained neutral, it would have been difficult for Mexico to sustain its nationalized oil industry. The Good Neighbor policy of the United States toward Mexico and Latin America was maintained despite pressures from the oil lobby and thanks to the fact that mining interests had remained untouched.

When the Second World War broke out, U.S. foreign policy with regard to Mexico was focused on the assistance that Mexico could provide. First of all, the United States needed access to Mexican petroleum, minerals, some manufactured goods, plus labor power to take the place of U.S. workers newly inducted into the military. Second, the United States required all possible cooperation from the Mexican military to protect the Pacific coast from a possible Japanese attack or any Japanese attempt to land troops in Mexico for a cross-border invasion of the United States.

This new situation was favorable to Mexico. In 1941, Roosevelt obliged U.S. oil companies to come to an agreement with Mexico over the expropriations, and using diplomacy he convinced British oil companies to do the same. As a result, Mexico and the United States were able to sign a new trade agreement and establish a bilateral Economic Cooperation Commission in 1942.

This newly cooperative relationship brought Mexico access to foreign credit that for all practical purposes had not been available since the revolution. The government of Ávila Camacho was therefore able to initiate, with foreign credits, major projects in industrialization and in irrigation, highway, and electrical infrastructure. Mexico's 1942 declaration of war against the Axis powers was a symbol of its definitive inclusion in the broad front of Allied countries and of its new relationship with the great industrial power of the United States.

The 1944 Bretton Woods Conference reorganized the international financial system, giving the dollar a central role and setting a fixed relationship between its value and that of gold. A Mexican delegation was present to sign this agreement. The new international order stemming from the victory of the Allies in the Second World War led to the 1945 Chapultepec Conference and the founding of the United Nations at a conference in San Francisco the same year.

Mexico's inclusion in the United States' sphere of influence, under the new bipolar system imposed by the superpowers, entailed certain rights and obligations. Mexico and the other Latin America countries required financial assistance in the form of easy credit and direct aid for their economic and social development. At the same time, Mexico criticized the enormous power assigned to the victorious United States, Britain, France, the Soviet Union, and China in the United Nations Charter and proposed a more democratic system for naming Security Council members.

At the Chapultepec Conference disagreements emerged between the United States and some Latin American countries, including Mexico. Several countries demanded that the United States make a greater financial commitment to the economic progress of Latin America. The U.S. delegation agreed to make that effort if the Pan-American conferences were transformed into a new regional organization, the Organization of American States. Other matters surfaced as well, such as the United States' criticism of certain protectionist economic postures taken by Mexico and other countries present. The U.S. delegation demanded that all States act in strict adherence to the Bretton Woods agreements.

The Chapultepec Conference did not meet all of the United States' expectations. The Organization of American States (OAS), formed in 1948 to replace the Pan-American Union, was not structured as the United States had wished. The United States had wanted to establish an OAS Security Council composed of a select group of countries. Instead, the OAS General Assembly was given decision-making authority and was composed of the member countries' foreign ministers based on equal representation: one country, one vote. The United States wanted to deal bilaterally with each Latin American country, including Mexico. This would have isolated each of these relatively small countries in a weak and disadvantageous position in relation to the superpower. Mexico was much more interested in negotiating a series of multilateral hemispheric agreements.

Mexican diplomacy was operating under enormous pressure, partly for the reasons described above, and also because, despite the Cold War environment, Mexico refused to abandon its foreign policy principles of nonintervention and the self-determination of nations. For example, Mexico refused to send troops to fight in the 1950–1953 Korean War, and at the 1954 Caracas Conference, the Mexican delegation dissented, on the basis of protecting constitutional rights, from the United States' proposition that any public disturbance in the OAS zone could be considered a "communist threat."

President Adolfo López Mateos took advantage of his term in office to reaffirm Mexico's foreign policy. Bilateral relations between the United States and Mexico became more flexible, and Mexican relations were expanded with many European and Latin America countries organized in blocs, by region, or as individual States. Charles de Gaulle paid an official visit to Mexico, and strong bilateral relations were established with France.

The Cuban Revolution and the ensuing confrontation between the United States and the Soviet Union presented the Mexican government with difficult foreign policy challenges. Former president Lázaro Cárdenas and much of the Mexican public enthusiastically supported the Cuban Revolution. At the same time, Mexico maintained a firm commitment to the principles of nonintervention and self-determination. To avoid a condemnation of revolutionary Cuba, Mexico asked the country to reaffirm its commitment to the inter-American system. But the Cuban government decided to align itself with the socialist camp. When the United States proposed to exclude Cuba from the OAS and the inter-American system, Mexico abstained and refused to participate in the commercial blockade imposed by the United States in 1961. In 1964, Mexico voted against the otherwise unanimous OAS decision for member States to break relations with Cuba, considering the move to be a violation of the principle of national sovereignty.

Relations between the United States and Mexico improved when President John F. Kennedy initiated the Alliance for Progress as his Latin American policy, but they quickly became strained when Mexico refused to vote for the creation of the Inter-American Peace Force to respond to the political crisis in the Dominican Republic.

A Diminished Federalism

We have seen how Mexico found its place in the international system and how its autonomous foreign policy was defined time and again by the principles of nonintervention and self-determination. We have also considered the national and international context at the end of the 1930s that transformed Mexican federalism into a centralist and corporatist arrangement. In the 1940s and afterward, Mexican federalism continued to survive in spite of the central State and government's attempts to make mere administrative units out of what had been sovereign states.

This process was incomplete because the central State's capacity to guide society and the economy had its limits. The greatest limit was undoubtedly the State's inability to bring the entire population into a corporatist framework. Half of the population at the most could be so organized at the earliest stages. The other half, composed of small-scale and medium-scale farmers, industrial entrepreneurs, and independent merchants and professionals, operated in a separate economic context that the State could not capture.

The corporatist project did effectively absorb the workers and peasants, however. These sectors were so strategic that their organization created a false impression of State omnipresence and omnipotence. This apparent wide influence was dependent on the status of the State and its party—the Institutional Revolutionary Party, or PRI, successor to the PRM—as the only national bodies with functionaries throughout Mexican territory and society to communicate and implement their policies. These historical conditions allow us to understand the construction of a national-corporatist political culture centered around the figure of the president.

The image of the State as supremely powerful may tempt one to underestimate the political importance of federalism and the independent social entities that found refuge in the states and municipalities in this period. However, a closer examination of prevailing political practices paints a different picture. When a new president took office, a good half of the incumbent governors and deputies would be appointees of his predecessor, and he would proceed to appoint the other half or have an influence on their selection. This provided a certain degree of political continuity and contributed to the peaceful transfer of power. It also imposed limits on the power of the president, who was obliged to negotiate, respect agreements, and recognize the internal political mechanisms in the states of the union. Only in this way could he obtain the necessary consensus and the reciprocity with the governors that were indispensable for good relations between the federal and state governments. In addition, the president was free to select candidates of his choice for state governors and federal deputies only as long as he left it to local forces to choose state deputies and municipal authorities. Thus Mexican federalism provided room for a certain political give-and-take within recognized limits.

Even the corporatist bodies of the worker and peasant sectors, though they were mainstays of the political system, were by no means mere appendages of the government, nor were they subordinate to an all-powerful presidency. Between 1918 and 1962, the labor sector held an average of 52 seats in the Senate and over 250 seats in the Chamber of Deputies. The Confederation of Mexican Workers (CTM) was in a position to negotiate with the government over the number of political posts it would control, based on its strength in given areas. This gave additional leverage to local and statewide labor bodies, which were not entirely sub-

ordinate to their national organizations. The presence of labor representation was politically meaningful. The corporatization of labor, the expropriation of the oil industry, the nationalization of the electrical system,
and the creation of the Institute for the Promotion of Workers' Housing
(INFONAVIT) were all negotiated on the basis of reciprocity with the
demands of industrial and peasant labor organizations.

Congress was most definitely the weakest branch of government. In
1940, just 5 percent of the federal deputies represented opposition forces.
Despite a gradual increase, their effectiveness was ever limited by the
overwhelming power of the government party, the PRI. In addition,
their political-economic proposals sometimes lacked coherence, which
made them seem merely contrarian. Between 1935 and 1959, bills sent to
Congress by the president were almost always approved unanimously.
Even at the most contentious of moments, or when constitutional revi-
sions were at stake, the government position received at least 95 percent
support. This was the case during the 1934–1964 period. It seemed that
Congress had a merely symbolic function in the legitimation of presidential initiatives. But this impression is somewhat deceptive. Cabinet
secretaries and even the president frequently consulted with Congress
and with other political forces not directly represented in the legislative
bodies, in order to reach consensus on all aspects of bills being submitted for approval. Especially during and after the presidency of Lázaro
Cárdenas, the political process revolved around the activities of the president in consultation with other forces, convincing or compromising
with them and modifying legislation appropriately. Even sectors outside
the corporatist framework participated in these activities. They could not
be excluded, for they retained the power of disobedience and noncoop-
eration, which could endanger the stability of the State.

The autonomy of state governors is another phenomenon that tends
to be underestimated in studies of modern Mexican federalism, given the
image of governors as selected or imposed by the incumbent president.
The subordination of governors is relative. Their very real political power
and autonomy belie the idea of state governments as mere conduits of
federal power. The six-year incumbencies of state governors do not coincide with those of presidents, so that in the second half of their terms
they work with a new president to whom they do not owe their selection.
The governors' relative autonomy from presidential power allows them
to develop their own state policies and to themselves aspire to the highest office.

The states have notoriously weak access to economic resources. In fact, between 1934 and 1964, the proportion of state government revenues in relation to total government revenues decreased from 14.5 percent to 9.5 percent. As a result, the states depended increasingly on federal credits and subsidies. In 1963, the federal government was the source of 34 percent of state revenues, compared to just 8 percent in 1950.

The subjugation of the states to the federal government was due more to financial than political constraints. The same can be said of the municipalities, the fundamental building blocks of state and federal politics. In the 1950s, municipal revenues represented only 3 percent of total taxation; the municipalities, too, had to turn to federal credits and subsidies to ensure their financial solvency.

It would probably be accurate to say that the states and municipalities ceded some of their powers to the federal government in the 1950s in return for economic resources. But this was a passing phenomenon. Relations between the levels of government call for constant renegotiation; they are circumstantial and not structural.

Presidential Power and Its Limits

By the end of the Cárdenas period, the presidency had become more central to governing Mexico than at any time since the revolution. The newly powerful presidency contributed to the corporatist characteristics of the Mexican political system and seriously reduced the power of the other branches of government. Channeling the energies and ambitions of the social sectors into a specific set of government institutions had stabilized the Mexican political system. The presidency had attained more than enough power, authority, and flexibility to successfully balance multiple demands and pressures.

The institutionalization of the "imperial presidency," with its power and privilege, signaled a new government endeavor to respond effectively to popular demands. The presidency's efficiency was a function of its increasing capacity to organize and interpret those demands. It undoubtedly assumed a role superior to those of the other branches partly as a result of its increased effectiveness. Eventually it became preeminent; the president's responsibilities and legal authority grew exponentially. But the imperial presidency coincided with the specific historical period from the 1940s to the 1960s. In those years, each new president was endowed with the sum of powers accumulated by his predecessors. Six years later, though, he would pass those broad powers on to his successor and retire definitively from the political scene.

One may legitimately ask why the Mexican presidency, with its immense power, did not evolve into an authoritarian or personalist position but maintained and even consolidated its institutional nature. Not only did the constitutional functions of the presidency not expand in this period, they even contracted somewhat. In fact, the last president to exercise extraordinary constitutional powers was Ávila Camacho, and that was in 1942. The presidential veto was rarely used between 1941 and 1970, and while the president had overridden the authority of the states forty times between 1918 and 1938, this occurred only seven times between 1938 and 1957.

Limitations on the legislative function of the presidency did not mean that the executive branch was weak but only that it exercised its power and maintained its efficiency through the political-administrative means provided for in the constitution, specifically, the power to issue regulations and to execute the law. It must be said that the constitution did not explicitly assign the regulatory function to the presidency, but the Supreme Court during this period interpreted the constitution to mean that the president would be charged with the promulgation and execution of the laws emitted by the Congress, providing the administrative means for their strict observance. In other words, what the presidency lost in legislative functions was compensated for through its political-administrative prerogatives, with the clear advantage of a lower profile of power and increased control of State administrative bodies as well as public-sector and corporatist institutions.

Increasing political-administrative centralization helps explain why the cabinets of the period did not meet collectively with their respective presidents. The presidents considered it more efficient to govern based on individual consultations with cabinet secretaries and other advisors. The exercise of administrative authority by presidents generated an enormous problem when it came to coordinating government activities affecting cabinet secretaries, their departments, and decentralized State bodies. Since the presidents rarely acted in coordination with their full cabinets, closed power circles developed within federal departments and other State entities, based upon the authority of their chief administrators. This accounts for the very limited success of the new Secretariat of the National Patrimony, created in 1958, in controlling or coordinating the disparate federal entities that administered State and para-State properties and operations. It also explains the problems encountered by Antonio

Ortiz Mena, the secretary of the treasury and public credit from 1958 to 1970, when he attempted to account for the finances of decentralized State enterprises, especially PEMEX, the State petroleum company, in the federal budget.

The growing political-administrative authority of the presidency did not make it any more efficient. Instead, it created a significant confusion of functions that essentially weakened the office and reduced the effectiveness of its central directive function, as well as its ability to coordinate work with cabinet secretaries, government departments, and decentralized bodies. Presidential power would have declined even further had it not been for what was euphemistically called metaconstitutional authority, the power derived from the president's being not only the head of State and government but also the titular head of the party that selected him, the PRI. The exercise of the presidency in 1940–1970 has been characterized as "government by consultation." Presidents listened to and took into account the needs, wishes, and objections of the principal interests involved in a given policy issue. Political flexibility and self-restraint were important attributes in the exercise of power during the first years of a presidential term. The president's primary task was not to set his own course but to synthesize the political demands of others. The president effectively became the conciliator of diverse social and institutional pressures, and it was incumbent upon a presidential candidate nominated by the PRI to consider, in addition to the instructions of his party, the social demands of corporatist bodies and constituencies as well as those of social sectors outside the corporatist structures.

These practices constrained presidential power between 1940 and 1970. In addition, presidential authority was impersonal; it pertained to the office, not to the man, and it was limited to one six-year term. What is more, certain individuals and pressure groups were able to counter the power of the presidency. These included regional and local *caciques,* the army, the clergy, large-scale landowners, domestic and foreign capitalists, the PRI, and bureaucratic forces within the administrative apparatus. Each of these had a direct influence on governmental decision-making.

Some authors have written that the power of interest groups in the Mexican political system of 1940–1970 derived from their positions within the corporatist framework. These authors forget that the corporatist system was never able to absorb all existing interest groups. In fact, when they assert that the consultative presidential system provided an opportunity for diverse social interests to be heard, including those outside the sectoral divisions of the PRI, they forget that Mexican corporatism extended only as far as the government's finite capacity to redistribute economic resources in return for political adhesion.

The corporatist framework of this period limited the political, economic, and social power of the developing presidential institution. After all, limited material resources made it impossible to absorb all social sectors into the corporatist arrangement. At best, the corporatist sector upon which the legitimacy of presidential power depended included only half of the population, while the progress of the other half was based on social and economic growth outside the direct control of the presidency. We may take the number of individuals affiliated with the official party as a measure of the size of the corporatist sector. This number increased from 3.3 million to 5 million between 1940 and 1958, was stable in the 1960s, and grew to 6 million at the beginning of the 1970s. If we compare the number of party members with the size of the electorally active population, we see that party members were responsible for practically all votes cast between 1940 and 1946, decreasing to 66.6 percent of votes in 1958, and just 42.8 percent of all votes cast in 1970. Although this statistical evidence is imperfect, the numbers speak for themselves. Despite the consolidation of presidential power, it was impossible to continue integrating the population into the corporatist structures. The evidence also helps us to understand the strong dissidence that developed beginning in 1958. During the 1960s, says Daniel Cosío Villegas, there was resistance to corporatism enforced by "the extraordinarily broad legal and extralegal powers of the President and the overwhelming dominance of the ruling political party," with the result that "the most urgent and important political problem in Mexico [was] to somehow contain or even reduce this excessive power."[1]

Whatever limitations existed to presidential power could be attributed to one of two factors. First, there was a divide between a "corporatized" citizenry allied with the presidency and the ruling party, and an independent, "noncorporatized" sector with intermittent ties to opposition parties, especially in presidential election years. Second, there was tension within the corporatist ranks, where a set of political factions built bureaucratic bases in federal secretariats, departments, and other bodies. These bureaucratic bases defended their power against outside forces, including the presidency. At the regional level, centralized power was compromised by opposition parties, which were strong in some states; by re-

---

1. Daniel Cosío Villegas, *El Sistema Político Mexicano* (Mexico City: Joaquín Mortiz, 1972), p. 68.

gional political bosses; and by internal divisions in state PRI committees. All of these factors support the idea that the presidency was most powerful when the president engaged in dialogue, persuasion, and compromise, rather than coercion. In other words, the exercise of "government by consultation" may have strengthened the hand of the presidency by engaging the ruling party, its subordinate organizations, and the noncorporatized social sectors in the decision-making process, but at the same time it weakened the presidency's own autonomous decision-making authority. The presidency's Achilles heel may have been its excessive expediency, especially in the 1960s.

Public Opinion, Political Parties, and Elections

Literacy and other educational campaigns in the 1920s and 1930s had succeeded in spreading the use of the Spanish language, raising the general educational level of the population, and producing trained technicians. Hoping to further the same goals, subsequent governments took up the educational task as a priority. In the period covered by this chapter, every government channeled resources into education as the essential mechanism for elevating and uniting the nation culturally, and instilling the understanding that education was itself the necessary basis for social and economic betterment and the prerequisite to social mobility in a democracy.

The following data should illustrate the commitment of the government and the determination of society to improve itself. From the 1920s onward, including in the 1950s, over 10 percent of the federal budget was consistently spent on education. After 1960, public health was also prioritized, accounting for over 4 percent of the federal budget. Between 1960 and 1970, spending on education, culture, hospitals, health services, and social security grew dramatically, increasing by well over the rate of overall budget growth. While total spending grew by 12.7 percent between 1959 and 1970, social spending grew by 15.2 percent in the same period.

This great effort by government and society between 1940 and 1970 led to the increased importance of informed public opinion, which encouraged cultural and ideological pluralism throughout society. As federal education policy was applied throughout the country, the level of education across different regions became much more balanced. A tendency had been developing since the end of the nineteenth century for each state to regulate its own educational system, but this was now reversed. Jaime Torres Bodet, the secretary of public education, focused his efforts on converting the nation's schools into "schools for all Mexicans." The secretariat embarked on another literacy campaign and established effective programs for school construction and improved teacher education and quality of instruction. Article 3 of the constitution was amended to eliminate the requirement for a "socialist education" to be provided exclusively by the State to all students at the primary and secondary levels and in normal schools.

The 1946 reform of Article 3 reaffirmed the principles of the 1917 Constitution as they related to open and secular education, the basis of Mexico's educational system. It also enriched this concept by specifying that such education was to be based on the freedom of conscience and on democracy, understood as a way of life based on the constant economic, social, and cultural improvement of the people. The improvement of the nation and the people should be directed "with neither qualification nor exclusivity" toward the understanding of our problems, and should contribute to the enrichment of human coexistence "based on the ideals of brotherhood and equal rights for all."

Torres Bodet was named secretary of public education for a second term, serving again from 1958 to 1964. He extended his plan for basic education through that period, for a total of eleven years. He instituted a free textbook program, built thirty industrial-technical training centers, and initiated the construction of the National Museum of Anthropology and History and the National Museum of Modern Art. It was a climactic moment for education and culture, although certain problems did emerge. The centralization of the educational system led to a general merger of educational unions, which detracted from the quality of instruction by politicizing the curriculum. It was also difficult for the Secretariat of Public Education to communicate effectively with the thousands of schools in the country, and the expanding educational system could not keep up with the rate of population growth.

A decentralization of the educational system was first proposed in 1958, but not even such clear signs of trouble as the teachers' demonstrations of 1958–1959 and the student uprising of 1968 were able to break through the bureaucratic inertia. Education reform was postponed, although Mexico and its educational needs had changed dramatically. A vast and fully formed middle class was now a reality, and its members were concerned and even anxious about their cultural and educational needs in the present and those of their children in the near future. To this new generation, the revolution was but a historical event.

Between 1957 and 1963, Mexico experienced social crises previously unknown in its modern history. Railroad workers and teachers opposed government policies and publicly criticized the government and the PRI for their authoritarianism. These movements struck a chord and attracted support among the middle class. The PRI instituted a number of internal reforms, including the creation of political space within the party for individual citizens, without challenging its essentially corporatist structure. In 1963, Article 54 of the constitution was amended to introduce the proportional representation of minority parties. Minority party delegates could be elected without gaining a plurality in any given district—a change that was beneficial to the National Action Party (PAN), which increased its representation in 1964 from five to twenty delegates, and to the Popular Party, led by Lombardo Toledano, which increased its one seat to ten. The PRI, which had held 96.6 percent of all seats in 1961, occupied 83.3 percent of them as of 1964.

Mexico's closed political system was further shaken by the power of the communist movement and the impact of the Cuban Revolution. The Mexican left minimized the value of popular suffrage, opting for street demonstrations, strikes, and even guerrilla movements. The PAN, on the other hand, founded in 1939 in opposition to the then ruling PRM (Party of the Mexican Revolution), began to move away from its deeply conservative positions. The party had responded ambiguously to the Cristero rebellion, but now Manuel Gómez Morín, a prominent attorney and an advisor to the Mexican central bank, led it to a more clearly institutional position within the political system and to full participation in electoral activities.

After the Second World War, the PAN began to move away from its Francoist positions and to center its discourse and political proposals around a secular, anti-statist, free-market, and reformist posture. From this new position it attracted some support from business and middle-class forces. For the first time, PAN won seats in the Chamber of Deputies—four out of 146. When the left opposition flourished in 1957–1963, the PAN moved first toward the Church and then, in the 1960s, in the direction of a centrist and antigovernment electorate. Its continued relationship with the Church cast it in a Christian democratic light, which it maintains still. Christian democracy has been highly successful in Chilean and European politics, but it has not established an explicit position in Mexico. The political shift by the PAN and the 1963 electoral reform enabled the party to double its representation from an average of five deputies between 1946 and 1961, or 2.8 percent of total deputies, to 9.5 percent of the total.

The governing party, though still enjoying a comfortable majority, now had competition from both the right and the left. In 1940, after the six years of Cárdenas's presidency, the Mexican Communist Party (PCM) had a highly disciplined, militant, and experienced base. During its Popular Front period, the Communist International had led the movement into maximum resistance to fascism and Nazism. The Mexican party had finally emerged from clandestinity and been legally recognized. The principle industrial unions, under Communist leadership, had affiliated with the CTM. The Communist Party maintained its collaboration with the government until the beginning of 1950.

Between 1940 and 1950, the Mexican union movement produced a phenomenon known as *charrismo,* referring to the connections that developed among corrupt union leaders, business interests, and government forces. The decline of the PCM, the principal party of the left, continued throughout the 1950s, until the rail workers' movement gave the party a jolt that led to a new political direction. With the liberalization of international Communism in the 1960s, and in the wake of the tragic experience in Czechoslovakia and the student movement of 1968, the PCM sought to build unity with other leftist movements and parties.

New social conditions, a new political culture, and the changed direction of opposition parties also led the PRI to consider changes to its own structure. Founded in 1938 along corporatist lines, under Ávila Camacho the PRM had moved away from radicalism and begun to accommodate itself to middle-class interests. Given the effective unity among unions, business, and government during the Second World War, and with an eye toward its fortunes in legislative elections, the governing party had abandoned its working-class and anticlerical discourse in favor of a tone more amenable to middle-class interests and voters. In 1946 the PRM transformed itself into a new party, the Institutional Revolutionary Party, or PRI.

The PRM was dissolved with the idea that the revolution should consolidate its institutions and undergo a process of renovation in the party, in the government, and in the worker, peasant, and popular sectors that were its social base. Under the organizational arrangements of 1946, each sector in each state had one member on the party's National Council, and a system of internal primary elections with individual and secret ballots was organized in order to select candidates for public office. This scheme, however, was never put into practice.

It was expected that the new party would more efficiently channel demands from the sectoral bases in the states to the party National Coun-

TABLE 11.2. National Convention of the Party of the Mexican Revolution, 1946

Sector	Number of Delegates	Number of Votes Represented
Worker	581	1,748,805
Popular	667	1,938,715
Peasant	719	2,063,962
TOTAL	1,967	5,751,482

SOURCE: Robert K. Furtak, *El Partido de la Revolución y la Estabilidad Política de México* (Mexico City: UNAM, 1974), p. 90.

cil. The function of the union and agrarian apparatuses in the transmission of demands made them crucial links in the overall political system. In fact, they became major mechanisms of social participation and mobilization. PRI candidates for Congress continued to receive 81–96 percent of the vote, and PRI presidential candidates did as well or better. Presidential candidate Adolfo Ruiz Cortines received the lowest percentage in 1952, about 76 percent of the votes cast.

The period of continued State expansion and the fine-tuning of the political apparatus generated a unique political culture in which debate centered on the different social sectors and their contention for relative advantage within the party. Each sector sought to expand and more closely control its base in order to wield maximum strategic weight in internal party debates and negotiations. The relative strength of each sector determined the level of federal funds that would be available to it and the number of legislative and gubernatorial positions its representatives could expect to occupy. Thus the political imperative of each sector was to demonstrate its own strategic value to the leadership by delivering the greatest number of votes to party candidates in general elections. This mechanism, the result of internal party and government dynamics, resulted in electoral victories for the PRI with majorities of 80 percent and more. Because of this structural imperative to maximize their influence, PRI forces replaced political persuasion with steamroller tactics and a crude dictatorship of the majority to crush all opposition.

Figure 11.2 illustrates the relative strength of union organizations. The CTM (Mexican Confederation of Workers), as the organizational expression of the PRI's working-class sector, was easily the largest, and imposed its characteristic politics and culture on the entire union movement. Fidel Velásquez headed the CTM and the union movement from the 1940s until his death in 1998. If any aspect of Mexico's political life

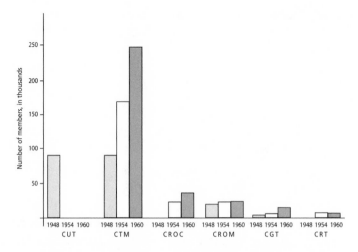

FIGURE 11.2. Membership of the principal union federations, 1948–1960. CUT = Central Workers Federation, CTM = Mexican Confederation of Workers, CROC = Revolutionary Federation of Workers and Peasants, CROM = Regional Confederation of Mexican Workers, CGT = General Federation of Workers, CRT = Regional Federation of Workers. (Sources: Fernando Talavera and Juan Felipe Leal, "Organizaciones Sindicales 1: Organizaciones Sindicales Obreras de México, 1948–1970: Enfoque Estadístico," in *El Trabajo y los Trabajadores en la Historia de México,* compiled by Elsa Cecilia Frost et al. [Mexico City: El Colegio de México and University of Arizona Press, 1979]. For further information, see José Luis Reyna, Francisco Zapata et al., *Tres Estudios sobre el Movimiento Obrero en México* [Mexico City: Jornadas 80, El Colegio de México, 1976].)

was dominated by one way of practicing politics and exercising power, it was the labor movement under Fidel. He directed the sector for half a century as a virtual minister without portfolio.

But the working-class movement was broader and more complex than its official bodies would have it. Outside the CTM and the orbit of the PRI were the CGT, with an anarchist orientation, and the CROC and the CRT, which had emerged from the independent left. Even the unions affiliated with the CTM represented different political and union tendencies. The Union of Miners and Metalworkers was Trotskyist. It broke away from the CTM in 1938, and by 2003 still maintained its independence, with a membership of some ninety thousand workers. The same can be said of the strategically important Mexican Union of Electricians, or SME. The Mexican Communist Party was enormously important in labor organizing and in the PRM until 1939, when it broke with the Cárdenas government to support the Hitler-Stalin pact. The PCM regained some influence within industrial unions during the Second World War. As the Cold War was developing in 1949, the party organized its own union confederation, the General Union of Workers and Peasants of Mexico, or UGOCM. The PCM maintained its strength among railroad and petroleum workers, electricians, and cinematographers and in the agrarian sector. Nonetheless, the CTM and the CNC (National Confederation of Peasants) remained dominant.

The Popular Party also played a somewhat significant role in these decades. The party had been founded in 1949, and in 1961 was reorganized as the Popular Socialist Party, or PPS, under the leadership of Lombardo Toledano.

The independent left formed several organizations and attempted a number of different political tactics, operating as an institutional opposition or presenting a radical critique. Leftists used the mass media to promote causes such as a more equitable distribution of income and resources, increased salaries, and improved educational opportunity. In general, organizationally unaffiliated intellectuals, journalists, professionals, artists, and teachers had important individual influence on public opinion, and enjoyed great popularity.

When the opposition sought to chastise the government of Miguel Alemán in 1952 by refusing to accept his successor, Adolfo Ruiz Cortines, the vote for PAN and for a coalition of two independent left parties came to a total of 24 percent, or 838,000 votes out of a total of 3.5 million. However, the opposition parties were unable to present candidates in every congressional district, while the PRI presented candidates for all sixty Senate seats and for 178 seats in the Chamber of Deputies. The PAN was able to compete in just two-thirds of the districts and the PPS in just half of them, so that electoral efforts had only limited value as a form of political opposition.

Economic Performance

In order to measure the economic performance of workers, peasants, business, and government between 1940 and 1970, I present selected indices that describe the evolution of the gross domestic product (GDP), real per capita income, and productivity. The change in real per capita income is obtained by adjusting the GDP to account for demographic growth. A figure on productivity is reached by describing the change in the GDP as a function of either additional labor input alone, or of

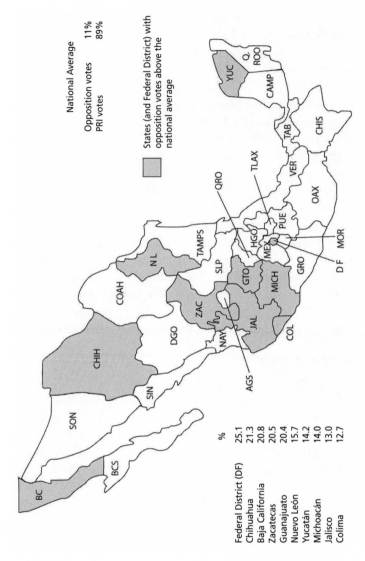

National Average

Opposition votes	11%
PRI votes	89%

States (and Federal District) with opposition votes above the national average

	%
Federal District (DF)	25.1
Chihuahua	21.3
Baja California	20.8
Zacatecas	20.5
Guanajuato	20.4
Nuevo León	15.7
Yucatán	14.2
Michoacán	14.0
Jalisco	13.0
Colima	12.7

MAP 11.1. States with the highest percentages of opposition votes (including the Federal District), 1964. (Source: Pablo González Casanova, coordinator, *Las Elecciones en México* [Mexico City: Siglo XXI, 1985], p. 167.)

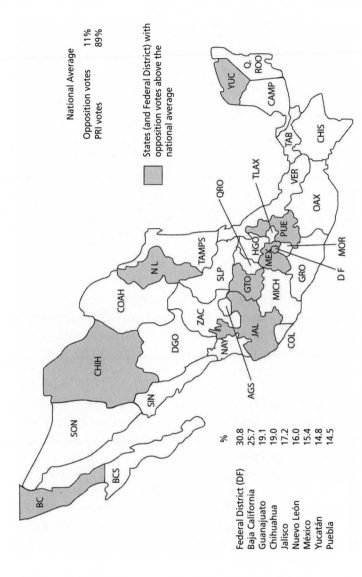

National Average

Opposition votes	11%
PRI votes	89%

States (and Federal District) with opposition votes above the national average

	%
Federal District (DF)	30.8
Baja California	25.7
Guanajuato	19.1
Chihuahua	19.0
Jalisco	17.2
Nuevo León	16.0
México	15.4
Yucatán	14.8
Puebla	14.5

MAP 11.2. States with the highest percentages of opposition votes (including the Federal District), 1970. (Source: Pablo González Casanova, *Las Elecciones en México*, op. cit., p. 329.)

TABLE 11.3. Economic Indicators, 1940–1969 (Annual Rate of Growth)

Years	GDP	Per Capita Income	Productivity	Employment	Urban Salaries	Industrial Salaries
1940–1944	5.7%	3.8%	2.3%	n/a[a]	−3.5%	n/a
1945–1949	4.5	1.6	1.1	n/a	−6.3	n/a
1950–1954	6.3	1.9	3.4	n/a	3.1	n/a
1955–1959	6.2	2.1	2.9	n/a	2.4	n/a
1960–1964	6.6	3.2	4.4	2.4%	5.3	5.9%
1965–1969	6.4	2.8	3.9	2.4	4.5	1.5

[a]n/a = Information not available.

SOURCES: Bank of Mexico, *Indicadores Económicos: Monetarios, Financieros y de Finanzas Públicas* (Mexico City, Banco de México, 1991); Rafael Izquierdo, *Política Hacendaria del Desarrollo Estabilizador, 1958–1970* (Mexico City: Fideicomiso Historia de las Américas—El Colegio de México—Fondo de Cultura Económica, 1995), pp. 156–61.

additional labor together with increased capital investment. I also present two other variables: the growth of manufacturing employment in principal industrial areas, and the increase in real industrial wages, which is the nominal increase in wages adjusted to account for price inflation.

Table 11.3 illustrates the economic performance of the three decades between 1940 and 1970, the most positive economic period in Mexican history, perhaps comparable to the 1880s, during the Porfiriato. Growth was rapid, sustained by constantly increasing productivity. These basic figures point to the 1940s as the period in which Mexico consolidated its capitalist economy, a qualitative leap that was possible thanks to the cumulative effort of the previous economic period, which was one of domestic market construction. The data on productivity indicate the point at which the Mexican economy began to grow not merely on the basis of natural resource and labor inputs, which is known as *extensive* growth, but also as a result of *intensive* growth, incorporating capital investment and the application of new technologies.

These economic figures provide an edifying lens through which to view the demand for improved education and technical training in the period. They describe a virtuous circle of new and intensive economic growth that was capital intensive in both economic and social terms, social demands for quantitative and qualitative improvements in educational opportunity, and the evolving sectoral composition of the labor force. Census figures indicate that the number of professionals and technicians grew 44.4 percent between 1950 and 1960, the number of office workers grew by 31.6 percent, and the number of workers and artisans engaged in the production of goods and the provision of services grew by 13 percent. On the other hand, the number of unskilled urban workers declined by 21.7 percent and the number of agricultural workers declined by 8.6 percent.

These changes in the structure of the labor force can be deduced from the growth in value added per economically active individual as workers migrated from relatively unproductive to more productive employment. In moving from noncommercial agriculture to urban employment, workers took up better-paid industrial positions that also provided social security and other employment benefits. They did not make the transition directly, however. First they required technical training, which could explain the increase in productivity relative to the increase in real wages. In a context of *intensive* economic growth, the most important factor is not an increased number of industrial workers, but the technical training of workers transitioning from agricultural to industrial employment. But the combination of technological and human capital has a cost, and intensive growth requires an institutional framework with clear rules of the game, well-defined property rights, equality of opportunity for foreign and domestic investors, and a new production regime organized to best exploit the inputs of capital, labor, and natural resources.

The economic growth of the 1940s was nurtured by a growth in federal spending and a monetary policy designed to stabilize the peso in relation to the dollar. The austerity policies of President Ruiz Cortines slowed it down, however. Between 1952 and 1958, a dearth of private investment and sluggish growth required increased federal spending. By 1954, it became necessary to devalue the peso from 8.5 to 12.5 to the dollar, an exchange rate that would be maintained until 1972. The devaluation and the fixed exchange rate were protectionist mechanisms intended to stimulate new investment, exports, and domestic demand.

The government's protectionist course elicited different responses from business, labor, and the middle class. Labor was of course represented by unions and peasant leagues such as the CTM, the CNC, and the CROM. The National Chamber of Manufacturing Industry, or CANACINTRA, was an organization of small and medium businesses, with ties to the PRI. Its membership benefited from protectionism. The Confederation of Chambers of Industry, or CONCAMIN, was an organization of large foreign and domestic businesses that did not always support the fixed peso-to-dollar exchange rate because of the difficulties it presented on the international market. The other social sectors and sectoral organizations arrived at a position that equated nationalism and protectionism. The governments of the 1940–1970 period attempted to reconcile these varying interests and positions, maintaining the fixed exchange rate and protectionist policies. Thanks to these policies, inflation was controlled and real wages protected.

The government consistently constrained public spending in order not to overheat the overall economy. Since 1959, the International Monetary Fund had been recommending a convertible currency, control over the deficit, and credit and monetary policies compatible with domestic and international economic stability. Spending was restrained during the presidential term of López Mateos, except when the government responded to worker unrest in 1959 with increased spending for that year and for 1960, and when significant credits were received from the Export-Import Bank in 1961.

The policy of the secretary of the treasury and public credit was to carefully maintain a balanced budget. While consciously avoiding excessive fiscal stimuli, it was still possible to relieve new industries from some taxation, and to control current spending so as to direct a sufficient amount of resources into public investment, especially into infrastructure. In distinction from all the other Latin American countries, Mexico had no budget deficit until 1952, and even then the deficit was very low, just 1.5 percent of GDP until the end of the 1960s.

The government employed a particular mechanism known as Mexicanization in its relations with domestic and foreign investors in key industries such as mining, electricity, fertilizers, and airlines. The government designed the Mexicanization policy in order to convert privately held businesses into majority Mexican ownership—at least 51 percent—but retain the participation of international capital. If insufficient domestic investment capital was available for this purpose, then domestic investors would receive State assistance. The Mexicanization policy succeeded in ensuring the application of new technologies and stimulating large-scale foreign reinvestment in the country. It also accelerated industrialization and strengthened the Mexican business sector. On the downside, it reduced or eliminated competition among domestic industrial firms and was a deterrent to competition on international markets, since high profits were easier to achieve in the protected domestic market. Mexican consumers paid for Mexicanization through higher prices on domestically produced goods that were not necessarily of the highest possible quality. Firms like PEMEX and FERTIMEX, the State fertilizer company, paid for the policy when their profits were invested in other areas of the economy, either through subsidized pricing structures or by their direct exploitation as a source for government spending needs in other areas.

Protectionist policies designed to promote social harmony generated economic growth at the end of the 1950s and throughout the 1960s, but also produced structural weaknesses that negatively affected economic development in following years. Reduced competitiveness in Mexico's productive apparatus translated into higher consumer prices. Direct foreign investment fell off because the law requiring 51 percent domestic ownership was not always compatible with efficient management. As a result, the need for government financing or financing by international institutions grew, increasing the foreign debt from 6.1 percent of GDP, or 813 million dollars, in 1960, to 9.2 percent of GDP, or 3.2 billion dollars, in 1970. Figures 11.3 and 11.4 illustrate that the difference between domestic savings and total investment was relatively minor between 1950 and 1962, so there was not a great need for foreign borrowing to meet domestic investment needs. In fact, foreign investment was insignificant between 1950 and 1956, just 0.74 percent of GDP. The recourse to foreign capital rose a bit in 1957–1962 to 1.81 percent of GDP, and stayed at approximately that level in subsequent years: 1.4 percent in 1959–1962 and 1.7 percent in 1962–1970.

Figures 11.5 and 11.6 indicate high rates of private investment, primarily domestic, until 1960. In fact, this kind of investment between 1950 and 1960 increased from 8 percent to 11.4 percent of GDP. Between 1960 and 1970, this form of investment stalled, and the State stepped in to make sure that total investment requirements were met. The lack of private investment was due to international capital flight in response to the Mexicanization policy, the strike wave at the end of the 1950s, the radical tone of Mexican political discourse, and the government's refusal to break commercial ties with Cuba. Since the Mexicanization policy benefited industrial workers, they were its firmest defenders, convinced that it protected the domestic economy from the fluctuations of the international business cycle and the disequilibria that such fluctuations would impose on the balance of payments, on employment, and on prices.

In a protected market whose political expression was economic nationalism, private investors and free enterprise were suffocated by the high cost of doing business. According to the secretary of the treasury at the time, the financial sector, including banks, insurance companies, and equity markets, should be the fundamental piece of the economic strategy in the 1960s. In fact, the financial sector financed the government as well as public and private business between 1962 and 1970. Manufacturing,

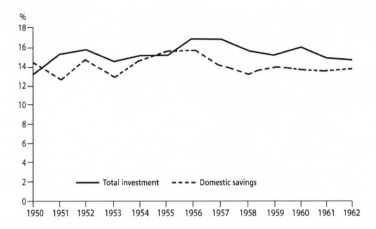

FIGURE 11.3. The gap between savings and investment, 1950–1962, expressed as a percentage of GDP. (Source: Enrique Cárdenas, *La Política Económica de México, 1950–1994* [Mexico City: Fideicomiso Historia de las Américas—El Colegio de México—Fondo de Cultura Económica, 1995], p. 29.)

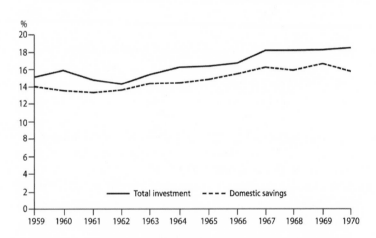

FIGURE 11.4. The gap between savings and investment, 1959–1970, expressed as a percentage of GDP. (Source: Enrique Cárdenas, *La Política Económica de México, 1950–1994,* op. cit., p. 79.)

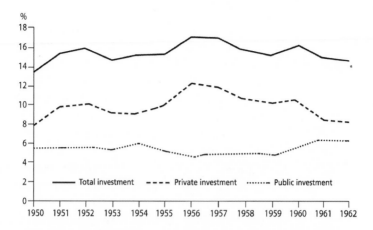

FIGURE II.5. Investment in 1950–1962, expressed as a percentage of GDP. (Source: Enrique Cárdenas, *La Política Económica de México, 1950–1994,* op. cit., p. 29.)

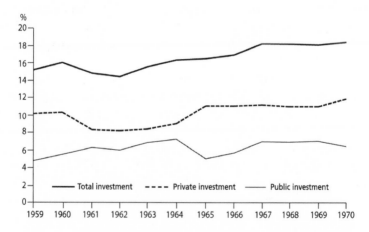

FIGURE II.6. Investment in 1959–1970, expressed as a percentage of GDP. (Source: Enrique Cárdenas, *La Política Económica de México, 1950–1994,* op. cit., p. 63.)

mining, and commercial enterprises received the greatest total credits. The public sector would begin to be systematically financed by banks as the Bank of Mexico authorized them to consider government bonds in their accounting of legal reserves.

The financial system represented a new and powerful factor in the productive economy, as those who saved using the banking system were now also indirect investors in domestic enterprise. It was the first time in Mexican history that the real economy was sustained by the financial economy.

The so-called Mexican miracle was produced by the factors discussed in this chapter. But there were limits to growth. One problem was the high rate of population growth, about 3 percent annually in 1950–1960. The economy grew 4 percent annually in that period, so real annual economic growth was 1 percent—certainly not insignificant, but insufficient to produce general economic prosperity.

In fact, the unequal distribution of income was probably responsible for generally reduced economic well-being. Half of domestic income was going to less than one-fourth of the economically active population, which meant that more than half the population did not experience any increase in purchasing power at all. The rate of growth in consumer industries began to slow in 1955–1965, and profits in heavy industry tended to fall. The simplest explanation is that once consumer demand—meaning the demand of the 15 percent to 20 percent of the population with sufficient purchasing power—was saturated, business began to design schemes to induce the other 80 percent of the population to purchase their goods by going into debt at near usurious rates that frequently led to bankruptcy and property foreclosures.

The government attempted to correct these social and economic imbalances, evocatively described by Oscar Lewis in *The Children of Sanchez,* by offering improved health and education services. This required an increase in social spending from 15 percent to 31 percent of the federal budget between 1952 and 1960. In addition, an attempt was made to implement the profit-sharing provisions of Article 123 of the constitution. What was not addressed, and what has not *been* addressed, was a reform of the tax structure in order to achieve a more satisfactory distribution of income.

CHAPTER 12

Into the New Millennium

In the last part of the twentieth century, Mexico saw a variety of political, economic, social, and cultural projects. The late 1960s and the 1970s saw extremes of wealth and poverty, the exercise of privilege, and the arbitrary rule of law, as well as street confrontations, guerrilla movements, and resistance to the growing demands for political representation and the full implementation of the 1917 Constitution. A cleavage began to open within Mexico's political system in the late 1950s, climaxing in 1968, when student and middle-class protests and the army's violent intervention illustrated the constraints imposed by authoritarianism. The incoming government of staunch populist Luis Echeverría first reacted with huge increases in government spending. Money flowed to university circles, *ejidatario* leaders, and labor unions. The spending increased as oil reserves were said to be boundless. In 1976, Mexico's recently elected president euphorically declared that Mexico's problem was not scarcity but how to administer abundance.

Mexico and the World

The vicissitudes of Mexican politics, society, economics, and culture cannot be understood in isolation from the international context. The end of the Cold War produced a new international instability but also ushered Mexico into the global market, setting it on an entirely new historical trajectory. As the twenty-first century dawned, Mexicans, like other peoples around the globe, were adjusting to a relatively uncertain and insecure existence in a world of rapid change. This is the age of the communication revolution, in which ideas and information travel at the speed of light. Even people, goods, and cultural forms can be moved rapidly, putting us all in contact with one another. Some people are still outside the electronic communications network, but the economic reasons for this should diminish as technology becomes ever more affordable. Mexicans receive information from other countries on a daily basis, integrate it, and make it their own. Mexican culture enriches people elsewhere, and Mexicans are enriched by the cultures of others. The most significant change that Mexico experienced in the twentieth century was to find itself a part of the larger world and to receive a plurality of messages, a wealth of new information that affected its politics, economy, culture, society, and national life.

Mexico is at the end of a historical cycle that saw its dramatic transformation from a corporatist society to a secular society of individuals operating in a market economy. Political practice in Mexico has produced a minimalist version of economic liberalism. Since the 1980s, this liberalism has been expressed essentially as a movement toward Mexico's reinsertion into the international economic order and in favor of attracting outside investment—two goals that bring the country in line with the parameters set out by international trade and financial institutions. At the same time, the crisis of the corporatist State has opened the political space for citizen movements and organizations to demand the effective exercise of their civil and political rights. These demands were co-opted by the government and addressed by means of gradual reform.

From 1946 to the beginning of the 1970s, the international situation was generally stable, largely due to the bipolarity born of the Second World War. The Soviet Union and the United States maintained order within their respective spheres of influence, and a third world war was avoided by the very real possibility of nuclear annihilation. Wars were fought on the margins, such as in Korea and Vietnam, and other international crises, such as the Cuban missile crisis, were resolved without recourse to war. At the same time, the Great Powers transferred enormous financial and technological resources to other countries in order to extend their own economic power and that of their allies. The reconstruction of Europe, for example, would not have been possible without the Marshall Plan. In addition to material aid, Asian and African countries received their independence. Every Latin American country benefited from the massive amounts of capital and technology that arrived during this time.

Unlike in the three decades between 1940 and 1970, the international situation of the thirty years between 1970 and 2000 had inconsistent effects on domestic conditions. While cultural internationalization was continuous, Mexico's political and economic life was punctuated by alternating periods of expansion and recession. The periods of expansion stimulated economic growth. For example, oil prices rose in the middle of the 1970s and again at the beginning of the 1990s when Mexico was able to renegotiate and reduce foreign debt. In the 1980s, on the other hand, a period of reduced trade and an international recession produced an economic crisis so severe that Mexico was still paying for it at the close of the century. The U.N.'s Economic Commission for Latin America and the Caribbean (ECLAC) famously termed the 1980s the "lost decade."

The instability of the business cycle reduced economic growth to a process of fits and starts. This began to change only after the demise of the bipolar world system. The symbolic date of this event was in 1989, when the Berlin Wall came down and the United States finally prevailed over the Soviet Union in their military and economic rivalry.

At that time, the United States thought that the world would be unipolar and under its control. Instead, the end of the bipolar system brought about the emergence of midsize powers. Some of these, such as the European Union, Japan, and China, would enter the ranks of the big powers, while others, such as Mexico, Brazil, Chile, and Australia, would consolidate their midsize status. Still others, such as Argentina and South Africa, would be considered *potential* powers. This is current history in development, but what is certain is that a new hierarchy has emerged in the international order. Within this new framework, countries such as Mexico have more freedom to maneuver because of policy differences between the United States and the European Union. The new international diplomacy confers special importance upon international organizations, such as the United Nations, the World Trade Organization, and the Food and Agriculture Organization, and regional bodies and agreements, such as NAFTA, MERCOSUR, the Organization of American States (OAS), and the Rio Group. Global and regional organizations and agreements play an ever more crucial role. They are the new organs of international collaboration, within which each State, without sacrificing or compromising its own national sovereignty, can benefit from international cooperation. They can participate in the mechanisms established by these institutions and access the resources made available to ease the potentially harmful effects of what are termed external shocks—events such as an increase in import prices at a time of decreasing export values, or a spike in the rates of interest for hard currency. These are events that could affect Mexico's public debt and impinge on the government's ability to provide for social spending and public services.

It should be made clear that Mexico has a proud diplomatic tradition. It has participated actively on the international stage in the consolidation of multilateral and open institutions and practices—despite the special and bilateral relations preferred by the United States since the Second World War. In 1971, Mexican President Luis Echeverría addressed the U.N. General Assembly to emphasize two guiding principles of a new international diplomacy: a multilateralist approach, and support for the proposals of the so-called Third World. These principles were not incompatible, as an international forum existed in UNCTAD, the United Nations Conference on Trade and Development, which represented the views of Third World countries that had declared themselves "nonaligned" with either of the international blocs, that of the United States and that of the Soviet Union. Mexico was one of seventy-seven countries—the Group of 77—that committed themselves to formulate a Charter of Economic Rights and Responsibilities of States to protect themselves from domination by the developed countries.

Despite the excesses and ultimate failure of the nonaligned movement, two of its important principles did take root. The first, which endures still, was the multilateral orientation of Mexico in its diplomatic and trade relations with all countries, regardless of their political or economic systems. The second, which was maintained until the second half of the 1980s, was the idea that Mexico's diplomatic posture was a basic supporting pillar of Mexican nationalism.

The implications of the idea that foreign policy strengthens nationalism were demonstrated between 1976 and 1982. At that time, Mexico had enormous oil reserves, a fact that was believed to increase the country's potential for power. The petroleum wealth also generated closer economic relations with the United States, Mexico's major energy market. Natural gas from the Mexican southeast was sent to the United States by means of the new Cactus-Reynoso pipeline. At the same time, Third-Worldist and ultranationalist critics divided Mexican public opinion and generated tension between Mexico and the industrialized countries. This was at a time when the entry of Mexico into GATT was being considered; Mexico initiated discussions in 1979, but there was no unanimity about joining GATT in either the PRI or the government. CANACINTRA, the National College of Economists, leftist parties, and nationalist intellectuals were among those favoring protectionism. The forces of economic liberalization were on the other side of the debate; they favored joining GATT. These forces included the largest business organizations, such as CONCAMIN, COPARMEX (Employers Federation of the Mexican Republic), and ANIERM (National Association of Importers and Exporters of the Mexican Republic), as well as centrist parties and some intellectuals.

Mexico also demonstrated its multilateral orientation, this time toward Central America and the Caribbean, by signing the San José Pact in 1980. In this agreement, which is still in effect, Mexico and its fellow oil exporter Venezuela agreed to sell petroleum to Costa Rica, Jamaica, Nicaragua, El Salvador, Guatemala, Barbados, Panama, Belize, and the Dominican Republic under favorable credit terms, if those countries agreed to purchase other products as well. This reinforced both Mexico's and Venezuela's political and economic positions in the region. Mexico's posture in Central America enabled it to play an important role in the 1980s in the resolution of the subregional crisis that accompanied the difficult transition from long-term dictatorships to new democracies.

The 1982 financial crisis over the "petroleumization" of the Mexican economy led Mexico to strengthen its presence in Latin America and improve relations with the United States. The government of President Miguel de la Madrid sought a larger role for the Mexican productive apparatus in the international economy. Mexico's trade and cultural relations were also diversified and expanded through the development of a mass tourism industry.

After 1982, Mexico promoted a new idea in international relations: that a country could maintain its independent foreign policy even if it was in a vulnerable economic position. Mexico took up a new regional focus, wanting to prevent foreign interventions that could be harmful to Latin American peace and coexistence. Representatives of Mexico, Panama, Venezuela, and Colombia met on the Panamanian island of Contadora in early 1983 to implement this position, and they took for themselves the name of the island, the Contadora Group.

The Contadora Group played an important role in the direction of Latin American regional relations. The effort was expanded by the 1985 formation of an additional support group, composed of Argentina, Brazil, Peru, and Uruguay and called the Friends of Contadora, which focused on two goals: elimination of foreign military forces from Central America and acceleration of the disarmament process of the Central American countries themselves. There was a strong element within the United States government that favored military intervention in the region to defeat a perceived "communist threat." Though the United States had virtual veto power over multilateral Central American negotiations, this interventionist group had sufficient power to circumvent any nego- tiated solution to the conflict. The negotiating position of the Latin American group was supported by Spain, France, and those elements in the United States that favored a peaceful solution to what had become a crisis. This was enough to enable the Contadora Group to achieve its goals and for the Central American peace process to move forward. A set of agreements signed at Chapultepec in 1991 brought an end to a long conflict.

The positive achievements of the Contadora Group created favorable conditions for the formation of the Cartagena Group in 1985. Represen- tatives of Mexico, Brazil, Argentina, and Colombia met in that Colom- bian port city seeking a common approach to the problem of external debt, which was impeding their economic development. They hoped to prevail upon international financial institutions to recognize their finan- cial needs and capacities and to negotiate a set of agreements that would provide for debt service more in keeping with their goals for economic development.

At the end of 1986, the Rio Group was set up as a permanent body for consultation and coordination, incorporating both the Contadora Group and the Friends of Contadora. Sensitive to the political weight of this new hemispheric body, the OAS began to institute its own reforms toward the end of the decade.

The failure of the United States to pay its OAS dues precipitated and contributed to the "Latin Americanization" of that organization. The OAS gradually took on new but crucial hemispheric responsibilities in- volving the defense and promotion of human rights, the supervision and coordination of drug control efforts, and electoral monitoring and ob- servation.

Mexico joined GATT in 1986 and took an active role in the liberaliza- tion of trade, a process that was crystallized in 1994 with the formation of the World Trade Organization. Mexico's active participation in this process and its enthusiastic promotion of the free trade agenda repre- sented a convergence of interests with the United States that helped alle- viate tensions over the U.S. "certification" of Mexico in the war on drug trafficking.

In 1988, the recently elected presidents of Mexico and the United States, Carlos Salinas de Gortari and George H. W. Bush, met for bilat- eral discussions in Houston, establishing a basis for expanded political cooperation between the two countries. A set of understandings reached in what was known as the "spirit of Houston" coincided with the demise of the bipolar world order and recognized the regional role that Mexico could play. A new Mexican foreign policy blossomed as of the late 1980s as the country developed cooperative relations with the United States, the European Union, Japan, and the countries of Latin America. Mexico also participated in the reform process within the United Nations system and played an active role in the development of the unfolding World Trade Organization.

Salinas's goal at the Houston meeting, held just weeks before he assumed office, was to reduce Mexico's foreign debt. Bush focused on security issues, fighting drugs, and establishing a free trade zone similar to the one agreed upon by the United States and Canada shortly before. As former president George H. W. Bush commented in September 2002 (at the ten-year celebration of the signing of NAFTA in Washington, D.C.), Salinas had shrewdly put Mexico's foreign debt on the front burner; only afterward did the three countries negotiate a free trade zone. In 1992, the Mexican government reached a historic landmark. A debt reduction of nearly 7.2 billion dollars heralded a new economic and financial era. The North American Free Trade Agreement, or NAFTA, which came into effect in 1994, was promoted by Canadian Prime Minister Brian Mulroney and Presidents Bush and Salinas. NAFTA was important to Mexico in a number of ways. It opened the U.S. market to Mexican products and led to Mexico's full and equal participation in international diplomacy. It reduced the level of ideological confrontation between Mexico and the United States, and it established Mexico and NAFTA as pivotal factors in the Latin American political economy. The NAFTA treaty became a template for bilateral and multilateral agreements throughout the hemisphere.

Mexican diplomacy moved into high gear as free trade agreements were negotiated and signed with Central America and then with Chile. Under the terms of NAFTA, the United States guaranteed Mexico access to the advanced technology it needed to maximize economic productivity and guaranteed the access of Mexican products to the most lucrative market in the world. This was expected to accelerate the transformation of Mexico into an exporter of industrial goods with high technological content. NAFTA also established mechanisms for the discussion and resolution of differences concerning the regulation of the North American market. The cooperative relations established among Mexico, the United States, and Canada proved beneficial during Mexico's 1994–1995 financial crisis, when Mexico obtained a substantial loan from the United States government. The efforts of other Latin American governments to sign on to agreements similar to NAFTA are evidence of their desirability. It is to be expected that Mexico will enter into additional trade agreements to strengthen Mexico's path toward globalization in the twenty-first century.

The Populist Episode

When Luis Echeverría became president in 1970, there were clear signs that the existing economic and political model was not responding to the country's real needs. The student movement and its violent repression were just two years in the past. The movement's central demand had been for greater political participation within structures less rigid than those of the traditional parties. The movement had been composed of students from the middle strata of the public university system, representing the different sectors of society that were demanding better salaries, improved education, health and other services, and above all, a full democracy. Although the corporatist interests of certain radical parties and organizations provided a subtext to the movement, its explicit demands did address new conditions and problems. No political party inside or outside the government was able to represent or channel the discontent of the students or the broad social forces that supported them.

The tendency of the government was to increase State participation in economic life by means of public investment and public-sector expansion. This led to one of the longest populist episodes in Mexico's modern history, lasting from 1970 to 1982 and spanning the presidencies of Echeverría and José López Portillo. Echeverría turned to populism rather than attempting to channel popular demands and discontent into a democratization of the political system. During the term of López Portillo, cash was flowing into the country as a result of the petroleum boom. He squandered these resources and the development potential they represented in a cross-class strategy that he called "shared development," under which the State operated virtually alone as society's economic motor.

The State sector was already a major economic player, yet the number of State productive and service enterprises more than quadrupled during these two presidential periods. The 273 such enterprises existing in 1950 nearly doubled under Echeverría in 1971–1976 with the addition of 232, and 651 new enterprises were then added under López Portillo in

1976–1982, for a total of 1,156. Taxation of private wealth was increased in order to improve the standard of living for middle and lower sectors. The policy was described as a set of measures intended to please everyone. "Everyone" would have included urban workers and their unions by means of salary increases; the middle class by means of price subsidies and an overvalued currency in order to facilitate the purchase of imported goods; and the agrarian sector, with cheap fertilizer, other subsidies, and improvements to rural infrastructure. Big business objected to neither the subsidies nor the overvalued currency, and the bureaucratic stratum benefited from the expansion of employment in the vast State and public sectors.

The architects and supporters of the populist experiment justified it as a way to improve wealth distribution in a country where a small number of people had very large incomes and the vast majority barely subsisted. They argued that the redistribution of wealth assured the general well-being of the society and that the least advantaged should by rights benefit more from the social wealth that existed. Some even suffered from the delusion that the populist episode was the beginning of a new era in Mexico that would be comparable to European social democracy. Others saw it as the wasteful exercise that it was. For its part, the political right sought to discredit populism entirely and encouraged opposition on the basis of a supposed communist threat.

It must be said that the populist policies were neither the saving grace of 1930s revolutionary nationalism nor a path to communism. Populism was an expensive attempt to detain the reform of an increasingly unproductive bureaucratic State and to close the door to any political reform of a strongly presidentialist regime.

In this period of arbitrary government decision-making, resources were unloaded on the countryside without any provision for control or oversight. Land in the Yaqui and Mayo valleys in Sonora state was expropriated and redistributed in the form of *ejido* collective farms. Later, in an attempt to repair the national unity that had been battered by extremists, the Alliance for Production was established. The need for a government response was real, because the government itself had provoked social conflict. Radicals had organized rural mobilizations and land occupations. Capital flight was one reaction, and private businesses gathered under corporate-based associations to defend themselves collectively. These included CONCANACO (Confederation of National Chambers of Commerce), the Mexican Council of Businessmen, and the Bankers' Association.

The populist policies also had repercussions on politics, including electoral politics. A 1977 electoral law expanded the number of deputies from three hundred to four hundred (though not all seats were filled until 1982; see table 12.2, page 314) in order to include one hundred deputies elected from regional and plurinominal lists, the latter a mixture of direct and proportional representation weighted to favor minority parties. This reform also increased congressional power with regard to the overseeing of elections. The requirements that political parties had to register were eased, which allowed two leftist parties to qualify, the Communist Party and the Socialist Workers Party, or PST for its initials in Spanish. However, in 1982 it was the centrist PAN that increased its vote to 12.7 percent from the 8.4 percent it had polled in 1976, while the various parties of the left divided their votes. The PPS (Popular Socialist Party) won 2.55 percent of the seats; the PSUM/PCM/PMS (a coalition of the three major socialist parties: the United Socialist Party of Mexico, Mexican Communist Party, and Mexican Socialist Party) won 4.25 percent; and the PST won 2.75 percent. Surprising as it may seem, it was the governing party whose vote decreased the most, despite its support for populist measures. The PRI vote dropped from 80.1 percent in 1976 to 69.3 percent in 1982.

Maps 12.1 and 12.2 contrast the electoral results in 1970 and 1982. The retreat of the PRI from the north to the center, south, and southeast is very clear. In addition, the party lost support in Jalisco, Michoacán, the state of Mexico, the Federal District, Querétaro, and Guanajuato. Outside of Chiapas, Campeche, and Quintana Roo, where the PRI still obtained over 90 percent of the vote, the days of 80 to 90 percent or higher support were a thing of the past.

The populist years contributed to an ongoing diversification of public opinion. The process had begun years before with the early stages of the rural-to-urban social transformation. This shift was reflected in a demographic modernization that culminated in the 1980s. Birth rates dropped in almost every state, with a few notable exceptions such as Chiapas, which has a high birth rate even today. Populist agitation stimulated both support and opposition in the cities and in the countryside. Populist policies had the effect, not consciously intended, of nationalizing the debate over what kind of nation Mexico wanted to construct. Disputes over rural policy were introduced into urban political discourse.

More or less between 1960 and the early 1980s, there was a prolonged rural crisis that battered agricultural production and peasant family income. This affected the corporatist political and associational ties of rural society with the National Confederation of Peasants (CNC), and with organizations intended to support the rural economy, such as the

Bank of Ejidal Credit and the National Food Support Program, or CONASUPO.

The economic crisis in agriculture is signaled in table 12.1. The consistent decline of the agricultural sector is evident, as is the decline of its contribution to growth. This decline is even more notable in comparison to the weight of the industrial sector with regard to GDP, and its continually increasing contribution to overall growth. In the populist decade of 1971–1981, the crisis in the agricultural sector and the sector's decreasing contribution to industrial growth led to a totally unexpected phenomenon. Agriculture had long supported the industrial economy with a supply of staple foods at subsidized prices and with other inputs, but the moment arrived when the price disparity between these goods and market-priced industrial goods had a negative overall effect. Agricultural backwardness came to be a burden on the industrial sector.

The Mexican Agrarian System, or SAM, was a program launched by President López Portillo to guarantee national food self-sufficiency. This was said to be a priority, since the sovereignty of a country dependent on food imports would always be at risk. Much was made of the program, and enormous amounts of resources were invested in it, but the results were thoroughly unsatisfactory. In 1968, 10.6 percent of federal investment went to the countryside, increasing to 16.9 percent in 1975 and to 19 percent in 1980. Nevertheless, as agricultural output increased, the State apparatus expanded even more, particularly the Bank for Rural Credit, or BANRURAL. Thus government policies never managed to reverse the decline of the agricultural sector. Despite all the attempts to support the population's buying power, a 1982 revaluation of the peso in relation to the dollar was enough to cut the real value of salaries by over half.

The rural crisis accelerated the migration to the cities (see maps 12.3 and 12.4). Between 1970 and 1980, while the Mexican population was growing at the high annual rate of 3.2 percent, the urban population grew by thirteen million and the rural population by only five million. Internal migration produced large rings of slums around Mexican cities.

Other political mechanisms were created in an attempt to exert some control on the rural situation. The new Permanent Agrarian Congress tried, with only limited success, to link independent peasant organizations to the CNC, the National Confederation of Peasants. Instead, peasant organizations such as the General Confederation of Mexican Workers and Peasants (CGOCM) and the Independent Peasant Organization (CCI) were firm in their opposition to the government.

Ejidatarios, small-scale landowners, and small-scale agricultural mer-

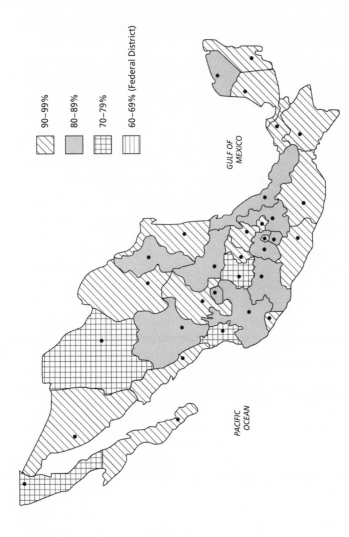

MAP 12.1. Presidential elections: percentage of votes for PRI presidential candidate by state, 1970. (Source: Silvia Gómez Tagle, *Las Estadísticas Electorales de la Reforma Política* [Mexico City: El Colegio de México, 1990], p. 46.)

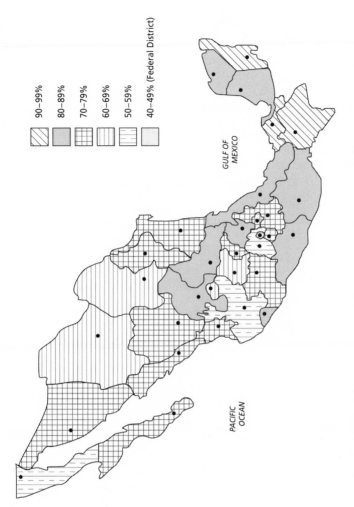

MAP 12.2. Presidential elections: percentage of votes for PRI presidential candidate by state, 1982. (Source: Silvia Gómez Tagle, *Las Estadísticas Electorales de la Reforma Política*, op. cit., p. 120.)

90–99%
80–89%
70–79%
60–69%
50–59%
40–49% (Federal District)

GULF OF
MEXICO

PACIFIC
OCEAN

TABLE 12.1. Contribution of the Agricultural, Industrial, and Service Sectors
to GDP and Economic Growth, 1962–1981

	% of GDP			% of Contribution to Economic Growth	
Sector	1962	1971	1981	1962–1971	1971–1981
Total agriculture:	15.3	11.5	8.8	7.0	5.7
Farming	9.8	7.0	5.2	3.8	3.4
Livestock, forestry, and fishing	5.5	4.5	3.6	3.2	2.3
Total industry	29.6	34.1	35.7	39.5	33.7
Total services	55.1	54.4	55.5	53.5	60.6
TOTAL	100.0	100.0	100.0	100.0	100.0

SOURCE: Nacional Financiera, *La Economía Mexicana en Cifras* (Mexico City: 1984), table 2.5, pp. 61–62, cited in Enrique Cárdenas, *La Política Económica en México, 1950–1994* (Mexico City: Fideicomiso Historia de las Américas—El Colegio de México—Fondo de Cultura Económica, 1995), pp. 60, 92.

chants began to seek associational mechanisms to improve their market competitiveness, but they came up against huge obstacles put in their paths by the banks and the government bureaucracy. At this point, many began to participate actively in the local political life of their municipalities in order to promote their interests through channels other than the CNC, the Ejidal Bank, and State insurers. The cause of their frustration was the banking practice of using property titles as collateral, thus excluding *ejidal* holdings from eligibility for credit.

The populist governments squandered precious and nonrenewable resources. The presidencies of Echeverría and López Portillo spanned the years from 1970 to 1982, and both of them led the Mexican economy astray. In 1970, public foreign debt had been 4.26 billion dollars. It increased to 19.6 billion dollars by 1976 and 58.87 billion dollars by 1982. Interest payments on foreign debt in 1982 were 14 billion dollars. Between 1983 and 1988, Mexico transferred the equivalent of 7 percent of its national product to meet interest payments on debt—more than the total sum spent on education and health combined. A series of unique opportunities went unexploited. Nevertheless, the situation awoke public opinion in the states and municipalities and gave democratization a helpful push forward.

The Democratic Option

The process of democratization was the most salient development at the end of the twentieth century. It had many historical roots in preceding decades—most recently, the awakened force of public opinion, increased political autonomy on the part of the citizenry, and institutional reforms promoted by state legislatures and municipalities. These reforms came to be supported by the government and the political parties, including the PRI itself.

The new pluralism resulted from a freedom of movement among the country's political forces after a rupture of the PRI-dominated interclass alliance and the breakdown of the party's sectoral political apparatus. The entire society had never been brought into the corporatist system, even at its most inclusive moments. There were always social sectors that the government was unable to organize. The breakdown of corporatism was accelerated by urbanization, which diminished the social distance between peasants and workers. With declining performance in the State sector and the State's inability to include the new urban populations in its corporatist structures, it became ever more difficult to hold onto even the forces within the traditional PRI sectors.

There are various explanations for the breakdown of the central State and the rebirth of federalism. State-run enterprises provided expensive and unreliable services, and some were facing insolvency. This was due both to their inefficiency and to the expanded bureaucracy that absorbed well over half of their budgets in administrative costs alone. At the same time, federalism's historical roots were strong and deep, as we have seen in earlier chapters. But circumstances intervened as well. The tendency of the omnipresent central State was to convert the states of the union into mere administrative units. A state governor could do very little, apart from arguing for state sovereignty, when the federal allocation for a single trusteeship was higher than his entire state budget, and President Echeverría tended to address social or economic problems with federally funded projects headed by a member of his entourage. One reaction to the invasiveness of the central government was a revived defense of state sovereignty. The growing strength of municipalities and of public opinion also shifted the balance of power within Mexican federalism and increased the power of Congress, as constitutional reforms in 1977 discreetly tempered the excesses of the presidency.

The new balance between the legislative and executive branches was furthered by 1982–1983 constitutional reforms submitted to the Chamber of Deputies by President Miguel de la Madrid. Election results led to a

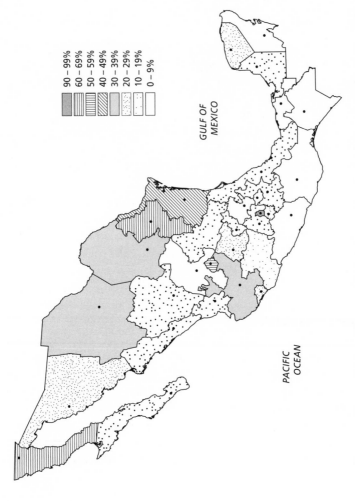

90 – 99%
60 – 69%
50 – 59%
40 – 49%
30 – 39%
20 – 29%
10 – 19%
0 – 9%

GULF OF
MEXICO

PACIFIC
OCEAN

MAP 12.3. Urbanization: percentage of population in urban areas by state, 1960. (Source: Silvia Gómez Tagle, *Las Estadísticas Electorales de la Reforma Política*, op. cit., p. 49.)

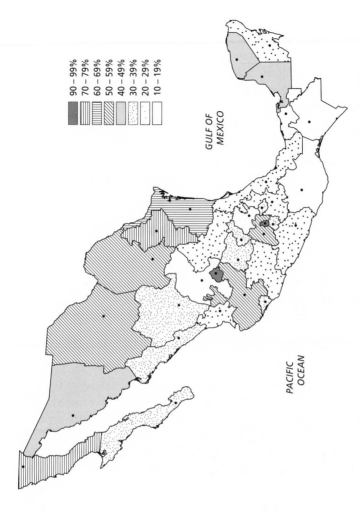

MAP 12.4. Urbanization: percentage of population in urban areas by state, 1980. (Source: Silvia Gómez Tagle, *Las Estadísticas Electorales de la Reforma Política*, op. cit., p. 50.)

90 – 99%
70 – 79%
60 – 69%
50 – 59%
40 – 49%
30 – 39%
20 – 29%
10 – 19%

GULF OF
MEXICO

PACIFIC
OCEAN

more pluralist and proactive Congress. The debates in congressional commissions now reflected the divisions in political life between statism and liberalism. The same contradiction emerged even within the PRI, leading to the formation of corresponding factions and ultimately to the departure from the party of one of those factions, led by Cuauhtémoc Cárdenas, the political beneficiary of the strong and continuing popularity of his father, former president Lázaro Cárdenas.

Politically, the opposition parties were more important qualitatively than quantitatively. Table 12.2 illustrates their rapid growth beginning in 1985. Legislative deliberations took on a renewed vigor that enriched the level of debate and, ultimately, of new legislation. The new pluralism and its active expression in the Chamber of Deputies had a fundamentally democratizing effect. With its new vigor and autonomy, Congress would be able to shift the balance of powers and exert pressure on the presidency to hew more closely to its role as defined and limited by the constitution. This process was enhanced by the existence of a better informed and politically more active public, and by the increased transparency of elections. Citizens could now vote because they felt that their vote counted for something. The results reflected their desire for political balance and for organized institutional change.

The Chamber of Deputies became a laboratory for democratization. The centrist opposition party, PAN, increased the quantity and quality of its representatives. But the most notable change came from the parties of the left, which in 1988 joined forces in the National Democratic Front, or FDN. The FDN won 27.8 percent of the seats, second to the PRI. Soon thereafter, the parties of the FDN organized the Party of the Democratic Revolution, or PRD. At this point the party system came to reflect the three major political and economic tendencies, organized into the PRI, the PRD, and the PAN.

It seemed that a culture of dialogue had been established in Mexican political life. Public opinion was better founded on reliable information, and a plurality of social groups was participating in public life, their voices heard in Congress through the political parties represented there. The politics of confrontation seemed to have given way to an appreciation of the vote as an organizing factor in political life.

The new electoral culture took hold at the municipal, state, and federal levels. In 1995, out of a total of 2,412 municipalities, 1,527 were governed by the PRI, 224 by the PAN, 178 by the PRD, 15 by the Labor Party (PT), and the remaining 468 by either a coalition or local parties. These figures highlight the municipal roots of the states' demand for a more balanced federalism. It is generally acknowledged that the 1988 elections had been a turning point for the transition to democracy, a process that deepened throughout the 1990s. (See tables 12.2 and 12.3.)

One aspect of democratization was the demand for a new federalism that would define and thereby limit presidential prerogatives and, indeed, limit the power of the federal government, its administrative apparatus, and the public sector. The political competition among the three main parties, the PRI, the PAN, and the PRD, led each of them to take up this same general goal, although each party formulated it differently in keeping with its own approach and political imperatives. But they all favored increased cooperation among the municipal, state, and federal levels of government to optimize the provision of basic security and other services, such as education, economic security, and health care.

The new phenomenon of meaningful voting was a positive factor in the movement toward a new federalism and political pluralism. It generated institutions such as the Federal Electoral Institute (IFE) and the Federal Electoral Tribunal (TRIFE). The IFE is completely autonomous; it is made up of a citizens' council, part of which is nominated and elected by a two-thirds majority of the Chamber of Deputies, and part of which is named by the political parties. The IFE is responsible for ensuring the organization, transparency, and legality of elections, while the TRIFE is responsible for resolving election-related conflicts at all three levels of government. These two institutions were formed through a set of constitutional amendments in 1990 and 1994, and their work is complemented by that of corresponding state electoral bodies. They are largely responsible for the orderly consolidation of the democratic process that Mexico has experienced, and thanks to their autonomy, the citizenry is confident of the legitimacy of the process.

The free exercise of the right to vote, the transparency of elections, and citizen confidence in the legitimacy of the vote were reflected in the geographical distribution of power after the elections of 1997 and 1999. The PRI governed in twenty-two states, the PAN in seven states, and the PRD in three states plus the Federal District. Congressional deputies were elected from these parties and from other parties that did not win any governorships. In 1997, the votes for congressional seats were distributed across the political parties, as illustrated in figures 12.1–12.4.

In 1999, almost all of the congressional representatives were from the three largest parties: in the Chamber of Deputies, the PRI held 47.8 percent, the PAN held 24.2 percent, and the PRD held 25.0 percent of the seats, while in the Senate the PRI held 59.8 percent, the PAN 25.2 percent, and the PRD 12.6 percent of the seats.

The relationship between the state and federal governments is far from being resolved, particularly when it comes to the allocation of tax revenues, for which institutional mechanisms are lacking. A VAT, or Value

TABLE 12.2. Federal Congress/Chamber of Deputies, Parties and Number of Seats and Percentage of Total, 1961–1994

Year	Total Seats	PAN Seats	PAN %	PRI Seats	PRI %	FDN Seats	FDN %	PRD Seats	PRD %	PPS Seats	PPS %	PARM Seats	PARM %	PFCRN Seats	PFCRN %	PT Seats	PT %
1961	178	5	2.81	172	97.19	—[a]	—	—	—	1	0.56	NA[b]	—	—	—	—	—
1964	210	18	8.57	178	84.76	—	—	—	—	9	4.29	5	2.38	—	—	—	—
1967	211	20	9.48	175	82.94	—	—	—	—	10	4.74	6	2.84	—	—	—	—
1970	213	20	9.39	178	83.57	—	—	—	—	10	4.70	5	2.34	—	—	—	—
1973	231	23	9.96	192	83.12	—	—	—	—	10	4.32	6	2.60	—	—	—	—
1976	236	20	8.44	194	81.86	—	—	—	—	12	5.07	10	4.22	—	—	—	—
1979	431	43	9.98	291	67.52	—	—	—	—	18	4.18	20	4.64	—	—	—	—
1982	399	51	12.75	298	74.50	—	—	—	—	10	2.50	NA	—	—	—	—	—
1985	400	41	10.25	289	72.25	—	—	—	—	11	2.75	11	2.75	NA	—	—	—
1988	500	101	20.20	260	52.00	139[c]	27.80	—	—	c	c	c	c	NA	—	—	—
1991	500	89	17.80	320	64.00	—	—	41	8.20	12	2.40	15	3.00	23	4.60	—	—
1994	500	119	23.80	301	60.20	—	—	70	14.00	NA	—	NA	—	NA	—	10	2.00

Year	Total Seats	PSUM (PCM-PMS)		PST		PDM		PRT		PMT		PCM		PSD		PVEM	
		Seats	%	Seats	%	Seats	%	Seats	%	Seats	%	Seats	%	Seats	%	Seats	%
1961	178	—	—	—	—	—	—	—	—	—	—	—	—	—	—	—	—
1964	210	—	—	—	—	—	—	—	—	—	—	—	—	—	—	—	—
1967	211	—	—	—	—	—	—	—	—	—	—	—	—	—	—	—	—
1970	213	—	—	—	—	—	—	—	—	—	—	—	—	—	—	—	—
1973	231	—	—	—	—	—	—	—	—	—	—	—	—	—	—	—	—
1976	236	—	—	—	—	—	—	—	—	—	—	—	—	—	—	—	—
1979	431	—	—	16	3.71	16	3.71	—	—	—	—	27	6.26	—	—	—	—
1982	399	17	4.25	11	2.75	12	3.00	NA	—	—	—	[d]	—	NA	—	—	—
1985	400	12	3.00	12	3.00	12	3.00	6	1.50	6	1.50	—	—	—	—	NA	—
1988	500	[c]	—	[e]	—	NA	—	NA	—	—	—	—	—	—	—	NA	—
1991	500	—	—	—	—	NA	—	NA	—	—	—	—	—	—	—	—	—
1994	500	—	—	NA	—	—	—	—	—	—	—	—	—	—	—	—	—

NOTE: From 1967 to 1976, all seats were held by party deputies and deputies chosen by plurality. From 1979 to 1994, seats were chosen by plurality and by proportional representation. PAN = National Action Party, PRI = Institutional Revolutionary Party, FDN = National Democratic Front, PRD = Party of the Democratic Revolution, PPS = Popular Socialist Party, PARM = Authentic Party of the Mexican Revolution, PFCRN = Party of the Cardenista Front for National Reconstruction, PT = Labor Party, PSUM = United Socialist Party of Mexico, PCM = Mexican Communist Party, PMS = Mexican Socialist Party, PST = Socialist Workers Party, PDM = Mexican Democratic Party, PRT = Revolutionary Workers Party, PMT = Mexican Workers Party, PSD = Social Democratic Party, PVEM = Green Ecological Party of Mexico. Some percentages do not sum to 100 percent due to rounding.

[a] A dash indicates that the party did not contest this election.

[b] NA: Party not accredited. It did not win the 1.5 percent of the total vote required to obtain a seat.

[c] In 1988, the FDN coalition of parties included the PPS, PARM, PFCRN, and PMS.

[d] In 1982, the PCM participated in a coalition of parties known as the PSUM.

[e] In 1988, the PST changed its name to the Party of the Cardenista Front for National Reconstruction (PFCRN).

SOURCE: Sylvia Gómez Tagle, Las Estadísticas Electorales de la Reforma Política (Mexico City: El Colegio de México, 1990), pp. 67–72.

TABLE 12.3. Party Alliances and Mergers

Acronym	Name in Spanish	Name in English	Year of Founding	Alliances and Mergers
PST	Partido Socialista de los Trabajadores	Socialist Workers Party	1975	—
FDN	Frente Democrático Nacional	National Democratic Front	1987	Cuauhtémoc Cárdenas is presidential candidate of PARM. PST, PARM, PPS, PMS, and PFCRN establish collective leadership and merge to form FDN.
PMS	Partido Mexicano Socialista	Mexican Socialist Party	1987	Formed out of PSUM, PMT, PPR, UIC, MRP, and PST.
PRD	Partido de la Revolución Democrática	Party of the Democratic Revolution (sometimes translated as Democratic Revolutionary Party)	1988	Formed out of components of FDN. In 1989, Heberto Castillo renounces his presidential candidacy, PMS officially merges into PRD, and PMS as such is dissolved.
PT	Partido del Trabajo	Labor Party (also translated as Workers Party)	1991	—
PFCRN	Partido del Frente Cardenista de Reconstrucción Nacional	Party of the Cardenista Front for National Reconstruction	1998	Formed from PST.

Added Tax, was introduced during the populist period. This kind of tax is levied on the exchange of goods and services. At the time of its intro-duction, the states were responsible for collecting the VAT, but the asso-ciated revenues reverted to the federal government, which redistributed them to the individual states in proportion to the effectiveness of their tax collection efforts, the volume of their contributions, and, beginning in 1989, their population numbers.

One obstacle to a more effective federalism is that the states depend on these revenues for 80 percent of their spending needs and the municipalities also depend on them for 60 percent of their budgets. Federal investment in the states is sometimes inequitable, and unfortunately, strong lobbies rep-resenting corporatist, nationalist, and statist interests persist. Together with radical and ideologically motivated elements, they continue to oppose a transparent, democratic, and institutionally sound federalist framework.

Another factor favorable to Mexican democracy is the abundance of new civil society and nongovernmental movements and organizations that participate in the formation of public opinion and affect the decision-making processes of the political parties. The growing weight of individ-ual and organized opinion helps Mexicans to disseminate their concerns and problems over the electronic media, as was illustrated in the case of the Chiapas movement in 1994, when the Zapatista National Liberation Army, or EZLN, communicated its case to the wider public over televi-sion and the Internet.

Voter behavior at the state level is more complex and pluralistic than in the past, shedding light on other political tendencies pertinent to dem-ocratic change. The electoral results in plurinominal districts illustrate the country's political pluralism. Out of a total of five hundred deputies, two hundred are elected from party lists. To elect candidates from a pluri-nominal list, a party must receive a plurality in one-third of the three hun-dred uninominal districts (where only one member is selected from each electoral district) and also has to receive at least 2 percent (amended from a previous threshold of 1.5 percent) of the total votes for all the party lists in the plurinominal regions.

Significant changes took place between 1982 and 1997. By 1985, the PRI enjoyed a plurality but no longer an absolute majority of political repre-sentation. The electorates of PAN and the leftist parties (referred to as PIZQ, *partidos de la izquierda*) were stronger in some states, and the PRI retained control of the states of the south-central region. Maps 12.5–12.9 il-lustrate the geographic distribution, by party, of delegates winning elec-tion with a plurality but not a majority. They demonstrate the alternation

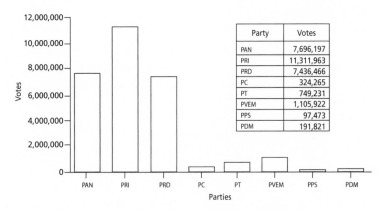

FIGURE 12.1. Results of the 1997 federal election. Federal deputies elected by plurality: national totals (not including null votes or votes for unregistered candidates). PAN = National Action Party, PRI = Institutional Revolutionary Party, PRD = Party of the Democratic Revolution, PC = Communist Party, PT = Labor Party, PVEM = Green Ecological Party of Mexico, PPS = Popular Socialist Party, PDM = Mexican Democratic Party. (Source: Mexico City: Instituto Federal Electoral, 1997.)

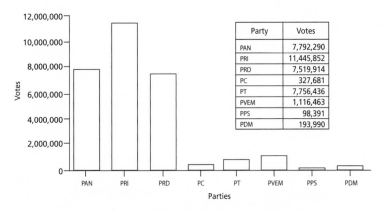

FIGURE 12.2. Results of the 1997 federal election. Federal deputies elected through proportional representation: national totals (not including null votes or votes for unregistered candidates; see figure 12.1 for party acronyms). (Source: Mexico City: Instituto Federal Electoral, 1997.)

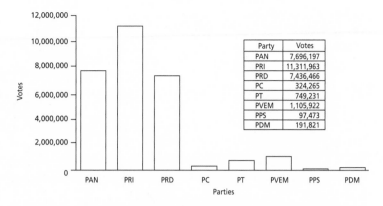

Party	Votes
PAN	7,696,197
PRI	11,311,963
PRD	7,436,466
PC	324,265
PT	749,231
PVEM	1,105,922
PPS	97,473
PDM	191,821

FIGURE 12.3. Results of the 1997 federal election. Federal deputies elected by plurality, votes obtained by political party: national totals (not including null votes or votes for unregistered candidates; see figure 12.1 for party acronyms). (Source: Mexico City: Instituto Federal Electoral, 1997.)

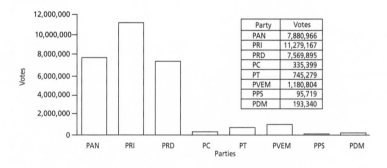

Party	Votes
PAN	7,880,966
PRI	11,279,167
PRD	7,569,895
PC	335,399
PT	745,279
PVEM	1,180,804
PPS	95,719
PDM	193,340

FIGURE 12.4. Results of the 1997 federal election. Senators elected through proportional representation: national totals (not including null votes or votes for unregistered candidates; see figure 12.1 for party acronyms). (Source: Mexico City: Instituto Federal Electoral, 1997.)

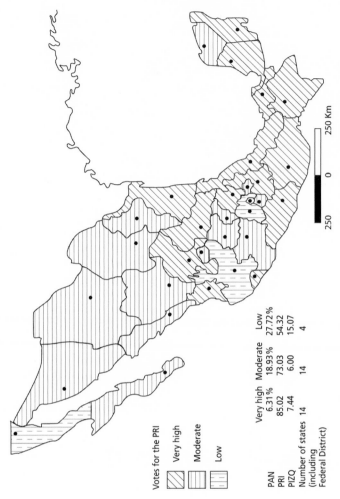

Votes for the PRI

⧄	Very high
⫴	Moderate
⸬	Low

	Very high	Moderate	Low
PAN	6.31%	18.93%	27.72%
PRI	85.02	73.03	54.32
PIZQ	7.44	6.00	15.07
Number of states (including Federal District)	14	14	4

250   0   250 Km

MAP 12.5. Deputies elected by plurality, 1982. PAN = National Action Party, PRI = Institutional Revolutionary Party, PIZQ = *partidos de la izquierda*, leftist parties. Numbers in the table do not always sum to 100 percent because the number of votes obtained, recorded by the Federal Electoral Institute (FEI), did not always reach the threshold for proportional representation. (Source: Silvia Gómez Tagle, *La Transición Inconclusa: Treinta Años de Eleccones en México* [Mexico City: El Colegio de México, 1997], p. 119.)

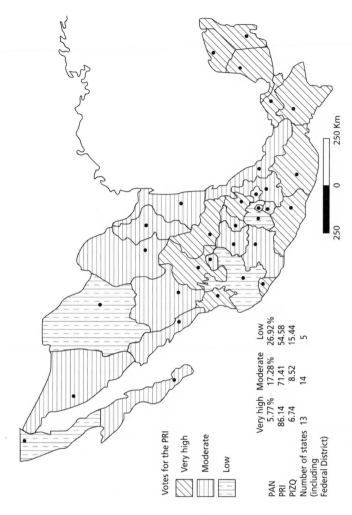

Votes for the PRI

		Very high	Moderate	Low
		5.77%	17.28%	26.92%
PAN				
PRI		86.14	71.41	54.58
PIZQ		6.74	8.52	15.44
Number of states (including Federal District)		13	14	5

Very high

Moderate

Low

250 0 250 Km

MAP 12.6. Deputies elected by plurality, 1985. Numbers in the table do not always sum to 100 percent because the number of votes obtained, recorded by the FEI, did not always reach the threshold for proportional representation. (See map 12.5 for party acronyms.) (Source: Silvia Gómez Tagle, *La Transición Inconclusa: Treinta Años de Elecciones en México*, op. cit., p. 121.)

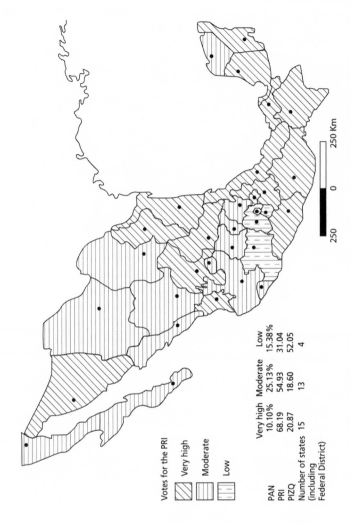

MAP 12.7. Deputies elected by plurality, 1988. Numbers in the table do not always sum to 100 percent because the number of votes obtained, recorded by the FEI, did not always reach the threshold for proportional representation. (See map 12.5 for party acronyms.) (Source: Silvia Gómez Tagle, *La Transición Inconclusa: Treinta Años de Elecciones en México*, op. cit., p. 123.)

Votes for the PRI

Very high

Moderate

Low

	Very high	Moderate	Low
PAN	10.10%	25.13%	15.38%
PRI	68.19	54.93	31.04
PIZQ	20.87	18.60	52.05
Number of states (including Federal District)	15	13	4

250   0   250 Km

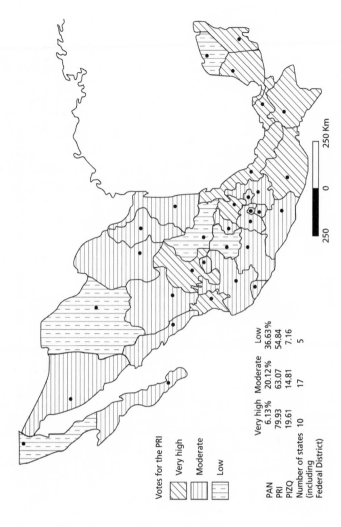

MAP 12.8. Deputies elected by plurality, 1991. Numbers in the table do not always sum to 100 percent because the number of votes obtained, recorded by the FEI, did not always reach the threshold for proportional representation. (See map 12.5 for party acronyms.) (Source: Silvia Gómez Tagle, *La Transición Inconclusa: Treinta Años de Elecciones en México*, op. cit., p. 127.)

Votes for the PRI

	Very high	Moderate	Low
PAN	6.13%	20.12%	36.63%
PRI	79.93	63.07	54.84
PIZQ	19.61	14.81	7.16
Number of states (including Federal District)	10	17	5

Very high

Moderate

Low

250   0   250 Km

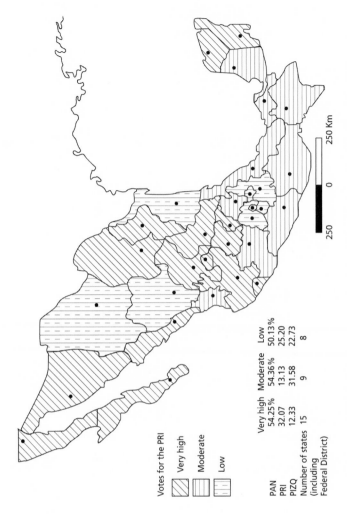

	Very high	Moderate	Low
	54.25%	54.36%	50.13%
PAN	32.07	13.13	25.20
PIZQ	12.33	31.58	22.73
Number of states (including Federal District)	15	9	8

MAP 12.9. Deputies elected by plurality, 1994. Numbers in the table do not always sum to 100 percent because the number of votes obtained, recorded by the FEI, did not always reach the threshold for proportional representation. (See map 12.5 for party acronyms.) (Source: Silvia Gómez Tagle, *La Transición Inconclusa: Treinta Años de Elecciones en México*, op. cit., p. 131.)

in power of parties in some states, particularly in Chihuahua, where the PRI and the PAN were winning and losing elections by margins of under 5 percent. Nationally, the electorate was divided three ways among the PRI, the PAN, and the PIZQ, but on the state level it can be observed that two of the three parties tended to strongly predominate over the third, with the particular parties in question depending upon the state.

The Government as Agent of Democratization

In the 1950s, 1960s, and 1970s, the pressure to express political and social demands was frustrated by a rigid regime with little desire to create democratic spaces for the opposition. Government policies, even those in the areas of social welfare, were decreasingly effective. The presidency and the government were politically out of step, unable to anticipate or channel social demands. Budget needs rose alarmingly, for as problems accumulated and worsened, increasingly large sums were required for their amelioration. Certain presidents made dramatic, unexpected, and seemingly arbitrary decisions that were left unexplained. President Echeverría, for example, expropriated the rich agricultural holdings in the Mayo and Yaqui region in Sonora toward the end of his term, and López Portillo nationalized the banking system in his last months in office, even though there was a president-elect in the wings. The secrecy that surrounded government decisions led to a cleavage between government and society, especially the best-informed citizenry, who got their information about what was going on in the government from the foreign press or foreign universities and research centers. The government's paralysis probably stemmed from fear of a split within the PRI or a loss of support from its traditional political sectors, including the business establishment.

The 1981–1982 nationalization of the banking system, the massive capital flight that followed, and the subsequent devaluations were shocks that left the country politically demoralized, dearly costing the government in credibility. It was left to the incoming government of Miguel de la Madrid to pull the country out of this crisis of confidence and restore the morale and predictability that were so sorely lacking. De la Madrid's strict adherence to the constitutionally defined powers of the presidency banished the specter of arbitrary presidential decision-making. He made no recourse to the extraordinary powers of the institutional presidency that had accumulated over the preceding half century, what some Mexicans have called metaconstitutional powers. Another confidence-building measure was de la Madrid's break with the practice of announcing presidential decisions after they had already been made. He went to the opposite extreme of explaining planned measures ahead of time.

President de la Madrid put together a legislative package designed to organize, clarify, and guarantee the roles of the public and private sectors. The package called for consultation between the president and the PRI parliamentary delegation, and consultations between the latter and the delegations of opposition parties. Not surprisingly, at this time the most intense activity in Congress was within the PRI delegation itself, where the resistance of the most statist and ultranationalist elements within the party had to be contained.

The domestic and international situations were not promising, especially in economic terms. A strong earthquake rocked Mexico City in 1985, and international economic crises in 1982 and 1986 had intense domestic ramifications. Strong political reforms had been introduced, but they had to be implemented gradually and deliberately, with the appropriate administrative measures that would lay down the institutional basis for change. The economic reforms were more immediately successful. They accelerated beginning in 1986, as a result of the drastic reduction of hard currency available to the government after a collapse in oil prices. Subsidies and other protectionist policies were abandoned. A more stable and dependable economic environment was promoted through market liberalization and the deregulation of economic activities.

Political and economic liberalization met with resistance and opposition, in part within the government itself and within the PRI, since the profits of powerful corporatist and business groups were contingent on the continued protection of their markets. At this point, a large segment of the PRI split off under the leadership of Cuauhtémoc Cárdenas and Porfirio Muñoz Ledo, giving rise to the first coalition of leftist parties, the FDN, or the Nation Democratic Front. PAN, the traditional opposition party, was also strengthened.

The 1988 elections were a product of the movement toward democracy. They were a heartening accomplishment, regardless of the debate over whether Cuauhtémoc Cárdenas or Carlos Salinas de Gortari won a majority of the presidential vote. First of all, the results demonstrated that the days of PRI's absolute hegemony were over. Second, the election reinforced confidence in a new democratic culture based on the popular vote, which also nullified certain insurrectional tendencies on the left. Third, difficulties inherent in PRI's management of the electoral process led to plans for fundamental reforms in that arena. Finally, the election restored the constitutional power of Congress, which represented a radical shift in the institutional life of the country. From 1988 onward, both the government and the opposition were aware that to formulate and pass legislation, their congressional delegations would have to negotiate cooperatively and form alliances with their adversaries around specific points.

Perhaps for the first time since the Maderista Congress of 1912, Mexico underwent a process familiar in every democratic country: the formulation, discussion, and approval of a national budget. Plans for State spending and the revenues and credits necessary to pay for it had to be explained and discussed with the parties represented in Congress. Above all, any constitutional change had to be negotiated and required alliances with opposition parties. While a constitutional amendment required a two-thirds majority in the Chamber of Deputies, the PRI held only 52 percent of the seats; the FDN had 27.8 percent, and the PAN 20.2 percent.

When Carlos Salinas succeeded Miguel de la Madrid in the presidency on December 1, 1989, relations were extremely strained among the congressional delegations themselves and between Congress and the presidency. The first statements emanating from the new cabinet stressed continuity with the economic policies of the outgoing administration. The next president, Ernesto Zedillo Ponce de León, made similar assurances of continuing economic liberalization immediately upon taking office.

The presidential style of Carlos Salinas de Gortari was a departure from the austerity and discretion of his predecessor. He instituted changes quickly, often acting against all odds. He was an extremely able and intelligent negotiator with both the rightist opposition in the PAN and the independent left. He promoted unprecedented social, political, and economic reforms—guaranteeing electoral transparency, creating the National Solidarity Program, modernizing public and private finance, and establishing clarity in the titling of rural *ejido* property. Salinas's constant appearances in all parts of the country created ties with the common people that inspired popular confidence in the possibility of a better future. He brought sympathizers of the opposition PAN and leading independent left intellectuals into his government or into close collaboration with it. His personal style of governing recalled the days of populism. For example, the social, political, and economic reforms he established served to divide the opposition and to attract progressive elements from the PAN and sectors of the left to the project of revitalizing the PRI. At the same time, he emphasized economic change, as though economic modernization could in itself propel democratic change. He quickly established new organizational forms for workers, the unemployed, and peasants. His idea was to create new popular organizations for these sectors in order to build a new social pact conducive to reform in the PRI.

The enormously popular and powerful National Solidarity Program, or PRONASOL, emerged from the office of the presidency to win back the support of the landless, the slum dwellers, and the peasantry. It was hoped that this new population of poor Mexicans could be organized through PRONASOL with programs to combat poverty, promote popular participation in setting up local service infrastructures, grant credit to those who could not provide collateral, and generate community organization and cooperation. In 1992, the Solidarity Program spent 1 percent of the GDP, or nearly 6 percent of the federal budget. The program was directed at pockets of extreme poverty. It addressed the most pressing needs of the poor and cushioned the negative effects of economic liberalization. It was hoped that the experience of participation in PRONASOL would demonstrate to new generations the value of self-organization and active participation in solving the country's problems.

Progress for the Countryside, or PROCAMPO, went into operation in 1993. PROCAMPO and PRONASOL sought to provide political counterweight to the CNC, which remained a sectoral organization of the PRI, and to modify the alliances between bureaucratic sectors and corporatist organizations. They began to organize the new poor, the squatters whose informal settlements, the slums known as *colonias,* surrounded many cities and towns and clustered near border areas. These rural immigrants and other poor townspeople were organized by the presidency via PRONASOL, creating a new set of social structures parallel to those of traditional authorities and *caciques.* PRI itself felt highly threatened, and demonstrated the limits to its stomach for change at its Sixteenth Regular National Assembly in March 1993.

The 1988–1994 economic reforms built upon the structural changes that began in 1986, when the collapse of oil prices had accelerated privatization and paved the way for a first debt renegotiation. The Salinas government inherited an economic regulatory mechanism that was key to the success of the economic transition. The Economic Solidarity Agreement had been signed in December 1987 by President de la Madrid and representatives of industrial workers, peasants, and business. The ability to reach wage and price agreements and lower inflation without provoking a recession was maintained during the Salinas presidency. Under the Economic Agreement, employers, workers, and peasants met periodically with the president and his economic cabinet to negotiate wage and price adjustments.

The Salinas government's capacity to generate consensus and establish alliances with PRI reformers and progressives within the PAN made possible the impressive economic liberalization and the complete dismantling of protectionist structures that culminated with NAFTA, signed in 1992 and launched as of 1994. The liberalization was broad-based. It included the modernization and deregulation of the financial sector (banks, insurance firms, and brokerages), which primarily benefited Mexican businesses. It also provided for the State's retreat from the industrial sector through the sale of 261 public-sector enterprises, and the opening to foreign investment, which immediately brought about the modernization of transport, communications, and production technology. Granting autonomy to the Bank of Mexico was another important step, the result of an agreement between the PRI and the PAN to guarantee the autonomy of monetary mechanisms in the new financial order. This prevented the government from having the Central Bank emit new currency to pay its debts, which had been the practice of the populist presidents. Instead, the government was forced to reduce spending or increase taxes. Significantly, President Salinas conceived of NAFTA as a test case for integrated economic development when asymmetrical economies are drawn together.

Despite its success in a number of places around the world, structural adjustment often brought negative social consequences, even in some of the most industrialized countries. In Mexico, with its extremely unequal income distribution, the situation was particularly egregious. However, other deep and long-neglected problems, not entirely attributable to structural adjustment, burst into the open shortly after midnight on the morning of January 1, 1994, with an armed uprising in the state of Chiapas. As fighters of the Zapatista National Liberation Army strode through the streets of San Cristóbal de las Casas, the international media transmitted live images of the rebellion and broadcast an interview with Subcommander Marcos. From its very birth, this new kind of insurgency was determined to use the electronic media to its advantage.

There was no lack of historical underpinnings for the rebellion. Long-standing problems within and among Indian communities had certainly been left to fester. What was new was the militancy of the Church under Bishop Samuel Ruiz. In the early 1990s, the independent left had abandoned the terrain in Chiapas to the proponents of armed struggle under Marcos and to the catechists working under don Samuel, who preached the attainability of the promised land through a theology of liberation. A shaken Mexican public awoke from its Salinista dream that the country was on the threshold of First World status. Some condemned the reversion to arms at a time when much of Mexican society was defending its nascent democratic institutions and the right to vote. Others supported the EZLN's demands for justice and denunciations of the extreme poverty of Chiapas. Some people, however, supported the EZLN out of on their own long-standing insurrectionist and antidemocratic propensities. Several bombings put people on edge, and many in the capital were unnerved by the menacing EZLN declarations that they were "already here." Yet this must have been the briefest guerrilla uprising in history. President Salinas immediately declared a unilateral cease-fire on the part of the government. In response, Subcommander Marcos declared himself prepared for war but not for peace, which led to an ongoing limited cease-fire and apparent stalemate.

The government immediately mobilized on many fronts. It took advantage of its credibility with international financial institutions to minimize the capital flight that threatened to empty the country's coffers. It opened negotiations with the guerrillas and strengthened the Federal Electoral Institute (IFE) to guarantee a peaceful process in the coming transfer of presidential authority. The presidential election was to be held in July 1994, and the change of government would follow in December. The recent reforms to the IFE had guaranteed its complete autonomy with respect to the government and eliminated any danger of electoral fraud. The government sought and almost obtained a "civility agreement," to be signed by all political parties in defense of the franchise and ongoing democratization, for the peaceful conduct of the 1994 presidential election process.

Despite Mexico's recent economic accomplishments, the Chiapas rebellion did enormous damage to its international credibility. The March 1994 assassination of Luis Donaldo Colosio, the PRI candidate for the presidency, was another terrible blow to most Mexicans. The circumstances behind this crime have yet to be clarified.

Ernesto Zedillo Ponce de León was PRI's replacement candidate. He was elected president in free elections by a resounding majority. PAN increased its vote and moved into second place, while the PRD lost ground, probably because the urban middle and upper classes were terrified of the EZLN. The new president inherited Mexico's moral crisis and financial fragility, as well as a PRI that had been victorious in the elections but was internally divided. Slander was a widespread form of political discourse, and the judicial branch was conspicuously absent in the midst of what was the worst crisis in modern Mexican history.

President Zedillo had the advantage, however, of working with a disciplined society that longed for domestic peace and tranquility. All political actors, the opposition parties included, felt and demonstrated great loyalty to the democratic system. The president, most business forces, and the PAN championed policies in favor of economic liberalization. Society strongly supported the solution of conflicts by means of dialogue and negotiation. The recent approval of NAFTA quickly bore fruit. International financial institutions and foreign governments, particularly the government of the United States, gave Mexico the necessary support so that the process of economic adjustment would not negatively impact the democratic framework that was then being developed.

From a Statist to a Market Economy

Between 1970 and 1982, the Mexican State dominated the economic life of the country. The most salient change since that time has been the construction of an economic system that promotes the economic freedom of the individual, and, implicitly, of future generations, within a regulatory framework established by the State. The legal basis for this economic freedom is crucial, for if it were disrupted, the foundations of the democracy Mexico has constructed would be endangered.

What did this change mean? In the 1970s, nearly half of government spending subsidized the public sector, that complex of manufacturing, businesses, trusts, and companies organized and managed by the State to keep the economy functioning. This meant that of every peso spent by the federal government, one half went to subsidize public-sector institutions such as CONASUPO and the national telephone company (Teléfonos de México), as well as industries such as sugar production and the generation of electricity by the Comisión Federal de Electricidad. About 90 percent of those fifty centavos came from taxes, and the other 10 percent was obtained through foreign credits, increasing Mexico's level of indebtedness.

Steps were taken beginning in 1982, but above all in 1986, to subject prices to market forces. This was intended to free up federal investment for priority areas such as public health, education, the provision of safe drinking water, and public transportation. These are areas of investment that benefit the entire population, without regard to income. In addition, these changes would reduce the government deficit and reduce inflation, which was the worst enemy of the peasants, the working and middle classes, and the urban poor. Inflation is like an additional tax paid by salaried workers and wage earners, as labor compensation always lags behind the price curve. Combating inflation became the one of the government's most important goals.

Figure 12.5 illustrates the reduction of Mexico's foreign debt, which dropped dramatically once the State reduced its direct participation in the productive economy and instituted realistic economic policies that encouraged investment based on savings.

The new economic environment did not bring Mexico the wide accessibility to consumer goods at affordable prices that we see in Europe and the United States. This was due to some obstacles that were international in origin and others that stemmed from the legacy of economic populism. Of course, mistakes have also been made by successive governments, and institutional deficiencies persist. A combination of negative legacies, omissions, incomplete measures, and errors has slowed down the process. The insufficiency of mechanisms to compensate for the short-term effects of deregulation has made the transformation more costly in social and economic terms. Nevertheless, government spending is monitored and controlled as never before, now that Congress is fulfilling its constitutional obligations in that regard. The business sector has expanded, and growing foreign investment in Mexico has compensated for a lack of domestic savings.

Table 12.4 illustrates the positive and negative elements with regard to the financing of the Mexican economy from 1982 to 1994. Savings were the basis for the financing of economic development. Saving translates into investment in the productive activities of the different economic actors who contribute to the gross domestic product. The table indicates that domestic saving was the most dynamic variable. Savings include (1) the resources that remain available to individuals, families, businesses, and the government after all consumption is paid for; (2) all the resources generated by businesses after they have distributed their profits among shareholders and primary owners; and (3) the reserves held by the public sector.

Between 1982 and 1984, domestic saving grew, but later it began to drop, first because of continuous government deficits and later, beginning in 1991, because private domestic saving decreased. It is interesting to note that between 1991 and 1994, foreign investment was responsible for the overall positive investment figures.

By 1991–1992, Mexico had been fully integrated into the international market, and external savings could be added to the savings generated by

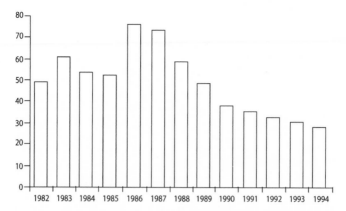

FIGURE 12.5. Total external economic debt as percentage of GDP, 1982–1994. (Source: Pedro Aspe Armella, *El Camino Mexicano de la Transformación Económica* [Mexico City: Fondo de la Cultura Económica, 1993], p. 130.)

the public sector. We do not have the necessary data, but one can suppose that private saving had not yet recovered the level reached in the previous decade. Recent studies of domestic saving indicate that it decreased due to inflation in particular between 1982 and 1988, and due to negative real interest rates in 1986–1988 and 1995–1996. In addition, between 1984 and 1992, more than 70 percent of all savings was concentrated in the hands of just 10 percent of the population, while 19.5 percent of all households represented only 1.3 to 3.5 percent of total savings. Figures from 1984–1994 indicate that family saving increased more rapidly than business saving, only to drop significantly in 1995–1996.

The Mexican savings rate was the highest in Latin America in relation to total investment, but this was still unsatisfactory for a developing economy. The rate at the century's end was much healthier than in the 1980s, though. After 1990, the public sector no longer ate away at resources. Investment fundamentally originated from public- and private-sector saving, and the combined investment of domestically and externally generated private resources was directed toward maximizing production.

The economic liberalization introduced a model of efficiency and competitiveness in every area of production. Private foreign investment was also a modernizing force, introducing new forms of technology that, once adapted to the Mexican context, produced knowledge and encouraged the formation and growth of human capital. This took place in the "traditional" maquiladora sector and even more so where the electronic

TABLE 12.4. The Financing of the Productive Economy, 1982–1994 (as Percentages of GDP)

	1982	1983	1984	1985	1986	1987	1988	1989	1990	1991	1992	1993	1994
Total investment	22.9	20.8	19.9	21.2	18.5	19.3	20.4	21.4	21.9	22.4	23.3	22.0	22.2
Foreign savings	3.4	-3.9	-2.4	-0.4	1.1	-3.0	1.4	2.8	3.1	5.3	7.5	6.6	7.9
Domestic savings	19.5	24.7	22.2	21.6	17.5	22.3	19.0	18.6	18.7	17.1	15.7	15.4	14.3
Private investment	12.5	13.1	12.2	14.8	12.6	13.7	15.5	17.1	16.9	17.8	19.1	17.8	17.9
Private-sector savings	26.1	25.7	23.1	24.8	27.6	32.7	26.6	19.8	17.7	10.5	8.1	10.5	10.1
Balance	13.6	12.6	10.9	10.0	15.0	19.0	11.1	2.8	0.8	-7.3	-11.0	-7.3	-7.8
Public investment	10.4	7.6	7.7	6.4	5.9	5.6	4.9	4.4	4.9	4.6	4.2	4.2	4.3
Public-sector savings	-6.6	-1.0	-0.8	-3.2	-10.1	-10.5	-7.6	-1.2	1.0	6.6	7.6	4.9	4.2
Public-sector balance	-16.9	-8.6	-8.5	-9.6	-16.0	-16.0	-12.5	-5.6	-3.9	-2.0	3.4	0.7	-0.1

SOURCE: Enrique Cárdenas, *La Política Económica en México, 1950–1994* (Mexico City: Fideicomiso Historia de las Américas—El Colegio de México—Fondo de Cultura Económica, 1995), p. 182.

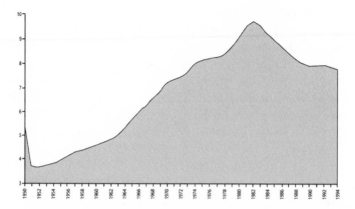

FIGURE 12.6. Average labor productivity, 1950–1994 (real GDP/EAP, moving averages). Note: The basis of the real GDP is 1980 = 100 percent. (Source: Enrique Cárdenas, *La Política Económica de México, 1950–1994* [Mexico City: Fideicomiso Historia de las Américas—El Colegio de México—Fondo de Cultura Económica, 1995], p. 199.)

component and automobile industries had taken root, in the new industrial corridors of Jalisco, Aguascalientes, and Coahuila.

Figure 12.6 concerns average labor productivity, a factor that is often overlooked in considering the obstacles to strong economic performance. In fact, increased investment and the incorporation of new technology would be largely futile in combination with unimproved measures of average labor productivity. Conversely, successfully increasing productivity should raise individual incomes and generate savings, that irreplaceable source of wealth. Any economic opening will have been in vain if productivity does not begin to rise, because it will not have created that economic virtuous circle that transforms investment into production.

My major concern is that in marked contrast to its rapid growth between 1952 and 1970, average labor productivity has not improved since 1982, according to ECLAC and others. Yet according to INEGI, the national statistical center, productivity increased by 1.2 percent between 1991 and 2000. Nonetheless, inadequate labor productivity may be a result of deficiencies in human capital development; in other words, the long-standing efforts of the State to improve education at all levels have not produced the desired results.

The performance of the real GDP from 1950 to 1994 demonstrates that average economic growth slowed in the 1980s from 6 percent to 1.7 percent annually due to a dramatic decline in oil prices and the negative impact of the government having expropriated all private commercial banks in 1982. At the beginning of this chapter, I mentioned the alternating expansion and contraction in the international economy. This cycle has followed a pattern within which the Mexican gross domestic product doubled on the average of every fifteen years. At current growth rates, however, it would take nearly half a century for the GDP to double.

I do not believe that growth rates are a good measure of economic performance, however. The Western economies have been going through a period of macroeconomic realignment for over twenty years. The expectation is that the long worldwide recession will come to an end in the first decade of the twenty-first century and that the Mexican national economy will enter a new period of sustained growth. It is true that the path has been long, but the transition from an economy on State life support to a healthy, sustainable, and self-sufficient economy begins with certain positive symptoms such as reduced inflation in a newly free market. The new economy reduced speculative income, which benefited some but was prejudicial to the majority, and freed export trade from its petroleum dependency with a diverse set of export goods, including industrial products. Mexico progressed from a cycle of currency devaluations—the result of a fixed and overvalued exchange rate—to a floating currency whose value is determined by supply and demand. The balance of payments was restored, the budget deficit was reduced, and an attempt was made to compensate increased productivity with higher salaries. Not all of these steps have been successfully consolidated.

If we take into account the macroeconomic adjustments and the two serious economic crises of the late 1990s, we can take some satisfaction in observing that Mexico's economy neither collapsed nor stagnated. The gross domestic product is still unsatisfactory and continues to be a concern. The extended period of slow growth is not a uniquely Mexican problem, however. It is a widespread phenomenon, affecting even the most industrialized economies.

The events of the mid-'90s still cry out to be explained coherently and comprehensively. The year 1994 was a turning point and probably a moment of lost opportunities. An uneasiness swept over most Mexicans that year, as though the country was on shifting sands or even being sucked into a whirlpool. A highly motivated and well-trained guerrilla force, equipped with an appreciation for new communications technologies, erupted onto the Mexican political scene and onto television sets around the world. Subcommander Marcos appeared to personify a social volcano

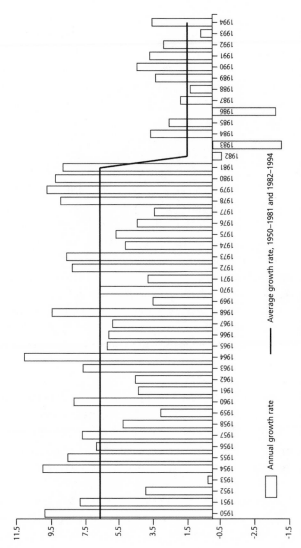

FIGURE 12.7. Percentage growth of real GDP, 1950–1994. (Source: Enrique Cárdenas, *La Política Económica de México, 1950–1994*, op. cit., p. 197.)

of local Indian communities from southern Chiapas who had ample reasons for rebellion. Yet he was an outsider, a middle-class university graduate from Tampico, with historical links to guerrilla pockets in northern Mexico. Extremes tend to converge. Could such a violent reaction have been intended to hamper Mexico's opening to the world? Could self-interested groups have been maneuvering to obstruct external oversight and transparency in government and in business? Recently enacted reforms such as NAFTA, and impending reforms in party politics, had undoubtedly endangered the livelihood of extreme conservative factions, minority factions within the ruling party, and large-scale drug traffickers. In Mexico, drug mafias and criminal forces have multiplied. Meanwhile, in Chiapas, the struggle of Indian communities for a better world once again faces oblivion. Its staunchest allies within the Church seemed to have stepped back, Bishop Samuel Ruiz has retired, and the government prefers not to rock the boat.

The year 1994 was also the year of Luis Donaldo Colosio's assassination. Colosio was a PRI modernizer and the president's designated successor. Salinas had been supremely confident of a Colosio victory, and PRI politicians foresaw and feared a continuity of policy after the change in government. Months later, José Francisco Ruiz Massieu, a staunch Salinas-style PRI modernizer with plans for major party reforms, was also gunned down.

Ernesto Zedillo, the succeeding PRI candidate, won in a transparent and democratic election. If questions of transparency and democratic governance had been the fundamental causes of the political assassinations and the rebellion led by Marcos, then violent political instability should likewise have characterized President Zedillo's term. From the very beginning of his presidency, however, the process of democratic change was overshadowed by a critical economic crisis. The new president would dedicate his six-year tenure to major macroeconomic issues.

In addition to the problem of the domestic and foreign debt, the peso was also overvalued. A liberalization of the currency exchange rate was overdue and inevitable. Yet Mexico's problems were foreseeable and manageable, and international credibility was at its peak. The intensity of the crisis was the result of several poorly explained and ill-advised government decisions. Zedillo was experienced, having been a leading economic policymaker during the previous government. His treasury secretary was Jaime Serra Puche, a member of Salinas's cabinet and a leading negotiator of the NAFTA agreement. This is to say that these men were not naïve. When Zedillo was sworn into office, business and investors were braced for a firm monetary policy. International monetary reserves were high, some 12.5 billion dollars, but treasury bond debt was also high, about 16.1 billion dollars. Bond issues were linked to the dollar at the then-current rate of about 3.44 pesos per dollar, and were due to mature in 1995.

But during his first presidential speech, a moment when most incoming Mexican presidents define their main differences from their predecessors, Ernesto Zedillo explicitly confirmed the continuity of previous policies. He did not even acknowledge the already foreseeable monetary adjustment.

Business and investor confidence wavered and monetary reserves began a silent exodus. The first, huge 855-million-dollar withdrawal came in mid-December due to a lack of confidence in the government's economic program. A second huge withdrawal of 701 million dollars took place five days after the Ministry of the Interior exaggerated the severity of a new Zapatista guerrilla uprising in the south. But the worst was yet to come. Serra Puche called for an extraordinary meeting with business and labor leaders on December 19 and 20. He had not discussed the economic situation with the cabinet members principally concerned with economic matters, nor, as it appears, with the president himself. In these December meetings, he proceeded to ask labor and business leaders for their advice! Was the government to devalue the peso or maintain a flexible flotation band? Business leaders suggested a controlled devaluation within a 15 percent flotation band. Privileged information had been disclosed, and the government agreed to a time limit before full devaluation, sending Mexican businesses running for the banks' international reserves. Fidel Velásquez, the lifelong labor leader, is said to have left the meeting bracing for the worst. In a single day, half of all international reserves were withdrawn. Between December 19 and 21, over 4.63 billion dollars were withdrawn from the reserves. Added to the nearly 1.4 billion dollars represented by an emergency issue of treasury bonds, the total loss of international reserves was over 7.7 billion dollars. The International Monetary Fund ascertained that there had been no speculation or withdrawals by foreign investors, that Mexicans were themselves solely responsible for the depletion of Mexico's international reserves.

Zedillo accepted Serra Puche's resignation and offered a revised explanation for the mishandling of the economic situation. He blamed the past administration and Salinas for an overvalued peso and the short-term debt that he had inherited, although the Bank of Mexico contradicted his protestations. Confusion and mixed messages further eroded the already-sinking confidence of investors. A series of devaluations reduced the value of the Mexican peso from 3.44 to 7.55 to the dollar within a period of three months, a devaluation of 120 percent. Interest rates increased from 15 percent in December 1994 to as much as 110 percent. Bank failures were common, and business and personal bankruptcies hit all sectors of society. Low-income families who had invested their life savings, and those who had obtained low-interest bank loans to obtain a car, a house, or a small business, lost everything.

One could dispute the long-term effects of the 1994–1995 crisis. But what seems clear, to me at least, is that Mexico's economic performance failed at a moment when a successful convergence with the U.S. boom of 1994–2000 could have bolstered its economic transformation.

Since the crisis, Mexico has seen both positive change and serious challenges. Without a doubt, its most important advance has been the democratic opening. Elections have been democratic nationwide, and the seventy-year rule of the PRI came to an end peacefully. The candidate of the PAN, Vicente Fox, became the first post-PRI Mexican president, serving in the 2000–2006 period. The 2000 elections transformed Mexico's political geography. Fox obtained 42.5 percent of the vote for the PAN, the PRI candidate won 36.1 percent, and the PRD, headed by Cuauhtémoc Cárdenas, garnered 16.6 percent. In the five-hundred-member Chamber of Deputies, the PRI won 211 seats, the PAN 207, and the PRD 50, while small parties won the remaining 32 seats. In the Senate, the PRI won 59 of a total of 128 seats, the PAN 45, and the PRD 17. The Federal District of Mexico City has its own elective assembly, where the PRI won no seats at all, the PAN won 38, and the PRD 36. Public life is more transparent and has given birth to an informed public opinion that accompanies the nascent democratic process. States and municipalities governed by different parties are reclaiming their constitutional roles in policymaking.

All the parties are represented in the state and federal legislative bodies, while the PRI retains a plurality. Although reforms had been approved in the past by an alliance of convenience composed of the PAN and the PRI, the Fox government appears to be disregarding this precedent. The blunders of the inexperienced Fox government have instead transformed a potential ally into an opposition force. This has delayed most constitutional reforms, which require a two-thirds vote for approval. In its first two years, the government of Vicente Fox showed itself incapable of promoting sorely needed reforms in fiscal policy or providing for new investment in the underdeveloped energy sector. Inexperience has taken its toll on government credibility.

A full democracy would mean much more than free elections. Government transparency and accountability have been bolstered but are still wanting. The rule of law is honored more in the breach than in practice. Corruption is intransigent. A reliable police force remains a dream.

The World Bank recently published a report on Mexico's economy from which I have drawn the following data: Exports tripled from 52 billion to 161 billion dollars between 1993 and 2002. Production grew in both manufacturing and agrobusiness. The value of processed agricultural goods increased at an annual rate of 9.45 percent in the first eight years of NAFTA. Imports grew at an annual rate of 6.9 percent. Direct foreign investment recovered to $11 billion annually.[1]

A tight and fairly independent monetary policy, a flexible foreign rate exchange regime, and single-digit inflation seem to have facilitated Mexico's convergence with its NAFTA partners. A manageable foreign debt, and debt control with careful oversight by Congress, have enabled Mexico to ride out various world financial crises, such as the 1997 East Asia crisis, the 1998 crisis in Russia, Brazil in 1999, and Argentina in 2003. Monetary reserves are at an all-time high.

As of the year 2005, macroeconomic indices are far from optimistic, however. Savings are continuing to diminish. The initial euphoria over the PAN presidency has evaporated as constitutional reforms have been consistently blocked by Congress and potential investors in the electrical power and petroleum sectors have diverted their initial enthusiasm toward greener pastures.

Foreign investment has also slackened in a climate of global stagnation. Sluggish U.S. economic performance and a downturn in Mexican market expectations have without a doubt been responsible for diminishing investment volume. According to INEGI, productivity grew 1.1 percent annually between 1988 and 1993, and 1.8 percent in 1994.[2] Between 1996 and 2000, productivity increased at an annual rate of 2.2 percent. In President Fox's first year in office, productivity grew an anemic 0.2 percent.

Mexico's most urgent pending issue is tax reform, followed by a fiscal policy conducive to more equitable wealth distribution, and a strong and sound budgetary policy able to ride out the wave of economic turbulence. The country's non-oil tax revenues amount to about 10 percent of the

---

1. Marcelo M. Giugale, Oliver Lafourcade, and Vinh H. Nguyen, *Mexico: A Comprehensive Development Agenda for the New Era* (Washington, D.C.: World Bank, 2001).

2. Productivity is defined by the relation between total production—measured in relation to the gross domestic product—and total labor remuneration.

GDP. PEMEX, the State petroleum company, requires new legislation leading to a complete overhaul of managerial practices in order to operate competitively by world standards. While it is true that the Mexican balance of payments is only partly dependent on the 10 percent of exports represented by petroleum, its fiscal accounts are dominated by the industry, since one-third of total tax revenue is oil-related.

Both public and private investment in the electrical and petroleum sectors are urgently needed and must be provided for. All educational sectors must be funded, and university authorities must be held responsible for their performance. A new labor force has yet to be trained and freed from the constrictions of union and statist-dominated labor policies.

One fundamental issue is the public debt. Explicit debt, meaning the legally recognized debt of Mexico's federal government, is low, about 25 percent of GDP. Additional implicit debt, however, held by the Institute for the Protection of Bank Accounts, or IPAB, and the fund established to bail out money-losing private highway construction concessions, known as FARAC, increases the total to about 46 percent of the GDP. The process by which this other debt was taken up by the public sector was far from transparent. Thus the mechanisms to incorporate these debts, and the list of private debtors who are protected, are not public information. The debt, both explicit and implicit, creates a burden for society, as it limits the government's ability to provide for social needs and to budget for new priorities.

Under current conditions, and under the tax policies currently in place, the above-mentioned 46 percent of GDP total public debt is unpayable. However, the OECD (Organization for Economic Cooperation and Development) maintains that Mexico's debt is within manageable parameters as measured by current government revenues: 15 percent of GDP as compared to a 35 percent average in the OECD countries.

Other liabilities cloud Mexico's prospects for economic recovery. Mexico's banking system has produced an alarming portfolio of bad loans equivalent to just under 20 percent of the GDP, a burden that is absorbed by taxpayers. The IPAB has an equally serious cash flow problem in the servicing of its own debt. This must be dealt with in the near future. Foreign banks have virtually bought out the Mexican banking system. Worse yet, weak regulations, the lack of transparency, and inadequate incentives for debt repayment have resulted in insufficient lending. Bank loans to the private sector have fallen by 40 percent in real terms since 1994, and private banks have ceased to provide consumer credit. While export-oriented corporations have access to foreign financing, small firms serving the domestic market operate under severe cash constraints, which has caused resentment. Most federal pension funds and social agencies are insolvent. Pension funds have been diverted to cover other spending needs, so pension payments require government transfers.

Mexico suffers from deficient public services and infrastructure. As of 2005, the energy sector alone requires an investment of 10 billion dollars per year for the next ten years. An investment of 37 billion dollars is required for electrical capacity alone. This is a need that can be met only through a combination of public and private investment, but constitutional reform is required to allow for private investment in energy, and the necessary changes have encountered resistance from unions and in Congress.

Transportation and public services such as water provision are far from adequate. Of the country's 257 aquifers, more than one hundred are overutilized, and less than one-tenth of the waste water is properly handled. Only 35 percent of solid waste is adequately treated. The growing infrastructure gap must be addressed, and it is now clear that public investment alone would be insufficient. The status of Mexican agriculture is another liability. The rural economy today generates barely 5 percent of the country's GDP, yet employs 20 percent of its labor force.

The most positive economic factors attributable to government policy are a tight and fairly free monetary policy and a flexible foreign exchange rate. The growing dependency on the U.S. economy is problematic, linking Mexican economic performance as it does to an economy in recession.

Better government has been promised, but we are still waiting to see an independent judiciary accompanied by an aggressive stand against corruption. The debt to Mexico's growing poor population is overdue and unpaid. According to World Bank data, between 1984 and 1994, Mexico had painstakingly obtained a 10 percent point reduction in poverty that was lost with the 1994–1995 crisis. By 1996, roughly two of every three Mexicans were poor, and one in three was extremely poor.

Mexico's Legacy:
A Transformed Geographical and Historical Space

Unlike other social sciences, history does not describe mechanisms that govern behavior, and can neither predict nor anticipate as yet unobserved tendencies. Thus I end this description of the recently concluded millennium

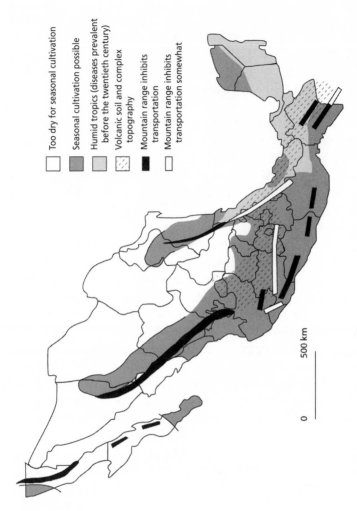

MAP 12.10. The natural environment of Mexico: overview of land use as of the 1990s. (Source: Claude Bataillon, *Espacios Mexicanos Contemporáneos* [Mexico City: Fideicomiso Historia de las Américas — El Colegio de México — Fondo de Cultura Económica, 1997], p. 77.)

Too dry for seasonal cultivation

Seasonal cultivation possible

Humid tropics (diseases prevalent before the twentieth century)

Volcanic soil and complex topography

Mountain range inhibits transportation

Mountain range inhibits transportation somewhat

0   500 km

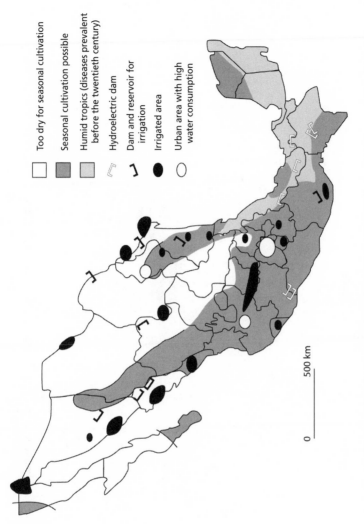

	Too dry for seasonal cultivation
	Seasonal cultivation possible
	Humid tropics (diseases prevalent before the twentieth century)
	Hydroelectric dam
	Dam and reservoir for irrigation
	Irrigated area
	Urban area with high water consumption

0   500 km

MAP 12.11. The natural environment of Mexico: water use as of the 1990s. (Source: Claude Batail-lon, *Espacios Mexicanos Contemporáneos*, op. cit., p. 77.)

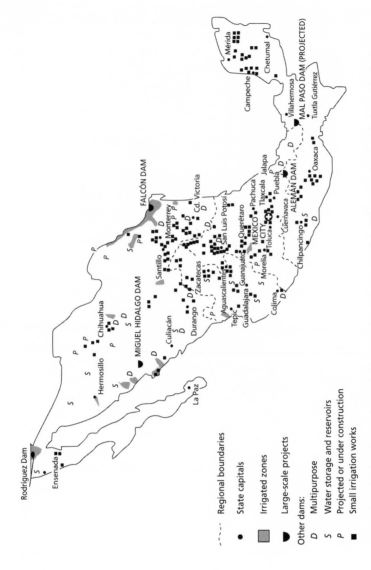

MAP 12.12. Hydraulic works, end of 1960. (Source: Howard F. Cline, *Mexico: Revolution to Evolution* [New York: Oxford University Press, 1962], p. 70.)

with a recapitulation of what it has brought, and the physical changes it has wrought on the geohistorical space that we call Mexico.

The primary theme that runs throughout this book is that human actions transform the rural and urban landscape. Even those who oppose certain transformative processes leave their mark on those changes that in the end do take place.

Mexico's natural environment has never provided its inhabitants with an abundance of natural resources. Indeed, those who have lived here have had to struggle against inherent natural obstacles. A rugged mountain chain runs from north to south, there is an expanse of humid tropics unsuited to intensive human activity, and more than one-third of the country is desert, where even seasonal agriculture is impossible without the benefit of irrigation infrastructure and intensive labor input.

Map 12.10 describes a landscape that is the result of half a century of technological, capital, and labor investment in order to carve habitable areas out of the land's generally inhospitable geography. Maps 12.11 and 12.12 illustrate the large-scale irrigation projects, completed by 1960, that were built to sustain Mexican agriculture and produce a large proportion of the country's hydroelectric power. The resulting irrigated farmlands became the nation's breadbasket, producing the food that made possible its initial industrial development in the postwar period and the decades that followed.

Mexico's transportation infrastructure remained underdeveloped for decades, hampering or slowing the delivery of goods, services, and labor. Map 12.13 illustrates the limited extent of a rail system that was already antiquated and inadequate by 1930. Map 12.14 illustrates the decision to deemphasize the rail infrastructure and strengthen the primary highway system, which was nearly complete by 1960. Map 12.15 illustrates the construction of modern superhighways and regional highway systems, mostly between 1988 and 1994. However, new investment and maintenance are urgently needed. These roads are increasingly valuable for interregional transportation, regional development, and transportation to and from the United States.

New oil and gas pipelines were constructed in the same period (see map 12.16). At the same time, there was a failure to improve the energy supply or to adequately exploit natural resources in western Mexico, which also has much less intrinsic potential for the generation of hydroelectric energy.

Transportation infrastructure, energy distribution networks, and major irrigation and hydroelectric projects all enriched the productive

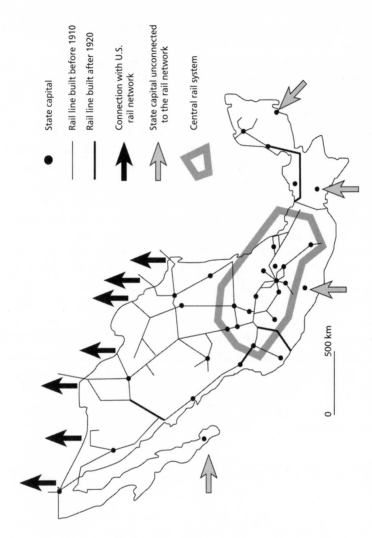

- • State capital
- ——— Rail line built before 1910
- —— Rail line built after 1920
- ⬆ Connection with U.S. rail network
- ⬆ State capital unconnected to the rail network
- ▭ Central rail system

0   500 km

MAP 12.13. The rail network as of the 1990s. (Source: Claude Bataillon, *Espacios Mexicanos Contemporáneos*, op. cit., p. 66.)

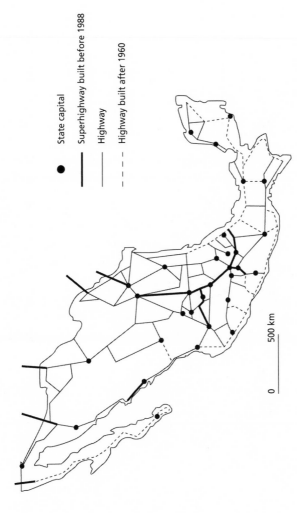

MAP 12.14. The highway system as of the 1990s. (Source: Claude Bataillon, *Espacios Mexicanos Contemporáneos*, op. cit., p. 67.)

State capital

Superhighway built before 1988

Highway

Highway built after 1960

0   500 km

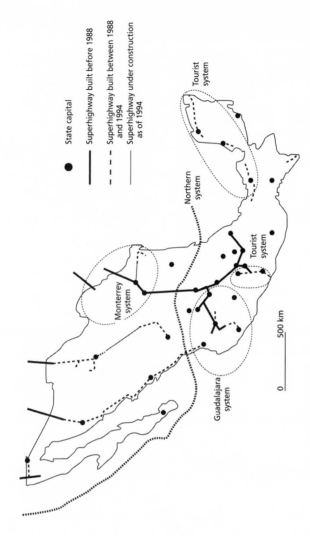

MAP 12.15. Superhighways: peripheral systems as of the 1990s. (Source: Claude Bataillon, *Espacios Mexicanos Contemporáneos*, op. cit., p. 68.)

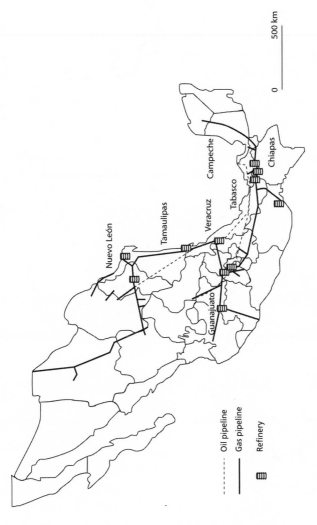

MAP 12.16. Gas and petroleum: refining and distribution as of the 1900s. (Source: Claude Batail-lon, *Espacios Mexicanos Contemporáneos*, op. cit., p. 70.)

Nuevo León

Tamaulipas

Veracruz

Campeche

Tabasco

Chiapas

Guanajuato

- - - - Oil pipeline
———— Gas pipeline
▦ Refinery

0   500 km

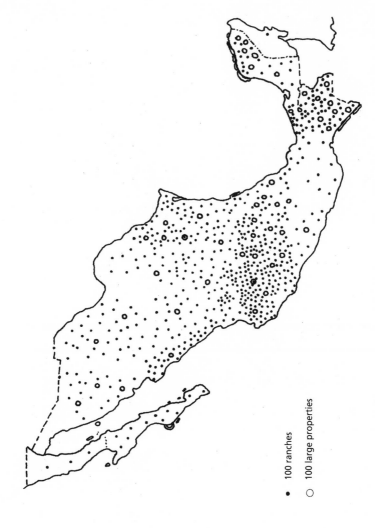

• 100 ranches
○ 100 large properties

MAP 12.17. The 1950 census of rural Mexico. (Source: Howard F. Cline, *Mexico: Revolution to Evolution*, op. cit., p. 109.)

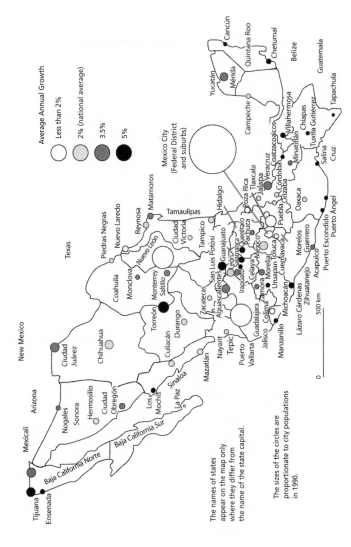

MAP 12.18. Urban growth, 1980–1990. (Source: Claude Bataillon, *Espacios Mexicanos Contemporáneos*, op. cit., p. 53.)

Average Annual Growth

○ Less than 2%

◔ 2% (national average)

◕ 3.5%

● 5%

Mexico City (Federal District and suburbs)

The names of states appear on the map only where they differ from the name of the state capital.

The sizes of the circles are proportionate to city populations in 1990.

0   500 km

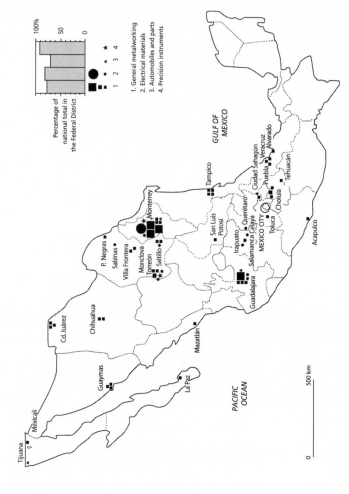

MAP 12.19. Metal industries, 1940–1960. (Source: Claude Bataillon, *Les Régions Géo-graphiques au Mexique* [Paris: University of Paris, 1967], p. 72.)

Percentage of national total in the Federal District

100%
50
0

● 1
■ ▲ ★ 2 3 4

1. General metalworking
2. Electrical materials
3. Automobiles and parts
4. Precision instruments

GULF OF MEXICO

PACIFIC OCEAN

Tijuana
Mexicali
Cd. Juárez
Chihuahua
Guaymas
La Paz
Mazatlán
P. Negras
Sabinas
Villa Frontera
Monclova
Torreón
Saltillo
Monterrey
Tampico
San Luis Potosí
Irapuato
Querétaro
Salamanca Celaya
Guadalajara
MEXICO CITY
Toluca
Cholula
Puebla
Ciudad Sahagún
Veracruz
Alvarado
Tehuacán
Acapulco

500 km
0

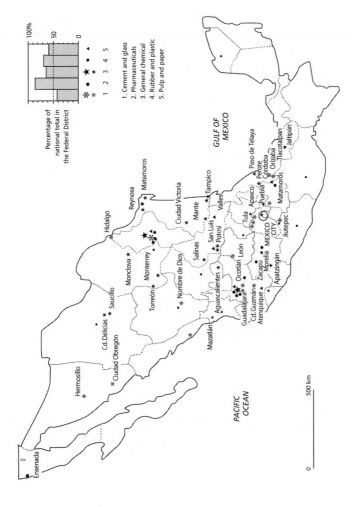

MAP 12.20. Chemical, cement, and glass industries, 1940–1960. (Source: Claude Bataillon, *Les Régions Géographiques au Mexique*, op. cit., p. 74.)

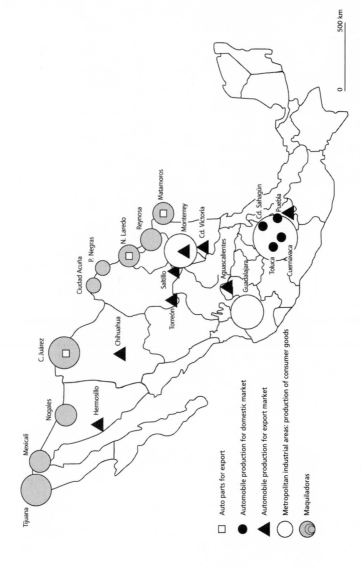

MAP 12.21. Industrial strategy, 1980–1990: automotive industry and maquiladoras. (Source: Claude Bataillon, *Espacios Mexicanos Contemporáneos*, op. cit., p. 71.)

□ Auto parts for export

● Automobile production for domestic market

▲ Automobile production for export market

○ Metropolitan industrial areas: production of consumer goods

◐ Maquiladoras

potential of Mexico's geophysical space. They also made possible an even greater change: the transformation of a country of towns and ranches into an urban society. Map 12.17 illustrates the rural nature of Mexico in 1950. Map 12.18 presents a transformed country in 1980–1990, with a new and complex urban geography and rapid growth in outlying regions.

Maps 12.19 and 12.20 illustrate the spread of the mechanical, metal-working, chemical, automobile, cement, and other industries from 1940 to 1960. This first phase of industrialization, which intensified in the following two decades, laid the groundwork for the second stage of intensive industrialization in the automobile, electronics, and maquiladora sectors, illustrated in map 12.21.

With this quick graphic overview of the country's transformation, which represents the daily efforts of Mexicans over the course of the last half century, I hope to have conveyed some idea of the magnitude of the human and material patrimony that is Mexico's. One hopes that the wealth Mexico has produced and accumulated will guarantee the Mexicans of the twenty-first century at least the potential for fuller and more satisfying lives.

Selected Bibliography

This is in no way an exhaustive listing of authors; it is only a guide to books that may invite the reader to inquire further into Mexico's history.

General Histories

The most useful general histories date from the 1970s, yet some have been brought up to date; recently, various authors have summarized the different periods in general texts or books. By far the best introduction to Mexico's history is Octavio Paz, *The Labyrinth of Solitude: Life and Thought in Mexico* (New York: Grove, 1961).

WORKS IN ENGLISH

Cosío Villegas, Daniel, et al. *A Compact History of Mexico*. Mexico City: El Colegio de México, 1974.

Hamnett, Brian R. *A Concise History of Mexico*. New York: Cambridge University Press, 1999.

MacLachlan, Colin Mackay, and William Beezley. *El Gran Pueblo: A History of Greater Mexico*. Englewood Cliffs, NJ: Prentice Hall, 1994.

Meyer, Michael C., and William Beezley, eds. *The Oxford History of Mexico*. Oxford: Oxford University Press. Contains 20 essays.

Meyer, Michael C., and William L. Sherman. *The Course of Mexican History*. New York: Oxford University Press, 1995. Successive reprints have incorporated new material.

Parkes, Henry Bamford. *A History of Mexico*. Boston: Houghton Mifflin, 1969.

WORKS IN SPANISH

On economics, see Enrique Cárdenas, compiler, *Historia Económica de México,* 4 vols. (Mexico City: Fondo de Cultura Económica, 1989–1994).

Since Mexico is a large country with distinct regions, it is best understood through a study of its individual states. Each of the thirty-two *Breves Historias de los Estados de la República Mexicana* (Mexico City: Fideicomiso Historia de las Américas—El Colegio de México—Fondo de Cultura Económica, 1994–2004) presents a summary history of a state. Beginning with the Indigenous past and continuing through the twentieth century, the books published in this series have greatly enriched this brief history of Mexico.

Mexico's history must also be understood in a broader context that includes the history of the Americas and of Europe. For this, I highly recommend the following works:

Carmagnani, Marcello. *El Otro Occidente: América Latina, de la Invasión Europea a la Globalización.* Mexico City: Fideicomiso Historia de las Américas—El Colegio de México—Fondo de Cultura Económica, 2003.

Carmagnani, Marcello, Alicia Hernández Chávez, and Ruggiero Romano, eds. *Para una Historia de América,* 3 vols. Vol. 1: *Las Estructuras.* Vol. 2: *Los Nudos 1.* Vol. 3: *Los Nudos 2.* Mexico City: Fideicomiso Historia de las Américas—El Colegio de México—Fondo de Cultura Económica, 1999.

Mexico's Indigenous Past

A recent and most original approach to the understanding of all three great cultural areas of pre-Hispanic North America is Alfredo López Austin and Leonardo López Luján, *Mexico's Indigenous Past* (Norman: University of Oklahoma Press, 2001). Other valuable works include the following:

Carrasco, Pedro. *The Tenochca Empire of Ancient Mexico: The Triple Alliance of Tenochtitlan, Tetzcoco, and Tlacopan.* Norman: University of Oklahoma Press, 1999. Thanks to this study, we better appreciate the relationships between society and the territory within which it exists, and between politics and the same territory. The conceptual framework that underpins my view of these historical dimensions stems from this extraordinary work.

Freidel, David, Linda Schele, and Joy Parker. *Maya Cosmos: Three Thousand Years on the Shaman's Path.* New York: William Morrow, 1993.

Schele, Linda, and David Freidel. *A Forest of Kings: The Untold Story of the Ancient Maya.* New York: William Morrow, 1990. This book offers a wholly new vision of Mayan civilization, a vision I have utilized in summarizing the relationship between religious beliefs and social organization.

OTHER IMPORTANT BOOKS ON INDIGENOUS HISTORY

Adams, Richard E.W., and Murdo J. McLeod, eds. *Mesoamerica: Cambridge History of the Native Peoples of the Americas,* vol. 2. Cambridge: Cambridge University Press, 2000.

SELECTED BIBLIOGRAPHY   361

Conrad, Geoffrey W. *Religion and Empire: The Dynamics of Aztec and Inca Expansionism.* Cambridge: Cambridge University Press, 1984.

Katz, Friedrich. *The Ancient American Civilizations.* New York: Praeger, 1972.

Rojas Rabiela, Teresa, and William T. Sanders. *Historia de la Agricultura: Epoca Prehispánica, Siglo XVI.* Mexico City: INAH, 1985.

Spores, Ronald. *The Mixtecs in Ancient and Colonial Times.* Norman: University of Oklahoma Press, 1984.

Three Centuries of Colonial History

The most important study on population history remains Sherburne F. Cook and Borah Woodrow, *Essays in Population History: Mexico and the Caribbean* (Berkeley and Los Angeles: University of California Press, 1971). I believe that the best social history remains Mario Góngora, *Studies on Colonial History* (Cambridge: Cambridge University Press, 1976). Also see the following:

MacLachlan, Colin M., and Jaime E. Rodríguez. *The Forging of the Cosmic Race: A Reinterpretation of Colonial Mexico.* Berkeley and Los Angeles: University of California Press, 1980.

Miño Grijalva, Manuel. *El Mundo Novohispano: Población, Ciudades y Economía, Siglos XVII y XVIII.* Mexico City: Fideicomiso Historia de las Américas—El Colegio de México—Fondo de Cultura Económica, 2001.

OTHER IMPORTANT BOOKS ON COLONIAL HISTORY

Society and Economics

Aguirre Beltrán, Gonzalo. *La Población Negra de México, 1519–1810: Estudio Etnohistórico.* Mexico City: Fondo de Cultura Económica, 1972.

Bakewell, P. J. *Silver Mining and Society in Colonial Mexico: Zacatecas 1546–1700.* Cambridge: Cambridge University Press, 1971.

Baskes, Jeremy. *Indians, Merchants and Markets: A Reinterpretation of the Repartimiento and Spanish-Indian Economic Relations in Colonial Oaxaca, 1750–1821.* Stanford, CA: Stanford University Press, 2000.

Brading, David A. *Miners and Merchants in Bourbon Mexico, 1763–1810.* Cambridge: Cambridge University Press, 1971.

Carmagnani, Marcello. *El Regreso de los Dioses: El Proceso de Reconstitución de la Identidad Etnica en Oaxaca, Siglos XVII y XVIII.* Mexico City: Fondo de Cultura Económica, 1988.

Chevalier, François, Alvin Eutis, and Lesley Byrd Simpson. *Land and Society in Colonial Mexico: The Great Hacienda.* Berkeley and Los Angeles: University of California Press, 1952.

Farriss, Nancy M. *Maya Society under Colonial Rule: The Collective Enterprise of Survival.* Princeton, NJ: Princeton University Press, 1984.

Gibson, Charles. *The Aztecs under Spanish Rule: A History of the Indians of the Valley of Mexico, 1519–1810.* Stanford, CA: Stanford University Press, 1964.

Hamnett, Brian R. *Politics and Trade in Southern Mexico, 1750–1821.* Cambridge: Cambridge University Press, 1971.

Hassig, Ross. *Trade, Tribute and Transportation: The Sixteenth-Century Political Economy of the Valley of Mexico.* Norman: University of Oklahoma Press, 1985.

Hoberman, Louisa S. *Mexico's Merchant Elite, 1590–1660: Silver, State, and Society.* Durham, NC: Duke University Press, 1991.

Kicza, E. John. *Colonial Entrepreneurs: Families and Business in Bourbon Mexico City.* Albuquerque: University of New Mexico Press, 1983.

Marichal, Carlos. *La Bancarrota del Virreinato: Nueva España y las Finanzas del Imperio Español, 1780–1810.* Mexico City: Fideicomiso Historia de las Américas — El Colegio de México — Fondo de Cultura Económica, 1999.

Powell, Phillip Wayne. *Soldiers, Indians, and Silver: The Northward Advance of New Spain, 1550–1600.* Berkeley and Los Angeles: University of California Press, 1969.

Romano, Ruggiero. *Moneda Seudomonedas y Circulación Monetaria en las Economías de México.* Mexico City: Fideicomiso Historia de las Américas — El Colegio de México — Fondo de Cultura Económica, 1998.

Taylor, William B. *Landlords and Peasants in Colonial Oaxaca.* Stanford, CA: Stanford University Press, 1972.

Politics and Culture

Alberro, Solange. *El Águila y la Cruz: Orígenes Religiosos de la Conciencia Criolla, México, Siglos XVI–XVII.* Mexico City: Fideicomiso Historia de las Américas — El Colegio de México — Fondo de Cultura Económica, 1999.

Brading, David. *The First America: The Spanish Monarchy, Creole Patriots and the Liberal State, 1492–1867.* New York: Cambridge University Press, 1991.

Estrada, Dorothy Tanck de. *Pueblos de Indios y Educación en el México Colonial, 1750–1821.* Mexico City: El Colegio de México, 1999.

Gruzinski, Serge. *La Colonización del Imaginario: Sociedades Indígenas y Occidentalización en el México Español, Siglos XVI–XVIII.* Mexico City: Fondo de Cultura Económica, 1991.

Israel, Jonathan I. *Race, Class, and Politics in Colonial Mexico, 1610–1670.* Oxford: Oxford University Press, 1975.

Liehr, Reinhard. *Ayuntamiento y Oligarquía en Puebla, 1787–1810.* 2 vols. Mexico City: Colección SEP-Setentas 243, 1976.

Lockhart, James. *The Nahuas after the Conquest: A Social and Cultural History of the Indians of Central Mexico, Sixteenth through Eighteenth Centuries.* Stanford, CA: Stanford University Press, 1992.

MacLachlan, Colin M. *Criminal Justice in Eighteenth-Century Mexico: A Study of the Tribunal de la Acordada.* Berkeley and Los Angeles: University of California Press, 1974.

Menegus Borneman, Margarita. *Del Señorío a la República de Indios: El Caso de Toluca.* Mexico City: Consejo Nacional para la Cultura y las Artes, 1994.

Miranda, José. *Las Ideas y las Instituciones Políticas Mexicanas.* Mexico City: UNAM, 1952.

O'Gorman, Edmundo. *The Invention of America: An Inquiry into the Historical Nature of the New World and the Meaning of Its History.* Bloomington: Indiana University Press, 1961.

Pietschmann, Horst. *Las Reformas Borbónicas y el Sistema de Intendentes en Nueva España.* Mexico City: Fondo de Cultura Económica, 1996.

Taylor, William B. *Magistrates of the Sacred: Priests and Parishioners in Eighteenth-Century Mexico.* Stanford, CA: Stanford University Press, 1996.

The series *Historia de los Pueblos Indígenas de México*, edited by Teresa Rojas Rabiela and Mario Humberto Ruz (Mexico City: CIESAS-INI, 1994–), is valuable for the study of ethnicity in the colonial and contemporary periods. Various volumes have been published since 1994.

From Independence to Revolution

The best general study on the independence period is Jaime E. Rodríguez, *The Independence of Spanish America* (Cambridge: Cambridge University Press, 1998). For an excellent analysis of nineteenth-century liberalism, see Charles A. Hale, *Mexican Liberalism in the Age of Mora, 1821–1853* (New Haven, CT: Yale University Press, 1968); also Hale, *The Transformation of Liberalism in Late Nineteenth Century Mexico* (Princeton, NJ: Princeton University Press, 1989). For a well-balanced analysis of the period, see Friedrich Katz, *Mexico: Restored Republic and Porfiriato, 1867–1910*, vol. 5 of *The Cambridge History of Latin America* (Cambridge: Cambridge University Press, 1984). On rural protest, see John Tutino, *From Insurrection to Revolution in Mexico: Social Bases of Agrarian Violence, 1750–1940* (Princeton, NJ: Princeton University Press, 1986). On the economy, see L. Jeffrey Bortz and Stephen H. Haber, eds., *The Mexican Economy 1870–1930: Essays on the Economic History of Institutions, Revolution, and Growth* (Stanford, CA: Stanford University Press, 2002); Luis de Villoro, *El Proceso Ideológico de la Independencia* (Mexico City: UNAM, 1977); and Josefina Z. Vázquez, ed., *La Fundación del Estado Mexicano* (Mexico City: Nueva Imagen, 1994). Another important reference is Daniel Cosío Villegas, ed., *Historia Moderna de México,* 7 vols. (Mexico City: Hermes, 1955–1963).

ECONOMIC AND SOCIAL PERFORMANCE DURING THE NINETEENTH CENTURY

Bulmer-Thomas, Victor. *Economic History of Latin America since Independence.* Cambridge: Cambridge University Press, 2003.

Carmagnani, Marcello. *Estado y Mercado: La Economía Pública del Liberalismo Mexicano, 1850–1911.* Mexico City: Fideicomiso Historia de las Américas—El Colegio de México—Fondo de Cultura Económica, 1994.

Coatsworth, John H. *Growth against Development: The Economic Impact of Railroads in Porfirian Mexico.* DeKalb: Northern Illinois University Press, 1981.

Garner, Richard L., with Spiro E. Stefanou. *Economic Growth and Change in Bourbon Mexico.* Gainesville: University Press of Florida, 1993.

Haber, Stephen H. *Industry and Underdevelopment: The Industrialization of Mexico, 1890–1940.* Stanford: Stanford University Press, 1989.

———. *Political Institutions and Economic Growth in Latin America: Essays in Policy, History, and Political Economy.* Stanford, CA: Hoover Institution, Stanford University, 2000.

Keesing, Donald. "Structural Change Early in Development: Mexico's Changing Industrial and Occupational Structure from 1895 to 1950." *Journal of Economic History* 29: 4 (December 1969), pp. 716–38.

Kuntz Ficker, Sandra. *Empresa Extranjera y Mercado Interno: El Ferrocarril Central Mexicano, 1880–1907.* Mexico City: El Colegio de México—Centro de Estudios Históricos, 1995.

Womack, John Jr. "The Mexican Economy during the Revolution 1910–1920: Historiography and Analysis." *Marxist Perspectives* (winter 1978), pp. 80–123.

POLITICS AND INSTITUTIONS

Carmagnani, Marcello, ed. *Federalismos Latinoamericanos: México, Brasil, Argentina.* Mexico City: Fideicomiso Historia de las Américas—El Colegio de México—Fondo de Cultura Económica, 1993.

Carmagnani, Marcello, and Alicia Hernández Chávez. "Dimensiones de la Ciudadanía Orgánica Mexicana 1850–1910." In *Ciudadanía Política y Formación de las Naciones en América Latina,* edited by Hilda Sabato, pp. 371–404. Mexico City: Fideicomiso Historia de las Américas—El Colegio de México—Fondo de Cultura Económica, 1999.

Hernández Chávez, Alicia. *Anenecuilco: Memoria y Vida de un Pueblo.* Mexico City: Fideicomiso Historia de las Américas—El Colegio de México—Fondo de Cultura Económica, 1993.

———. *La Tradición Republicana del Buen Gobierno.* Mexico City: Fideicomiso Historia de las Américas—El Colegio de México—Fondo de Cultura Económica, 1999.

Katz, Friedrich. *Riot, Rebellion, and Revolution: Rural Social Conflict in Mexico.* Princeton, NJ: Princeton University Press, 1988.

Rodríguez, Jaime, ed. *The Evolution of the Mexican Political System.* Wilmington, DE: Scholarly Resources, 1993.

Sinkin, Richard. *The Mexican Reform, 1855–1876: A Study in Liberal Nation-Building.* Austin: Institute of Latin American Studies, University of Texas at Austin, 1979.

The Mexican Revolution

Among the books that have contributed the most to a better understanding of the 1910–1920 period are the following:

Aguilar Camín, Héctor. *La Frontera Nómada: Sonora y la Revolución Mexicana.* Mexico City: Siglo XXI Editores, 1977.

Anderson, Rodney D. *Outcasts in Their Own Land: Mexican Industrial Workers, 1906–1911.* DeKalb: Northern Illinois University Press, 1976.

Clark, Marjorie Ruth. *Organized Labor in Mexico.* New York: Russell and Russell, 1973.

González y González, Luis. *Pueblo en Vilo: Microhistoria de San José de Gracia.* Mexico City: El Colegio de México, 1968.

Katz, Friedrich. *The Life and Times of Pancho Villa.* Stanford: Stanford University Press, 1998.

———. *The Secret War in Mexico: Europe, the United States, and the Mexican Revolution.* Chicago: University of Chicago Press, 1981.

Knight, Alan. *The Mexican Revolution.* Vol. 1: *Porfirian Liberals and Peasants.* Vol. 2: *Counter-Revolution and Reconstruction.* Cambridge: Cambridge University Press, 1986.

Levin, Norman Gordon. *Woodrow Wilson and World Politics: America's Response to War and Revolution.* New York: Oxford University Press, 1968.

Tannenbaum, Frank. *Peace by Revolution: Mexico after 1910.* New York: Columbia University Press, 1993.

Womack, John Jr. *Zapata and the Mexican Revolution.* New York: Vintage Books, 1970.

Contemporary Mexico

The monumental series *Historia de la Revolución Mexicana*, a project directed by Luís González, is an important resource published by El Colegio de México beginning in 1976. Twenty of the planned twenty-three volumes have been published, including my *La Mecánica Cardenista* in 1979. I also recommend Enrique Cárdenas, *Historia Económica de México*, 5 vols. (Mexico City: Fondo de Cultura Económica, 1989–1994).

It is difficult to choose just a few titles focusing on recent decades from the extensive bibliography available. Nevertheless, Pablo González Casanova, *La Democracia en México* (Mexico City: Era, 1972), is virtually required reading. See also Arnaldo Córdova, *La Ideología de la Revolución Mexicana: La Formación del Nuevo Régimen* (Mexico City: Era, 1973).

ECONOMICS AND SOCIETY

Aspe Armella, Pedro. *El Camino Mexicano de la Transformación Económica.* Mexico City: Fondo de Cultura Económica, 1993.

Blanco Mendoza, Herminio. *Las Negociaciones Comerciales de México en el Mundo.* Mexico City: Fondo de Cultura Económica, 1993.

Cárdenas, Enrique. *La Política Económica de México, 1950–1994.* Mexico City: Fideicomiso Historia de las Américas — El Colegio de México — Fondo de Cultura Económica, 1995.

Giugale, Marcelo M., Olivier Lafourcade, and Vinh H. Nguyen, eds. *Mexico: A*

Comprehensive Development Agenda for the New Era. Washington, DC: World Bank, 2001.

Lustig, Nora. *Mexico: The Remaking of an Economy.* Washington, DC: Brookings Institution, 1998.

Rogozinski, Jacques. *La Privatización en México: Razones e Impactos.* Mexico City: Editorial Trillas, 1997.

POLITICS AND CULTURE

Camp, Roderic Ai. *Mexico's Mandarins: Crafting a Power Elite for the Twentieth Century.* Berkeley and Los Angeles: University of California Press, 2002.

Cosío Villegas, Daniel. *El Sistema Político Mexicano.* Mexico City: Joaquín Mortiz, 1972.

Fowler Salamini, Heather. *Agrarian Radicalism in Veracruz, 1920–1938.* Lincoln: University of Nebraska Press, 1971.

Gilderhus, Mark T. *Diplomacy and Revolution: U.S.–Mexican Relations under Wilson and Carranza.* Tucson: University of Arizona Press, 1977.

González Casanova, Pablo. *La Democracia en México.* Mexico City: Era, 1977.

Hansen, Roger D. *The Politics of Mexican Development,* Baltimore: Johns Hopkins, 1971.

Hernández Chávez, Alicia. "El Estado Nacionalista, su Referente Histórico." In Trimestre Económico, Serie Lecturas, vol. 64.5, pp. 110–27. Mexico City: Fondo de Cultura Económica, 1994.

———, ed. *¿Hacia un Nuevo Federalismo?* Mexico City: Fideicomiso Historia de las Américas—El Colegio de México— Fondo de Cultura Económica, 1996.

———. *La Mecánica Cardenista, 1934–1940.* Vol. 16 of *Historia de la Revolución Mexicana.* Mexico City: El Colegio de México, 1979.

———, ed. *Presidencialismo y Sistema Político: México y los Estados Unidos.* Mexico City: Fideicomiso Historia de las Américas—El Colegio de México—Fondo de Cultura Económica, 1994.

Hernández Chávez, Alicia, with María Luna Argudín. *La Nueva Relación entre Legislativo y Ejecutivo: La Política Económica, 1982–1997.* Mexico City: El Colegio de México—Instituto de Investigaciones Legislativas de la Cámara de Diputados—Instituto Politécnico Nacional—Fondo de Cultura Económica, 1998.

Loaeza, Soledad. *El Partido de Acción Nacional, la Larga Marcha, 1939–1994.* Mexico City: Fondo de Cultura Económica, 1999.

Ojeda Gómez, Mario. *Alcances y Límites de la Política Exterior de México.* Mexico City: El Colegio de México, 1976.

Ronfeldt, David. *Atencingo: The Politics of Agrarian Struggle in a Mexican Ejido.* Stanford, CA: Stanford University Press, 1973.

Rozental, Andrés. *La Política Exterior de México en la Era de la Modernidad.* Mexico City, Fondo de Cultura Económica, 1993.

Salinas de Gortari, Carlos. *Mexico: The Policy and Politics of Modernization.* New York: Random House, 2002.

Schuler, Friedrich. *Mexico between Hitler and Roosevelt: Mexican Foreign Relations in the Age of Lazaro Cardenas, 1934–1940*. Albuquerque: University of New Mexico Press, 1998.

Schulz, Donald E., and Edward J. Williams. *Mexico Faces the Twenty-First Century*. New York: Praeger, 1995.

Smith, Peter H. *Labyrinths of Power: Political Recruitment in Twentieth-Century Mexico*. Princeton, NJ: Princeton University Press, 1979.

Wayne, Cornelius, Ann L. Craig, and Jonathan Fox, eds. *Transforming State-Society Relations in Mexico*. San Diego: Center for U.S.–Mexico Studies, 1989.

Womack, John Jr. *Rebellion in Chiapas: An Historical Reader*. New York: New Press, 1999.

Index

Text: 10/13 Galliard
Display: Galliard
Compositor: Binghamton Valley Composition, LLC
Printer and Binder: Edwards Brothers, Inc.